Praise for
PLAY YOUR BEST POOL

National Billiard Publications:

"*Play Your Best Pool* by Phil Capelle is the most thorough book on playing pool ever published. Every shot you can think of is discussed. It is clearly written and illustrated, and contains a huge amount of practical information to help you deal with improving and enjoying your game. This is a book to study and use. You'll love it."

--Tom Shaw,
Pool & Billiard Magazine

This one is one of those rare books from which you can actually learn something. Highly recommended".

--George Fels,
Billiards Digest

"*Play Your Best Pool* tops all previous 'how-to' books. Capelle...has compiled a thorough volume that is must reading for beginner, intermediate and professional players".

--The National Billiard News

"If you can only buy one pool instruction book, get this one".

--The American Cueist

Champion Players:

"Phil Capelle's knowledge of 8-ball and 9-ball strategy is particularily impressive".

--Buddy Hall,
Two Time World Nine Ball Champion

"*Play Your Best Pool* definitely has my vote! Never have I seen a more complete, detailed and easy to read book on pool. I've looked for advice on my weak spots and found help. Thanks, Phil for your thorough job. God Bless."

--Robin Dodson,
Two Time World Nine Ball Champion

"You can really profit from Phil's research. He has done his homework and come up with all A's."

--Lou "Machine Gun" Butera,
Member of the BCA Hall of Fame

"Reading this book is like playing several good players. You'll learn all their trade secrets. Anybody that plays Nine Ball should read this book."

--Jay "Swanee" Swanson,
Winner of Four Major Nine Ball Titles

"After reading parts of Phil's book, I am convinced that it is the most in depth book on pool there is. It is beneficial for all players; pros and amateurs alike. Thanks again Phil".

--Tommy Kennedy,
1992 U.S. Open Champion
Six Time Florida State Champion

"I found *Play Your Best Pool* full of valuable information and instruction. This combined with the hundreds of detailed diagrams makes this book a must if you're looking to improve your game.

--Darlene Stinson,
W.P.B.A. Top Ranked Touring Professional

Industry Experts:

"Kudos to Phil Capelle! *Play Your Best Pool* is perhaps pool's most complete, readable and practical teaching book! For those players at my workshops, I have quickly and proudly moved this valuable book to the top of my recommended reading list".

--Paul Gerni "The Ambassador of Pool",
18-times World Trick Shot Champion

"There's no better book for 8-ball and 9-ball strategy".

--Michael Shamos,
Curator of the Billiard Archive

"A truly awesome piece of work".

-- Bob Henning,
Author, Cornbread Red

"Destined to become a classic."

--John McChesney,
Chairman, Texas Express Promotion Group

"From the vivid, *artistic* cover to the last page, this book puts a "grip" on the reader and teaches "key" instructional points to advance anyone from the ranks of novice to the highest level of performance".

--Tom "Dr. Cue" Rossman,
World Masters Trick Shot Champion

PLAY YOUR BEST
POOL

Secrets to Winning Eight Ball and Nine Ball for All Players

PHILIP B. CAPELLE

First Edition

Billiards Press, Huntington Beach

Play Your Best Pool

Secrets to Winning Eight Ball and Nine Ball for All Players

By Philip B. Capelle

Published by: Billiards Press
            P.O. Box 400
            Midway, City, CA 92655

Fifth Printing

Printed in the United States of America

10   9   8   7   6   5   4   3   2   1

Library of Congress Catalog Card Number 95-092655

ISBN 0-9649204-0-9

Cover Illustration by David Harrington

Dedication

I dedicate this book to the Pool Gods, may they have mercy on all of us poor souls who doggedly continue our lifelong journey to excellence on the green felt.

ACKNOWLEDGEMENTS

Writing and producing this book was a constant reminder of the value of teamwork and being associated with people who shared my enthusiasm for the project. I was very fortunate to have them on my side. I would like to thank all the people mentioned below and any others who I may have missed for their help with this book.

I cannot say enough for the thankless devotion to duty of Chris Donnelly, who was largely responsible for the production of this book. Chris spent untold hours at the computer and was always one step ahead with suggestions for improving the book. Linda Hunt endured my handwriting while cheerfully typing the majority of the text. Thanks so much for a job well done. Susie Massard provided invaluable editing assistance and support for the project Melinda Snyder enthusiastically worked nights on the computer to ensure the book was completed on time.

David Harrington was responsible for the beautiful artwork on the cover. Jim Taylor of Taylor Made Videos provided the camera work for the photos. Danny Kuykendall was kind enough to allow us the use of his pool room for the photos. Thanks to you all.

A special thanks to BCA instructors Roy Yamane and Bob Jewett. Roy helped with ideas on league play and photography. Bob kindly allowed me the use of data from his tests on the throw effect on cut shots. Thanks to Jerry Moreno for his knowledge of the game. Karen Latham offered several ideas for improving the text. Vikki Armistead spent many hours working on ideas for the book. Mike Murad offered advice on the project while Scott Melsinker helped test some of my theories.

Brunswick Billiards of Bristol, Wisconsin provided the illustration of the regulation table. Scott Schrader and Martin Bohn of Valley Recreation located in Bay City, Michigan, were responsible for the drawing of the bar table. I would like to thank both of those fine organizations for their support.

Shirley Donnelly continuously evaluated the book while offering suggestions for its improvement. Thanks also to Chris Donnelly, Jr. and to Sean Donnelly. I appreciate the support of A. L. Johnson and Emil Egeling, who believed in the project from the start. Thanks also to Larry Schultz, Craig Wooldridge, Frank Howsare, Margaret Lukaszewicz, Kamal and Jennifer Sabeh.

Thanks also go to Jeffrey Bean, and to friends like John Houge and others who offered their encouragement. Finally, I appreciate the friendship of Wendy Becker, who has been a believer in my work and has shared her knowledge of the publishing industry with me. Thanks so much to each and every one of you.

Why I Love Pool

The Feeling of Being in "Dead Stroke"

Watching a Master play Precision Shape

Impossible Trick Shots

Learning from Defeat

The Strategy of Eight Ball

The Thrill of a Match that Stands Hill-Hill

Clutch Shots that Win a Match

The Sights and Sounds of a Powerful Nine Ball Break

Practicing in Solitude

Watching Players' Reactions to the Game

The Good Rolls and the Bad

English on the Cue Ball as it Hits the Rail

An Air-tight Safety

Running a Tough Rack of Nine Ball

The Beauty of a Well Made Cue

The Roll of the Balls Across the Green Felt

Meeting New People in a Social Environment

The Satisfaction of Playing Well and Winning

A Well Executed Draw Shot

Escaping a Trap with a Kick Shot

The Heat of Competition

Appreciating Your Opponent

The Endless Quest for Knowledge

INTRODUCTION

This book is about helping you play pool better, perhaps much better than you ever have before. It is both a blueprint for your game as well as a reference source to be consulted when needed. My goal is to provide players of all levels with the most complete and useful guide to pool ever published.

The fundamentals come first. Beginners and less experienced players are urged to start with the first two chapters as they lay the foundation for all that follows. Established players may wish to review those chapters from time to time when their game needs a tune up. Next comes the chapter on shotmaking, which provides you with practical techniques for pocketing a wide variety of gamewinning shots. The chapter on english will show you how sidespin affects the aiming process as a complete mastery of english is necessary to compete at the upper levels of the game.

You will be provided with a complete course on how to control the cue ball in the chapter on position play. This includes the basics of cue ball control (stop, draw and follow) as well as the twenty-one principles of position play. If you master these principles, you'll be well on your way to controlling the cue ball like a professional.

Two big chapters will give you the secrets and strategies for winning at the two most popular pool games: Eight Ball and Nine Ball. You'll learn all about position, patterns, strategies, safeties, kick shots and the break.

The biggest hurdle for most players is the mental game. Chapter eight will show you how to think like a top player. By changing your thoughts, you can change your game. It's within your power. The next chapter will prepare you to compete successfully in tournaments, money games and league play. Although some may disagree with including a section on money play, I feel that as a practical matter it's a necessity. Pool players of all levels will continue to wager on their skills so they may as well learn to do so without falling prey to the old time cons of the hustler.

I'm a big advocate of practice, especially for new players. It's during these early practice sessions that good habits are developed which can last a lifetime. Chapters ten and eleven show you how to set goals, improve, and how to make the most of your practice time. Lastly, chapter twelve discusses how to select and maintain your equipment.

Again, newer players are urged to start at the beginning and work their way back through the book, making sure to take the time necessary to master each section. Experienced players should refer to the expanded table of contents to locate the area of interest to their game.

In nearly every sport there is a wide spectrum of participants that span all groups of society. Golf is played by hustlers in tennis shoes on municipal "dog" tracks as well as by captains of industry amid the lush surrounding of a perfectly manicured country club. Similarly, basketball is played in pristine college gymnasiums as well as on cracked asphalt courts in drug infested neighborhoods. Although the stereotypical pool room still exists, more than ever before, the game is now played in pleasant surroundings in which anyone would feel comfortable.

Yes, it's time to bury pool's past image once and for all and, in fact, not mention it again. In place, I propose that participants and the media alike focus on the positive, and on what the game is really like for the vast majority of today's players.

Pool's new image:
- A beautiful and challenging game played in pleasant surroundings.
- A social game where members of both sexes can mingle freely.
- A game that requires precise physical skills
- A game of knowledge
- A thinking person's game.
- An endlessly fascinating and at times infuriating game.
- A game that participants can enjoy for a lifetime.

I was waiting in line to cash a check at the student union at U.C. Berkeley when my gaze wandered over to the double glass doors leading to the campus pool room. I remember becoming instantly intrigued with the sights and sounds of a pool room. Within a few moments I found myself checking out a rack of balls. Like most beginners I was lucky to make a ball. Nevertheless, a love affair was born. After a couple of days wearing out the cushions with my errant shots, I decided a trip to the campus book store was in order. I quickly discovered a copy of <u>Willie Mosconi on Pocket Billiards</u>.

I look back on this purchase as the turning point in my pool playing career, for the teachings of Mr. Mosconi gave me a solid understanding of the fundamentals. Twenty-six years later I continue to love both playing and watching pool, perhaps more than ever before. Over the pages of this book I hope to share my enthusiasm for the game and knowledge I've acquired through playing, practicing, watching, reading, teaching and talking pool since that spring day in 1969 when my story (and this book) began.

Every pool player has their own unique story of how they got started, why they play and what they hope to achieve from the game. What's yours? Like all pool players, no doubt you have a desire to improve your game, and in the process, derive maximum enjoyment from this great game.

I appreciate the opportunity to be a part of your journey through the teachings in this book. I hope you will come to view me as a friend who is sincerely interested in your game and that you will look to this book when you feel you need help with some portion of your game.

Let me know about your journey by writing to me at the address in the back of the book. Best of luck to you always as you continue your personal quest to play your best pool.

Philip B. Capelle

CONTENTS

CHAPTER 1   **Fundamentals**   1

CHAPTER 2   **How to Aim**   27

CHAPTER 3   **Shotmaking**   43

CHAPTER 4   **How to Use English**   85

CHAPTER 5   **Position Play**   101

CHAPTER 6   **Eight Ball**   191

CHAPTER 7   **Nine Ball**   253

CHAPTER 8   **The Mental Game**   339

CHAPTER 9   **Competitive Play**   357

CHAPTER 10   **How to Improve**   379

CHAPTER 11   **Practicing Pool**   391

CHAPTER 12   **How to Buy Equipment**   415

Appendix   429
Glossary   435

CHAPTER I   **Fundamentals**   1
Grip   2
Bridges   4
Stance   11
Stroke   18
A Short Course in Fundamentals   24

CHAPTER 2   **How to Aim**   27
Preshot Routine   28
Contact Point   29
Cue Ball at Contact   29
Pocketing a Shot   30
Margin for Error   30
Cut Shots   32
Fullness of the Cut   33
Target Size   33
Where to Aim in the Corner Pocket   34
Shooting Balls Down the Rail   34
The Feel Method   35
All Shots are Straight   36
Setting up a Ghost Ball   37
Watching Your Errors   37
Dispersion Patterns   38
Visualizing a Channel to the Pocket   39
Visualizing a Line of Cue Balls   39
Contact Induced Throw   40
Contact Induced Throw at Forty Degrees   40
Contact Throw at Long Distances   41
Different Degrees of Contact Throw   42

CHAPTER 3   **Shotmaking**   43
Basic Shotmaking   44
Missing Shots - Why it Happens   44
Cut Shots   46
Measuring the Cut Angle   46
The 90 Degree Test   46
The Distance Principal on Cut Shots   47
Cut Shots Angles   47
Pocketing Down the Rail Cut Shots   48
Spinning Cut Shots in with English   48
Frozen to the Rail Cut Shots   49
Close Together Cut Shots   50
Side Pocket Shotmaking   51
Combinations   54
How to Shoot Combinations   54
Combos and the Margin for Error   55
Four Combinations Shots - Degree of Difficulty   55
Ball in Hand Combinations   56
Frozen Combinations   57
How Throw Works   58

Three Ball Frozen Combinations   59
Rail First Kick Combos   60
Rail First Two Way Combos   60
Bank Shots   61
How to Measure Bank Shots   61
How Speed Affects Bank Shots   62
How English Affects Bank Shots   62
Typical Short Rail Bank Shots   63
Typical Long Rail Bank Shots   63
Three Uses of Outside English   64
Three Uses of Inside English   65
Crossover Bank Shots   66
Multi-Rail Bank Shots   67
Carom Shots   68
How to Pocket Carom Shots   68
Dead Carom Shots/Throw Caroms   69
Dead Carom Shots/Throw Caroms   69
Easy Carom   70
Touch Cut vs. Easy Carom   70
Rail First Frozen Carom   70
Billiards   71
The Theory of Making Billiards   71
How to Alter the Cue Ball's Path   71
How to Pocket Three Billiards   72
Cutting in Billiards with Centerball   73
Cutting in Billiards with Centerball (2)   73
Dead Billiards and Throw Shots   74
Rail First Billiards Using Draw and Follow   75
Draw Back Billiards   76
Rail First Shotmaking   77
How to Pocket Rail First Shots   77
Aiming Rail First Shots   78
Using your Cue to Measure Rail First Shots   79
Rail First Thin Cut Shots   79
Miscellaneous Shotmaking   80
Cue Ball Frozen to the Rail   80
Jump Shots   81
Curve Shot   82
Push/Throw Shot   82
Frozen/Frozen Shots   83
Two Combo Bank Shots   84
Four Assorted Shots   84

CHAPTER 4   **How to Use English**   85
Shooting Down the Vertical Axis   86
The Six Positions Using English   88
Throwing Balls in with English   90
Outside and Inside English   91
Allowing for Deflection   92
Deflection Test Results   93

Deflection and Throw   94
Missing Shots Because of Throw   95
Missing Shots Because of Deflection   96
How Curve Affects Aim   97
Throwing in Shots Around Obstructions   97
Pocketing Balls with English   98
How English Affects the Cue Ball off the Rails   99
A Short Course on English   100
Rules of Thumb   100

CHAPTER 5   **Position Play**   101

Basic Position Play   103
Stop Shot   103
Slight Angle Stop Shots   104
Ball in Hand Stop Shots   104
Force Shots   105
Fine Tuning Force Shots   106
The Draw Shot   107
The Affect of Stroke Force on Angled Draw Shots   109
Draw Off the Side Rail with English   110
Drawing up the Side Rail with English   110
Back to the Rail Draw Shots with English   111
Force Draw   111
Power Draw   112
Nip/Draw Shot   112
The Jack-Up Draw Shot   113
The Follow Shot   114
Follow Shot Drills   115
Force Follow   116
Soft Follow Shots   116
Nip Follow Shots   117
Straight-In Cheat the Pocket Follow Shots   117
Follow with English   118
Principles of Position Play   119
The Principles in Action   120
Speed Control   122
Ideal Angle and Distance Equals Position   124
Know the Shape of Position Zones   126
Play Natural Shape as much as Possible   127
Right Side/Wrong Side - The Master Key to Playing Position 128
Allowing for a Margin for Error   130
When to Play Area Shape   132
Enter into the Wide Area of a Position Zone   133
Playing Down the Line of a Position Zone when Possible   134
Ball In Hand Shape   135
Play to the Long Side when Possible   136
Use Rail Targets   138
Avoid Scratching   140
Plan Your Route - Avoiding Obstructions   142
Play the High Percentage Sequence   144

Plan for Three Balls at a Time	145
Keep the Cue Ball away from the Rail	146
Survey the Table before Shooting	147
Pay Attention to Details	148
Use Your Imagination	149
Play Your Game	150
Playing Position off One Rail	151
Drawing the Cue Ball Down the Table	152
The Kill Shot	153
The Soft Draw Creeper Shot	153
Slight Angle Force Shot	154
Force Shots off a Side Rail	155
Side Pocket off the Rail Position	155
Side Pocket Inside English Follow Shots	156
Side Pocket Cut Shots off the End Rail	156
Using English off the Rail	157
Getting a Better Angle with English	157
Multi-Rail Position	158
Two More Two-Railers	159
Two Rail Inside English Follow Shot	159
Power Two Rail Follow	160
Two Railer with Draw and Force	160
Basic Three Rail Position	161
Four Rail Position	161
Inside English Three Railer	162
Three Rails with Inside Follow	162
Three Railer with Outside English and Draw	163
Around the Table	163
Thin Cut Cross the Table Shot	164
Twice Across with Inside Follow	164
Drawing Across the Table Twice	165
Inside English off the Rail Draw Shot	165
Up and Down the Table	166
Around the Table Three Railer	166
Side Pocket Two Railer	167
Side Pocket Three Railer	167
Side Pocket Shape Using Inside English	168
Four Rail Side Pocket Shape	168
Balls Near The Pocket	169
Balls Deep in the Jaws	170
Playing Shape with English	171
Draw Shots on Balls Near the Pocket	171
Using Rail First Position on Pocket Hangers	172
Back to the Rail Follow Shot	172
Change of Direction Follow Shot	173
Variety of Position Plays	174
Playing Up Close to get an Angle	174
Using Tangent Lines to Control the Cue Ball	175
Hit or Miss Using Tangent Lines	175
Playing Shape on the Short Side	176
Cheat the Pocket for Shape	176
Thick or Thin will Alter the Cue Ball's Path	177

When to Play the Extra Rail 177
The Lag Shot 178
Go Rail First to Gain an Angle 179
Avoiding Balls coming Across the Table 179
Frozen/Frozen Position Plays 180
Bumping Your Next Ball into Position 181
First Rail Target Zones 182
Playing Position Down the Length of the Table 183
Using the Side Rails for Position 184
Playing Position off Other Balls 185
Drawing Off an Object Ball for Position 186
Using Balls as Backstops 187
Backstops - Part Two 187
Playing Shape off Combinations 188
Combos with the Balls near the Pocket 189
Combos with a Ball in the Jaws 189
A Checklist of Common Mistakes 190

CHAPTER 6   Eight Ball

CHAPTER 6   **Eight Ball** 191
What Can Make You a Winner 192
Assessing the Table 193
Your and Your Opponent's Balls are Easy 193
One Group is Easy - The Other is Hard 194
Assessing the Trouble Spots 195
The 8-Ball is in a Precarious Position 196
Strategy 197
The Big Mistake - The Failed Runout 197
Winning A lost Game 198
Tightening the Screws 199
Saving Balls for a Specific Purpose 200
Let Your Opponent do the Dirty Work 201
Creating an Edge;
     Making Things Tougher for your Opponent 202
Setting up the Rack 203
Taking Care of a Trouble Ball with Ball in Hand 204
Breaking Open Balls with Ball in Hand 205
Offensive Play 206
Basic Pattern Play 206
Simple Pattern Play 207
Easy Runout Patterns 208
Medium Tough Runouts 209
Advanced Pattern Play 210
A Tough but Runnable Pattern 211
Run Killers - What Could Stop Your Run? 212
Clearing Out an Area 213
Up and Down the Table 214
Three Balls at a Time 215
Three Balls at a Time (II) 216
Proper Sequence 217
Plan B - Changing a Runout 218
End Game Position - Weaving Through Traffic 219

Saving a Key Ball 220
Consider all Six Pockets 221
Two Balls to the Same Pocket 222
Near Pocket vs. Far Pocket Shape 223
Using an Easy Shot to Play Difficult Shape 224
Don't Break Up Balls Unnecessarily 225
Playing Tough Position on Purpose 226
Playing for a Roll and Position 227
Playing for a Roll on a Breakout 228
Defensive Play 229
Stake Your Claim - Then Play Safe! 229
Missing on Purpose 230
Hooking Your Opponent 231
Soft Hit Safety Play 232
Keeping a Blocker in Place 233
Lagging the 8-Ball on a Tough Shot 234
Unblocking Pockets and Playing Safe 235
Plan B - Abandoning a Runout 236
Blocking Pockets 237
Playing Defensive Position 238
Shotmaking 239
Gamewinning Shots 239
Using a Carom to Remove a Blocker 240
Lining Up Banks Through Traffic 241
Breaking Balls Apart 242
Nudging Balls Apart 242
Breaking a Tight Cluster on the Rail 243
Keeping an Insurance Ball 244
Blasting into a Poorly Broken Rack 245
When to Break up a Cluster 246
Kick Shot Strategy 247
Which Ball to Kick for 247
The Lag Shot Kick Shot 248
Soft Kick Safety 249
Kicking at a Group 250
The Forced to Kick Shot 251
Break Shots 252
The Control Break Shot 252
Breaking to Make the 8-Ball 252

CHAPTER 7   **Nine Ball** 253
Shotmaking 254
Winning Nine Ball 254
Adjusting to the Competition 256
Nine Ball Strategies 257
Planning to Break a Cluster 257
Don't Break Balls That Don't Need to be Broken 258
When to Play a Tough Combo 258
Moving a Trouble Ball 259
Breaking Up a Cluster in Traffic 259

Playing for a Roll on a Breakout 260
When to Ride the Money Ball 260
When to Pass on a Combo 261
Playing Two at a Time 261
Knocking a Ball Closer to the Pocket 262
Trouble Balls in the Middle of the Table 262
Winning with the Three Foul Rule 263
Evaluating the Layout 264
Easy Runout 264
A Tough Rack that can be Run 264
Potential Run Stoppers 265
Potential Run Stopper (II) 265
Weighing the Options: Offense vs. Defense 266
No Possible Runout 266
Play the Table ; Don't Force the Issue 267
Position Play/Patterns 268
Playing for Three Balls at a Time 268
Playing for the Correct Angle 269
The Importance of Speed Control 270
Pattern Play 271
Advanced Pattern Play 272
When to Play Straight-In Position 273
The "Out Shot" - Getting in Line 273
The Last Three Balls 274
The Importance of the Last Three Balls 274
Going the Extra Rail for Position 275
A Difficult Three Ball Run 275
Push Out Strategies 276
Push Outs 276
Push Out Principles 277
Push Out Strategies 278
Pushing Out to a Shot 279
Sucker Shot vs. Smart Safety 280
Beware of the Easy Hook 281
Get the 9-Ball out of the Pocket 281
Free Shots - Accepting Them 282
No Good Push Out - The Forced Kick 282
Push Out to a Tough Shot 283
Shoot In and Easy 1-Ball 283
The Break 284
Goals for the Break 284
The Break Stroke 285
Setting up the Shot for the Break 286
Where the Balls go on the Break 288
Safety Play 289
What is a Safety? 289
Required Skills 290
How Much Ball to Hit 291
Stopping Distance of the Object Ball 292
Thin Hit vs. Bank Shot 292
Leaving Tough Shots 293
Drag Draw from a Distance 294

Inside English Kill Shot	294
Soft Follow Hook Shot	295
A Situation to Avoid	295
Using a Holding Ball	296
No Shot Thin Hit Safety	296
Hook Zones	297
How to Determine the Side of Hook Zone	298
Frozen Hook Zones	298
Multiple Ball Hook Zones	299
Two Rails to a Hook Zone	299
Double Bank Hook Shot	300
Three Rail Hook Shot	300
Freeze Against the Object Ball	301
Pass on Tough Combo	302
Ball Near Rail Create Large Hook Zones	302
Three Rail Thin Hit Safety	303
Thin Hit Hook Behind a Ball	304
Cluster Racks offer Hook Shots	305
Thin Hit Safeties	306
Large Target Safety Plays	306
Thin Hit Double Cross Safety	306
Down the Side Rail Safety	307
Thin Hit with a Soft Touch	307
Thin Hit with a Ball in Hand	308
Setting up the Rack	309
Set up a Combination	309
Getting Easier Position on the Next Ball	310
Breaking up Clusters	310
Running Out to a Hook	311
Pass On Shot	312
Thin Hit Double Bank Safety	313
Pass on an Easy Shot that Leads Nowhere	313
½ Shot/½ Safety	314
Thin Cut Shot Safeties	314
Safety Cross Corner Bank Shots	314
Cross Side Bank Safeties	315
Long Rail Bank Safeties	315
Cross Table Bank/Hook Shot	316
How to Play Kick Shots	317
Notes and Strategies on the Kicking Game	317
Improve Your Skills with Kick Pool	319
Short Rail Kick Shot Target Size	320
Kick Shot Approach Angle	321
Trapping the Object Ball	322
Size of Kicking Channels	323
Kick Routes	324
Kick Shot Safeties	326
Soft Hit Safety Kick	326
One Rail Safety Kick	326
Sticking the Cue Ball with follow	326
Sticking the Cue Ball with Draw	327
Avoid the Open End of the Table	328

Kicking with Speed and Accuracy 328
Splitting the Cue Ball and The Object Ball 329
Kick to Hit 330
The Triangle Method 330
Using English to Avoid other Balls 331
Difficult to Aim Kick Shots 332
Curve Kick Shots 332
Kick to Pocket 333
Kicking Balls in Using the Triangle Method 333
Kick Shots Along the Rail 334
The Power Ride Kick Shot 334
The Forced Kick Shot 335
Short Rail Kick Shots 335
Adjusting Your Aim on Kick Shots 336
Playing Position on Kick Shots 337
Sucker Kick Shots 337

CHAPTER 8   **The Mental Game** 339
Realizing Your Potential with a Positive Attitude . . . 340
Confidence 341
Concentration 342
Self Image 343
Mental Toughness 344
Excuses 345
The Luck Factor 347
Opponents 347
Self Talk 349
Goals and Hurdles 350
Dealing with a Slump 351
The Mental Side of Pocketing Balls 352
How to Make Pressure Shots 355
Spiritual Pool 356

CHAPTER 9   **Competitive Play** 357
Opponents 358
Sharking 360
Tournaments 362
Preparing for a Tournament 363
Winning Tournaments 363
The Score 364
Hill - Hill 367
Tactics 367
Money Games 368
Money Management 369
Format 370
Spotting 371
Backers 372
Playing Conditions 373
Hustles and Shark Moves 374

League Play 376
  Competition 376
  Getting Involved 376

CHAPTER 10   **How to Improve** 379
  The Learning Curve 380
  The Learning Sequence 382
  Mastering Change 383
  Setting Goals 384
  Working with an Instructor 385
  The Pyramid of Excellence 386
  The Champion's Checklist 388
  Sources of Knowledge 389

CHAPTER 11   **Practicing Pool** 391
  The Stroke 392
  Perfecting Your Stroke 394
  Perfecting Your Stroke (II) 396
  Straight-In Shot Stroke Check 397
  Down the Rail Straight-In Shot Drill 398
  The "Field Goal" Drill 399
  Shotmaking Practice 400
  Progressive Cut Shot Drill 401
  Progressive Distance on Cut Shots 401
  Blocking Part of the Pocket 402
  Side Pocket Shotmaking 402
  Position Play 403
  Speed of Stroke Drill 404
  Progressive Distance - Stop, Draw, Follow 405
  Varying the Hit on the Cue Ball 406
  Zig Zag Drill 407
  Zig Zag Drill (II) 407
  Side Pocket Circle Drill 408
  One Corner Pocket Drill 408
  Ball in Hand Runouts - Eight Ball 409
  Ball in Hand Runouts - Nine Ball 409
  Varying the Size of Shape Zones 410
  Ball in Hand - Choose the Best Route 410
  Safety Practice 411
  English 411
  Pool Games That Can Improve Your Play 412
  Eight Ball 412
  Nine Ball 412
  Rotation 412
  Bank Pool 413
  Straight Pool 413
  One Pocket 414

CHAPTER 12   **How to Buy Equipment**   415
   Tables   415
   Room Size Requirements   417
   Items for Your Home Pool Room   417
   Table Care   418
   Cue Sticks   418
   Selection Criteria   419
   Choosing a House Cue   420
   The Parts of a Cue   420
   Maintaining Your Cue   421
   The Tip   422
   Cue Cases   424
   Accessory Items   425
   Jump Cue   425
   Break Cue   426
   Tip Maintenance   426
   Special Glasses   426
   Practicing Your Aim   426
   Practicing Your Aim and Stroke   426
   Cue Maintenance   427

Appendix

   Playing on Bar Tables   430
   Recommended Books   431
   Where to Play   433
   Publications   434
   Glossary   435
   About the Author   442
   For More Information   442

CHAPTER 1

FUNDAMENTALS

Laying The Foundation

For Your Game

Mastering the fundamentals can lay the foundation for a lifetime of enjoyment of pool. When you play better, the game is simply more fun. This chapter offers you a complete course on the fundamentals of pool. I urge newer players to take the time to learn these fundamentals thoroughly. Make them a part of your game. Don't rush the process. Make sure that you feel comfortable with your grip, bridge, stance and stroke before leaving this chapter.

Advanced players should use this section as a refresher course. Perhaps a new approach can raise your game to a higher level, or help you break out of a slump. Learn them thoroughly. Practice them diligently. And check them regularly throughout your career. Your game will benefit accordingly.

The game of pool is both an art and a science. As such, you will discover there is some room for working outside the accepted fundamentals. However, I advise newer players to stick closely to the basics recommended in this chapter. This will keep you from developing bad habits that may be tough to break. Try to be as natural as possible. Let your game develop it's own style. And be sure to follow the three P's: practice, patience and persistence. In order for these lessons to work, you've got to put in time at the table. The good news, especially for newer players, is that your practice time can lead to immediate and rapid progress.

The Grip

How you hold the cue with your backhand will largely determine your success as a pool player. With the proper grip, you can shoot with deadly accuracy and perform wondrous feats of cue ball wizardry. On the other hand, a poor grip will largely negate any other positives in your game and severely limit your progress as a player. Therefore, I am issuing an urgent plea for you to pay special attention to your grip.

A good grip must have the right feel. It will allow the cue to do most of the work. When your grip and stroke are really in tune, your cue will serve as an extension of your hand, arm and brain. Your cue will become part of your body. When your grip feels great, you will be unaware of how you are holding the cue. You will be on automatic pilot.

A light grip allows you to whip the cue through the cue ball in a straight line for accurate shotmaking. It also promotes action on the cue ball. To form the correct grip, stand erect and allow your shooting arm to hang down relaxed at your side. Notice that your fingers are turned slightly upward. Now lay the cue along the cradle that's formed naturally by your fingers. Your thumb acts as a support to keep the cue from falling. Make sure you do not squeeze your fingers too far upward as this will tighten your grip. There should be some daylight between the top of your cue and the skin between your thumb and index finger.

The Grip

The Loose Grip

The cue is primarily held by your first two fingers and your thumb. Some players also use the third finger. Almost all the experts, however, agree that your little finger is not to be used in the grip. It may lie alongside the grip. Some players intentionally remove it from the cue altogether. Your thumb should be pointing nearly straight down at the ground and slightly inward.

Where you place your grip hand on the cue depends both on your physical characteristics and the type of shot you are playing. Your first step is to locate the balance point. Lay the cue across your index finger and adjust its position until it balances on its own. The balance point serves as a point of reference. Shorter players will position their hand only a few inches behind the balance point while taller players and those with longer arms will need to hold the cue at least eight to ten inches past the balance point. Carrying this to an extreme, very tall players (6'4" or above) often will grip the cue at or very near the end of the cue to accommodate their large wing spans.

Let's assume you have found your ideal grip location for average or normal shots. We'll assume your ideal grip is six inches behind the balance point. A couple of adjustments can help refine your technique. For shots requiring a fine touch you may wish to move your grip hand up to within three inches or so of the balance point. For a power shot you should grip about nine inches past the balance point. Your grip position is also related to the length of your bridge (the distance between your front hand and the cue ball). The shorter your bridge, the closer your grip to the balance point and vice versa. I'll go into more detail on this in another section.

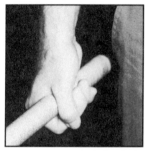

The Death Grip

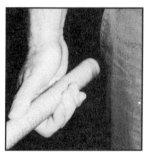

Thumb on Top

The power in your stroke comes largely from the grip hand and your wrist. If you use a death-grip on the cue, you will retard your wrist action and rob your stroke of power. Your hand, wrist and arm all work together to provide needed power. So don't lock your wrist by placing the thumb on top of the cue or by squeezing the cue too tightly. Stay loose and learn to whip that cue.

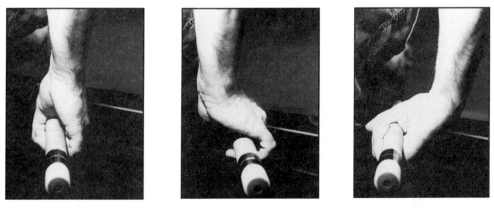

Correct Grip   Outward Wrist Cock Inward Wrist Cock

There are some very fine players who cup their wrists inward and others who cock their wrists to the outside (see illustration). Newer players who don't have ten hours a day to work on their game are urged to stick to the recommended grip. Also beware that your grip will tend to tighten under pressure. A grip that's tight at the start of competition may become immobilized later on. Meanwhile, a loose grip that tightens up somewhat should remain very functional under pressure. As a test of grip pressure, I'll have a student take hold of my hand with the same pressure that they use to grasp their cue. Fully 80% to 90% hold their cue too tightly. Do you? If so, lighten up.

Bridges

The main purpose of the bridge is to provide a secure guide for the cue stick. The bridge may seem insignificant to beginners, but it is an integral component, along with grip, stance and stroke, of any successful shot. New players can often get by with a couple of basic bridges. To truly master this game, however, you will need to become familiar with perhaps a dozen or more.

Some players tend to favor a particular type of bridge, such as the open or closed bridge, for the majority of their shots. Certain types of shots, such as rail shots, will dictate which bridge to use. Your physical characteristics can also affect your choice of bridges as well as how you construct them.

The Open Bridge
The open bridge is very popular with newer players and a number of experienced players as well. To build this bridge, place your left hand flat on the table. Spread your fingers as far apart as possible. Now pull your fingertips in so that the first two or three knuckles of your hand raise up slightly. Next, position your thumb alongside your index finger between the second joint and the knuckle. The cue is then placed in the vee formed by the index finger and the thumb. Be sure to press your entire hand down on the table with enough pressure to add some stability to your bridge.

The open bridge is most commonly used on follow shots and on shots when you must stretch across the table. It is also useful on shorter shots. A primary advantage of this bridge is that it gives you an unobstructed view of the cue ball. Snooker players use this bridge for nearly every shot (snooker is similar to pool and requires great accuracy).

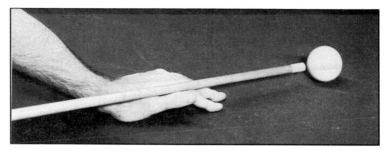

The Open Bridge

Closed Bridge

The closed bridge is used by nearly all of the better players. It offers several advantages: it insures against miscues, it helps you stay down on the shot, it's good for precision shooting and it is especially useful on power shots. I hope I've convinced you to use this bridge whenever possible.

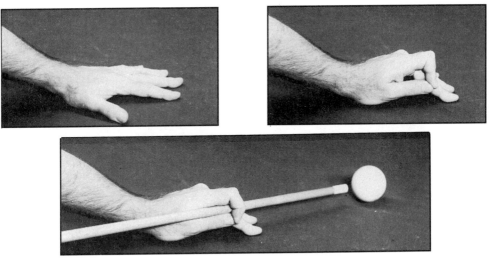

The Closed Bridge

The closed bridge is formed by placing your hand flat on the table, and spreading your fingers. Bring the tips of your thumb and forefinger together so they rest on your middle finger. Bringing the thumb and index finger together automatically raises your hand. Notice that a loop is also formed. Insert the cue through this loop.

You should exert some downward pressure on the table to add stability to your bridge and to keep your hand from wobbling. Even the slightest sideways movement can cause a missed shot. It may help to think of your bridge as a miniature version of the Rock of Gibraltar. Weight should be evenly distributed through your fingers, the heel of your hand and the base of your thumb.

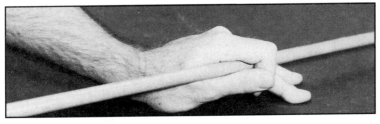

Modified Closed Bridge

Players with especially long fingers may wish to adopt a second version of the closed bridge. This bridge is constructed the same as the one above with one difference; the loop is formed by placing the index finger between the thumb and middle finger. This bridge can help reduce the opening in the loop for players with long fingers so that their bridge remains snug.

You can increase the effectiveness of the closed bridge by making sure you place your hand nearly parallel with the cue stick. In this position the cue will have two contact points with your hand. This can help to guide the cue in a straight line.

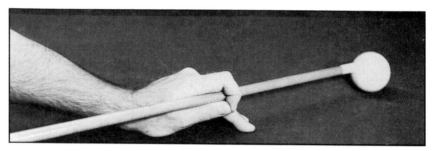

Follow Bridge

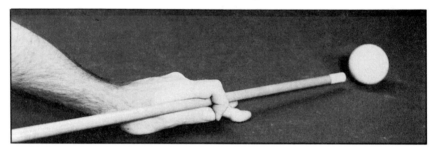

Draw Bridge

The closed bridge can be used for a variety of purposes. In the normal position your cue should be level. The tip should be even with the center of the cue ball. You can raise your bridge to hit the cue ball above center by bringing the tips of your fingers in closer to the rest of your hand. To hit the cue ball below center, lower your bridge by extending your fingers out as far as possible. One of your goals should be to keep the cue as level as possible at all times. Therefore, don't make the mistake of raising your grip hand to lower the tip of your cue. Draw shots (below center) are best accomplished by lowering your bridge and cue, not raising your grip hand.

The length of your bridge is defined as the distance from the cue ball to the loop. It can be adjusted to meet a variety of purposes. For soft shots and greater accuracy, use a short bridge. When a long, power stroke is called for, lengthen your bridge two to three inches past normal. As a rule of thumb, eight ball players should use a short bridge on most of their shots (about 8"). Nine ball players, due to the number of power shots, would tend to use a longer bridge (9"-12").

Whatever game you play, your bridge length should be a compromise between accuracy and power. A bridge that's too short may provide plenty of accuracy but it will also limit your power. An inappropriately long bridge will provide plenty of power. However, any errors in your stroke will be greatly magnified. For example, if you twist your hand or arm slightly during the forward stroke, the cue could easily be a half tip off at impact. Because pool requires great precision, an error of this size could easily lead to a missed shot. Newer players should use a short bridge until they develop a dependable stroke. As the stroke develops and matures, the bridge can be lengthened and adjusted according to each players' preference.

The closed bridge provides solid support for the cue. In addition, the cue should slide smoothly through the loop in your bridge. Many beginners are turned off by the closed bridge because their cues stick in the loop. This problem can be solved easily enough. The solution is to keep the shaft of your cue clean. There are many fine products on the market designed specifically for that purpose. Some players also find it helpful to shoot with a pool glove on their bridge hand. And still others resort to talcum powder to reduce unwanted friction. Whichever solution you choose, remember that a closed bridge is well worth the small inconvenience of keeping your shaft clean and smooth.

Elevated Bridge
Obstructing balls require a bridge that can provide stability while elevating the cue stick. Place the tips of your fingers down first with your palm elevated at about a forty-five degree angle (in relation to your fingertips). Position your fingers as close to the obstructing ball as possible without touching it. Spread your fingers for added stability. Now rest your thumb high up on your index finger near the knuckle. The cue is placed in the vee. Out of necessity, you must adopt a more upright stance. Use a short stroke and avoid using any sidespin whatsoever.

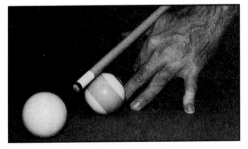 

Elevated Bridge

Rail Bridges

There are a wide variety of bridges you can use when the cue ball is near or up against the rail. These bridges should be used only when you are prevented from using the standard closed bridge.

When your cue rests on the rail, it is automatically raised to above the center of the cue ball. That's assuming that the cue is held level. You can still use a level stroke on follow shots when your cue is resting on the rail. However, you will need to raise your grip hand on draw shots in order to stroke the cue ball below center. You should refrain from using english on draw shots off the rail. It's not a bad idea to avoid english altogether on all of your rail shots because it can easily lead to miscues and missed shots.

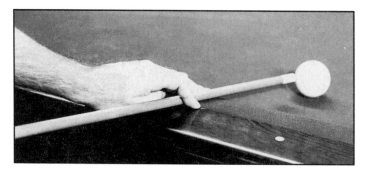

Closed Rail Bridge

The basic closed rail bridge is formed by placing your hand flat on the rail. Now raise your index finger. Tuck your thumb underneath your index finger. Place the cue so that it touches your thumb and the tip of your middle finger. Finally, put the tip of your index finger on the rail on the opposite side of the cue (the right side) from the rest of your hand.

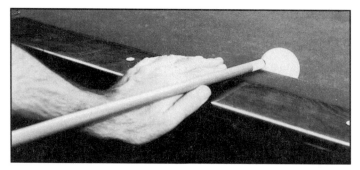

Open Rail Bridge

The open handed rail bridge is very useful, especially when the cue ball is near to or frozen to the rail. This bridge gives you an excellent view of the top part of the cue ball, which helps to avoid miscues. It is formed by placing your hand flat on the table. Lift your thumb slightly so that it forms a vee with your index finger. Then place the cue in the vee. Make sure not to crowd the rail with your bridge when the cue ball's close to the cushion or this will severely reduce your backstroke.

Assorted Rail Bridges

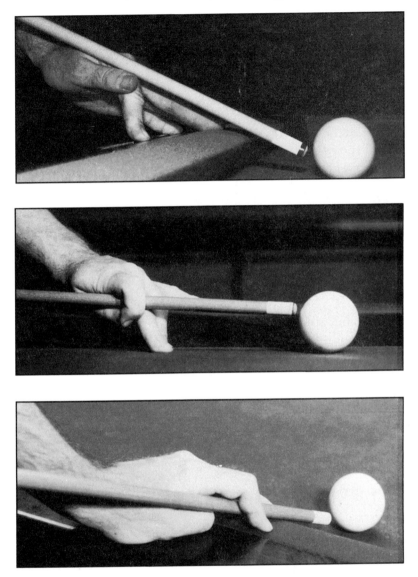

    The illustrations demonstrate a couple of other rail bridges that will come in handy. On unusual or difficult bridges, be sure to take a little extra time to get settled in. Don't shoot until your bridge feels comfortable and secure. Sometimes you may need to consider two or three bridges until you come up with a creative solution to an unusual position.

Mechanical Bridge

Most players will go to just about any lengths to avoid using the mechanical bridge. However, this implement can occasionally enable you to pocket a shot that can't otherwise be reached. Therefore, I would advise that you learn how to use it properly. Start by placing the bridge down carefully so as not to disturb any other balls. Place the bridge as close to the cue ball as possible while still allowing for the required stroke force. Hold the bridge securely on the table with your left hand. Your stance will be fairly upright. In addition, your cue will be inclined, so you should avoid using any english as it will be very difficult to control. Hold the cue between the thumb and your first two fingers. The stroke should be fairly short and mostly with the wrist.

Mechanical Bridge Over a Ball

The mechanical bridge offers a variety of possible positions. The lower rungs are for draw shots. The upper rungs are for follow shots. You can elevate the bridge further by turning it on its side. This will enable you to shoot over obstructing balls at a distance. At times you may need to place one bridge on top of another when extra elevation (over obstructing balls) is required.

The Stance

No two players stand exactly alike at the table. This is partly due to differing physical characteristics and to personal preference. So, while it is difficult to say what's exactly right for each and every player, there are still a number of goals and objectives that each player's stance must meet. They include:

Room to allow the arm to swing freely
Balance
Providing a solid foundation that minimizes unwanted movement
Allows aiming accuracy
Comfortable - avoid feeling cramped or tense
Sets the cue level and straight

The distance that you stand from the table depends entirely on the position of the cue ball. On certain rail shots you will be a couple of feet from the table while on stretch shots you may lean your entire upper body over the table. The distance you spread your feet apart depends on your height and on how far you position your head over the cue. Taller people will naturally have to spread their feet more than shorter people. At the same time, players who crouch low over the cue generally will spread their feet more than those who assume a more upright shooting position.

You should spread your feet far enough apart so your stance is very stable. It should keep you from rocking off balance even the smallest amount. Your weight should be evenly distributed on both feet. To complete the tripod you should be leaning slightly forward so that part of your weight is distributed onto your bridge hand.

Over time you will develop a routine that allows you to automatically assume a correct stance. Newer players may wish to adopt the following procedure. Stand facing the table with your cue held at your side in your grip hand. The cue tip should be placed within a fraction of an inch of the cue ball along the intended line of sight. Now turn your body forty-five degrees to the right. Next step six to eight inches straight forward with your right foot (your right hip may now be touching your right hand). Now step about one and a half feet forward and slightly to the left with your left foot. At the same time, bend forward at the hips and extend your left arm and form your bridge. This basic procedure gives you a solid foundation from which to adapt your stance to your personal requirements.

I recommend that you stay within the confines of the stance we discussed above. It will help you avoid either of two extremes which can be damaging. In position #1 both feet are along the line of sight, which puts your body in the way of your arm swing. At the other end of the spectrum, both feet and your entire body are facing the shot. This position can lead to an awkward push stroke. Ideally, the placement of your feet and legs will get your body lined up correctly <u>and</u> out of the way of your arm swing.

Forming a Stance

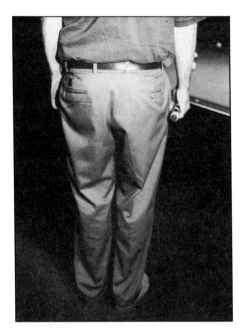

Step 1

Step 2

Step 3

Step 4

The Side Saddle (Incorrect)   **Facing the Shot (Incorrect)**

It is most common for the back leg to be straight and for the front leg to be bent slightly. However, some players flex both knees to lower their stance and/or to achieve greater relaxation. Other players prefer the rock-like stability of having both legs straight. Again, it's a matter of personal preference.

Three Popular Stances

The Classic Stance   **The Double Flex**   **Both Legs Straight**

Extremely Upright Stance

There are several possible head positions for your stance. Here again, it's a matter of choice. Many pros currently shoot with the cue directly under their chins. Some even place the cue to the side of their chin, directly under their dominant eye.

A low stance is best for aiming accurately. However, some players feel they can aim just as accurately with their head eight to ten inches above the cue. A higher stance provides more room to swing the arm freely. It is generally preferred when a powerful stroke is called for. A higher stance also lessens the chance of a player jumping up prematurely to make additional room for their shooting arm. I would advise, however, that you avoid the extremely upright stance in the illustration.

It's not a bad idea to vary your head position slightly. You can lower your head for precise aiming and raise it for power shots, such as the break. There is one constant, however, when it comes to the stance. Either your nose or your dominant eye (if you have one) should be lined up directly over the cue. If you're even the slightest bit doubtful about your position, have your house pro or a friend check this out. Also make sure to keep your head perfectly level. Cocking the head to one side or the other creates unwanted distortions.

One of the primary objectives of the stance is to get your shooting arm in the proper position so that it can deliver the cue squarely into the cue ball with maximum effectiveness. I recommend that your stance put you into the position that will promote a pendulum arm swing. It is easiest to use a pendulum like stroke when your arm begins in a straight up and down position. Your right arm should hang straight down from your elbow. In this position, your cue and arm will be fairly close to, but not touching, your right side.

The ideal setup for a pendulum stroke will find your right shoulder, arm, elbow, wrist and hand all resting on an imaginary pane of glass. They will be lined up along with the cue precisely down the intended line of aim. In this position you have the best chance of executing a perfectly straight stroke. No midstroke compensations should be needed to keep the cue moving in a straight line.

The Pendulum Position

Arm Angled Inward (Incorrect)

Arm Angled Outward (Incorrect)

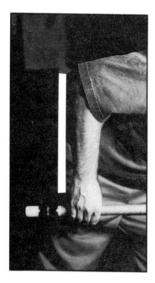

The 90 Degree Position   **Grip Hand Forward**   **Grip Hand Back (Incorrect)**

There are three basic positions in which you can place your shooting hand at address. They relate to the elbow position. Two are recommended, one is not.

In the first position, the grip hand rests directly beneath the elbow. This promotes a long fluid stroke. Players who hold the cue in this position will generally require a longer bridge. A big advantage to this position is that the stroke begins with the cue perfectly level at the impact position.

Nearly all of the great straight pool players, including Willie Mosconi, have used the classic position where the grip hand is a few inches <u>ahead</u> of the elbow at address. This produces a short bridge and a compact stroke. It also largely eliminates the chance of lifting the grip hand during the backstroke. This address position also helps to promote a level cue. The stroke can be lengthened by moving both the bridge and grip hands further back on the cue. One word of caution: don't place your grip hand too far forward (definitely not beyond the balance point) as this may create a choppy stroke and an abbreviated follow through.

The last position ruins many pool players' games. When the grip hand is past the elbow excess lifting will occur in the backstroke, which will create a choppy stroke. In order to maintain any semblance of a level cue, you would need to drop your elbow on your backstroke. This is virtually unheard of! I can't remember any great players who addressed their shots with their grip hand in this position.

Your left arm completes the stance. It should be kept as straight as possible. However, a slight bending at the elbow doesn't hurt and is preferred by many good players.

Special Stances

So far we've discussed the standard stance that you'll be using on the majority of your shots. However, when the cue ball is extremely close to the object ball at an angle, it often helps to stand higher to better judge the proper cut angle (more on this later). As we mentioned earlier, power shots often require a higher stance to permit maximum cue stick acceleration. The illustration shows how to stretch for a shot. Use an open bridge and a short stroke while holding the cue at the end of the butt. Also pictured is a stance with a leg on the table that can enable you to reach a shot that you would otherwise be unable to reach.

Stretching Across the Table

Leg Up On the Table

The Stroke

The stroke is quite simply the most important fundamental in the game. Your ability to pocket balls and play shape is in direct proportion to the quality of your stroke and your ability to aim correctly. I can't emphasize enough the importance of developing a consistent, dependable stroke.

Confidence plays a major role in the overall quality of your game. When you are confident, relaxed and stroking smoothly and effortlessly, the balls seem to find the pockets on their own. There's nothing to it. You can't miss. Players refer to this euphoric state as being in "dead stroke". On the opposite end of the spectrum, if your confidence is low and your stroke is jerky, each shot becomes a struggle.

Several pros on tour have strokes which are distinctive. Their strokes work because of years of practice. There is no single, correct method of stroking; rather, it is an individualized process unique to each player. And yet, I would advise newer players to adopt the principles of stroking I have set forth in this section until they are comfortable with the fundamentals of the game. By following the "textbook" stroke, you can develop a stroke that will render very positive results. You will also have a set of guidelines to refer to when you are in a slump or "out of stroke".

The ideal stroke will send the cue ball along a precise path to the object ball and enable you to shoot with a wide variety of speeds.

Your preshot routine will prepare you to successfully execute the stroke. Take some time to size up the table. Make a decision on exactly how you intend to play the shot. Then and only then are you ready to take your stance at the table. Make your approach to the shot the same every time. This will help you "move into the shot" and position yourself consistently. Relax from your right shoulder to the tips of your fingers. This will help promote a smooth, fluid and powerful stroke.

Once you are settled into your stance, you are ready to fine tune your aim and to begin your warm-up strokes. Warm-up strokes serve a number of purposes. They allow you to build muscle memory and to get your stroke on track. Getting a feel for the length and speed of the stroke is another primary purpose. Ideally your warm-up strokes will be smooth, rhythmic and straight. Some players use a series of short strokes (2-3 inches) while others will pull the cue tip all the way back to within an inch or so of the bridge. A series of rapid strokes is favored by a number of players while others use slow, deliberate warm-up strokes. You must find the method that works for you.

The shot you are facing dictates largely how many warm-up strokes you should use. If you use too few strokes, you can't complete your routine. This will cause you to miss even easy shots. On difficult shots, such as thin cuts, where aiming is a top priority, you may need to take a few extra warm-up strokes to really zero in on the target. Be aware that you can spend too much time warm-up stroking. As you complete your final warm-up stroke, your eyes should lock onto the object ball. It's now time to execute the perfect pool stroke.

The pendulum stroke, which involves swinging the arm straight back and straight through, is highly recommended. It will keep you from having to make any compensating moves, such as twisting your arm and/or wrist, during your forward stroke. In other words, you won't have to cancel out one flaw with another flaw in order to successfully execute your shot. The pendulum stroke gives you greater consistency.

The only moving parts during your backstroke should be from the elbow on down of your right arm. The rest of your body should remain motionless. It's good practice to concentrate on keeping your body still during your stroke. This will allow you to gain a heightened sense of what your stroke feels like. Of course, if you don't like what you feel, by all means make the needed adjustments. Beware also of a common tendency to lift the right elbow during the backstroke. This can throw the cue off track. You can generate plenty of power with only your lower arm.

Your backstroke should be long enough to provide sufficient power. You want to avoid having to hurry up your forward stroke. At the same time, the stroke should be short enough so that you can avoid decelerating through the shot. The secret is to find the proper balance. Some players are able to use the same length bridge while varying the length of their backstroke from shot to shot. Others benefit by changing the length of their bridge to match the length of the backstroke on each shot.

The tempo of your stroke should be as smooth and even as possible. Unfortunately, many players ruin their stroke during the transition from the backstroke to the forward stroke. A little voice tells them, "I've got to really hit that cue ball". This causes a jerky stroke. The results are often disastrous. As a remedy, some top players have been known to pause ever so slightly at the conclusion of their backstroke. I recommend that you develop an awareness of the transition phase of your stroke. If your stroke lacks fluidity and power, slowing down your transition may solve the problem.

As the arm swings forward, the right elbow should drop. The elbow drop begins at contact with the cue ball. This is a vital component of a fundamentally sound stroke. By dropping your elbow, you are ensuring that the cue will travel on a level and straight line. The elbow drop will prevent you from dipping the cue tip into the cue ball. This is especially crucial on draw shots.

The wrist acts in concert with your arm to produce a powerful stroke. In turn, a more relaxed grip on the cue will increase the snap of your wrist at impact. Even a little wrist action can add substantial power to a stroke that is all arm powered. Your final stroke should be related to the speed of your warm-up strokes. However, the final stroke will move faster through impact because of the snap of the wrist.

We discussed the grip at the address position earlier in the chapter. As the stroke progresses, the grip will undergo a couple of significant changes. This is no cause for alarm. During the backstroke your grip hand will open up. This helps keep the cue level. Be sure to maintain a constant grip pressure during your back stroke and as you complete the transition to the forward stroke. As your arm swings forward, your grip hand will return to the address position at impact. It's only natural to expect some increase in grip pressure during the forward stroke. However, your stroke will produce more action on the cue ball if you can maintain a light grip into your follow through.

A full and graceful follow through is the signature of a superior stroke. A full follow through prevents an abrupt stab at the ball. It also gives the cue ball much of its action. Let the cue stick come to a natural stop. Don't cut the follow through short and, definitely avoid recoiling the cue backward. Your follow through should extend at least as far as your backstroke, possibly even further. This is especially true on long draw shots. Be sure to stroke through the cue ball smoothly. Don't let its presence or the shock of impact cause you to quit on your stroke. As a practice exercise, try stroking through the cue ball pretending it's not even there. You can learn a lot about your stroke by observing your follow through. It helps to hold your follow through as if you were posing for a picture. Now check to see if the cue is level and pointing down your line of sight. If your follow through and arm swing are perfectly straight, you won't be able to see the back end of the cue under your arm.

You will need to eventually raise up from the table. You may even have to remove yourself rather quickly to avoid fouling the cue ball or an object ball. You should learn to raise up from the table smoothly and quickly when necessary, but only after you have completely finished your follow through. Avoid jumping up in the middle of your shot as this can totally destroy your stroke.

We've covered a lot of ground on the last few pages. Obviously, you can't think of everything when executing a shot. I advise you to work on one or two fundamentals at a time. When you've made those an integral part of your game, move on to the next. Keep adding pieces to the puzzle. With sufficient practice you will no longer need to consciously think about what to do on each shot. Your warm-up strokes, grip, stance, and the other components of your game will be executed unconsciously. A solid stroke that's well grounded in the fundamentals will enable you to experience peak performance on occasion. When you enter the state of mind where you're in "dead stroke", you will experience the pool player's equivalent of runners high. You will experience the great joy of playing this game easily and effortlessly.

It's very important to develop an accurate stroke that consistently delivers the cue straight through the cue ball. Of equal importance is your ability to vary the speed of your stroke. One of the great fascinations of pool is the seemingly infinite variety of the types of shots you must play. On one shot you may need to nudge the object ball gently into the pocket. On the next, you may have to execute a powerful table length draw shot. And so it goes. Easy stroke. Hard stroke. Medium soft follow shot. Power force shot. Shot after shot you will need to apply just the right amount of force to send the cue ball to the desired location. Keep this in mind.

The Complete Stroke

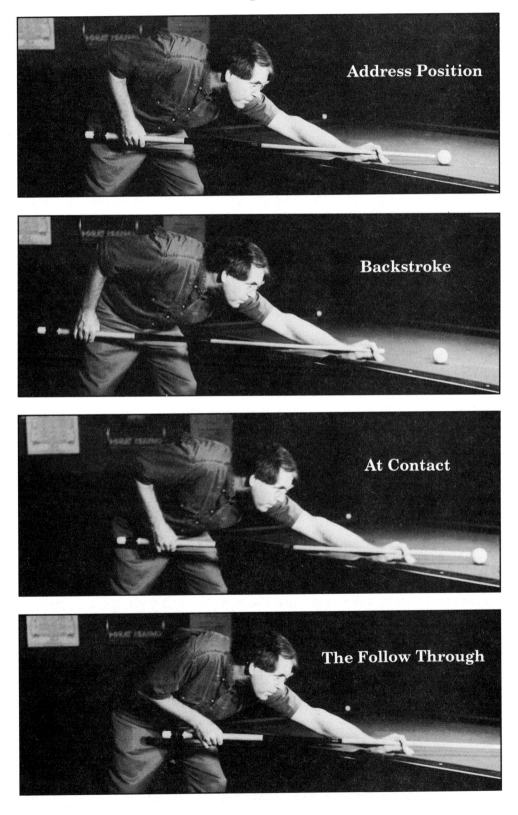

Don't develop a stroke that's one dimensional. Learn to vary the speed of your arm swing and the amount of wrist action. On some shots an easy swing of the arm with little or no wrist action will get the job done. On others, you will need to whip your arm and wrist to generate the necessary force. The ability to vary the speed of your stroke is directly related to your ability to play position. Make speed of stroke a top priority as you develop your game.

While learning the game or during a slump, it can help to focus on something positive. Top golfers use swing keys. These may relate to tempo or some mechanical part of their swing. Similarly, pool players should use one or two stroke thoughts. These can help groove a fundamental technique. Stroke keys can and often do change. A new key can correct a flaw and produce immediate results in your game. The list below gives you some stroke keys that are designed to help your stroke:

- Use a smooth stroke
- Slowly complete the transition to the forward stroke
- Stay down until the ball is in the pocket
- Focus on moving your arm only
- Point your tip at the target on follow through
- Feel the tip at impact
- Pay extra attention to where you strike the cue ball
- Look at the object ball intently on your last stroke

You can do many things right and still miss balls. Here's where a stroke key can come in handy. Stroke keys have a way of focusing your attention on one vital aspect of the stroke that may be causing you to miss balls. In addition, a stroke key can free up your mind so your stroke can function as naturally as possible. For example, if you are concentrating totally on the object ball, you won't be worrying about what your arm swing feels like. You will free up your arm to make the best stroke possible.
There are a number of drills that can help you ingrain the fundamentals and monitor your progress. Some you can do alone, some with a partner, either an instructor or a friend.

- Slow your stroke way down. Observe how straight it is. Gradually build the speed up to normal.
- Look back at your right arm while taking practice strokes. Is your arm moving in a straight line? Is your wrist twisting out of position?
- Have your partner stand behind you, directly in line with your cue and watch for flaws.
- Try pushing the cue through the cue ball.
- Experiment with different length bridges. Start with a six inch bridge and move back.
- Do a stroke check. Is your arm completely covering the butt of your cue on the follow through as it should be?
- Shoot straight-in shots - have the cue tip point directly at the pocket.

Imagine this sequence: you've decided on the correct shot, you've settled into a perfectly comfortable stance that's dead in line, you've taken several even, smooth warm-up strokes, and then, at the moment of truth, you jump up, and miss...badly. What did you accomplish? Many positives, one negative. The net result is a missed shot. Perhaps you have one particular flaw that's hurting your game. If so, find it and remove it as soon as possible. The following checklist gives you some of the many common mistakes. Match your game against the items included in the checklist. This will help evaluate your weaknesses versus your strengths. Remember, you can do a lot of things correctly; all it takes is one fatal flaw to miss a shot.

- Indecisiveness - no clearcut plan of action.
- Thinking negatively
- Faulty preshot routine
- No preshot routine
- No warm-up strokes
- Too many warm-up strokes
- Inappropriate warm-up strokes for the shot
- Twisting your arm
- Twisting your wrist
- Jerking or jabbing at the ball
- No arm drop on forward swing
- Freezing over the shot
- Jumping up prematurely
- Speeding up the final stroke
- Excess tension
- Abbreviated follow through or lack of follow through
- Crooked follow through
- Head or body movement during the stroke

A Short Course in the Fundamentals

We've covered a lot of ground over the last several pages. It will be important for you to review this material again and again until you become well-grounded in the fundamentals. I've prepared a short course in the fundamentals which covers the grip, bridge, stance and stroke. I encourage new players to refer to this list often. You may even want to copy the list and carry it with you for use during your practice sessions.

The Grip

- It must have the right feel.
- Use a light grip.
- Cradle the cue in two or three fingers and your thumb.
- Allow some daylight between your cue and hand.
- Find the ideal spot to hold the cue in relation to the balance point.
- Adjust your grip hand for soft shots (forward) and for power shots (back).

The Bridge

- Provides secure guidance for the stroke.
- Open bridge - place cue on the vee formed by the thumb and index finger. Good for follow shots and stretch shots.
- Closed bridge - used most often. Place the cue through a loop formed by pressing the tips of the thumb and index finger together on the middle finger.
- Raise the bridge for follow shots by bringing in the tips of the last three fingers.
- Lower the bridge for draw shots by extending the fingers as far as possible.
- Use a short bridge for control and a long bridge for power.
- Keep your shaft clean and/or use a glove to prevent stickiness during the stroke.
- Elevated bridge - place your fingers securely on the table and raise your hand off the table. Place the cue in a vee formed by your thumb and index finger.
- Rail bridge - slide your thumb underneath your index finger, placing the cue alongside your thumb and tip of your middle finger, then wrap the index finger over the cue.
- Open rail bridge - place the cue in a vee formed by the thumb and index finger.
- Mechanical bridge - place as close to obstructing balls as possible. Secure it to the table with your left hand. Use a short stroke, mostly powered by the wrist.

The Stance

- Stance objectives - balance, comfort, accuracy of aim (head over cue), alignment, freedom of arm movement, and consistency.
- Distance - from the table depends on position of cue ball.
- Stability - spread your feet wide enough for stability.
- Head position - distance from cue largely a matter of preference. Keep head low for aiming, high for power shots.
- Weight distribution - should be spread evenly between your feet with some also on the bridge hand.
- Develop a routine for settling into your stance.
- Position your shooting arm straight up and down in the pendulum position.
- Position your grip hand even with, or a few inches in front of your elbow.

The Stroke

- Trust and confidence are the keys to a successful stroke.
- The ideal stroke will send the cue ball along a precise path, have a variety of speeds, be silky smooth and deliver results!
- Plan your shot.
- Follow your routine as you settle into your stance.
- Warm-up strokes should be of the correct type and number.
- Warm-up strokes should be smooth and rhythmic.
- Use the pendulum (straight back and straight through) arm swing.
- No unnecessary body and head movement.
- Smooth transition to the forward stroke.
- Maintain a light grip pressure.
- Drop right elbow as cue contacts the cue ball.
- Stay with the shot - don't jump up.
- Follow through completely.

CHAPTER 2

HOW TO AIM

Developing An Eye For The Pocket

In chapter one we discussed the fundamentals of a solid, dependable stroke. When you combine a good stroke with aiming skill, you have the ingredients necessary to become a shotmaker. Nearly all of the top players possess fundamentally solid strokes. Some, of course, are a little more pleasing to the eye than others. What sets the Pros apart is an uncanny sense of aim. The best players are by and large the best aimers. From long hours of practice they know how to aim each shot.

The Pro's also have exceptional hand/eye coordination, partly acquired, partly god given. And when they settle in over a shot, they mean business. You can see the fierce determination in their eyes. Similarly, you can learn to zero in on the target and to pocket a wide variety of shots with consistency. The good news is that the method we'll cover is used by the majority of leading Pros. And since you enjoy practicing (you <u>do</u> enjoy practicing, don't you?) there's more good news: our method simply requires the necessary hours at the table and your attention on what you are doing. Nothing more, nothing less.

Preshot Routine

Before you settle into your stance and fire away you need to decide what shot you're going to play, and how you're going to play it. The most important thing is to be decisive. Once you've chosen your shot it's time to enter into your preshot routine.

A set routine for approaching the table will help you develop a consistent stance, which in turn will enable you to aim with greater accuracy. Don't approach the table in a haphazard manner. Don't assume your stance from one direction, then the other. Establish a set routine and follow it on all shots.

Remember our procedure for building a stance? It involved laying the cue precisely along the line of aim, and then constructing our stance around the cue stick. Forming your stance should be automatic by now. However, you should face each shot directly down the intended aiming line and approach your stance from that angle. This will help you not only to move into each shot with ease but also to line up your shot with much greater consistency. This will decrease the number of adjustments in your stance once you're down over the shot.

Top players are so good at picking out their line of aim that they require few, if any, adjustments once they are down in their stance. Any alterations they do make are nearly undetectable. With time you can develop a sense of aim that will enable you to settle in at the table in the correct position. For now, however, recognize that minor adjustments in your stance can bring you closer and closer to perfect alignment, and perfect aim.

When you settle down into your stance, the cue tip may not be positioned exactly where you want it. You will need to adjust its position. This may cause another part of your body to feel out of position, which will also need to be adjusted. In short, once you bend down into your stance, take a moment or two to wiggle and settle various body parts into perfect alignment. Make sure everything feels just right. Don't dally too long, but don't rush the process either. After awhile, you will begin to settle into a comfortable stance without even thinking about it. Just be aware that if you go ahead and pull the trigger when the cue's pointing off center, your head is to the side, or your bridge feels funny, you shouldn't be too surprised if you miss your shot.

So far we've chosen our shot, made a firm decision on how to play it, and followed our routine while settling into our stance. It's now time to aim and shoot the ball into the pocket.

Finding the target is a challenge to many new players. After all, we are being asked to shoot one round shiny object into another and have it disappear into a rather small opening. However, it's not as difficult as it seems.

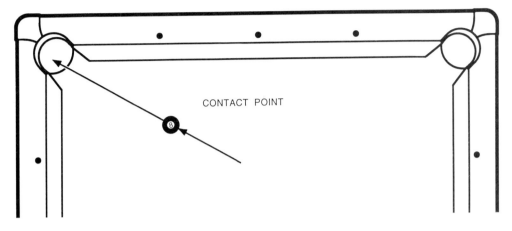

The Contact Point

The diagram above shows how to find the contact point on the object ball. Draw an imaginary line from the pocket through the center of the object ball and out the other side. The arrow shows the contact point on the 8-ball.

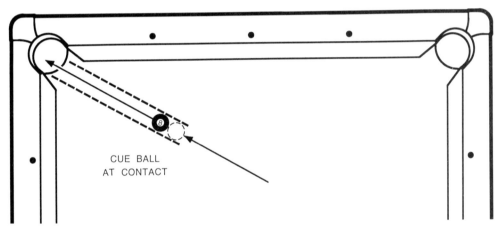

Cue Ball at Contact

To make the 8 in the corner pocket, the cue ball need only strike the 8 at the contact point. The diagram above shows the exact location of the cue ball at contact. Notice that the two parallel lines drawn down the edge of each ball form a channel. The 8-ball will travel through the channel and into the pocket.

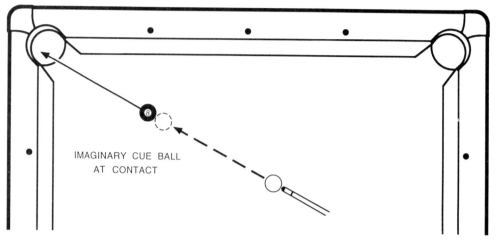

IMAGINARY CUE BALL
AT CONTACT

Pocketing a Shot

We've now added a cue ball and cue stick to demonstrate a successful shot. The cue ball has been shot along the dashed line directly into the contact point. As a result, the 8-ball will disappear into the corner pocket. Notice the imaginary cue ball at contact. Many excellent players have learned to aim by imagining a "ghost ball" at the desired point of impact. Many players still use this method of aiming with excellent results. Perhaps it will help your aiming. My feeling is, whatever works, use it.

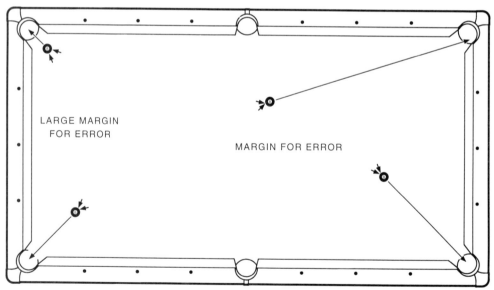

LARGE MARGIN
FOR ERROR

MARGIN FOR ERROR

Margin for Error

The contact point on the object ball will vary in size depending on its distance from the pocket. When the object ball is close to the pocket, you have a fairly large margin for error. Notice how the arrows, which depict the target on the object ball, get closer and closer as the object gets further from the pocket. The 8-ball in the top right portion of the diagram should give you some appreciation of the precision aiming that this game requires.

Straight in shots are highly useful for improving your stroke and for learning the aiming process. They are the easiest to aim, as you need only shoot the center of the cue ball directly at the center of the object ball. Straight in shots allow you to devote a good deal of your energy to developing your fundamental skills.

As you settle into your stance and begin your warm-up strokes, consider exactly what is it that you should be looking at. The pocket, the cue ball, or the object ball? As you size up the shot you will initially look at all three. After you've played and practiced enough pool, you'll develop a sixth sense of where the pocket is. You must trust that this will take place, as it simplifies the aiming process. You will catch a glimpse of the pocket in your peripheral vision. From that point forward, your attention should focus back and forth between the object ball and the cue ball. As you begin your final backstroke, your eyes should lock onto the object ball and remain there until it's well on it's way to the pocket. And be sure not to peek at the shot before it's rolling towards the pocket or you may not like what you see!

It will help your game tremendously when you can learn to stroke confidently down you chosen line of aim through the cue ball. However, some players feel it's necessary to make minute adjustments in their aim on their final stroke. This approach can work as long as you are not violently twisting your arm and/or wrist through impact to compensate for incorrect aiming.

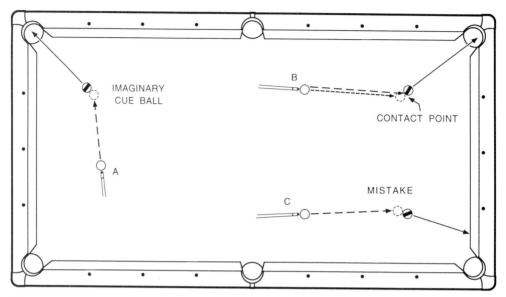

Cut Shots

Our discussion so far has focused on straight in shots. However, as a practical matter, nearly every shot that you'll encounter has at least some amount of cut to it. A cut shot is defined as a shot in which you aim for a less than full hit on the object ball. The diagram above demonstrates a basic cut shot (position A). Observe how the imaginary cue ball (ghost ball) and the object ball (the stripe) line up directly into the pocket. Again, many players aim by imagining a ghost ball at the precise point of impact. The cue ball need only be shot to the place occupied by the ghost ball for a successful shot.

You may find it helpful to place a second cue ball in the position of the ghost ball. Now settle into your stance to see what the correct contact position looks like. Then remove the ghost ball and try the shot. As you'll recall, the center of the cue ball is aimed at the center of the object ball on straight in shots. Not so with cut shots. In position B, the ghost ball and stripe are lined up at the pocket. Notice, however, that the far left side of the ghost cue ball contacts the stripe, <u>not</u> the center.

Position C shows what happens on cut shots when you mistakenly aim the center of the cue ball at the contact point of the object ball. The shot will always be undercut.

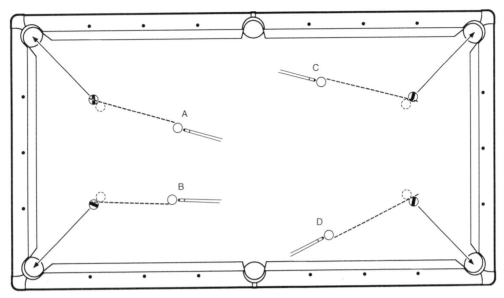

Fullness of the Cut

The diagram above illustrates a progression of cut shots. In position A, half of the cue ball contacts the object ball. This is called a half ball hit. In position B, ¼ of the cue ball hits the object ball. Only ⅛ of the cue ball contacts the stripe in position C. Finally, in position D the cue ball barely grazes the stripe. The lesson from these examples is clear: as the cut angle becomes greater, less of the cue ball will come in contact with the object ball.

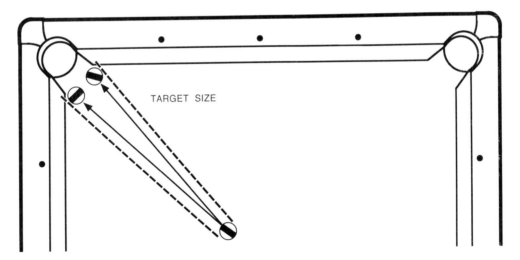

Target Size

This diagram shows the size of the target on a shot that's facing directly toward the pocket. You can strike the rail ½ inch on either side of the pocket and still make the shot. This makes the pocket's effective opening 5¾ inches wide. The size of the target becomes slightly smaller when the object ball approaches from an angle.

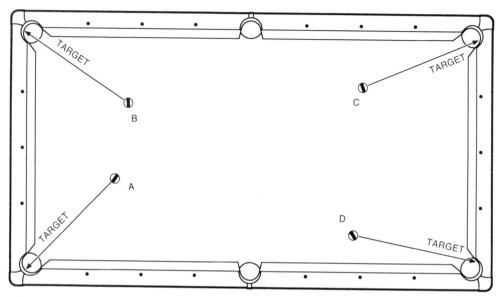

Where to Aim in the Corner Pocket

When the object ball is lined up directly in front of the pocket as in position A above, the target is the center of the back of the pocket. Example B shows how the target has shifted to the left with the object ball further to the right. Examples C and D show how the target shifts further away from the center of the pocket as the object ball rests closer to the rail. Remember to adjust your target in the pocket to the location of the object ball.

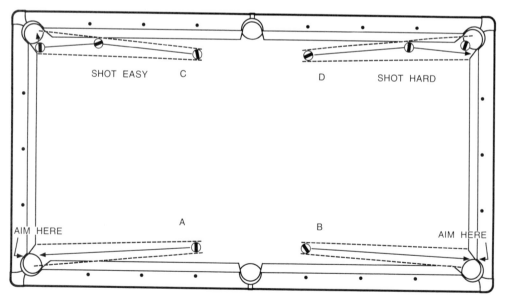

Shooting Balls Down the Rail

There are a few things to consider when choosing your target on shots near the rail. Position A in the diagram above shows where to aim the stripe on tables with pockets of average difficulty. Notice that the channel allows for contacting the rail in front of the pocket. Under normal playing conditions, the pocket's effective opening remains 43/4". Notice how far the target has shifted to the right (marked aim here).

Position B demonstrates the same shot, this time on a table with tight pockets. Observe how the target has shifted even further away from center. This is because you can barely graze the rail (if at all) on shots down the rail into tight pockets. Position C shows how you can hit up the rail and still make the shot when shooting softly on tables of average difficulty. Position D demonstrates how the same shot on the same table will stay out of the pocket when shot with a hard stroke.

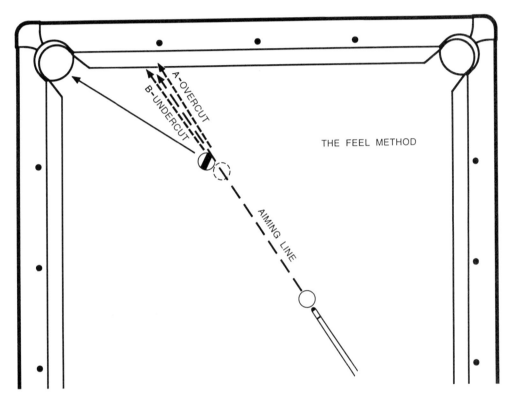

The Feel Method

We've identified the target for the pocket and the contact point on the object ball. Now we're ready to discuss a method of aiming that's simple and very natural. I call it the "feel method". The first step is to settle into your stance along your chosen line of aim. This should position the cue on a straight line that extends through the center of the cue ball to the center of where the cue ball will be at impact (the ghost ball). The diagram depicts the aiming line.

How do you know where to aim? The answer comes from hours and hours of practice. You simply develop "an eye" for each shot. Something in your brain clicks as you line up a shot that tells you "this is the correct line of aim". Hundreds of previous observations of the same shot tells you that you are now aimed correctly.

In our example, let's assume you settled into your stance and aimed along either line A or B. Using the feel method, your brain would tell you that you are aimed improperly. You would then make the appropriate adjustments until your brain tells you that your aim is on the mark. Let's assume you were mistakenly aiming along Line B. On this shot you can tell that the shot is not being cut enough. Your aim will need to be adjusted to the <u>right</u> on the object ball so that it will go more to the <u>left</u> and into the pocket. The feel method involves adjusting your aim in small increments until it looks just right. But what if you are a new player who has no idea where to aim? The answer is to practice. Set up easy cut shots to start. Shoot the same shots over and over again. You can easily mark their position by using hole reinforcers. Observe each shot carefully. Learn from your failures and your successes. Learning to aim is largely a self corrective process. Trial and error. Trial and success. Keep shooting balls, lots of balls and you will quickly begin to develop an "eye".

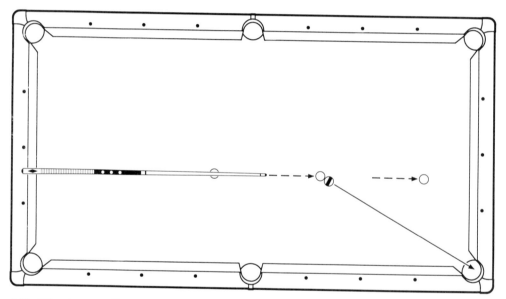

All Shots are Straight

Once you have developed a feel for how to aim a wide variety of cut shots, aiming will become a simple, natural process. You won't have to think about it much. Your instincts will guide you into the proper line of aim. Then you can concentrate on making the straightest stroke possible! This, of course, gives you your best chance of making the shot. Perhaps it will help you by remembering this phrase, "once I am lined up correctly, all shots are straight shots". The diagram above demonstrates this concept. The shot has been lined up correctly. All you have to do is follow straight through as indicated. Imagine you are shooting the cue ball along the indicated line and it will slice the stripe into the corner pocket.

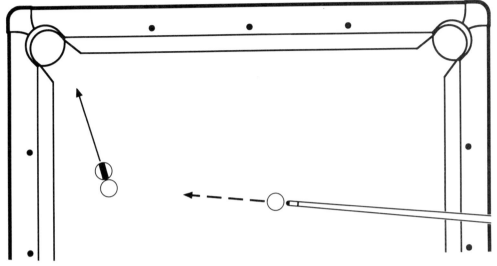

Setting up a Ghost Ball

You may find it helpful at first to imagine a ghost ball at impact. You can also speed up the learning process by placing a second cue ball in line with the object ball when you initially setup a new shot. Observe it's position carefully and then remove it prior to shooting. This will eliminate some of the guesswork and reduce your number of unsuccessful attempts.

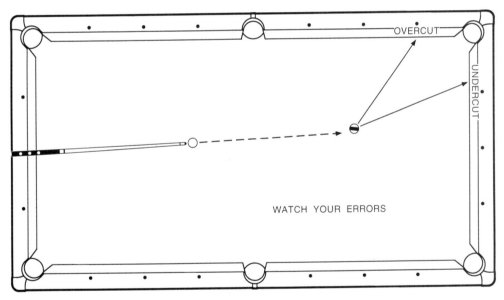

Watching your Errors

Look for tendencies when you practice a specific shot. The example shows the two errors possible: undercutting and overcutting. An undercut shot comes from hitting the object ball too fully. Most beginners tend to undercut most of their shots. An overcut results from hitting the object ball too thinly.

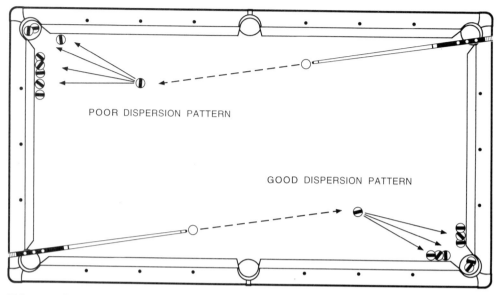

POOR DISPERSION PATTERN

GOOD DISPERSION PATTERN

Dispersion Patterns

The dispersion pattern that your shots form can help you detect flaws in your aim. The pattern at the upper left shows a player with a definite tendency to undercutting. When the vast majority of your misses are to one side of the pocket, you simply must make the necessary adjustment. The player in our example needs to start cutting this shot more until the dispersion pattern begins to resemble that of the player at the lower right.

Player B has a much better dispersion pattern. The misses are generally closer to the pocket. This player is honing in on the target. In addition, player B is not committing the same mistakes over and over. Instead, player B is constantly refining his/her aim. The process goes like this: overcut, undercut, undercut a little less, overcut a little bit, hit the pocket.! Back and forth. The misses move from one side of the pocket to the other. The ball comes closer and closer to the pocket. As your eye develops you start pocketing the shot, sporadically at first. Then the balls begin to fall on a much more regular basis. Pretty soon you know where to aim. You know the shot.

Learning to aim is simply a matter of creating as many successful impressions in your minds eye as possible. Lots of practice while paying close attention will enable you to develop a feel for each shot. There's simply no substitute for practice. You'll hear this over and over throughout this book. If you want to develop your aiming skills as quickly as possible, space your practice sessions as close as possible.

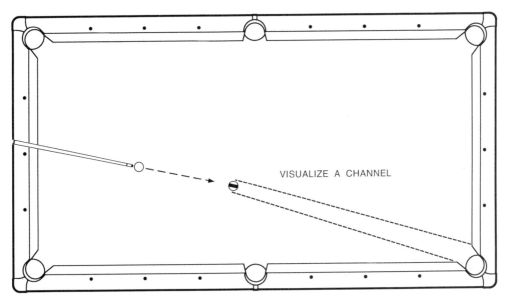

Visualizing a Channel to the Pocket

There are a couple of visualizations that may help you to locate the pocket. The diagram illustrates a channel to the pocket. Notice how it expands toward the pocket, which is more than twice as wide as the object ball. This visualization makes the target seem larger and more inviting than it may otherwise appear. This can raise your confidence and lower your anxiety level.

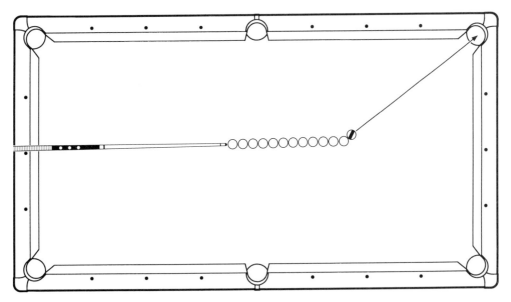

Visualizing a Line of Cue Balls

Try to visualize a line of cue balls that extends precisely to the point of contact. Visualizations such as these are good tools for learning to aim. They may also be useful under game conditions. One of the beauties of visualization is that it gives you something positive to think about.

Contact Induced Throw

On all cut shots you will need to know about a phenomenon I shall refer to as contact induced throw. At contact there is friction between the cue ball and object ball. The friction that develops will alter the path of the object ball.

When you are cutting a ball to the left, friction will throw it to the right. When you cut to the right, friction will throw the object ball to the left. You must therefore allow for a little more cut on virtually every cut shot.

The table below is adapted from a study conducted by Bob Jewett. It shows that a soft stroke creates the greatest amount of throw. Perhaps that's because the cue ball and object ball are in contact slightly longer on a soft shot, which gives friction a little more time to work. Throw is least felt when a hard stroke is used.

Contact Induced Throw In Degrees
Stroke Force

Cut Angle	Soft	Medium	Hard
0	0	0	0
15	3	3	3
30	6	4	4
45	5	4	2
60	5	3	2
75	5	3	1

The table also demonstrates that contact induced throw is greatest at 30 degrees. On greater cut angles with a hard stroke, contact induced throw has very little affect on the aiming process.

Let's return now to our exercise where we placed a second cue ball at the desired point of contact. As you'll recall, the second step is to remove the second ball and then shoot directly at that spot. If you find that, despite your best efforts, you are not cutting the shot enough, you are probably a victim of contact induced throw. If you are cutting to the left, for example, adjust the position of the second cue ball so that it lines up with the object ball to a point at the left edge of the pocket. If this still doesn't work, adjust your aim a little further to the left.

Aiming is tough enough, so I certainly hope I have not confused the issue. However, we can't argue with the laws of physics. One way or another you simply must learn to adjust your aim for contact induced throw.

One of the reasons I recommend the feel method of aiming is that you can learn to make the necessary adjustments automatically. You will just know, through hours of practice, where to aim a shot without having to delve too deeply into the mysteries of contact induced throw. Nevertheless, a working knowledge of it's effects on your aiming should be helpful, especially for newer players.

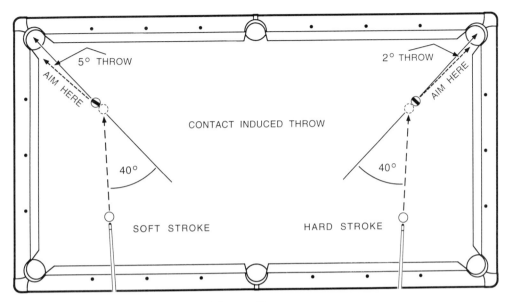

Contact Induced Throw at Forty Degrees

The diagram above demonstrates the effect of contact induced throw on a 40 degree cut shot at two different stroke speeds. In the position on the left, a soft stroke was used. Notice that 5 degrees of throw must be allowed for. The shot at the right is identical, only this time a hard stroke was used. As a result, the throw only amounted to 2 degrees.

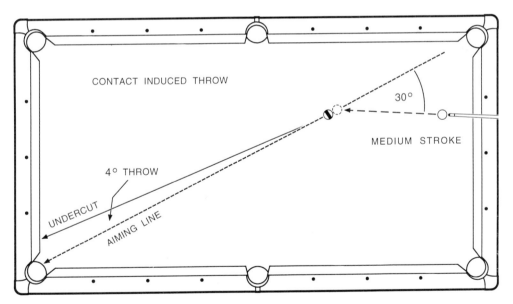

Contact Throw at Long Range

The effects of throw are magnified over greater distances. The shot above is a 30 degree cut which was hit with a medium stroke. The cue ball was aimed to cut the stripe into the corner pocket. Observe how the actual path of the object ball (represented by the solid line) deviated from the aiming line. Again, the solution to pocketing this shot is to hit the object ball a little bit thinner to compensate for this throw.

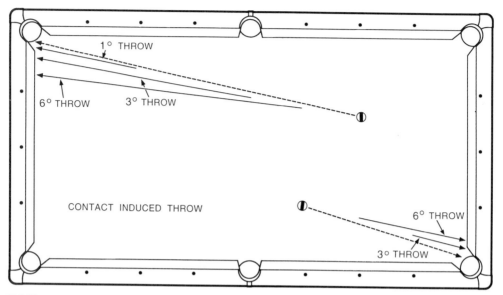

Different Degrees of Contact Throw

The table referred to earlier shows the magnitude of throw in degrees at different stroke speeds. The diagram above demonstrates how various degrees of throw can affect your shots. The stripe ball at the top of the diagram will miss badly with either 3 degrees or 6 degrees of throw. It may barely sneak into the side of the pocket if it is thrown one degree off line. The stripe ball in the lower portion of the diagram is considerably closer to the pocket. Nevertheless, it will still miss if it is thrown 6 degrees off line. The stripe may barely sneak into the pocket if thrown only 3 degrees off line.

CHAPTER 3

SHOTMAKING

Building An Arsenal Of

Gamewinning Shots

There's not much doubt that shotmaking is the most exciting aspect of pool. The thrill that's generated from the circular path of a well executed masse shot and other displays of cue wizardry helps to explain the popularity of professional trick shot artists. It also accounts for a growing library of books and tapes that are designed to teach the novice player wondrous feats of cue magic.

In this book, however, our goal is to learn to play pool, not to pocket spectacular shots that never come up in competition. What we'll be covering in the pages ahead are a host of practical shots that will add great depth to your game.

There's a vast difference between being a shotmaker and a pool player. Shotmakers may look very impressive to the untrained eye. The trouble with their game is that they are always being forced to make one tough shot after another. Expert shotmaking may win games at lower levels of play. However, if you aspire (as I certainly hope you do) to become a real player, you'll learn to regard yourself as a complete player, a player who can make the right shots when needed. After all, shotmaking does not exist in a vacuum. Excellent shotmaking skills must be combined with other important elements of the game, such as position play, safety play, and game strategy.

In this chapter we'll first discuss some of the basics of shotmaking. Then we'll move on to the specifics of how you can improve your game by mastering cut shots, combinations, banks, billiards, caroms, and other assorted gamewinning shots. Some shots require english, which is discussed in Chapter 4.

Basic Shotmaking

The quality of your shotmaking is largely dependent on your level of confidence. In turn, your confidence is directly related to your ball pocketing skills. They will both grow in tandem as your games progresses. The better you shoot, the more confidence you'll have. The more confidence you have, the better you'll shoot. Ideally you will develop a self-perpetuating cycle of improvement that will continue to boost your shotmaking capabilities to ever higher levels. But first you must build a solid foundation for your game. Your ability to pocket balls consistently will be directly related to the time you spend practicing and playing. Practice won't guarantee you ball pocketing wizardry, but without lots of hours at the table you won't even have a chance to fully develop your skills.

All players seem to have their favorite shots. These are the shots that they feel comfortable shooting, that they believe they can pocket. As your game improves, and your confidence grows, you will develop your own list of shots that you truly believe you're capable of making the majority of the time. It's a definite plus to have a number of shots that you can count on, but don't cut short the development of your shotmaking. Instead, keep adding to your list of those shots you feel confident playing until you become a well rounded shotmaker.

Missing Shots - Why it Happens

From beginner to expert, nobody enjoys missing shots. However, if you train yourself to learn from your mistakes, then your game will progress much faster. Top players are the best at looking for some positive feedback from their mistakes. They do this in hopes that they'll learn something that will prevent them from repeating the same mistake over and over again. We'll cover some of the common reasons why balls are missed. Perhaps you'll discover a flaw or two that's been hurting your shotmaking. Take some time to conduct an objective evaluation of your shotmaking skills. Are you guilty of committing one or more of these errors? If so, resolve to take the appropriate measures to correct any flaws that you may discover.

The primary reason for missing balls is faulty technique. A poor stroke may be keeping you from striking the cue ball precisely where intended. Perhaps you need to work on your aiming, which is a major cause of missed shots. Perhaps, you may be stroking <u>and</u> aiming poorly. To become an accurate shotmaker you will need to develop a fundamentally sound stroke and a keen sense of aim. So if you are having trouble pocketing basic shots, take some time to review the fundamentals in the first two chapters before moving on to the shots presented later in this chapter.

Poor shot selection is another cause of missed shots. If you are regularly shooting razor thin cut shots or other shots that are well beyond your skill level, you are throwing away games unnecessarily. Remember, the practice table is the time for working on tough shots and for expanding your repertoire. Only when you feel complete confidence in a shot should you be using it in game conditions.

Perhaps your fundamentals are sound but you still miss shots that are well within your capabilities. A poor preshot routine (or worse yet, the lack of one) is usually the culprit. Virtually any shot can be missed if not given the proper care and attention. A well rehearsed preshot routine that's followed religiously on each and every shot can keep you from committing needless shotmaking blunders. Your preshot routine will help you quell that little voice of doubt that roars up at the worst times and says, in effect, "you're going to miss it". This little voice of negativity has plagued everyone who's ever played the game at some point in their career. However, remember that the mind has room only for one thought at a time. Therefore, if you can develop a preshot routine that's full of the positive things that you need to do to execute each shot successfully, you'll reduce or eliminate the little voice that's saying "miss it".

Steady nerves play a big part in a successful game of pool. As the heat of competition increases, funny things can happen to that well oiled stroke that worked so well in practice. In addition, your sense of aim may suffer. As a mater of fact, it's been well documented by scientific studies that our muscles react differently under stress, and that our eyesight may become impaired. If you suffer from a case of the jitters under the pressure of competition that causes you to miss balls you wouldn't ordinarily miss, take heart and remember that your not alone. The best known cure is to keep on competing. As your experience grows and your skill rises you will get used to playing under pressure.

Shooting good pool takes your undivided attention. That's why even top players whose names you'd probably recognize are not above a subtle remark or gesture that may disrupt an opponent's concentration. They know if they can get to their opponent even once or twice in a match, that could tip the scales in their favor. So be forewarned that you will, throughout your pool playing career, encounter some form of sharking on a steady basis.

The post great shot letdown syndrome is another reason why balls fail to hit the pocket. After making a career shot, there's a natural tendency to carry the celebration over into the next shot, often with disastrous consequences. Here's the remedy: after taking your bows for a great shot, take a short breather before settling over your next shot. This will allow you to regain your equilibrium and to summon the concentration that's required for even the easiest of shots.

Cut shots are often missed because the shooter is trying to control the cue ball at the expense of the shot. Some players have trouble shooting the 6, 7, or 8-ball because they are dark and a little tougher to see when lighting is poor. And still other players will fail to check their equipment before shooting as they insist on using a flat tip cue that's crooked in three places. As you may have gathered, there are plenty of reasons (excuses?) for missing shots. To maximize your shotmaking all you need do is to evaluate the reasons for missed balls and to eliminate them one by one.

Cut Shots

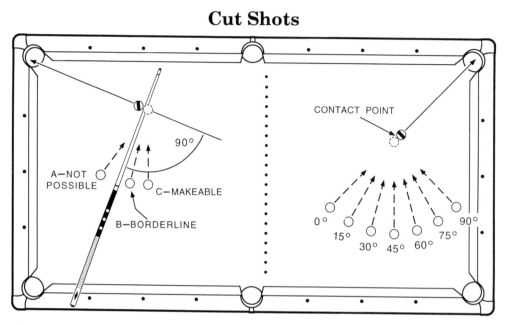

Measuring the Cut Angle

The are very few absolutely straight in shots. As a result, virtually every shot you'll encounter will require some angle of cut. Lots of practice will help you to develop and maintain an "eye" for the vast majority of cut shots that you'll normally be called upon to make in actual play.

Some cut shots are, of course, easier than others. It is very important for you to recognize what is and what isn't a makeable cut shot. An awareness of the degree of difficulty on cut shots can help you select the most probable shots, and to avoid cut shots that are nearly impossible, or that are beyond your comfort zone.

The diagram both illustrates the concept of possible and not makeable cut shots. A dead straight in shot is 0°. That's easy enough. Cut angles ranging from 1°- 45° are not much of a problem for most players with at least some experience. However, once the cut angle exceeds about 45°, cut shots rapidly become more difficult to estimate correctly. At about a 60° cut angle, a very small portion of the cue ball is contacting the object ball. This takes a very well trained sense of aim. A practical limit for even top players is about 70°- 75°.

It's important to know what your limits are on cut shots. As a practical matter, you should develop an eye for cut shots up to at least 65°- 70°. However, remember that on some shots your personal preference may be to shoot a bank shot or play a safety on a shot that another player would choose to cut in.

The left hand portion of the diagram shows how you can use your cue stick to determine if a cut shot is possible. Simply line the cue up at a 90° angle to the line the object ball will take to the pocket. In our example, the shot is impossible with the cue ball in position A, and extremely difficult from position B. Position C presents a makeable cut angle of about 65°.

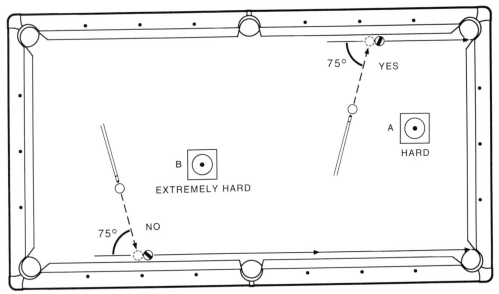

The Distance Principle on Cut Shots

Thin cut shots require a firm stroke so that enough force will be transferred to the object ball to get it to the pocket as shown in position A above. Although the cut angle is identical to (A), the cut shot in position B is not practical because of the distance that the object ball must travel to the pocket. An extremely hard stroke is tough to control on thin cut shots.

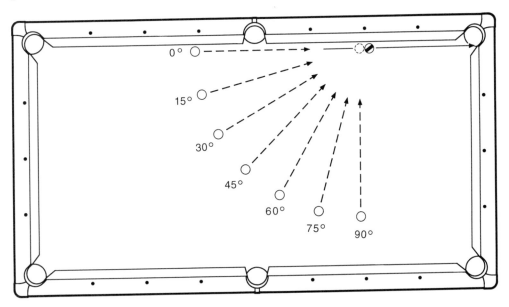

Cut Shot Angles

The diagram above gives you another perspective on cut shots. The rail serves as a handy guide. When the cue ball is directly opposite the point of contact (in this example, just above the second diamond), you have a 90 degree cut shot. Notice that a 75 degree cut shot looks very tough, but is makeable. Also, observe from this vantage point how relatively easy a 45 degree cut shot becomes.

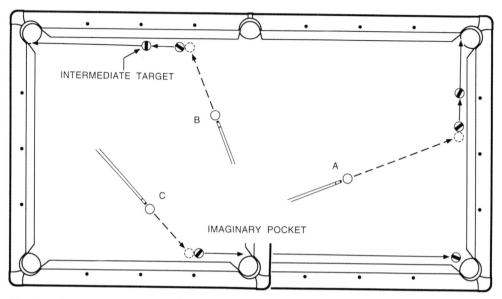

Pocketing Down the Rail Cut Shots

Sometimes it's hard to pocket thin cut shots down the rail. Here's a tip that should help: forget about the pocket. Try instead to get the object ball started down the rail for even a few inches on the proper line and it will run into the pocket (A). It may help to use an intermediate target (B) or to visualize an imaginary pocket that's only slightly up the rail (C).

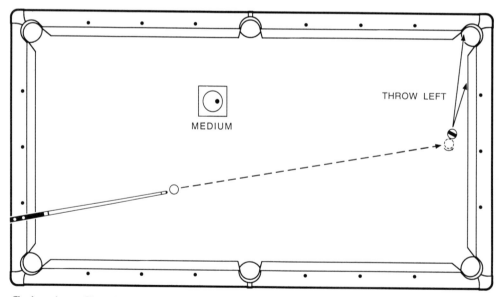

Spinning Cut Shots in with English

This somewhat frightening shot can nevertheless be pocketed with regularity. Use outside english (right in this example) and a medium-soft stroke. The key is to shoot hard enough to send the ball to the pocket, yet soft enough to allow the throw from the english to work. Avoid hitting down on the cue ball or it will curve off the intended line.

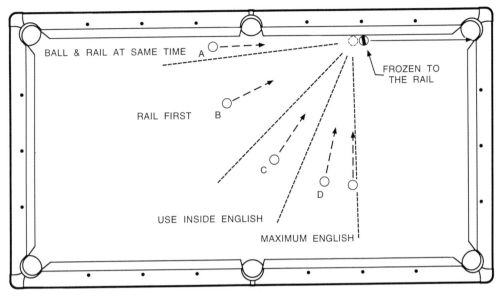

Frozen to the Rail Cut Shots

You are faced with a special challenge when the object ball is frozen to the cushion. However, these often troublesome shots can become rather routine when you employ the techniques we'll discuss below.

At the top of the diagram the cue ball is only a few inches off the rail. From this angle you can pocket the object ball by striking both the rail and the ball at the same time. Any errors that you make in aiming from this position should be in favor of hitting the rail ever so slightly ahead of the object ball.   Remember, on frozen to the rail shots: <u>never</u>, <u>never</u>, hit the object ball first!

As the cut angle grows, you will need to allow for contact induced throw. If you simply contact the object ball and the rail at the same time, contact induced throw will push the object ball into the rail, causing a missed shot. On cut shots of about 10° to 45°, you can neutralize the effects of contact induced throw by aiming to hit the rail first about ⅛" above the object ball.

On frozen to the rail shots with a cut angle greater than about 45° inside english makes this shot a simple matter. In our example, about ½ to 1 tip of right english combined with hitting the rail about ⅛" up from the object ball can enable you to easily pocket this shot.

On very thin cut shots (as diagrammed) continue to aim up the rail from the object ball and use plenty of inside english. Strangely enough, you can pocket what appear to be impossible cut shots (90°+) by employing this technique. These shots aren't easy, but they can be made. As a matter of fact, hustlers have won money by sinking these seemingly impossible cut shots.

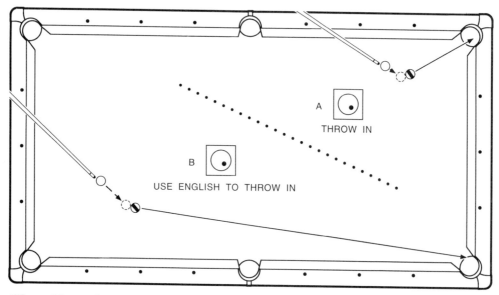

Close Together Cut Shots

Aiming cut shots can be difficult when both the object ball and cue ball are relatively close together. What makes these shots hard is that it's difficult to gain a sense of the correct cut angle from close range. Under these circumstances, many players find it useful to aim for a fuller hit on the object ball and throw the ball in with outside english (see Chapter 4). At close range you do not need to worry nearly as much about deflection and other assorted items that make using english a difficult proposition.

In position A, you are faced with a thin cut shot with the balls very close together. In addition, the object ball is close to the pocket (this shot is much more difficult at longer distances). A few changes in your approach to this shot can increase you chances for success. A more erect stance than you normally use will allow you to see the cut angle better. Use plenty of outside english (right). Elevate your cue slightly and hit down on the cue ball using draw. This will increase the throw effect of the english. Finally, use a little extra wrist action, but make sure not to hit the shot very hard. The stroke is mostly a short, smooth flick of the wrist. The object ball and the cue ball are further apart in position B, but this shot can still be troublesome because of the distance to the pocket. In this example, your only adjustment is to use outside (right) english to throw the ball into the far corner pocket. With outside english you will need to aim for a fuller hit on the object ball. Incidentally, the fuller hit should enable you to control the cue ball better.

Side Pocket Shotmaking

The side pockets are often misunderstood and avoided whenever possible by many players who consider them a necessary evil. However, the side pockets should not be ignored as they can help your game tremendously when played correctly.

Straight shots into the side pocket are among the easiest to make, as the diagram below demonstrates. In fact, the opening to the side pockets is about ½" wider than the corner pockets. Problems arise, however, once the approach angle decreases from 90° (straight in) towards the theoretical limit of about 21° as the diagram also demonstrates. At this angle of approach, you have virtually no margin for error. Between these two extremes (90°-21°) lies a number of shotmaking possibilities.

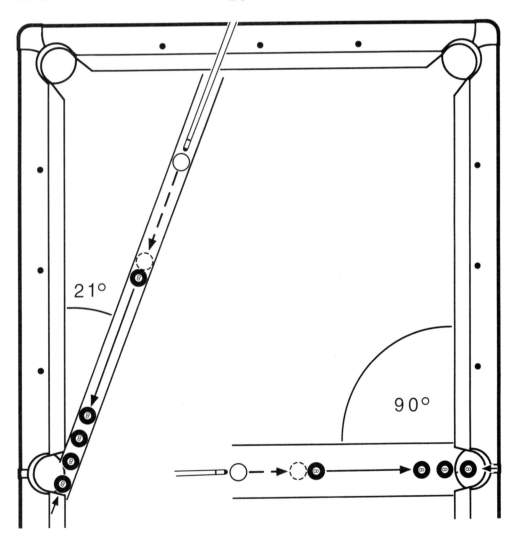

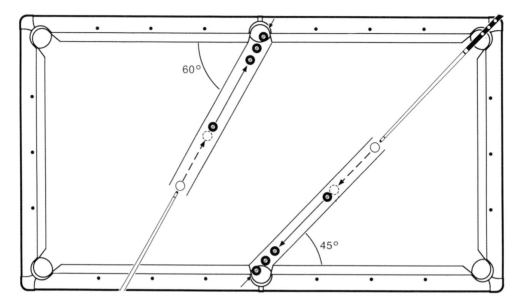

The two keys to pocketing balls in the side pocket are stroke speed and choosing the correct part of the pocket as your target. The diagram above demonstrates how your target shifts as your approach angle changes. At 90°, your target is the center of the back of the pocket. Notice at 60° and 45° how the target(arrow) has shifted around to the side of the pocket. At the 21° limit, your target is now barely inside the rail. Also observe that about ½" of the 8-balls' diameter is actually aimed outside the edge of the pocket!

A number of players have a visual perception problem when shooting into side pockets at an angle that causes them to miss on the near side of the pocket. This problem can be solved by making sure you change the aiming point <u>sufficiently</u> at the smaller approach angles as we just discussed.

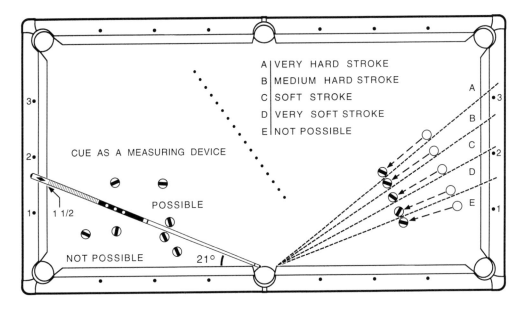

Stroke speed is also vital to playing side pockets correctly. When shooting directly at the pocket (90°) you can use a very hard stroke if needed. As the approach angle shifts, however, some allowance must eventually be made for the continuously decreasing size of the effective pocket opening. The diagram demonstrates this. From position A you can still pocket the ball with a very hard stroke. Moving to position B, you must now begin to reduce the maximum speed with which you can shoot the object ball into the pocket. At position B, a medium-hard stroke will pocket the ball. However, if you hit the shot along the exact same line, but with a very hard stroke, the pocket would reject the ball. At position D you can only make the ball by using a very soft stroke. At position E the shot is no longer possible.

You can use your cue stick as a measuring device to tell whether a ball can or can't be made in the side pocket. Line your cue up from the near edge of the pocket to a position 11/2 diamonds up from the corner pocket as shown. The diagram shows that the striped balls above the cue can be made, while those resting below the cue can't possibly made in the side pocket.

Combination Shots

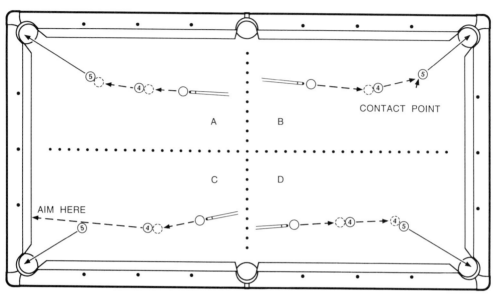

How to Shoot Combinations

A successful combination shot comes as a result of a chain reaction between the cue ball and two or more object balls. In a two ball combination, the cue ball contacts the first object ball, which then acts like a cue ball by driving the second object ball into the pocket. Combination shots can be very difficult or ridiculously easy. It all depends on the position of the balls. The easiest combos occur when the balls are close together and lined up toward the pocket. Combos quickly become much more difficult as the distance between the object balls and the cue ball increases.

Most players seem to go through cycles when they're either hot or cold when shooting combinations. The problem lies at least partly in finding a method that works, and then sticking with it. The diagram above demonstrates four different techniques for lining up and shooting combinations. Perhaps one of them will work for you.

In the first approach (A), your goal is to visualize a cue ball striking the object ball (the 5-ball, as in all of our examples) exactly where required to drive the second ball into the pocket. The imaginary cue ball is often referred to as a ghost ball. In position B, your first task is to locate a precise spot on the second ball that , if contacted, would drive it into the pocket. Your objective is then to drive the first object ball into this predetermined contact point. In our third approach (C), you pick a spot to aim at on the rail (perhaps it's 3" left of the diamond as shown). If you can shoot the first object ball toward this spot it will cut the second ball into the pocket. Using method D calls for you to visualize the first object ball as a second cue ball. Once you're lined up over the shot, forget about the cue ball and concentrate on shooting the 4-ball into the 5-ball. You should avoid using english on combinations as this adds an unnecessary variable to the equation. And be sure to stroke combos at a medium or medium-soft speed as this enhances your shooting accuracy and gives close shots a better chance to fall in.

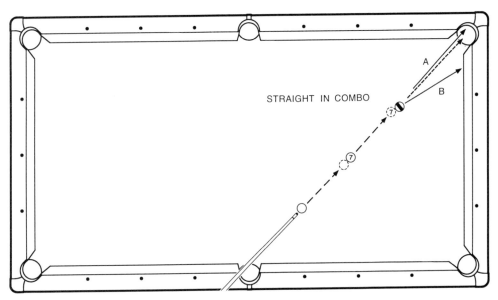

Combos and the Margin for Error

The diagram above should enhance your appreciation of the aiming process on combos. The cue ball, 7-ball, and striped ball are all lined up dead straight in. Line A shows where the 7-ball would enter the pocket if shot into the left side of the pocket. Now observe how badly the stripe would miss the pocket (line B) if the 7 was shot only slightly off course!!

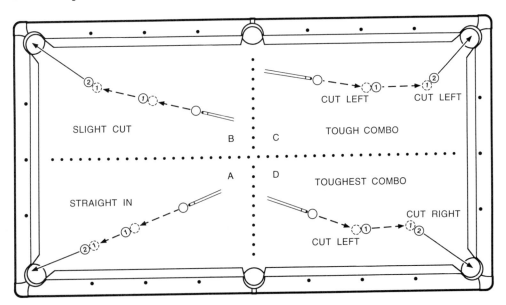

Four Combination Shots - Degree of Difficulty

Combination A in the diagram above is perfectly straight in. This is one of the easier combos you'll encounter. Combination B is only a little tougher as the cue ball and 1-ball are lined up to cut the 2-ball in. Combination C is not easy as the cue ball must cut the 1 into the 2- ball, which is then cut into the corner pocket. Toughest of all is combination D which requires cuts in two different directions.

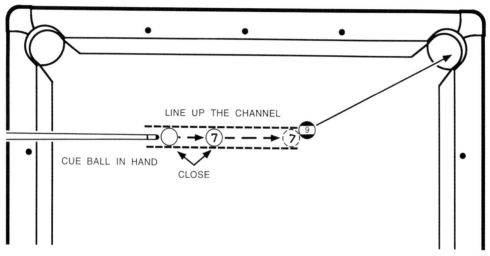

Ball in Hand Combinations

Ball in hand rules allow you to place the cue ball anywhere on the table after your opponent has committed a foul. When playing Nine Ball this can give you the opportunity for some quick and easy wins if you can effectively pocket combination shots with cue ball in hand.

The first thing you'll want to do when shooting combos with ball in hand is to set the shot up as straight as possible. The diagram illustrates the process. The cue ball is placed so that it can be shot directly into the 7-ball. The 7-ball in turn should contact the 9-ball precisely where needed to pocket the 9-ball and win the game! You've simplified the shot greatly by eliminating any cut angle on the 7-ball .

The cue ball should be placed close enough to the 5-ball to insure accurate contact, and yet far enough away so that you can stroke smoothly and avoid a double hit on the cue ball. Six to eight inches should do the trick.

Make sure that you don't decide to cut the first ball one way or the other while your down in you shooting stance. Line the shot up dead straight to the best of your ability, make sure that it looks "on" to you before you assume your stance, and then stroke down your chosen line of aim. Once you've completed the preliminaries, it's time to make the shot. One method is to shoot the cue ball at the second ball (the 9-ball in our example) as if the first ball (the 7-ball) doesn't exist. Another technique is to shoot the cue ball straight into the first ball (the 7-ball) as if the second ball was not there.

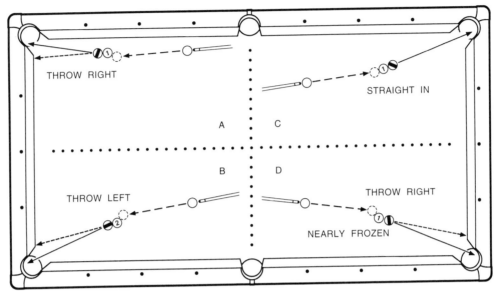

Frozen Combinations

A combination shot is said to be frozen when the object balls are touching each other. A number of frozen combination shots that appear to be impossible at first glance, are really quite simple once you understand how throw works. Take position A in the diagram above. The 1-ball and the stripe are lined up to the left of the pocket. The stripe can still be made by shooting the cue ball into the left side of the 1-ball. The 1-ball will spin as if hit with left english. Left english throws the object ball to the right. In this case, the stripe ball will be thrown to the right and into the pocket as indicated.

In position B, the 2-ball and stripe ball are lined up to the right of the pocket. The stripe ball will be thrown to the left and into the pocket if you shoot the cue ball into the <u>right</u> side of the 2-ball.

Position C illustrates what is one of the easiest shots in the game: a frozen combination that's lined up dead straight into the pocket. All you need do is to shoot the 1-ball as if the stripe ball wasn't there. Be sure not to aim carelessly on this shot as it can be missed if you apply throw by hitting either side of the 1-ball. You can also insure against a miss by hitting this shot with a firm stroke as this will minimize any effects of throw that you may unintentionally apply.

In example D, the two object balls are nearly frozen, but there is a discernable gap between the 1-ball and the stripe. This combination shot cannot be cut in. However, it can be thrown in as diagrammed if you play it as you would a frozen combination throw shot. Use a soft stroke to make sure that you get the desired throw effect from the 1-ball to the stripe ball.

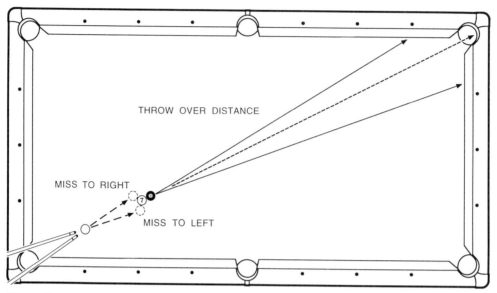

How Throw Works

The diagram above shows the possible effects of throw on a frozen combination at long range. The 7/8-ball combo is lined up straight into the pocket, as shown by the dashed line. At this distance, however, this seemingly dead combo can be missed and missed badly if the cue ball contacts either side of the 7-ball. Hitting the left side of the 7- ball causes the 8-ball to miss to the right, and vice versa.

This illustration demonstrates why you need to take care in aiming frozen combinations. At the same time you can also pocket frozen combos at long range that are lined up several inches wide of the pocket. In our example, the 8-ball could be thrown into the pocket if it were lined up along either of the solid lines.

Stroke speed also plays an important role in playing frozen combos. Everything else being equal, a soft stroke will create more throw than a hard stroke. So remember, you can change the amount of throw by adjusting your stroke speed. This will enable you to play a wider variety of frozen combos. You can generate more sidespin by hitting further away from the center of the cue ball when using english. Similarly, you can increase the throw effect on frozen combos by aiming further to the side of the first object ball. The diagram illustrates the maximum that you would want to purposely aim off center. The following table should help you in shooting frozen combos.

Stroke Speed	Amount of Ball Hit	Throw Effect
Soft	Full	None
Hard	Full	None
Soft	Half Full	Throw
Hard	Half Full	Very Little Throw
Soft	Thin	Maximum Throw
Hard	Thin	Some Throw

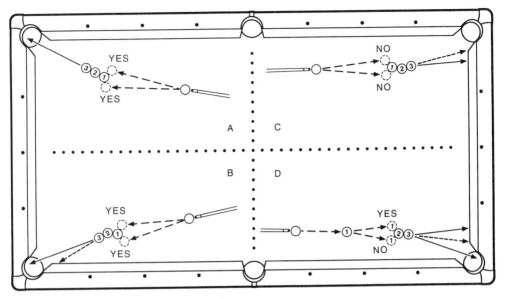

Three Ball Frozen Combinations

Remember when evaluating a three ball frozen combination that the shot in question is either "on" or "off". In other words, the position of the balls determines if the shot can or can't be pocketed. With that in mind, we'll now examine four different positions.

In example A, it's virtually impossible to miss this shot. All three balls are lined up straight at the pocket. Any possible throw that you may apply by contacting either side of the 1-ball has absolutely <u>no</u> effect on the third ball. The only way that you can miss this shot is to hit so far to either side of the 1-ball or shoot so softly that the 3-ball fails to reach the pocket! Although the 3-ball is lined up at the rail in position B, it can still be thrown into the pocket. When the cue ball strikes the 1-ball, the 1-ball will apply left english to the 2-ball. In turn, the 2-ball will then throw the 3-ball (because of the left english) into the pocket. You can make this shot by shooting anywhere between the two dashed cue balls.

There's no way to pocket this 3-ball combination as diagrammed (C). The 1-ball is going to apply left english to the 2-ball which will then throw the 3-ball even further to the right of the pocket. This shot is definitely "off" in pool parlance.

Position D differs from the first three in that the 1-ball (the first ball of the other three ball frozen combos) is not frozen to the 2-ball. This gives you some additional freedom in how you play this shot. The 2 and 3 balls are lined up to the left of the pocket. The 2-ball needs to be contacted on the left side by the 1-ball so that it can throw the 3 to the right and into the pocket. Of course, you wouldn't want to make the mistake of shooting the 1-ball into the right side of the 2-ball, as this would cause the 3-ball to miss badly to the left.

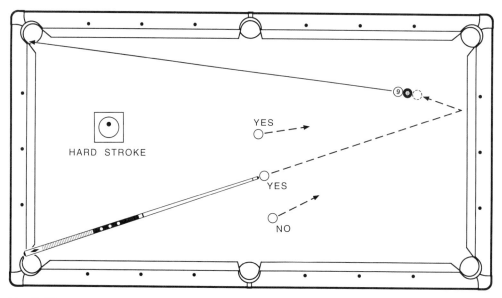

Rail First Kick Combos

This is a "go for it" shot when you have nothing to lose (or no other reasonable alternative). In the diagramed position, the 8 and 9 balls are lined up directly at the opposite corner pocket. Use a hard stroke to minimize any throw from an off-center hit on the 8-ball. This shot is easiest when the approach angle is relatively straight (Yes). You should avoid the shot from the angle marked "no".

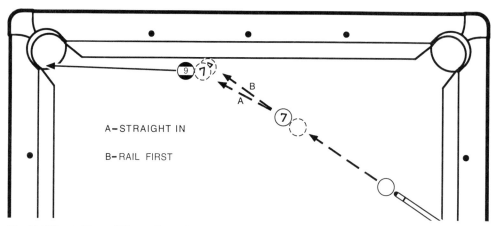

Rail First Two Way Combos

Even simple looking combination shots such as the one in the diagram above can be easily missed. So when the object ball is very close to the rail you might be wise to play a two-way combo. Instead of shooting the 7-ball directly into the 9, aim the 7 between the rail and the nine. Now you can make the 9-ball with a direct hit or by having the 7 rebound off the cushion into the 9. (What you're hoping for is to miss your intended line slightly to the left or right.)

Bank Shots

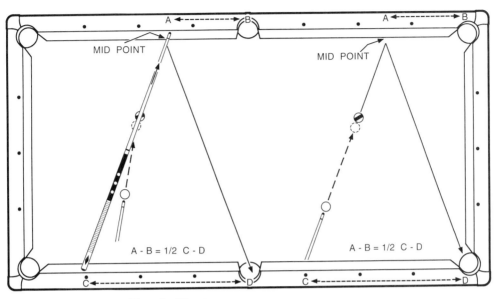

How to Measure Bank Shots

A bank shot is when the object ball first contacts one (or more) cushions before crossing the table into the pocket. Bank shots require great judgement and experience that comes from extensive practice. They are not easy, but over time you can develop a sense of aim for bank shots, just as you would any other shot.

There are a number of factors that can influence the direction of the object ball as it rebounds from the cushion. They include: cut angle, speed of stroke, english, contact induced throw (see Chapter 2) and the condition of the cushions. As you can see, there's a lot that goes into banking balls accurately.

In the righthand portion of the diagram our goal is to pocket the stripe in the opposite corner pocket. In theory, if the object ball follows along the path outlined by the triangle, it will disappear into the opposite corner pocket. Finding the mid-point of the triangle is the key. The left bottom of the triangle marked C-D is 3 diamonds from the center of the corner pocket. The apex is 1½ diamonds up from the top right corner pocket. That is your aiming point. In lining up a bank shot, your goal is to locate point A, which is half as far up the rail as point C on the opposite rail.

You can find the mid-point by using your cue stick as shown on the lefthand portion of the diagram. Place your cue tip on the opposite rail with the cue directly over the center of the object ball. Now adjust the position of the cue until the tip is half as far from the center of the pocket as the butt end is on the other side of the table. When the distance from A-B is half the distance of C-D and the cue is directly over the center of the object ball, you have found the mid-point. This is your target for the object ball. This method works best if you use a medium stroke and <u>no</u> english. If you apply english and/or shoot hard, you will need to adjust your aim accordingly.

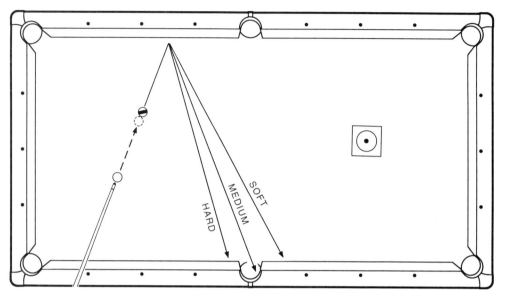

How Speed Affects Bank Shots

The rebound angle of the object ball is largely dependent on the speed of stroke. When a bank is shot hard, the object ball sinks further into the rail, causing it to rebound less sharply. At medium speed the bank will rebound at about the same angle that it contacted the rail at. A soft stroke will send the object ball out at a slightly wider angle.

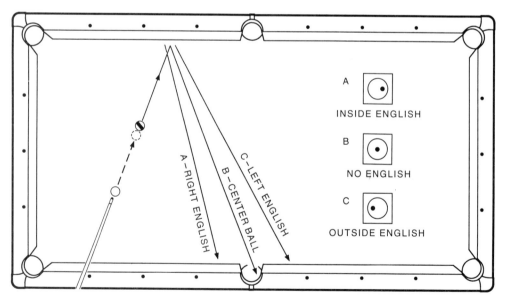

How English Affects Bank Shots

You can change the object ball's rebound angle by throwing it with english, just as you would throw a cut shot (See Chapter 4). The diagram illustrates how inside english (A) sharpens the rebound angle. At the same time, outside english (C) opens up the rebound angle. The same stroke speed was used for all three positions.

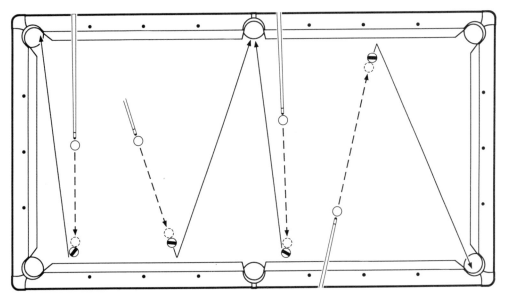

Typical Short Rail Bank Shots

The diagram shows four common short rail (across the width of the table) bank shots. If you can master these shots, or close variations, you will be well prepared for about 80% of the bank shots that you'll shoot in actual play. Practice time spent on these basic bank shots will help your game tremendously.

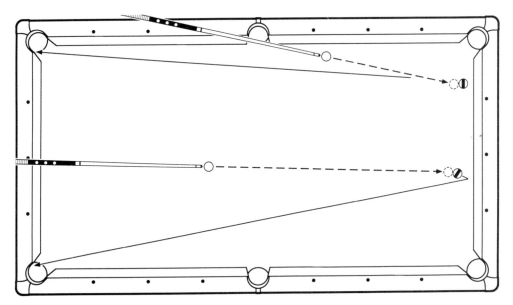

Typical Long Rail Bank Shots

Long rail (across the length of the table) bank shots are never easy because of the distance involved. However, you can learn to make a fair percentage of both of the diagrammed shots. Here's a tip: don't try so hard to make the shot. Instead, merely aim with your best guesstimate and then give the shot a pure stroke. Concentrate only on execution.

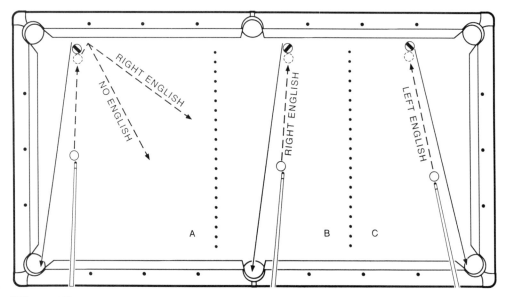

Three Uses of Outside English

Outside english, when used properly, can improve both your position play and your ball pocketing on bank shots. Position A demonstrates the path of the cue ball using follow as it comes off the rail after contacting the stripe ball. In some instances you may want the cue ball to follow the path labeled "No English". However, should you need position further down the table, outside english (right in this example) will open up the rebound angle sending the cue ball along the indicated pathway.

Position B demonstrates a favorite banking technique of many excellent players. The cross side bank is not difficult; it requires only a small cut to the right of center. With outside english you can aim for nearly a full hit on the stripe ball. The english will throw the bank shot to the left causing it to travel along the solid line and into the opposite side pocket.

The bank shot diagrammed in position C requires a fairly thin cut on the stripe ball that is somewhat difficult to gauge accurately. Again, outside english can make this bank/cut shot much easier. Reduce the amount of cut when aiming. Now add in a liberal dosage of outside (left) english. It will help bring the stripe ball back into the opposite corner pocket.

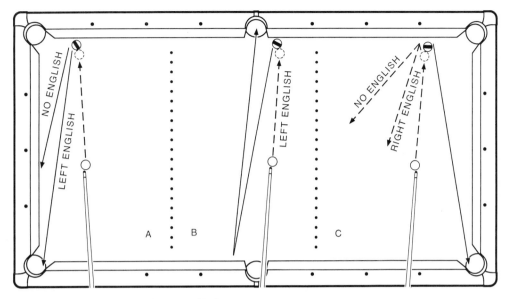

Three Uses of Inside English

Although inside english is used far less often on bank shots than outside english, there are times when it comes in handy. For instance, in position A, this bank shot could not be made without using inside english because the cue ball would double kiss the stripe ball. The trick to this shot is to hit the stripe ball thinner (i. e. more to the right) and apply a fair amount of inside (left) english. The english will "hold up" the object ball, causing it to rebound at a sharper angle. This of course allows you to pocket what seems like an unmakeable shot. It may help you to use a fairly hard stroke.

　　The shot in position B is another example of how you can use inside english to make a seemingly impossible shot. In this case, the object ball is too close to the side pocket to be banked into the opposite side pocket. You can, however, make this shot by using inside english (left) and hitting the stripe ball just thin enough to avoid a double kiss. The stripe ball will reverse course off the second rail and enter the side pocket next to its original position. This intentional two railer really works. Try it! Inside english can also be helpful in retarding the roll of the cue ball as it comes off the rail after contacting the object ball. Position C shows this. By using inside english, you can once again effectively reach your position play objective.

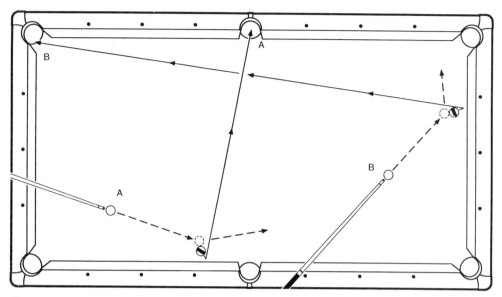

Crossover Bank Shots

A crossover bank shot is when the cue ball passes in front of the object ball a split second before the object ball rebounds off the cushion and across the table into the designated pocket. The diagram illustrates this concept.

Crossover bank shots can be an effective weapon when you are in a tough spot and your choices are limited. Strangely enough, however, many players tend to overlook this possible gamewinning bank shot. Not you, now that you've read this book.

There are a few things to keep in mind when playing crossover bank shots. First of all, they must be shot with a firm stroke because of the thin hit on the object ball. So don't baby this shot. Remember to plan the cue balls route carefully as it's going to travel some distance after contact. Because of the cue ball's angle of approach, the object ball will be thrown slightly forward before it contacts the rail. There are two things that you can do to counteract this contact induced throw. One is to hit the object ball a little thinner than you think is needed. The other is to apply some outside english.

A final work of caution. It's not hard to double kiss these shots if the object ball is on or very close to the rail, or if the cue ball is very far away from the cushion. It will therefore, pay for you to setup and shoot several possible crossover banks so that you can discover which shots are "on" or "off".

Multi-rail Bank Shots

Occasionally you might find yourself in a tough spot where one of the multi-rail bank shots diagrammed below will save the day. Practice them occasionally and tuck them away in your memory bank just in case they are needed, but don't spend too much practice time on them.

Oddly enough, the three-railers are easier to visualize and execute than the two-railers. Because of this, you should make them your first priority among these shots. Also become familiar with the two-railers presented below. The four and five rail bank shots may come in handy some day, but they don't come up enough to be worth devoting practice time.

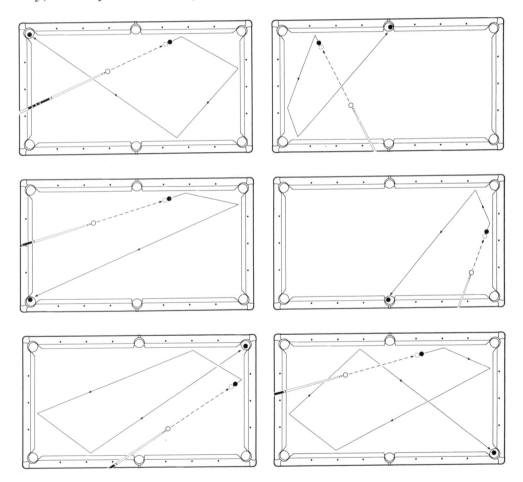

Carom Shots

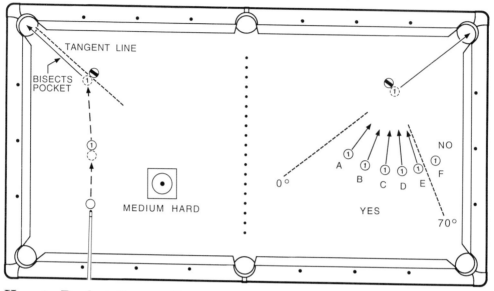

How to Pocket Carom Shots

A carom shot is when the object ball glances off a second object ball and into the pocket. In the diagram, the 1-ball has been shot towards the stripe ball. After contacting the stripe ball, the one ball has been diverted to the left and into the pocket.

A couple of easy steps will tell you where to aim the first ball. First, visualize an imaginary line that runs from the opposite side of the pocket to the edge of the second object ball (the ball you want to carom off). This line is called the tangent line. Where it touches the second object ball is your point of contact for the ball that you wish to pocket. The contact point is simulated by the dashed 1-ball. At contact, a line drawn from the center of the 1-ball to the pocket will bisect the pocket.

Carom shots should be shot with at least a medium hard stroke if the balls are more than a foot or so apart. At longer distances carom shots become impractical because the first object ball will pick up forward roll.

The right portion of the diagram illustrates the spectrum of possible carom shots. In this example, the 1-ball can be pocketed off the stripe ball anywhere within the borders labeled 0°-70°. Past 70° the shot can no longer be made as the stripe ball will "give way" to the full hit by the 1-ball. This will cause the 1-ball to miss to the left of the pocket. Although caroms can be made at shallow approach angles such as A and B, these are difficult to visualize because of the thin carom off the stripe. Approach angles C and D are the easiest angles to visualize and execute.

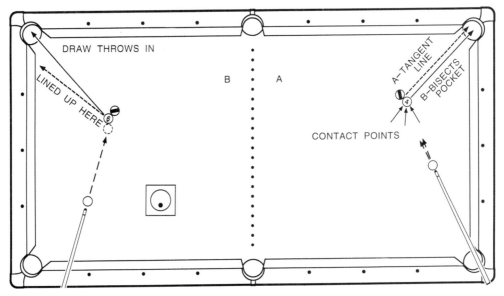

Dead Carom Shots/Throw Caroms

You should always be on the lookout for dead carom shots such as the one illustrated in part A of the diagram above. A carom shot is said to be dead when two object balls are frozen in this position. Once again, the tangent line (A) between the two balls is lined up into the far side of the pocket. As a consequence, a parallel line that runs from the center of the ball you wish to pocket (i.e. the 4-ball) will run directly through the center of the pocket at contact.

This shot is considered dead because it's lined up to go directly into the pocket (similar to the dead combinations discussed earlier). You can shoot the cue ball anywhere between the two outside arrows next to the 4-ball and the 4 will go into the pocket. However, if you to choose to aim at the right side of the target zone, be careful not to shoot too hard and make sure that you don't use draw. The shot is dead, but it can be thrown off line as you'll discover in a moment.

Position B shows a frozen carom shot that's <u>not</u> dead. The 6-ball is frozen to the stripe. If you shot a normal carom shot, the 6-ball would strike the rail to the left of the pocket. You can, however, still pocket the 6-ball. Simply apply sharp draw to the cue ball and aim to hit the 6-ball nearly full. The decisive draw action will push both the 6-ball and the stripe forward a critical few inches before the 6-ball squirts out to the left and into the pocket.

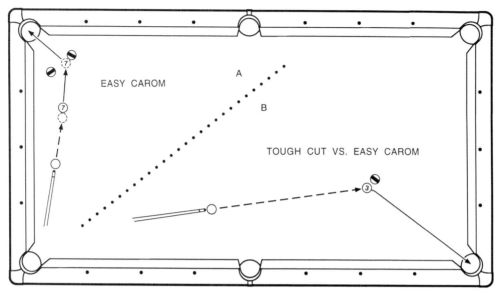

Easy Carom Shots

Position A shows what a fairly simple carom looks like. This highly practical shot allows you to pocket the 7- ball into the corner even though the stripe ball to the left is obstructing the 7-ball's pathway to the pocket.

Tough Cut vs. Easy Carom

In part B of the diagram you are faced with a long tough cut shot on the 3-ball. It will be tough to control the cue ball at this distance and angle. The solution is to carom the 3-ball off the stripe and into the corner pocket!

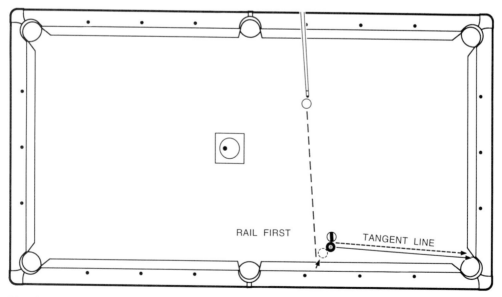

Rail First Frozen Carom Shot

You're playing a game of Eight Ball and you're faced with a super thin cut down the rail. But wait! There's a much easier shot at hand. Apply left english to the cue ball and strike the rail first. The 8-ball will then carom off the stripe and into the corner pocket, giving you the game.

Billiards

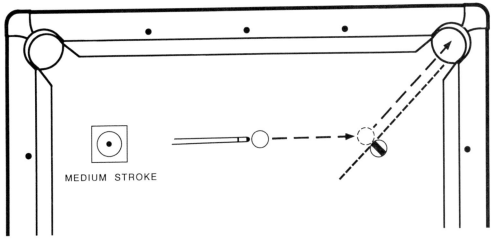

MEDIUM STROKE

The Theory of Making Billiards

On a billiard shot the cue ball is shot directly into an object ball. After glancing off the first ball, the cue ball then proceeds to pocket a second object ball. You will have numerous opportunities to use a wide variety of billiard shots in both Eight Ball and Nine Ball.

The first diagram shows the basic theory behind billiard shots. The cue ball is shot towards a point on the object ball that's lined up towards the far side of the corner pocket. From this position you can pocket a ball that's positioned on a direct line to the pocket. A medium stroke with centerball will send the cue ball along the predetermined pathway.

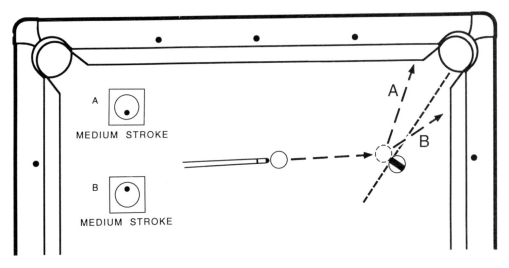

A

MEDIUM STROKE

B

MEDIUM STROKE

How to Alter the Cue Ball's Path

The diagram above shows how to alter the cue ball's path with either draw (A) or follow (B). By changing the cue balls path, you can cut in balls that are not lined up directly with the pocket.

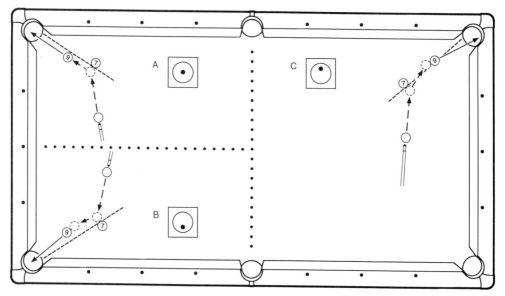

How to Pocket Three Billiards

The billiard on the 9-ball is lined up directly into the pocket in position A. A centerball hit with at least medium stroke speed will propel the cue ball along a line that's parallel to the heavy dashed line and into the 9-ball, sending it into the pocket. This is an example of a basic straight in billiard.

In position B the contact point on the 7-ball remains the same. On this shot, however, you need to apply some draw so that you can change the path of the cue ball slightly, enabling it to cut the 9-ball into the pocket. Take note that if you failed to draw the cue ball, you would overcut the 9-ball, missing it to the right of the pocket.

A follow shot will cause the cue ball to roll forward after contacting the 7-ball in position C. This will allow the cue ball to cut the 9-ball back into the corner pocket. Please take note that there is a practical limit to how accurately you can cut balls in that are not directly in line with the pocket as in position A. If the ball you're trying to pocket is more than 2-3 inches on either side of a direct line to the pocket, you may wish to reconsider shooting billiard.

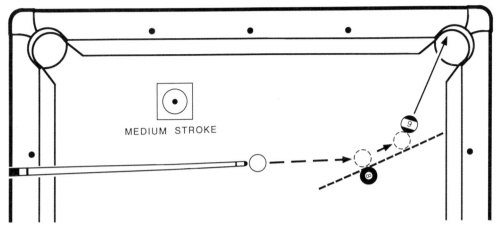

Cutting in Billiards With Centerball

The diagram above shows another method for cutting in a billiard shot. The cue ball is hit with centerball and a medium stroke. The cue ball is shot at the edge of the 8-ball that's in line with an imaginary cue ball that is located precisely at the desired contact point with the 9-ball. The aiming point is at a small part of the 8-ball.

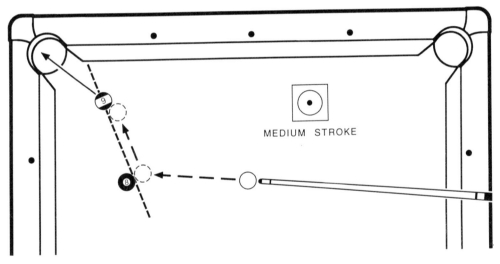

Cutting in Billiards With Centerball (2)

In this example you should aim for a fuller hit on the 8-ball. Use a medium stroke with centerball. Observe how the full hit sends the cue ball along the indicated path, which results in a game-winning billiard into the corner pocket.

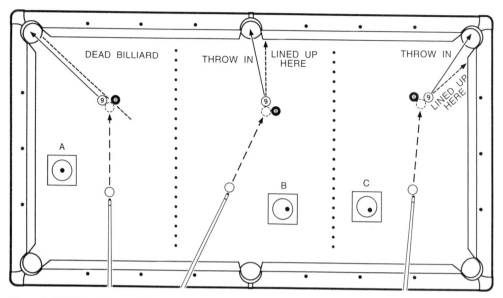

Dead Billiards and Throw Shots

Billiard shots can be fairly simple when the first object ball and the ball that you wish to pocket are right next to each other. Position A illustrates what could be called a dead billiard. If you contact the 8-ball just a whisker before the 9-ball, the 9-ball will head directly into the pocket. The key to this shot is to properly recognize the opportunity at hand. If the near edge of the first ball and the far side of the ball you wish to pocket are on the same line, and that line points towards the far side of the pocket (as the heavy dashed line does in the diagram) then you have a billiard that's tough to miss. Take care to hit the first ball first, if ever so slightly. If your opponent tends to question shots like this, be sure to have a neutral observer watch the shot.

The 9-ball can be pocketed in the second example (B), even though it appears that it will hit the rail first to the right of the side pocket. Use plenty of outside (right) english and a soft stroke. This will throw the 9-ball several inches to the left and into the pocket. It will help if you can come real close to the 9 when you initially make contact with the 8-ball.

Draw with inside (right) english will enable you to pocket the 9-ball in position C. Again you will want to use a fairly soft stroke so that the english can throw the 9- ball into the center of the pocket. And, of course, be sure to contact the 8-ball first.

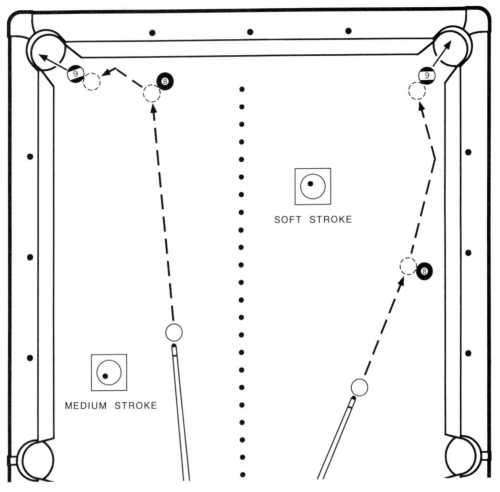

Rail First Billiards Using Draw and Follow

When the ball you are playing is close to the pocket, you should consider shooting a rail first billiard shot. By going rail first you can create a cut angle on the object ball that will help you avoid a scratch. In addition, your position on the next shot may possibly benefit from a rail first billiard.

It is very easy to scratch in the position on the left if you shoot a billiard directly into the 9-ball. The smart choice is to hit the 8-ball a little bit thinner (to the left) and play the shot rail first. A touch of left english will help to throw the 9-ball into the pocket.

In the position on the right, you should barely clip the 8-ball to create a rail first cut shot. Again, a little lefthand english helps to throw the 9-ball into the pocket.

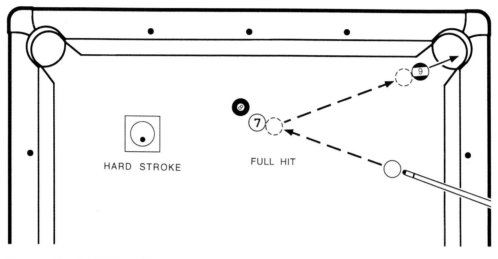

HARD STROKE

FULL HIT

Draw Back Billiards

The diagrammed position is from a game of Nine Ball. The 7-ball can't be made except on a lucky shot. Furthermore, the 7/8 combination is so difficult as to not be worthy of your consideration. You might be able to play safe, but there is no guarantee that it would work from this position. The solution to this quandary is to play a draw back billiard shot. The 9-ball is very close to the pocket, which makes this shot possible. If the 9 is more than a few inches from the pocket, this shot becomes especially difficult because it is very tough to gauge the return path of the cue ball with any great precision.

You will need to hit the 7-ball nearly full with a hard draw stroke, to create the desired path for the cue ball. If the 7 is hit even slightly too far to the right, the cue ball will wind up hitting the rail well above the 9-ball. This is largely a judgement shot that, you guessed it, comes from practice. Set up some balls in a similar position and give this shot a try. It could win you a game here or there when no better option is available.

Rail First Shotmaking

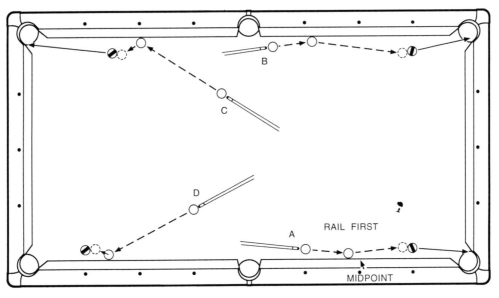

How to Pocket Rail First Shots

The two primary reasons for playing a shot rail first are to sidestep obstructing balls or to gain better position for the next shot. Rail first shots are not difficult at all when the object ball is within a 1/4" or so of the rail. When the object ball is this close to the cushion, you need only strike the rail a short distance up from the object ball.

Rail first shots become much more exacting when the object ball is one or two inches from the rail. These shots can be made. They just require a little know how. However, if the object ball is more than 21/2" to 3" from the rail, you should consider other available options.

As the name implies, your target on rail first shots is the cushion. The trick is to estimate accurately just how far up the rail you need to hit the cushion to pocket the object ball. In position A, both the object ball and the cue ball are the same distance from the rail (about 1"). The arrow shows the mid-point between the two balls. This serves as a starting point for your calculations. When the two balls are the same distance from the rail, you will want to aim at the point that's at least a few inches up from the mid-point as diagrammed. If you follow this rule of thumb, you will make, or come very close to making this shot.

In position B the cue ball is about 1" off the rail while the object ball is about 21/2" from the cushion. Notice how far up the rail you need to aim the cue ball to make the stripe on this shot.

Although the stripe ball is about 2½" from the rail in position C, this shot is makeable, but very difficult. That's because the cue ball is more than a foot from the rail. To make this shot you must aim a short distance up the rail from the stripe to cut the stripe ball back into the corner pocket from a fairly sharp angle.

Position D presents a similar shot. This time the object ball is only an 1¼" from the rail, which makes this shot considerably easier than the shot in position C.

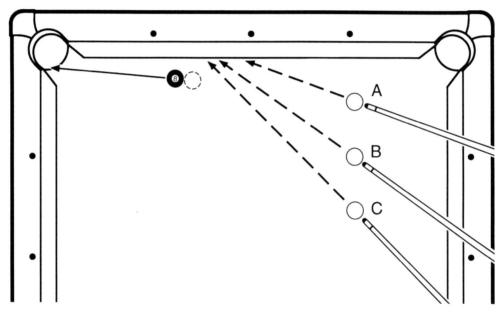

Aiming Rail First Shots

This diagram should give you some additional perspective on how to aim rail first shots. Your goal is to pocket the 8-ball, which is about 1¼" from the cushion, while playing the cue ball off the rail first from three different locations.

From position A at the top of the diagram you will need to aim about 8" up the rail so that the cue ball will rebound into the 8-ball as shown by the dashed cue ball.

Now here's the key. Observe how the contact point with the rail becomes closer (B) and closer (C) to the 8-ball as the distance of the cue ball from the rail becomes greater. This discussion should give you some understanding of approximate aiming points that will give you a reasonably good shot at pocketing rail first shots.

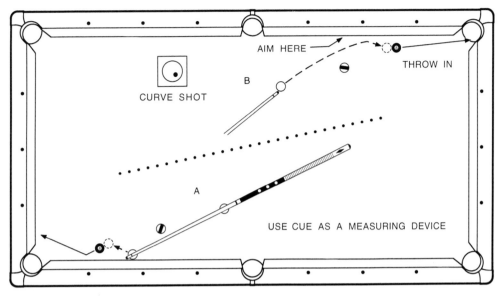

Using Your Cue to Measure Rail First Shots

The obstructing ball in position A may cloud your vision as to whether or not you can pocket the 8-ball by going rail first. You can gain some valuable information by laying you cue down <u>over</u> the cue ball as shown. Allow for just enough clearance past the stripe ball. In this example, the point at which the cue tip contacts the rail shows that you have an excellent chance of making this shot. If this test tells you that you can't cut the ball in rail first, don't give up yet. You can still make the shot by curving the cue ball around the stripe to play the 8-ball rail first (see position B).

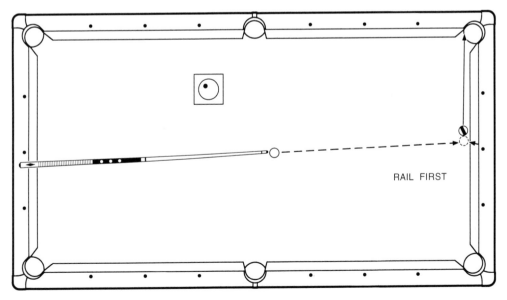

Rail First Thin Cut Shots

This shot would be extremely difficult (if not impossible) to cut in. The answer is to aim slightly to the right of the stripe ball and to cut the ball in coming off the rail with left english.

Miscellaneous Shotmaking

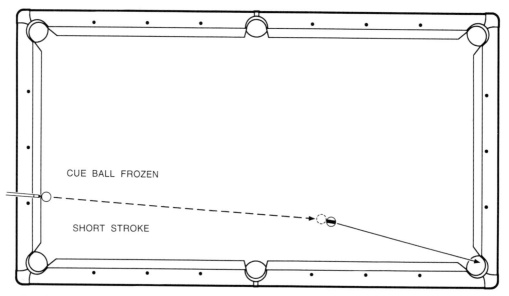

Cue Ball Frozen to the Rail

This shot is quite difficult because of it's length, and especially because the cue ball is frozen to the rail. However, there are some steps that you can take to increase your chances of success. Use a short bridge. Many players prefer an open bridge on this shot as it allows them to line up the shot better. Most importantly, make sure to use a short stroke, as this will increase your accuracy. Your backstroke should be no more than 3"-4". Don't try to power this shot. A medium or medium-soft stroke works best. A push-like tap on the cue ball is the best way I can describe the ideal stroking action. And lastly, have a positive attitude about your chances for success!!

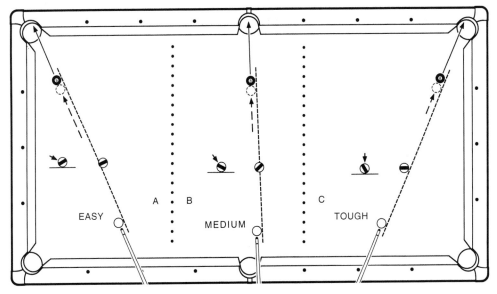

Jump Shots

The diagram illustrates three jump shots with varying degrees of difficulty. In all three examples, the stripe ball with an arrow next to it shows the spot on the ball that must be cleared. Position A is the easiest of the three as you need hurdle only the edge of the stripe ball. Position B is somewhat tougher as you must jump over about 75-80% of the height of the stripe. Toughest of all is position C, which requires that you jump the whole stripe ball. For starters, you should begin by shooting jump shots such as the one in position A. Continue to build your skill gradually until you can jump a full ball that's fairly close to the cue ball.

To execute the jump shot, elevate you cue to a 30-40° angle. Stroke firmly down on the cue ball just slightly below center using a snap of the wrist. The angle of your cue and the force of your stroke will largely determine how far the cue ball gets airborne. However, it's not necessary to slam the cue ball into the felt as some players do.

Lining up jump shots can also be tough because you have your shooting arm raised up in an unnatural position. It may help you to first line up the shot with your cue held level, and then raise the butt-end up to the proper elevation before shooting. When aiming, you should also determine if the cue ball will still be above the table when it contacts the object ball. If so, you should aim for a fuller hit on the object ball. This will compensate for the contact that's being made on the upper half of the object ball.

Other factors to consider include: the distance between the cue ball and the ball your jumping, the size of the cue ball's landing area, the distance between the object ball and the pocket, the possibility of the cue ball jumping off the table, and your ability to play position on the next shot.

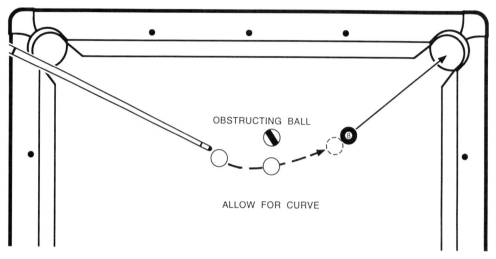

The Curve Shot

The stripe ball is blocking the cue balls path to the 8-ball. You can pocket the 8, however, by curving the cue ball around the stripe. Allow for the curve by aiming a few inches to the right of the stripe. Elevate your cue slightly and hit down on the cue ball with low left english. You can curve the ball the necessary amount in this example with a medium speed stroke. The key to this shot is to accurately gauge the amount of the curve.

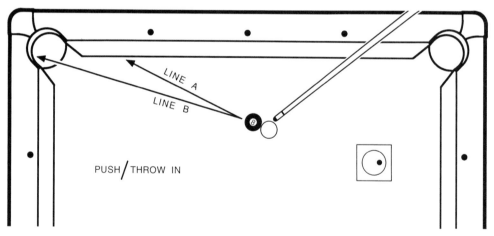

Push/Throw Shot

The cue ball and 8-ball are frozen together and pointing along line A to the right of the pocket. However, you can still pocket the 8- ball by shooting in the opposite direction of that which you would take to cut the ball in. You can actually push the ball towards the pocket. Right english will help to throw the ball into the pocket. Don't hit the 8-ball any fuller than shown in the diagram or you may commit a foul.

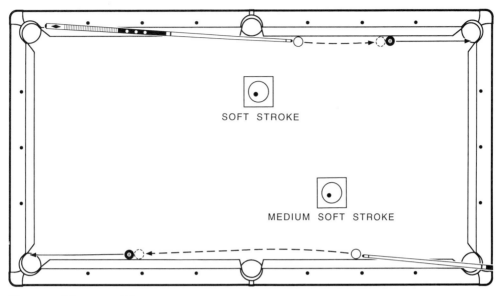

SOFT STROKE

MEDIUM SOFT STROKE

Frozen/Frozen Shots

One of the more unpleasant situations you will encounter is when both the cue ball and object ball are frozen to the same rail. Your first priority is to make the ball as playing position will be extremely difficult, if not impossible. In the position at the top, aim just a hair away from the rail. Use a soft stroke and hit slightly down on the cue ball a touch below center. The shot at the bottom of the diagram is much tougher because you must circumvent the side pocket. Use the same shooting technique as above, but with a slightly firmer stroke. You might also want to aim a little bit further outside of the pocket.

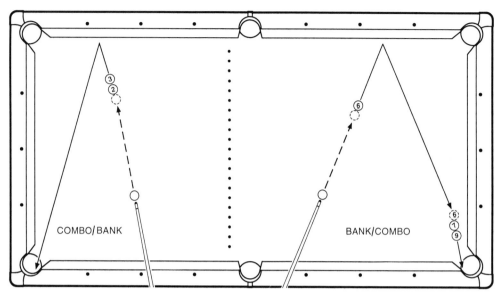

COMBO/BANK

BANK/COMBO

Two Combo Bank Shots

Often you will come across opportunities to pocket balls by combining a couple of the themes discussed previously in this chapter. For example, the shot in the left hand portion of the diagram is a blend of a combination shot and a bank shot. The shot at the right is a bank shot into a combination!

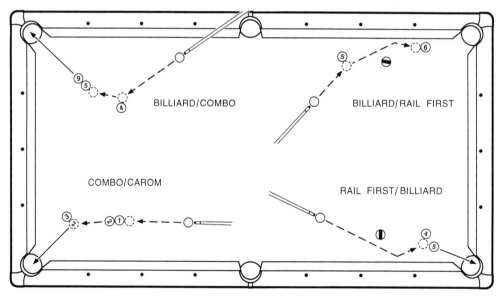

BILLIARD/COMBO

BILLIARD/RAIL FIRST

COMBO/CAROM

RAIL FIRST/BILLIARD

Four Assorted Shots

The diagram above presents you with four more unusual, yet highly makeable shots. All of them combine various types of shots discussed earlier in this chapter. Their titles are self explanatory. Always be on the watch for unusual, but highly possible shots like these and you will add another dimension of gamewinning shots to your repertoire.

CHAPTER 4

HOW TO USE ENGLISH

Understanding The Effects Of Throw, Deflection, Curve & Speed

English can be defined as the application of sidespin to the cue ball. English is applied by striking the cue ball on either side of its vertical axis. English can do wonderful things for your pool game. It can enable you to play better position, to spin the cue ball off the cushions and around the table for perfect shape. English can also make pocketing certain shots much easier. Although you can play a very respectable game using little or no english, you must master it to become a complete player.

There is a price to be paid for reaping the rewards of english, or "spinning your rock" as the players call it. You will need to learn how it affects your aiming process. This will happen much faster when you become familiar with such concepts as throw, stroke force, deflection, and curve.

At this point, I would like to wave a big caution flag for newer players. Learning to use english takes time and lots of practice. If you are not completely confident in your fundamentals, you will be much better off in the long run, waiting until your game is more solid. Improperly used, english can do more harm than good. If you're ready, let's get started. Take your time. Go at your own pace through these lessons to make sure you absorb the material thoroughly. And always remember to keep english in perspective: it is a useful tool that can add great depth to your game. Don't become an english addict who uses it on nearly every shot as some players make the mistake of doing. Learn to use it wisely and always be respectful of the challenge that it brings to the aiming process.

Shooting Down the Vertical Axis

The first diagram with the bullseye in the center of the cue ball gives you a point of reference for the discussion that follows. Chalk your tip and try to hit the cue ball in the dead center (note: there is an excellent training ball that's been devised for this purpose). It's not as easy as it looks. When you can consistently hit the cue ball within a couple of millimeters of center, your stroke is ready for english. We defined english earlier as sidespin, or striking the cue ball away from the vertical axis. The diagram below shows the vertical axis of the cue ball. When your tip contacts the cue ball on either side of the dashed line, you will apply english to the cue ball.

Before delving further into the mysteries of sidespin, we'll take a moment to talk about follow and draw. Topspin, or follow as it's called, is applied to the cue ball by striking it above the horizontal axis. The example shows what one full tip of topspin looks like. In all of the diagrams, we assume a standard 13 millimeter tip. you can cue the ball this high with no danger of miscuing. Draw, or backspin, is created by striking the cue ball below center. One and one quarter tip below center will give you decisive draw action. Neither follow nor draw is considered english when they are used along the vertical axis. Remember, english is sidespin, not topspin or backspin.

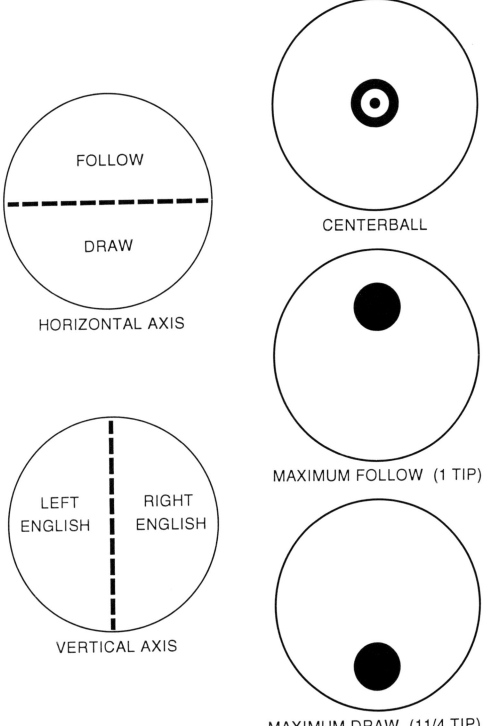

FOLLOW

DRAW

HORIZONTAL AXIS

LEFT
ENGLISH

RIGHT
ENGLISH

VERTICAL AXIS

CENTERBALL

MAXIMUM FOLLOW (1 TIP)

MAXIMUM DRAW (11/4 TIP)

The Six Positions Using English

The cue balls at the top of the next page demonstrate center left and center right english. In each example, the cue tip is positioned 1/2 tip off center. This is a good place to start the learning process. A 1/2 tip of english will teach you much about it's effects without severely changing your aim. The degree of difficulty factor rises geometrically the further off center that you strike the cue ball. Keep in mind that many top pros make it a policy to rarely go beyond 1/2 tip off center.

English is most often used in combination with either follow or draw. The illustrations demonstrate the four possible combinations. For example, left english and draw are shown at the bottom left of the page. This is commonly referred to as low left english. Your must be careful to limit the amount of sidespin that you use when playing combinations (of english and either draw or follow). If you were, for example, to place your cue one tip over and one tip below center, your tip would be perilously close to the edge of the cue ball. As a consequence, you would run a very high risk of a miscue (a miscue occurs when the tip fails to stick on the cue ball at the desired spot).

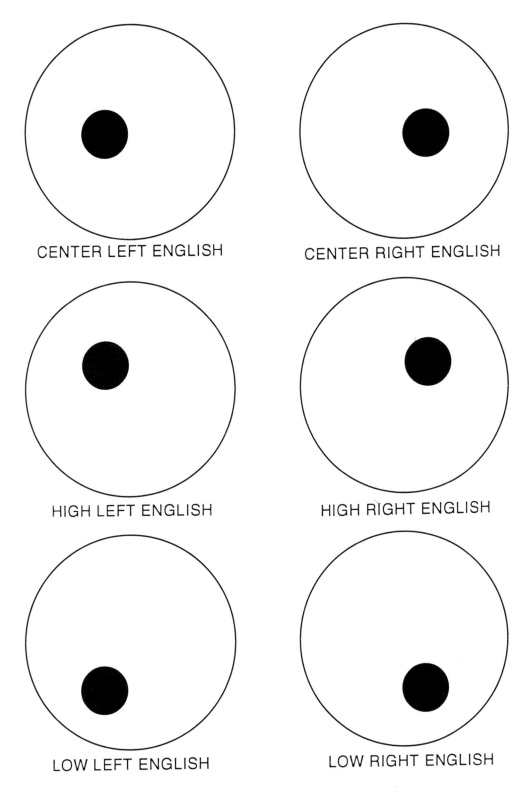

CENTER LEFT ENGLISH

CENTER RIGHT ENGLISH

HIGH LEFT ENGLISH

HIGH RIGHT ENGLISH

LOW LEFT ENGLISH

LOW RIGHT ENGLISH

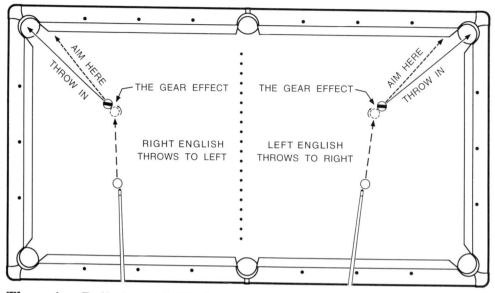

Throwing Balls in with English

English changes the direction of the object ball. The left portion of the diagram shows what takes place when right english is used. Upon contact the cue ball and object ball are momentarily locked together. Their meshing acts like gears. In this case, the cue ball, which is spinning counterclockwise (right), grabs hold of the object ball and throws it to the left. As you can see, you must compensate for the english by aiming to the right of the pocket. At contact the two balls are lined up slightly right of the pocket. The throw turns the object ball to the left and into the pocket.

The right side of the diagram shows the effects of left english. In this example, the clockwise spin of the cue ball throws the object ball to the right and into the pocket. The shot was aimed outside the left edge of the pocket to allow for the throw.

Both examples demonstrate the basics of throw. There are a couple of additional factors that will determine the magnitude of the throw. Throw is greatest on straight shots and those with a small cut angle. This is explained by the gear effect (or meshing), which is most felt upon full or near full contact with the object ball. As the cut angle grows, the cue ball begins to strike less and less of the object ball. This reduces the amount of throw and thus the effect of english.

The force of your stroke will also influence the level of throw. A soft stroke maximizes the effects of throw. Conversely, with a hard stroke, you will experience very little throw at all. In our examples, each ball was shot using medium stroke speed. With a hard stroke you would change your aim to the inside edge of the pocket.

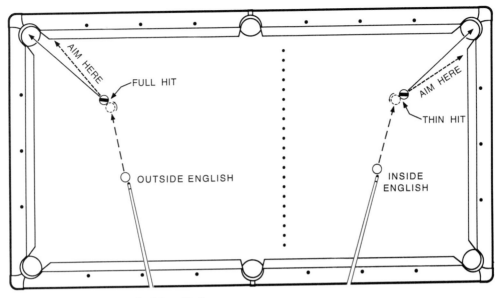

Outside and Inside English

English is commonly referred to as either outside english or inside english. In the previous diagram, both shots were hit with outside english. In the diagram above, the shot on the left is played with outside english. When a ball is cut to the left with right english, that's considered outside english. Conversely, cutting to the right with left english is also known as outside english. When using outside english, aim for a fuller hit on the object ball than normal. A number of players prefer to spin balls using outside english because it allows them to aim for less of an angle on cut shots.

The right portion of the diagram illustrates what's called inside english. Cutting to the right with right english is called inside english. And, of course, cutting to the left with left english would also be considered inside english. The object ball is hit thinner with inside english. As a result, inside english will not throw the ball quite as much as an equal amount of outside english on the same shot. Many players shy away from inside english because it requires a thinner hit, which seems to make aiming correctly especially difficult.

Newer players should first learn to use outside english. Only after you become quite proficient at outside english should you tackle the challenge of using inside english.

Allowing for Deflection

When the cue ball is struck with english, it <u>does</u> <u>not</u> travel in exactly the same direction as the cue was pointed at address. Hitting the left side of the cue ball causes it to go slightly to the right, and vice versa. This somewhat disturbing phenomenon is known as deflection, or squirt. Deflection is pool's one dirty word. Players have studied it, cursed it, and grudgingly come to accept it as a necessary evil that comes with using english.

All players who aspire to greatness must come to terms with deflection by gaining a thorough understanding of how it affects the aiming process. Before going any further, however, I will give you a short course on english and deflection that hopefully will relieve many of your concerns. Here it is: use english mostly on short shots, strike the cue ball no more than ½ tip off center and primarily use a soft stroke. If you follow these guidelines, much of the discussion that follows will not apply to your game. Furthermore, these few simple rules will enable you to play most of the shots on which a pro would use english.

There are many variables that affect the degree of deflection. They include the amount of english used, speed of stroke, distance of the cue ball from the object ball, and the shaft of your cue stick.

I went to the lab (my local pool room) to run a series of tests that hopefully would reveal some of the mysteries of deflection. I was completely armed with a training cue ball, laser sight, color coded target, protractor, rulers and the help of a friend. We tested deflection using three different speeds of stroke and two separate hits on the cue ball. Before we discuss the results, keep in mind that we used my cue, which may deliver slightly different results from your stick. In addition, my definition of a soft, medium, and hard stroke may not be quite the same as yours. With these thoughts in mind, here are the results.

English	Stroke	Degree of Deflection
½ Tip	Soft	.40
½ Tip	Medium	.78
½ Tip	Hard	1.25
1 Tip	Soft	1.03
1 Tip	Medium	1.37
1 Tip	Hard	2.03

As you can see, a 1/2 tip of english with a soft stroke yielded the least amount of deflection at .40 degrees. At the other end of the spectrum, 1 full tip of english and a hard stroke threw the cue ball 2.03 degrees off line. It is interesting to note that the cue ball is thrown more than a full ball's width off line from a distance of about five feet using a hard stroke with one tip of english. This rather sobering finding should persuade many of you to reconsider your plans for juicing up the majority of your shots.

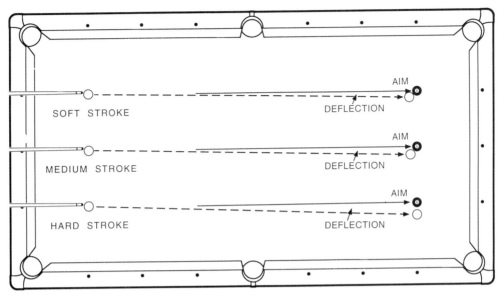

Deflection Test Results

The diagram above shows how far deflection can throw the cue ball off course, especially at longer distances. One full tip of english was used and each cue ball was aimed directly at the 8-ball. A hard stroke caused the cue ball to miss the entire 8-ball! Now you know why I've been warning you of the difficulties of using english.

The results of the test have been converted into the following table. The table gives you in inches, approximately how much you must adjust your aim for deflection. Here's an example of how it works: using ½ tip of english and a medium stroke with the cue ball three diamonds from the object ball, you will need to allow for .53" of deflection.

Cue Ball Distance from Object Ball/Deflection

(Distance Measured in # of Diamonds)
(Deflection Off Target Measured in Inches)

Tip	Stroke	#1	#2	#3	#4	#5	#6	#7
½	Soft	.08	.16	.26	.35	.44	.53	.61
½	Med.	.18	.35	.53	.70	.87	1.05	1.23
½	Hard	.28	.56	.84	1.12	1.40	1.69	1.96
1	Soft	.23	.46	.69	.92	1.15	1.38	1.60
1	Med.	.30	.61	.91	1.22	1.52	1.83	2.13
1	Hard	.45	.90	1.36	1.80	2.26	2.71	3.16

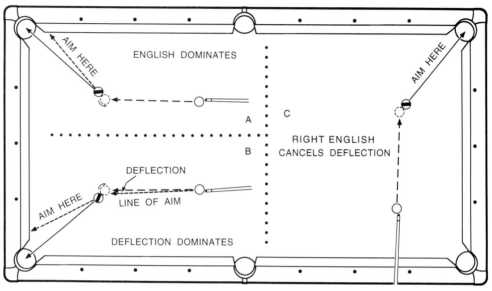

Deflection and Throw

So far we've covered the two primary factors that affect your aim when using english: throw and deflection. Perhaps you may have gathered that each factor exerts a different influence on your point of aim. Our goal is to resolve this conflict so that you can aim correctly using english. Let me first remind you of one thought: using english correctly isn't the easiest thing in pool, but it's well worth it.

In position A in the diagram above, we are cutting the ball to the right while using 1/2 tip of right (inside) english. Assume a soft stroke is being employed. In this case, deflection will be only about 1/8". Therefore, we should aim to the right of the pocket to allow for throw, which is greatest, as you'll recall, on a soft stroke.

Position B is the mirror image of position A. Again we are using 1/2 tip of inside english, only this time a hard stroke is being used. Now we must adjust our aim about 3/4" to the left to compensate for the deflection. Notice what this does to the line of aim. In position B, deflection dominates the aiming process (not throw). As a result, you will need to aim for a fuller hit on the stripe. The left english will deflect the cue ball to the right causing it to hit the object ball on the correct spot.

Interestingly enough, with the proper stroke speed you can aim your shot as if you were not using any english at all. In position C right english will deflect the cue ball to the left. However, the right english will also throw the object ball to the left. The bottom line is that the english and deflection have canceled each other out. Therefore, no adjustments in aim are required. When aiming with english, keep these guidelines in mind:

- On soft shots throw influences the shot more than deflection.
- The harder your stroke, the more deflection you must allow for.
- At some point deflection and throw cancel each other out.
- Deflection must be allowed for at longer distances.

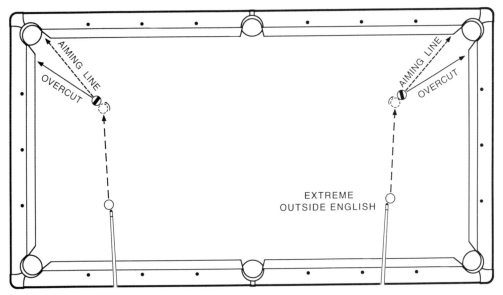

Missing Shots Because of Throw

Improperly gauging the effects of throw is a common reason for missing balls when using english. In the position at the left, the player used only ½ tip of right english, but failed to allow sufficiently for the throw. He/she should aim slightly outside the right edge of the pocket. In the righthand portion of the diagram the player aimed at the outside edge of the pocket. However he/she missed because the stripe was thrown too much. In this example, the player used too much (one tip) english. Remember to adjust your aim sufficiently for throw when using a soft stroke, and especially when you are applying extreme english to the cue ball.

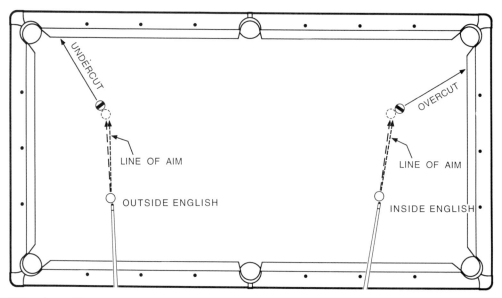

Missing Shots Because of Deflection

It's not hard to miss balls when using outside english with a medium or hard stroke. Deflection can easily send the cue ball into nearly full contact with the object ball. This causes the shot to be undercut, as the left side of the diagram demonstrates. There are two solutions. One is to use a soft stroke. This will reduce the deflection and increase throw at the same time. You could also aim for a thinner hit on the object ball and allow deflection to push the cue ball into proper contact. This is a theoretically correct solution, however, most players have trouble aiming for a thinner hit when using outside english.

It's been my observation that at least 80 to 90% of all players miss shots using inside english because they shoot too hard and fail to sufficiently allow for deflection. In the position at the right, the player used inside (right) english and a medium stroke. The cue ball traveled to the left of the line of aim (as you'll recall, right english deflects to the left). As a result, the stripe was overcut badly to the right of the pocket. Do you overcut balls using inside english? If so, aim for a fuller hit on the object ball and/or use less stroke speed.

You should expect to miss a number of shots when learning english. However, you can speed up the process by paying close attention to your missed shots. When you know the various effects of throw, deflection and speed of stroke, you can begin to make the appropriate adjustments. Awareness of the probable cause of missing shots is the first step towards curing the problem.

How Curve Affects Aim

At the risk of creating sensory overload, I feel you must know about one final factor that can affect your aim when using english. When the cue ball is struck with a level stick, it will travel in a straight line. The sidespin has virtually no effect on the path of the cue ball. However, is english is applied with a downward blow, the sidespin will cause the cue ball to curve in the direction of the english. For example, if you apply right english, the cue ball will curve to the right and vice versa. The problem of curve appears most often on draw shots with english. You can eliminate this variable from your calculations by stroking with your cue as level as possible. Using english is tough enough as it is so don't add to the difficulty by tossing curve into your preshot calculations.

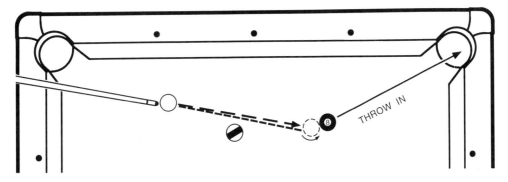

Throwing Shots in Around Obstacles

In this position, the 8-ball cannot be made with a centerball hit because the stripe is in the way. So, rather than aiming along the heavy dashed line, instead adjust your aim down the dashed line with the arrow. This allows you to avoid contacting the stripe. Now use a slow stroke with plenty of outside (right) english. This will throw the 8-ball to the left and into the pocket.

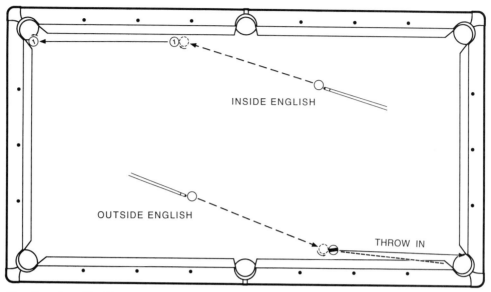

Pocketing Balls with English

A number of very fine players use english on a variety of routine shots as they feel it increases their accuracy and cue ball control. The position at the bottom of the diagram is a prime example. Here you have a cut shot of perhaps 20° or so down the rail into average sized pockets. Use a medium soft stroke and aim along the heavy dashed line. The outside english (right) will throw the stripe to the left and into the pocket.

At the top of the diagram you are faced with the same shot, only this time the pockets are very tight and unforgiving. Under these conditions you may find it helpful to apply a touch of inside (left) english to the cue ball. Upon contact, the cue ball will transfer a small amount of spin to the object ball. In this example, the cue ball was spinning clockwise, therefore, the one will be turning counterclockwise. The diagram shows the spin on the 1-ball as it hits the lip of the pocket. Sometimes a small amount of spin can mean the difference between success and failure when shooting into tight pockets.

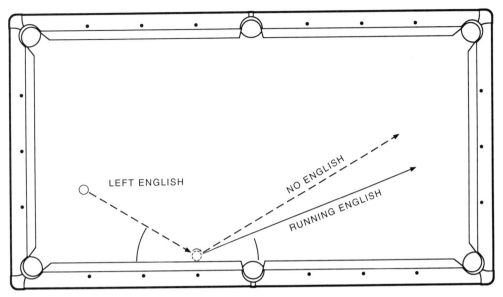

How English Affects the Cue Ball off the Rails

Although english can be used to pocket balls, it is primarily used for playing position. When the cue ball strikes the rails, english can have a profound affect on it's direction.

The diagram shows the path of the cue ball without english. Observe how the cue ball rebounds at an angle very close to it's angle of approach. Now we'll assume the same starting position and the same contact point on the rail. Only this time we're going to use some left english. Notice how the cue ball's rebound angle flattens out (solid line). This is what happens when running english is used. The rebound is less and the cue ball picks up speed when it hits the rail. One of the subtle beauties of pool is to watch a slow moving cue ball grab a rail with running english, build up a head of stream, and take off running down the table. If you have not yet experienced this sight, you then have something to look forward to.

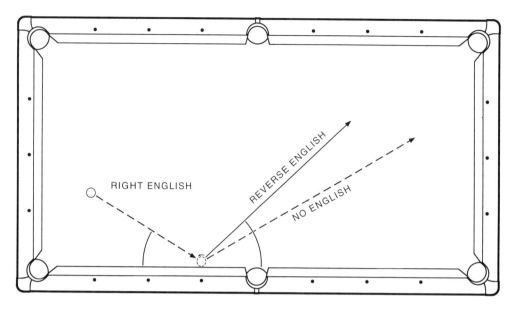

Reverse english exerts the opposite effect on the cue ball. The second diagram once again demonstrates the path of the cue ball without english (dashed line). The same position and angle of approach are taken, only this time reverse english (right) has been used. Reverse english digs into the rail and slows down the cue ball. It also increases the rebound angle. A number of players also enjoy watching the cue ball screech to a halt as it dies off the rail because of reverse english.

The approach angle and amount of spin determine the change in the rebound angle. At shallow angles of approach (15° or less) english has little effect on the rebound angle. In sharp contrast, when the approach angle nears 90°, the cue ball can change direction radically upon contact with the cushion. We will cover position using english in great detail in chapter five.

A Short Course on English
Left english throws to the right
Right english throws to the left
Soft stroke throws more than a hard stroke
Left english deflects the cue ball to the right
Right english deflects the cue ball to the left
Soft stroke deflects less than a hard stroke
½ tip of english creates less deflection than a full tip
Your cue stick affects the amount of deflection.
The cue ball will curve slightly in the direction of the english on a downward hit

Rules of Thumb
Use ½ tip or less of english
Use english mostly when the cue ball's within three diamonds or less of the object ball
Use a soft or medium stroke on nearly all of your shots with english

CHAPTER 5

POSITION PLAY

How To Control

The Cue Ball

I remember watching the legendary Willie Mosconi play an exhibition match of straight pool in San Diego back in the early 1970's. As his run of consecutive shots without a miss approached 140, I recall hearing a fellow spectator remark to his friend "He never has a hard shot. This is boring. I wish he'd do his trick shots".

Position, also known as shape, is the location of the cue ball relative to the next shot. Good position makes the next shot easy. Poor position leads to missed balls and lost games. What the observer mentioned above failed to realize and appreciate, was that Mr. Mosconi was playing perfect position on nearly every single shot.

To play position well, you simply need to know where you want the cue ball to go, and how to make it get there. In addition, you must be able to execute what you know. It is an absolute must for any player who wishes to rise above the level of beginner to gain at least some measure of control over the movements of the cue ball; in other words, to play shape. Good position play can turn a crowd pleasing shotmaker into a player. Good position play can also make the game substantially easier for anyone willing to apply a little grey matter towards improving this facet of their game. At this point, I trust that you are now sufficiently motivated to learn position play and to build on the basics covered in the first four chapters.

Our discussion on position play is divided into six sections. First we'll cover the basics of position play. This includes how to stop, draw, and follow the cue ball. Readers are urged to become well grounded in the basics as they provide the foundation for the remaining sections of the chapter.

Principles of position play comes next. This all important section provides you with the fundamentals necessary for a successful game of pool. Here you'll learn the importance of speed control, how to avoid scratching, and how to plan your shots successfully.

Off the rail shape will teach you how to control the cue ball as it rebounds off the cushion. Included here are the effects of english on the cue ball after it contacts the rail, the kill shot, force shots and more. After reading and practicing the position plays in multi-rail shape, you'll know how to send the cue ball around and across the table without fear of scratching. This section covers a wide variety of two, three, and four rail position plays.

Included is a special section on how to play position when the object ball is close to the pocket. All too often these shots are easier to make but harder to play good shape. Finally, you'll be taught a number of useful techniques for playing shape in a variety of position plays. Included in this section are the lag shot, playing shape off combinations, using balls as backstops, and much more.

It takes lots of time, practice, and patience to learn to play position well. So take your time and work through the lessons in this chapter at your own pace. It's okay to skip around from sections two through six, but only after the basics presented in the first section are mastered. And lastly, have fun and take pride in your increasing skills.

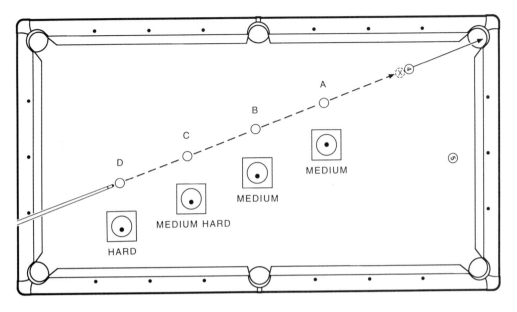

Basic Position

Stop Shot

When a stop shot is properly executed, the cue ball will come to rest precisely at its point of contact. One of the beauties of the stop shot is that you know, in advance, exactly where the cue ball will be positioned for the next shot. For example, in the diagram above, a stop shot on the 4-ball will leave the cue ball in ideal shape for an easy shot on the 5-ball. It is imperative that you master the stop shot, as you will be faced with it over and over again in actual play.

At short distances, a cue ball struck with centerball a level cue, and at medium speed, will slide across the felt into the object ball and, upon contact, stop dead in its tracks (position A). As the length of the shot increases, however, friction between the cloth and the cue ball will take over, creating topspin. With topspin, the cue ball will travel past the point of contact with the object ball. There are two methods for overcoming the effects of friction which will allow you to execute stop shots at longer distances. By increasing the force with which you strike the cue ball, you make the cue ball stop on longer shots. However, past about three feet, the cue ball will begin to roll forward. On longer stop shots, a more effective technique is to apply draw to the cue ball (positions B, C, and D). With practice you will learn to gauge the correct amount of draw and stroke speed that will allow you to shoot stop shots down the entire length of the table.

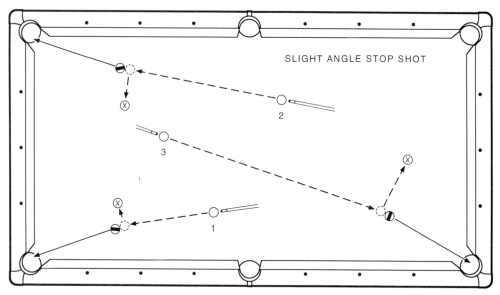

Slight Angle Stop Shots

You can minimize sideways drift on stop shots that have a slight cut angle. Use a slow and very smooth stroke while striking the cue ball as low as possible. By the time the cue ball makes contact with the object ball, friction will have removed the vast majority of the backspin, allowing the cue ball to stop quickly with a minimum of sideways drift.

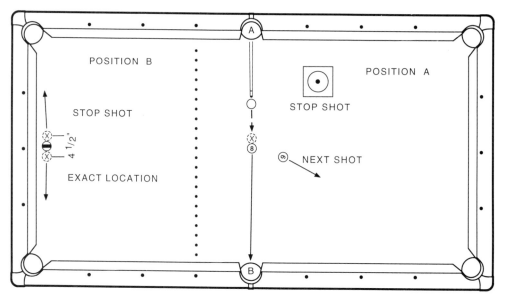

Ball in Hand Stop Shots

With ball in hand, the 8-ball can easily be shot into either pocket A or B. Pocket B is the better choice because you can stop the cue ball dead (at point X) for an easy shot on the 9-ball. Position B shows how you pinpoint your position by shooting a stop shot from either side of the object ball.

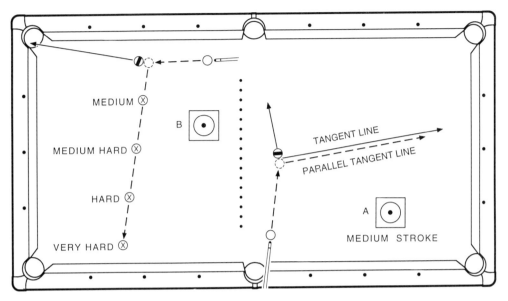

Force Shots

The force shot is vital to good position play. When you come across a nearly straight-in shot of 10° cut angle or less, the force shot will enable you to send the cue ball across the table to a variety of desirable locations with great precision. When a force shot is stroked correctly, the cue ball will travel directly along a line that's parallel to the tangent line between the cue ball and object ball at the moment of contact (see position A). This is called the parallel tangent line. The cue ball will travel along this line if you apply the same technique as for the stop shot: centerball hit, level cue, and at least medium force. The two key factors which determine how far the cue ball slides sideways are the cut angle and the speed with which you strike the cue ball. You will need to apply additional force to achieve greater cue ball movement. Part B of the diagram shows four variations of speed on the same cut angle. As you can see, the cue ball will crawl a few inches down the parallel tangent line with a medium hit. However, with a hard stroke, you can force the cue ball all the way to the opposite side of the table.

Force shots are most effective when the cue ball is reasonably close to the object ball, (about three feet or less). Once you go beyond this distance it becomes much more difficult to pocket the ball, as you will be using a harder stroke. This is especially true when shooting down the rail on a table with tight pockets. It's also tougher to hit the cue ball with the precise amount of draw (remember, stop shots need draw at longer distances) to get the cue ball to travel exactly along the parallel tangent line.

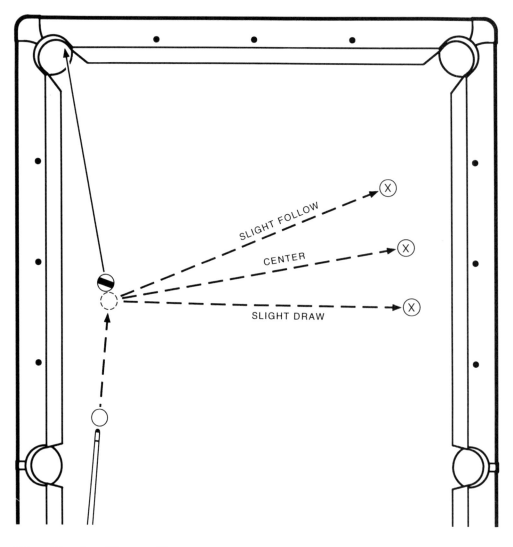

Fine Tuning Force Shots

You can fine tune your force shots by raising or lowering your tip slightly at address (about 1/4 to 1/2 tip) to produce a small amount of follow or draw. The diagram above shows you the effect this creates on the cue ball's path.

The Draw Shot

The draw shot, simply put, is a below center hit which creates backspin on the cue ball. Backspin will cause the cue ball to roll back toward the shooter after making contact with the object ball. Draw shots are fun to watch, very satisfying when executed properly, and are indispensable to good position play. In fact, you will be required to use draw in one way or another on at least 40-50% of your shots! Since a draw shot is a glancing blow to a slick object, your cue tip will need to be well maintained in order to achieve proper contact with the cue ball.   The even application of chalk before all draw shots is your best insurance against the sickening sight of an airborne cue ball caused by a miscue. Enough said? You should also check your tip regularly to make sure it is holding a sufficient amount of chalk. Run your finger or a napkin over the tip to remove the chalk. If the surface is slick and shiny, you should rough-up your tip immediately. Every so often you should also check the curvature of your tip. A nickel shaped radius works okay, but if you plan on drawing more than one tip beneath center, keep your tip shaped with the radius of a dime.

Now that your tip is in excellent condition, you are ready to approach the table and execute pool's most beautiful shot. Your first step will be to lower your bridge hand so that the cue is at least one tip diameter below center.   Once you get comfortable shooting at that position, you should consider lowering your bridge hand until your cue is 1 1/4 tips below center. Remember, the lower you are able to effectively stroke the cue ball, the more backspin and less forward momentum will be applied to the cue ball. Be sure not to make the mistake of raising your grip hand while setting up a draw shot. You'll want to keep your cue as level as possible.

Now for the stroke, the true secret to the draw shot. Keep a relaxed backhand grip as this promotes maximum wrist action. Avoid the so-called death grip like the plague. Stroke smoothly and accelerate smoothly through impact. In turn, make sure that you follow through completely. Your tip should come to rest anywhere from a few inches to a foot or more past the cue ball's original location. The amount of draw required and your speed of stroke will dictate the length of your follow through. By all means, avoid the temptation to pull back on your stroke!

Many novices worry when following through that they won't get out of the way of the returning cue ball in time, thus committing a foul. Two words on that subject: first, with practice, you will develop a sense of timing that will allow you to remove yourself from the table immediately after executing a complete follow through. Secondly, in most cases, the cue ball will not come straight back toward your bridge hand. Because of this you'll have plenty of time to lift your bridge hand.

The best way to learn the draw shot is to begin with the cue ball a foot or so away from the object ball. At short distances such as this, friction between the cloth and the cue ball will have little time to remove backspin from the cue ball. You can then progress to longer versions of the draw shot as your skill and confidence grow.

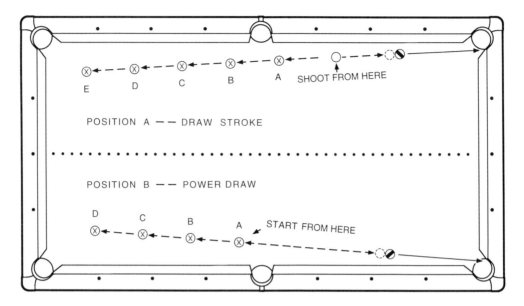

In example A above, you should keep the cue ball and object ball in the same position for each shot. At first, try to draw the ball just a few inches. You may surprise yourself by drawing the cue ball a couple feet back or more. Be sure to follow through completely before moving off the table to make room for the cue ball as it comes back toward you. Most important, stay in tune with your stroke. When you get the desired result, say to yourself, "Aha, that's how it's done"! Your first draw shot will truly be one of your magical moments in pool. Once you get the hang of it, begin to increase the speed of your stroke incrementally as you work your way back to points B, C, D and E. One thing you'll want to look for as your proficiency rises, is the delay effect. When you stroke a draw shot with expert technique, you will notice that the cue ball will hesitate just slightly before the backspin takes over and the cue ball rockets back down the table. This shifting of gears is one of the most delightful characteristics of the draw shot.

Once you've mastered the routine shown in position A, it is time to move on to the power draw shown in position B. When the distance between the cue ball and the object ball has grown to two feet or more, as in our example, friction will remove a good part of the cue ball's backspin before it reaches the object ball. This phenomenon of physics makes long draw shots particularly difficult. Obviously, your stroke and technique need to improve proportionally on longer draw shots. It's especially important to remember that maximum draw comes as a result of applying backspin smoothly. If you try to gain maximum draw with an especially hard stroke, you'll create excess forward momentum on the cue ball. With insufficient backspin, the cue ball will creep back only a few inches at best. In position B, start with the cue ball at A, and try to draw the cue ball back to A, then B, C, and D. Once you've got A down pat, place the cue ball at position B and progress backward again. By the time you can place the cue ball at D and draw it all the way back to D consistently, you may be ready to turn Pro.

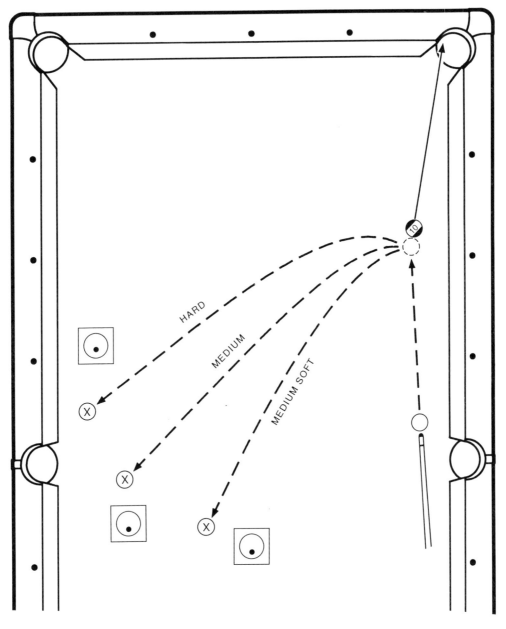

The Effect of Stroke Force on Angled Draw Shots

On draw shots with a cut angle, the cue ball will first travel for a short distance at a right angle from the point of contact. A harder stroke will cause the cue ball to slide further sideways before the draw takes over. On angled draw shots where you want to minimize this effect, hit at the maximum low point on the cue ball with a softer stroke. To maximize sideways drift, simply apply less draw than normal and use a firmer stroke.

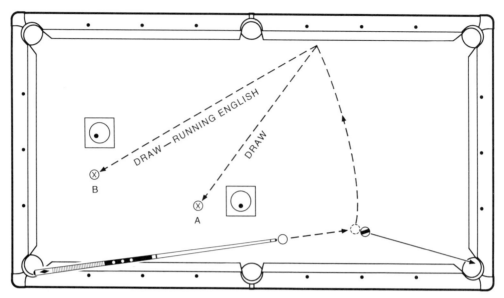

Draw off of the Side Rail with English

On angled draw shots, running english can help you easily move the cue ball down the table. Line A shows the path of the cue ball using draw, but no english. Line B demonstrates how running english (left in this case) can send the cue ball to the opposite end of the table.

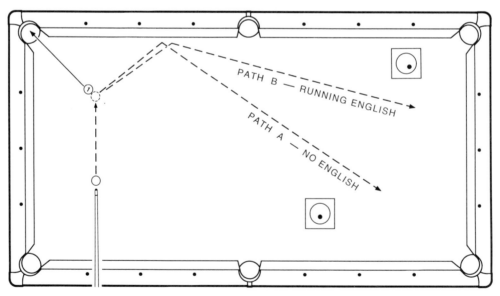

Drawing up the Side Rail with English

A firm stroke with minimum draw and no english will send the cue ball off the rail at a sharp angle, as shown by Path A. Now, if you adjust your draw lower, apply right english, and use less stroke force, the cue ball will strike further up the rail. In addition, the english will open up the angle, sending the cue ball down path B.

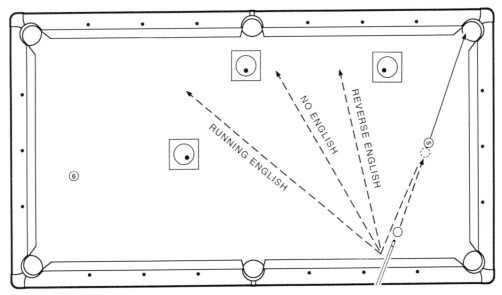

Back to the Rail Draw Shots with English

In our example, draw with running english (right) will serve to open up the rebound angle off the rail, sending the cue ball down the table for position on the 6-ball. Note how reverse (left) english sharpens the rebound angle. Lastly, observe the path of the cue ball without english.

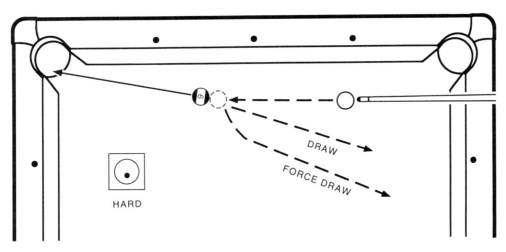

Force Draw

The force draw shot results from the skillful blending of two concepts: the force shot and the power draw shot. The first objective is to maximize the sideways movement of the cue ball. The next goal is to have the cue ball creep back toward the designated location. To execute this shot properly use a very firm stroke with minimum draw. Please note that because of the power required, this shot is most effective at close range.

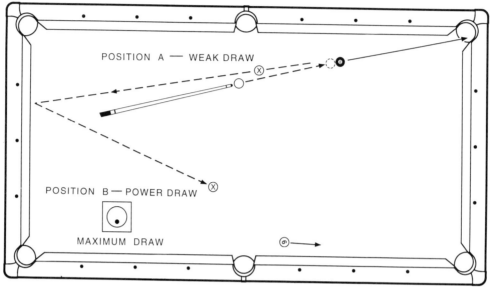

Power Draw

In our example, the player needs to pocket the 8-ball, then the game winning 9-ball. A player with a weak draw might opt to draw the ball slightly, setting up a bank shot into the opposite side pocket. A power draw shot to the end rail and back out would put the cue ball in position B for a much easier shot on the 9-ball. A longer bridge than normal will facilitate a longer, smoother stroke and fuller follow through. This will permit a lower hit on the cue ball for maximum draw.

The Nip/Draw Shot

Draw shots are a special challenge when the cue ball is but a few inches from the object ball (approx. 3-7 inches). You will need to accomplish two objectives: apply sufficient draw with a very short stoke and remove your bridge quickly before the cue ball returns. Your first adjustment is to curl the fingers of your bridge hand under at the knuckles. This will lower your bridge so that your knuckles are now resting on the table. Now you can easily strike the cue ball well below center. Your second adjustment is to shorten your bridge to about 5-6 inches. Your stroke on a nip shot is more like a quick jab, which allows you to exit the table rapidly. You'll be surprised how far you can draw the cue ball once you've got this very useful shot down pat.

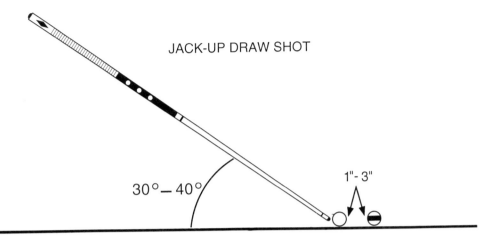

JACK-UP DRAW SHOT

30° — 40°

1"- 3"

The Jack-Up Draw Shot

When the cue ball is three inches or less from the object ball, both the nip draw and the standard draw shots are out of the question, as either technique would almost certainly result in a foul. The solution is the jack-up draw shot. Employ the same bridge that is used for shooting over a ball: elevate your bridge hand so that only the tips of your fingers are on the table. Now place the shaft of the cue in a groove formed by your thumb and index finger. Elevate your cue by raising your grip hand until the cue is at a 30 - 40 degree angle. As a rule of thumb, the closer the cue ball is to the object ball, the sharper the angle will need to be. This will allow you to shoot through the cue ball without committing a foul. You will want to strike the cue ball about one tip below center. Bear in mind that this means beneath center as you look down on the cue ball from your chosen angle of attack. Your stroke will, of necessity be very short, and mostly propelled with wrist action.

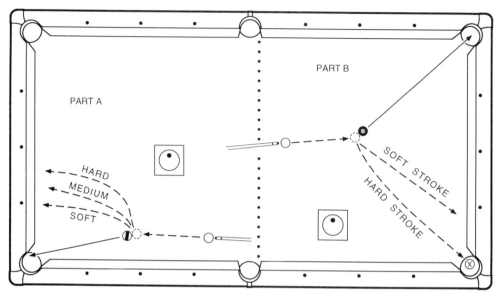

The Follow Shot

After making contact with the object ball the cue ball will continue to roll forward on a follow shot. Although follow shots are not normally as crowd pleasing as draw shots, knowledgeable observers will nevertheless applaud your control of the cue ball. The bottom line is that proper execution of follow shots is a fundamental element to playing expert position. So plan on mastering follow shots, just as you would any other essential element of the game.

The physics of the follow shot are relatively straightforward: by striking the cue ball above center, you will create topspin, which helps propel the cue ball forward. The excess topspin on the cue ball combines with friction from the cloth to create additional forward roll. When a follow shot is particularly well stroked, you may notice a momentary delay as the cue ball spins it's wheels prior to accelerating down the table. To the trained eye, this is one of the more visually rewarding characteristics of the follow shot.

To prepare for a follow shot, you simply need to raise your bridge hand so that your cue tip is above the center of the cue ball. One half tip above center should be enough for the vast majority of follow shots. For maximum follow, however, you should elevate your stick to a full cue tip's diameter above center. This will give you the decisive follow action required to send the cue ball great distances across the table. Don't be afraid to use maximum follow. You won't miscue as long as you take proper care of your tip.

Your elevated bridge hand will help you keep a level stroke on follow shots. Make sure you don't also raise your grip hand when setting up for follow shots. As always, use a smooth stroke and follow through.

On straight-in follow shots the cue ball, if stroked firmly enough, will follow the object ball into the pocket for a scratch. Almost all of your position plays using follow, however, will have at least some degree of cut angle. Because of this, it is imperative for you to grasp how the cue ball reacts immediately after contacting the object ball on all non straight-in follow shots. After contact, two forces are at work. The force that sends the cue ball at a right angle to the object ball after contact initially wins out. After the cue ball has momentarily drifted down the right angle line, however, topspin quickly takes over and causes the cue ball to begin it's forward roll.

Speed of stroke will also affect the cue ball on angled cut shots. A firmer stroke will increase sideways drift down the right angle line before the cue ball commences it's forward roll. Part A of the diagram above shows you how speed of stroke on follow shots affects the direction of the cue ball. Knowledge of how the angle and stroke force influences the path of the cue ball can be used for playing position, avoiding other object balls, and to avoid scratching. Part B presents a shot that newer players scratch on repeatedly. Instead of firing the ball in, shoot easier and the cue ball will begin its forward roll sooner, thereby avoiding a scratch in the corner pocket.

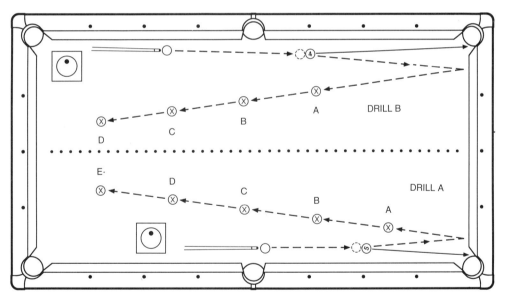

Practicing follow shots will help you build your stroke and refine your position play. The diagram shows you a progressive drill. With the balls lined up nearly straight in, practice shooting to position A, then B, C, D, and E (drill A). Don't move past any one location until you can consistently stop the cue ball near the target on the diagram. Next, move the object ball and the cue ball further from the pocket (drill B). Now try to achieve the same positional objectives as in the first exercise.

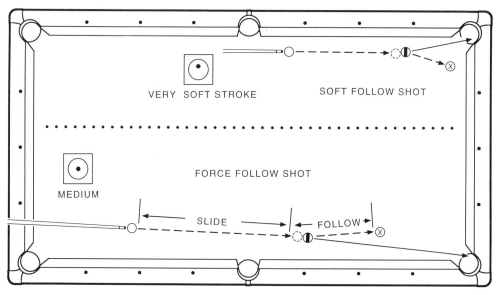

Force Follow

Sometimes you'll need the cue ball to travel a few inches to a couple of feet past the object ball on a long shot. Most players make the mistake of babying this shot. Slow rolling long follow shots make it easy to control the cue ball speed, but at a high cost. By soft stroking this shot, the cue ball may roll off due to a non-level table. In addition it's tough to make an accurate stroke when hitting the cue ball softly at longer distances. I recommend that you try the force follow shot on this position play. You'll recall that stop shots are hit with centerball and medium stroke speed and that the cue ball stops sliding after about two-three feet. The diagram shows that once slide has been removed from the cue ball, it will begin to roll forward. The trick to the force follow shot is to accurately gauge just how far the cue ball will keep rolling after slide has turned to follow. As you might have guessed, the correct stroke speed will come only with practice. At first, you may have a little trouble figuring out just how hard to hit the cue ball. However, once you've mastered this shot, you'll appreciate the results.

Soft Follow Shots

It's okay to stroke the cue ball very softly on follow shots as long as the object ball is reasonably close to the pocket, and the cue ball is within three feet of the object ball. At this short range, it would take a lopsided table to cause the object ball to roll off enough to miss (Caution: Lopsided tables do exist - it always pays to check the table roll before you begin play). On short follow shots, you should also be able to control your stroke. Complete mastery of the soft follow shot will enable you to position the cue ball consistently within a few inches of perfection. The good news is that the soft follow shot is one of the easiest shots to learn. The secret is to develop a heightened sensitivity for touch.

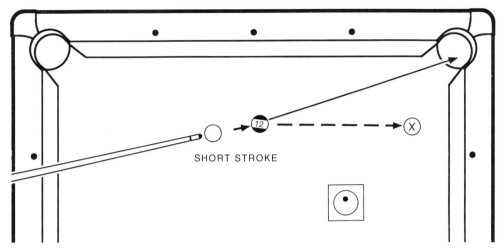

SHORT STROKE

Nip Follow Shot

The nip follow shot will enable you to follow the cue ball up to several feet when the object ball and cue ball are within just a few inches of each other without committing a double hit (a foul). Use a very short stroke and accelerate sharply using mostly your wrist. The trick is to follow through no more than 1" - 2" past the cue ball without flinching.

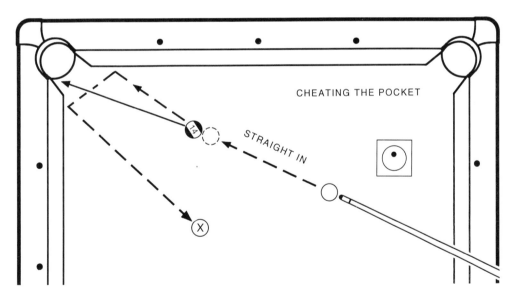

CHEATING THE POCKET

STRAIGHT IN

Straight in Cheat the Pocket Follow Shots

On straight-in follow shots it's possible to avoid scratching by cheating the pocket. Shooting intentionally into either side of the pocket requires great accuracy. Be sure to stay down on this shot until the object ball's in the pocket. Don't attempt this shot if the object ball is too far from the pocket.

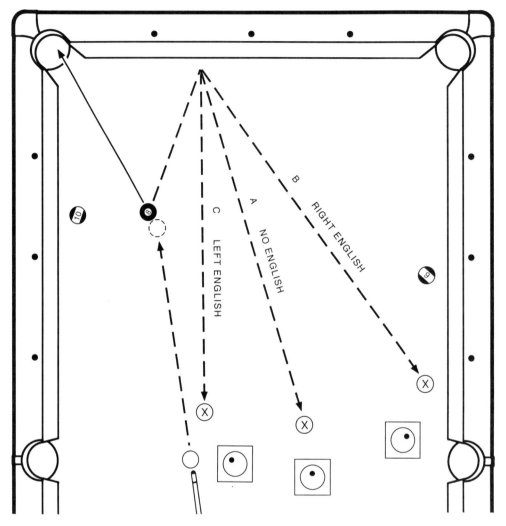

Follow with English

Applying english to a follow shot can make it possible for you to easily reach a variety of position play objectives. In the diagram above, a follow shot with a medium stroke would bring the cue ball up the center of the table to position A. Let's say, however, that you would like to have an easier shot on your next shot which is the 9-ball. Again, use a medium stroke and follow, but this time also apply some righthand english. Note how the english opens up the angle off the rail, causing the cue ball to veer to the right along line B. Now let's assume that our goal is to position the cue ball in the ideal spot for a simple shot on the 10-ball. Left english and follow at medium speed will cause the cue ball to rebound of the rail at a much sharper angle. This will carry the cue ball back along Line C. .

Principles of Position Play

You will need to master each of the principles of position to play your very best pool. The principles will serve as your guide on every shot you play. They will help you select the best route for the cue ball and they will keep you from costly mistakes. By using them you can avoid scratching the cue ball, getting hooked, and other assorted disasters. Some principles carry more weight than others, but all are vital to your developing a top caliber game of pool. If you overlook even one principle, that may just be the one that will cost you an important match. Therefore, I urge you to learn each of these principles thoroughly. Be sure to refer back to this section if you are having trouble with position play in the future.

The principles are best learned one at a time. Make sure that you understand each concept thoroughly before moving on to the next one. Bear in mind, however, that the principles all work together. You will use several of these concepts on every single shot. Perhaps this may sound unduly complicated. It's not. Over time, as you gain knowledge and experience, many of these principles will become second nature. Your mental computer will automatically sift through all possible options, selecting those principles you need to execute each shot to the best of your ability.

The diagrammed position demonstrates in what ways each of the principles of position work together to create a successful shot. In the example, at least eleven different principles can be identified. We'll go through them one by one. Note that the numbers on the table correspond to each principle.

1. Speed control- The cue ball was hit with perfect speed. As a result, the player now has a simple shot on the gamewinning 8-ball.

2. Ideal angle and distance equals position- The 8-ball is a very simple shot at this distance. In addition, no angle is required because this is the last shot of the game.

3. Play natural shape- The cue ball followed its most natural course by first contacting the two rails at the top end of the table.

4. Enter into the wide area of a position zone- The cue ball has entered the position zone (indicated by the heavy dashed line) near it's widest point.

5. Allow for a margin for error- The cue ball has contacted the rail well up from the corner pocket, which has minimized the chances of scratching.

6. Play to the long side- In this example, there was a big advantage to playing shape on the long side because the 8-ball was within a diamond of the lower left hand pocket.

7. Use rail targets- Notice the two rail targets that were accurately struck. These targets helped the player to avoid hitting the 10-ball or scratching.

8. Keep the cue ball away from the rails- The cue ball has come to rest midway between the two side rails.

9. Avoid scratching- The player has successfully avoided scratching in either the righthand side or corner pockets.

10. Plan your route- avoid obstructions- The player has skillfully avoided contact with the 10-ball, which would have ruined his/her position on the 8-ball.

11. Survey the table before shooting- Viewing the position zone from the side rail before shooting helped the player establish his/her position objective for the shot.

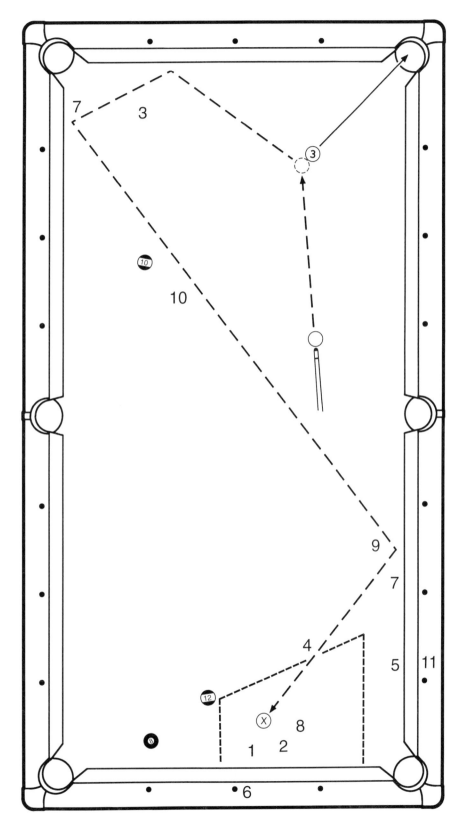

Speed Control

Knowing how hard to stroke each shot is called speed control. This is the single most important principle for playing position. If you can control the distance that the cue ball travels, you can compete at the upper levels of the game. On the other hand, if you stroke the cue ball like a blacksmith, you'll be forever facing one tough shot after another. In short, your control of cue ball speed will make or break you as a player.

Shooting pool with good speed control is quite similar to skills required in other sports. Golfers develop a feel that allows them to hit long putts close to the hole. Basketball players with a shooting touch can swish 20 foot jump shots. What makes pool especially challenging, however, is the wide variety of possible position plays, each one requiring just the right touch. With sufficient practice you will begin to develop a feel for distance. Something will click in your eye, hand, and brain computer. As your game develops, you'll gain control over an ever increasing array of position plays. Ultimately, the quality of your speed control will be directly related to the time you spend playing and practicing, in addition to whatever God-given talent you possess..

You can improve your speed control by becoming aware of the spectrum of force with which good players stroke the cue ball. The 1-10 scale should make it easy for you to visualize the different speeds of stroke. As the table shows, the spectrum ranges from extremely soft (1) to the break shot (10), where maximum stroke speed is employed.

1. Extremely Soft	6. Medium hard
2. Very Soft	7. Hard
3. Soft	8. Very hard
4. Medium soft	9. Extremely hard
5. Medium	10. The break shot

For some unknown reason, almost all beginners typically hit their shots way too hard. Their stroke speed falls primarily between levels 6-8. In sharp contrast, professionals players shoot much more softly. They confine their stroke speed to levels 3-7 for most shots, although they are capable of playing position across the entire spectrum of force. Pros tend to avoid shooting very easy (1-2) or very hard (8-9) because these speeds can lead to missed shots. You should become familiar with all the variations in speed, with particular emphasis on levels 3-7. Put some variety into your speed of stroke and witness the accompanying improvement in your cue ball control. As your skill rises, you'll come to value highly the position play possibilities that a refined sense of speed will bring to your game.

In this chapter you should take careful note of the force that's required to reach ideal position in each example. Also keep in mind that the force needed can vary widely, depending on the playing conditions. A fast table with lively rails will require much less stroke speed than a slow table with sponge-like cushions.

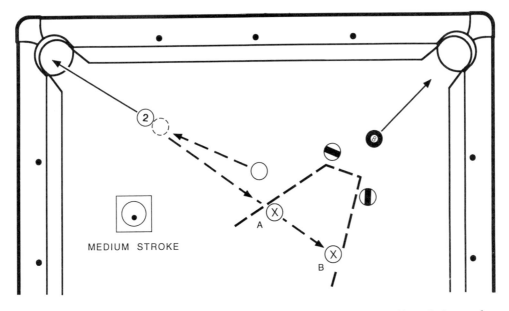

In the diagram above, your goal is to pocket the 2-ball and draw the cue ball back between the dashed lines (A-B) for position on the 8-ball. This is easier said than done, as good speed control using draw is one of the tougher shots to master.

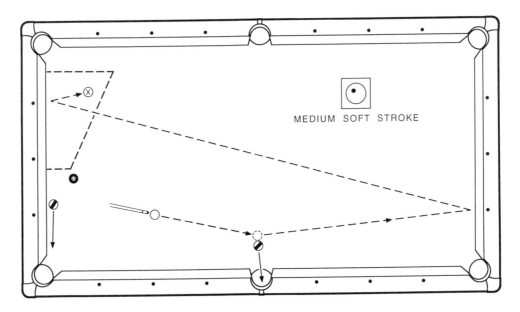

Most players have a much better sense of speed control on follow shots. As your game progresses, you may at first be wise to develop a sense of speed by emphasizing follow shots. Follow shots will help you develop a soft stroke as they require, for the most part, less force than draw shots. In our example, a medium soft-stroke was all that was needed to send the cue ball all the way to the end rail and back.

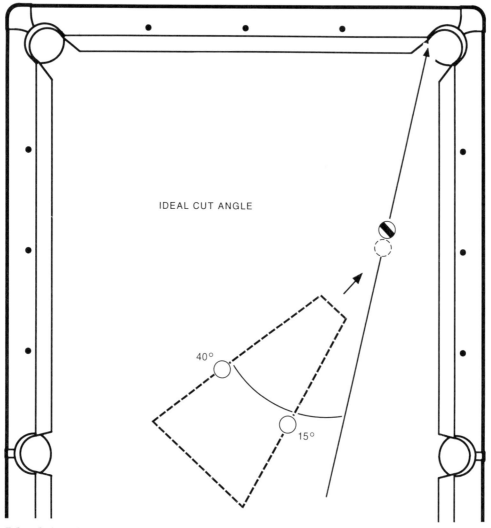

IDEAL CUT ANGLE

40°

15°

Ideal Angle and Distance Equals Position

When your position play is on track you will consistently shoot easy, or at least reasonably makeable shots. Furthermore, good position will allow you to send the cue ball to the next shot without too much effort. Your game will flow. On the other hand, if you fail to position the cue ball correctly, you will be faced with an unending series of difficult shots and position plays, and your run outs will be few and far between.

Proper distance and cut angle equals good position. Let's go over them one at a time. Playing good shape requires that you position the cue ball neither too close nor too far from the object ball. On long shots, your chances of missing the ball rise dramatically.   Furthermore, long shots require extra speed of stroke, which reduces the sense of touch that you need to play great shape. It's also much more difficult to apply english at long range. Problems also arise if you get too close to your work. At close range, you may have to use a special shooting technique to generate sufficient cue ball speed. You might also have to stretch uncomfortably or, worst of all, you may be so close to the object ball that you may not even have a shot.

The second component of good position play is the cut angle between the cue ball and the object ball. Most of the time you'll want a shot with a relatively modest cut angle. Thin cut shots are much more difficult to pocket, and they make it much tougher to control the speed of the cue ball. On shots with a shallow cut angle, you'll often be forced to use a harder stroke to develop adequate cue ball speed. You should be able to achieve maximum cue ball control on the majority of your position plays with a cut angle that ranges from 15° to 40°. The first diagram allows you to visualize what the optimal cut angle looks like.

You must learn to recognize when to follow these rules of thumb and when to make exceptions. That's the nature of the game. For example, a dead straight in shot or perhaps a thin cut at close range may be your best bet. Principles are designed to give you guidance, but you will need to recognize when to make appropriate exceptions to the rules. The second diagram presents a position play that comes up time and again in Nine Ball. Your objective is to pocket the 8-ball in the far corner and draw the cue ball across the table to the position marked X. We'll go over the merits of each of the five cue ball positions individually. Position A presents you with a long tough draw shot down the rail with virtually no angle to work with. The cue ball marked B is at the proper angle, but the shot is very missable at that distance. Position C is a tough cut shot that requires perfect touch to have a chance of getting good shape on the 9-ball. With the cue ball at D you will have to stretch across the table and poke at the cue ball with a very short stroke. As you might have guessed, the winner here is position E. The cue ball is reasonably close to the object ball so that pocketing the ball should be no problem. Furthermore, the cut angle makes it a simple matter to bring the cue ball to rest at X for an easy shot on the 9-ball. In all five cases you had a shot on the 8-ball, but only with the cue ball at E did you really have what players would call true position.

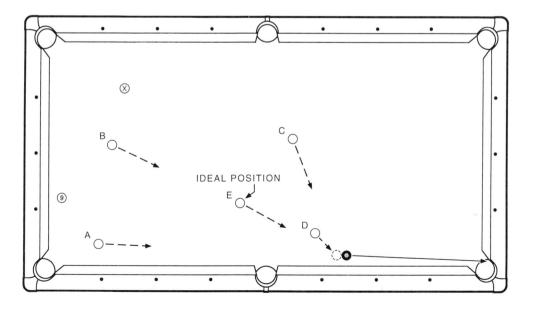

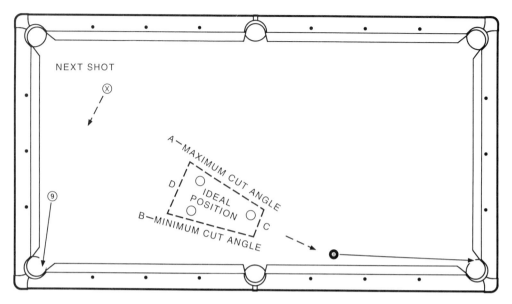

Know the Shape of Position Zones

Even the Pros make lots of mistakes. In fact, pool is a game of minimizing your mistakes. Because of this, top players instead play for zones, for areas where they'll have, at worst, at least adequate position. Perfect shape is usually a result of lucking into the middle of a shape zone. Similarly, a golfer who sinks a 40 foot putt was both skillful and lucky. Nobody can consistently hit the position zone bullseye. But close is good enough in almost all cases.

You'll recall from the previous section that position is comprised of a workable cut angle and the correct distance of the cue ball from the object ball. These principles come together to form the boundaries of the ideal position zone. In the diagram, we want to shoot the 8-ball in the corner and send the cue ball to position X for shape on the 9-ball. Line A forms the boundary for the maximum cut angle. Beyond that we'd have too much angle. Line B identifies the minimum acceptable angle for this particular position play. That takes care of our cut angles. We wouldn't want to be any closer than line C for a variety of reasons presented earlier. At the same time, line D shows the maximum distance that we'd like to have. Connecting the four lines together gives us the outer boundaries of the ideal position zone. Position zones vary in size and shape for every shot. It would take another book to demonstrate all of the possibilities. What's most important for you is to understand the concept: play for zones with the appropriate combinations of distance and cut angle. What you are after is a makeable shot <u>and</u> an angle that allows you to easily control the cue ball for the next shot. Your position zones will decrease in size as your ability to pinpoint the cue ball and your level of skill rises.

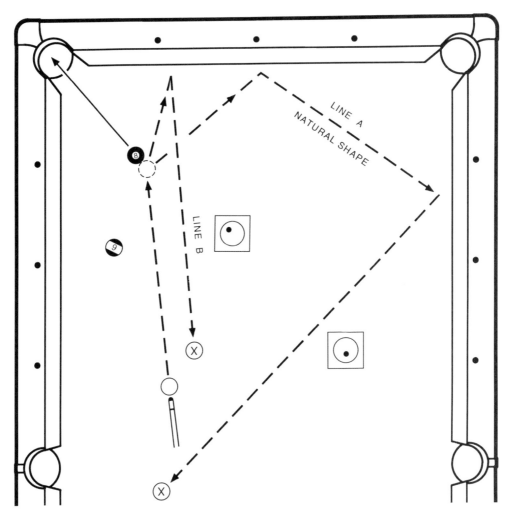

Play Natural Shape as Much as Possible

When the cue ball is struck in the dead center the position that results is called natural shape. By practicing a variety of position plays with center ball only, you will come to understand the natural roll of the cue ball. There are two major benefits to playing natural shape: it will increase your shot-making accuracy and your control of the cue ball.

In actual play, the natural roll of the cue ball is augmented with varying degrees of english, draw and follow so that you can position the cue ball with greater precision. The diagram best illustrates this principle. The play here is to pocket the 8-ball and get good shape on the 9-ball. Natural shape is indicated by line A. By using a slightly below center hit, we can gain good shape on the 9-ball. Line B shows the opposite of natural shape as we use follow and left english to turn the cue ball to the left off the rail, forcing it to roll in opposition to it's natural course.

There are a great number of variations of the two rail natural shape shot shown in the diagram. In fact, it is one of the most common and most important position plays in the game.

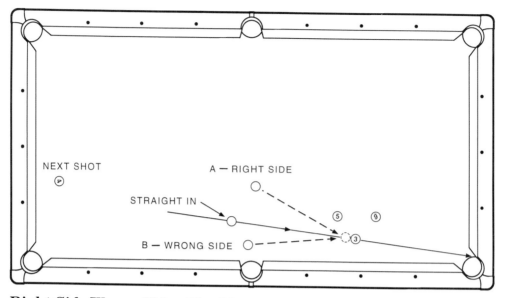

Right Side/Wrong Side - The Master Key to Playing Position

Once you master this position play principle, your game could be set for a quantum leap forward. The right side/wrong side principle is that important. We discussed earlier how position play becomes easier when you leave yourself an angle. Now you're going to learn on which side of the object ball to position your cue ball for optimal shape. You want to have the cut angle working for you, (the right side) not against you (the wrong side).

How do you go about determining the right side vs. the wrong side? Start by drawing a line from the center of the pocket, straight through the object ball and out the other side. This is shown in the diagram. If the cue ball is positioned on the line, you have a straight in shot. Remember that sometimes you'll want a straight in shot for position. More on that later. Now here's the key; if the cue ball is to the left of the line, it will veer to the right after contacting the object ball and vice versa. This simple bit of physics can greatly improve your game.

With the cue ball in position A, you can easily pocket the 3-ball and come off the rail with draw for the 4-ball. Now let's move over to the wrong side, to cue ball B. Here you have an equally simple shot. The trouble is, after contact, the cue ball will veer to the left. The 6-ball and 5-ball prevent you from either drawing or following the cue ball back for the 4-ball. By planning ahead and using the right side/wrong side principle you can avoid obstructing object balls.

Pool becomes much easier to navigate from the right side. Begin to analyze each shot with this thought in mind: which side of the line gives you the easiest position play while also allowing you to avoid other balls. With a little diligence on your part, you will learn to pick the correct side, the right side, nearly every time. Good luck!

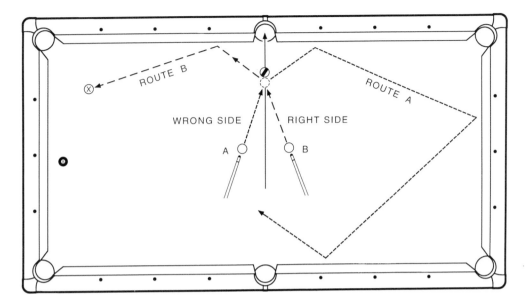

In the second example, your goal is to pocket the stripe in the side and get good position on the 8-ball. From position A, you will need to send the cue ball all the way around the table for position. Notice how much easier it is to get shape on the 8 from position B, which is the right (correct) side.

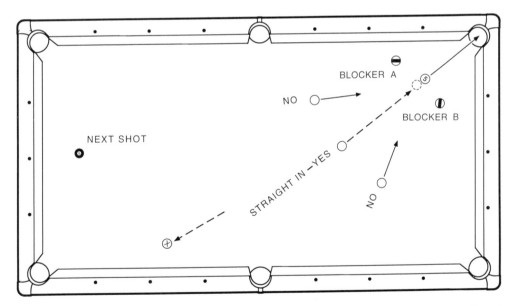

Now for the exception to the rule. In the diagram below you are faced with the dreaded double blockade. If your cue ball veers left after contact, you'll run into blocker A. From the other side, you'll crash into blocker B. The only solution is to get straight-in on the 5-ball so that you can draw back away from the obstructing object balls.

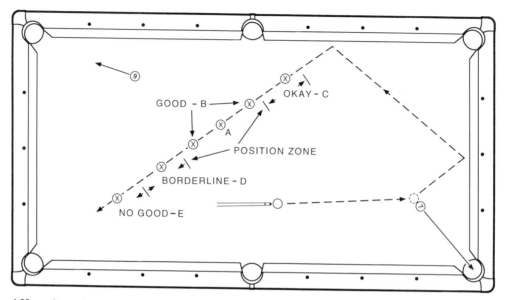

Allowing for a Margin of Error

Shape zones give you an inviting target that allows for imperfections when positioning the cue ball. Similarly, the principle of allowing for a margin of error can also provide you with a safety net which insures that you'll at least have a decent shot on the next object ball.

Our goal on the shot in the diagram above is to pocket the 7-ball and get good position for a high percentage shot on the game-winning 9-ball. The dashed line lays out the route of the cue ball and identifies several possible outcomes. We'll go through them one by one. Position A is the bullseye. Perfect speed of stroke will take the cue ball here. Great job! The other cue balls that are within the borders of the position zone have given you a margin for error. Any shot within this zone is nearly as good as a bullseye. We'll now venture out of the shape zone. In position C, you've come up short of the ideal. This is the lessor of two evils. From position C you still have a very makeable shot, however your pocketing percentage may now be down to perhaps 75-90% as compared to 95-100% in the shape zone.

Overrunning shape on this position play can lead to sheer disaster. From position D, you now must make a tough cut shot and avoid scratching in the opposite side pocket. Further down the line things change completely. At position E you are faced with a particularly tough cut, a bank shot, or a safe. Beyond position E, your options are down to a bank shot or a safe. In this example, all good players would allow for a margin of error by aiming to the front half of the position zone as a further refinement to their game.

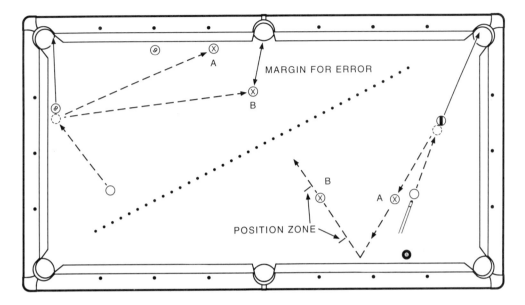

You won't always want to play to the short side when you use the margin of error principle. In the second example shown in the right position diagram above, the position play calls for a draw shot back to the rail for shape on the 8-ball. This time if you come up short of your position zone (at point A), you'll be left with a bank shot. The smart move on this shot is to err toward the long side of the position zone. If you overshoot the shot and the cue ball winds up at position B, you'll still have a pretty easy shot.

You can also use the margin for error principal to avoid scratch shots. In the left portion of the diagram above, the player needs to pocket the 8-ball and get position on the 9-ball, to win the game. Ultimate shape would be at position A. Getting to this point, however, runs the risk of scratching in the side pocket. A better choice would be to send the cue ball to position B. This provides for a wide margin for error, as indicated, and still leaves a very easy shot on the 9-ball.

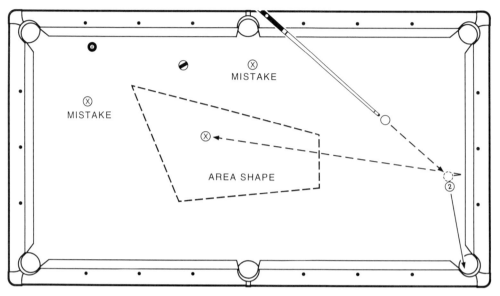

When to Play Area Shape

On some shots you will need to thread the needle through traffic to a small shape zone. The majority of your shots, however, will be aimed toward a sufficiently large position zone that provides you with a workable margin for error. Best of all, however, are those shots that permit you to play what's called "area shape". When playing area shape, your margin for error is huge. You are simply trying to place the cue ball anywhere within a very sizeable area and at the same time avoid disaster. The diagrammed example will illustrate this concept.

      The game is Eight Ball. To win the game you need only pocket the 2-ball and then the 8-ball. This is no time to get fancy and try for perfect shape when it's not required. The 8-ball is a very easy shot from anywhere within the very sizeable area shown. If you went for a straight-in shot, you might wind up behind your opponent's striped ball. Another mistake would be to overrun your position while trying to get too close to the object ball. When used at the right time, area shape guarantees your next shot while helping you to avoid a costly blunder.

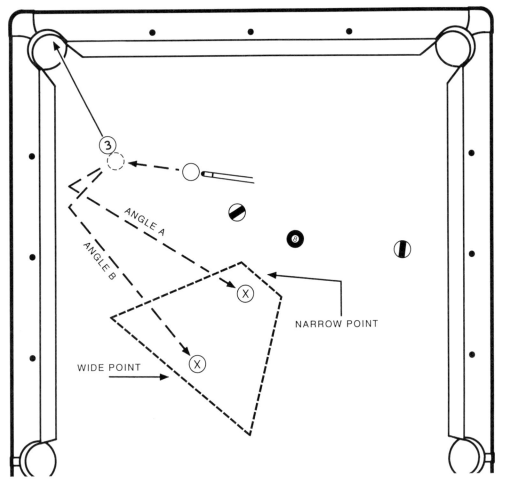

Enter into the Wide Area of a Position Zone

Let's assume that you've identified your ideal position zone such as the one shown in the diagram. The cue ball will be approaching the side of the position zone from off the cushion after pocketing the 3-ball. Your goal is position on the 8-ball. Notice the two different angles of approach. From angle A the cue ball will be crossing the position zone near it's narrowest point. Your speed control has to be nearly perfect to land the cue ball in this tiny area. Now lets look at angle B. In this case, your target within the shape zone is much wider, which of course gives you a greater margin for error. Crossing into (but hopefully not through) a shape zone is one of the more exacting position plays in pool. It demands precision cue ball control. Make it as easy on yourself as possible by favoring the wide part of a position zone when you're faced with this situation.

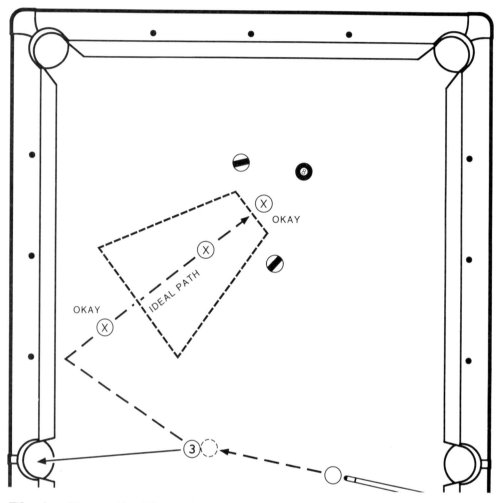

Playing Down the Line of a Position Zone when Possible

Crossing into a shape zone is a demanding position play because of the small margin for error. I'll introduce a much more preferable means of obtaining shape. Whenever possible you will want to play what we'll call down the line shape. When using this principle, the cue ball will approach the next object ball and position zone in a direct line.

After cutting the 3-ball in the side pocket, the cue ball has rebounded off the cushion and is now approaching the shape zone. Notice that the cue ball is heading directly through the heart of the position zone. While the cue ball's traveling on this line, it is maintaining a perfect angle for the next shot. Even is you don't hit the cue ball at the perfect speed, you will still have the ideal angle for the next ball!

There are several good reasons why down the line shape is preferable. You have a much larger margin for error. If you come up short of the shape zone, you'll still have pretty good position, just a little longer shot. You can overrun the shape zone slightly and also have decent position. Best of all, once you're coming directly down the line at the object ball, you no longer have to worry about getting behind other object balls.

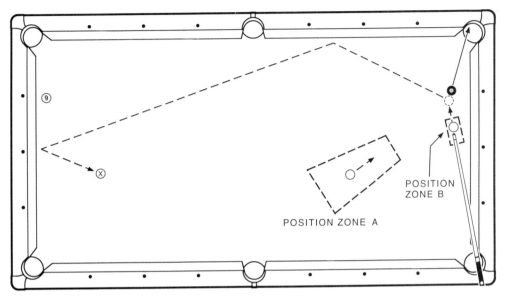

Ball in Hand Shape

Every pool player literally jumps to the table when their opponent commits a foul that gives them ball in hand. With this most cherished commodity, you are allowed to place the cue ball <u>anywhere</u> on the table. Because virtually all tournament Eight Ball and Nine Ball matches are now played using ball in hand rules, it behooves you to learn to take full advantage of the opportunities that ball in hand affords you.

There is a huge difference between ball in hand position and the shape you have to play for. When playing shape, you must factor in an assortment of possible human errors, problem balls, and scratches. All of these shot calculations go out the window when you are given ball in hand. Instead, you can now minimize your chances for a mistake by precisely placing the cue ball anywhere you want to.

You'll recall that good position play is made up of two elements: distance and cut angle. When positioning the cue ball with ball in hand, you have exact control over both distance and cut angle. As a rule of thumb, I would recommend that you place the cue ball anywhere from 6"-8" up to about two feet from the object ball. At this range, every shot with ball in hand should be a simple matter. An obvious exception to this rule would be that you not purposely stretch for a shot. Be sure also to choose your cut angle precisely. You may put the cue ball up close with a sharp angle, if that's your best play. You can also set up for a straight in shot if that's what will make it easiest for you to get shape on the next ball.

In the diagram, our goal is to pocket the 8-ball and play shape for the 9-ball. Position zone A shows an area that most good players would shoot for when playing shape. However, there is a danger of scratching in the corner pocket opposite the 9-ball. With ball in hand, position B becomes the better choice. A centerball hit with a little left english will make it easy to control the cue ball as you send it down the table to position X. It is important to note that it would be extremely difficult to position the cue ball at B when you have to play for shape.

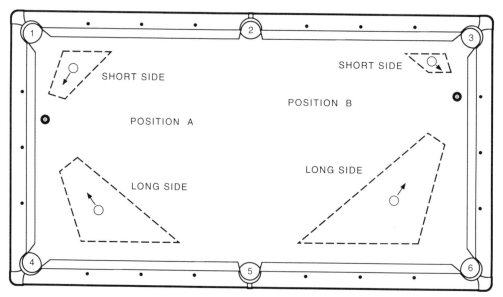

Play to the Long Side when Possible

The diagram above depicts clearly why, whenever possible, you should play position to the long side of the object ball. When the object ball is opposite the middle diamond, position for either pocket works equally well. However, once the object ball is on one side or the other of the center point, then the odds, in most cases, begin to favor playing position on the long side. We'll define and illustrate the long side whenever possible principle with the aid of the diagram.

The 8-ball in position A is one full diamond closer to pocket # 1 than pocket # 2. Because of the location of the object ball, you have much more room to play shape on the 8-ball into pocket # 1. This can be seen easily by the comparative sizes of both the long side and short side shape zones. In position B, the 8-ball is now only one diamond away from pocket # 3. As you can see, the short side shape zone in this example is extremely small. At the same time, observe how big the long side shape zone has become!

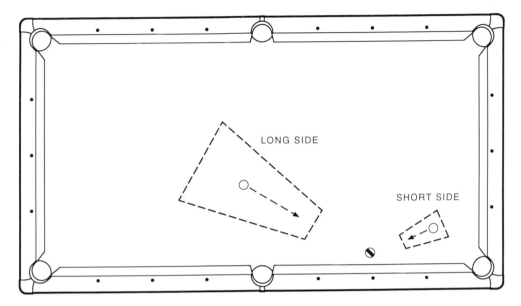

The second diagram further illustrates the play to the long side when possible principle. In this example, the object ball is located next to the side rail at the second diamond. Notice the corresponding sizes of the long side and short side shape zones. Because a pool table is twice as long as it is wide, you have a greater number of opportunities to play short side shape when the object ball is on the side rail. However, once an object ball on the side rail is within 1 1/2 to 2 diamonds of either corner pocket, you should position the cue ball so that you can shoot the object ball into the closest pocket.

As always there are exceptions to the rule. You should favor short side shape when other object balls considerably reduce the size of the long side position zone, or when the easiest and most natural position route will only take the cue ball to the short side. Keep in mind, however, that once the object ball is within one diamond or less of the pocket, playing shape on the short side greatly increases the possibility of scratching the cue ball.

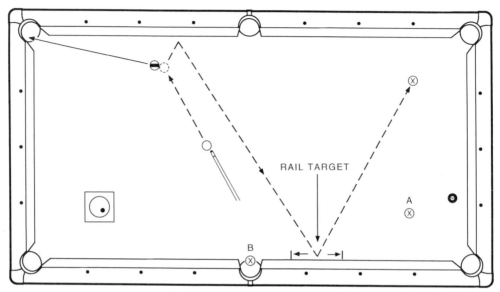

Use Rail Targets

A very high percentage of the position plays in Nine Ball (and to a lesser extent in Eight Ball) require that you send the cue ball long distances around or across the table. Often the cue ball will contact 2-3 rails or more before arriving at it's destination. Of course, you'll first want to identify where you want the cue ball for your next shot. But it's also critical for you to know just how you are going to get from point A to point B. Before sending the cue ball on its journey, stop for a moment and consider exactly where the cue ball will be striking the rails. The rails give you shorter, intermediate targets to aim for. If you can hit your rail targets at the right speed, then the cue ball will in all likelihood arrive safely at your predetermined shape zone. Rail targets will also help you sidestep scratches and intervening object balls.

The diagram above gives you a good example of how to use a rail target. Your goal is pocket the last striped ball and gain position for the 8-ball on the long side marked by the cue ball with an X. The plan is to cross the table twice by applying low right english to the cue ball. Without proper planning and execution, the cue ball could wind up at position A, or even worse, in the opposite side pocket(position B). The intelligent use of rail targets will help to avoid these mistakes. Before shooting, simply identify an area on the rail that, if hit, will enable the cue ball to continue onward to the position zone.

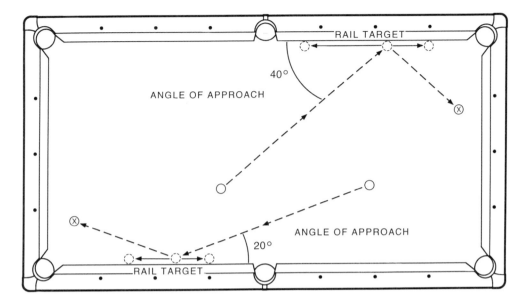

If the cue ball is traveling only a short distance, then you can set your rail targets closer to the pocket. However, on longer shots you should allow for possible errors in executing your shot when setting your rail targets. The angle of approach has a lot to do with your choice of rail targets. The diagram above shows two possible angles of approach. With a shallow angle of approach (lower portion), you'll want to set your rail targets further from the pockets because of the danger of a scratch. With a sharp angle of approach (upper portion) you can set your target closer to the pocket because there is less danger of scratching.

Avoid Scratching

Most new players, and even some who should know better, scratch the cue ball over and over again. The reason for their "scratchitis" is that they simply don't know where the cue ball's going to end up. It takes a lot of practice and know how to keep the cue ball from disappearing into one of the six pockets. Over time you can cut down on your scratch shots by learning to recognize the routes that most often lead to a scratch. Once you become aware of the most common scratch shots, you are ready to apply the appropriate cures. Sometimes a little english here, a bit of draw there, or perhaps a little less cue ball speed is all that's necessary to avoid scratching on any given shot. Just remember that your education in position play is not nearly complete until you can consistently maneuver the cue ball around the table without fear of scratching.

Over the next couple of pages I've diagrammed some of the most common scratch shots in the game, as well as some possible remedies. These should help get you started towards what will hopefully be a near scratch-free game of pool. Set up some of these shots yourself and observe closely the path the cue ball takes. If it scratches, adjust your english, draw, follow, or speed accordingly. Good luck!

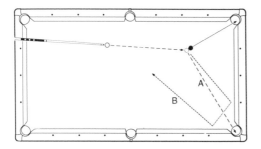

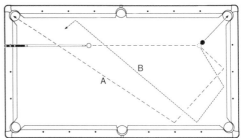

Draw and/or too much force will cause this scratch. Try using a softer stroke and follow.

Use draw to avoid a corner pocket scratch. It may also help to apply some outside (right) english .

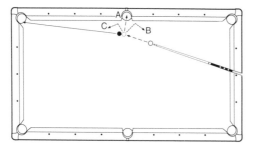

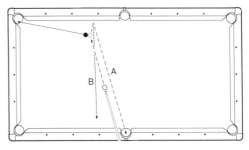

Use soft follow to arrive at point C. A smooth soft draw stroke with outside english will result in Pt. B.

Inside English (left) will make the cue ball travel directly across the table (B), not into the side pocket.

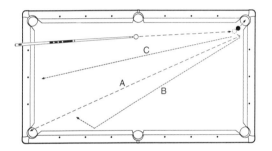

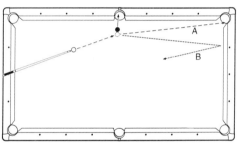

Hitting the right portion of the ball is the key. A thin hit leads to (C). A thicker hit results in (B).

Draw and/or outside english (right) will send the cue ball down Path B, avoiding the corner pocket.

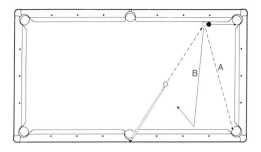

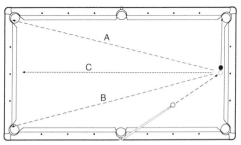

This is a very troublesome scratch shot. Draw combined with inside (right) english does the trick (B).

Scratches here come from using inside (A) or outside (B) english. Centerball will lead to path C.

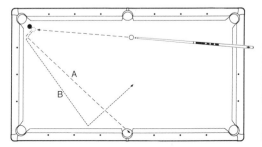

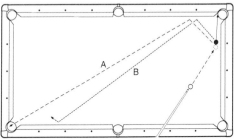

Centerball leads to a scratch (A). Draw with 1/2 tip of outside (left) english will result in (B).

This can be a difficult shot. Try using less force and a little more inside (left) english to give you (B).

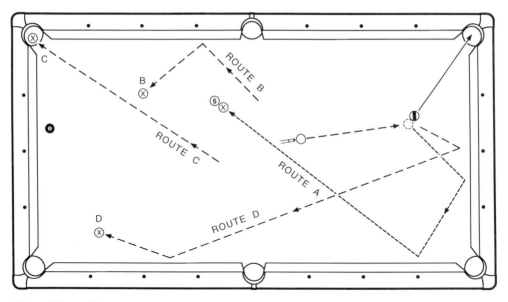

Plan Your Route - Avoiding Obstructions

A big part of position play is the proper routing of the cue ball through a maze of object balls. In your quest to arrive at your position zone, you must avoid all other object balls in the way that could throw the cue ball wildly off course. This problem can pop up at any stage of the game. Early in a rack you must normally negotiate your way through a labyrinth of balls. The challenge is a little less taxing in the later stages of a game when you are facing an uncluttered table. Nevertheless, just one solitary ball that's planted smack in the middle of your position route can completely mess up your shot. You must make appropriate allowances for obstructing balls. When making plans for the cue balls journey from point A to B, your thinking should be as follows:

- You can play your most ideal route because no other balls stand in the way of the cue ball.
- Your route carries with it a high possibility of scratching.
- You may be able to play your chosen route, but with some slight adjustments.
- You will, upon consideration, have to abandon your first choice and devise a plan B for obtaining position.

The diagrammed position demonstrates each of these possible options. The game is Eight Ball. You need to simply pocket your remaining stripe ball and get position on the eight for a win. Route A would normally be preferred by all top players. As you can see, however, your opponent's 6-ball stands directly in the cue ball's path. You might now consider route B, which circumvents the 6-ball. The problem with this choice is that you'll probably leave yourself with a very tough cut on the 8-ball. Route C around the other side of the 6-ball is hardly much better. If you pull the shot off, you'll have an easy shot on the 8-ball. However, the danger of scratching in the corner pocket is high. At this point, you may want to junk these routes and consider route D, which offers no obstructions whatsoever. It's not the easiest shot, but it beats the alternatives.

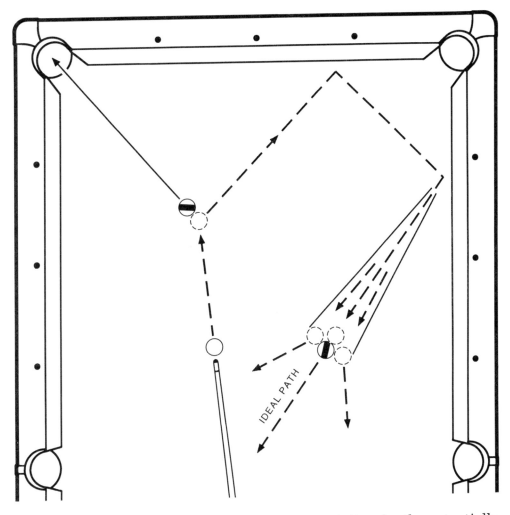

The second diagram gives you an appreciation for the potentially damaging effects of object balls that are in route to your position zone. Notice how one ball that's in your way, really takes up much more room than just a ball's width. The cue ball can be diverted from its destination from contact with any part of the intervening object ball, so plan accordingly. Give possible obstructing balls a wide berth.

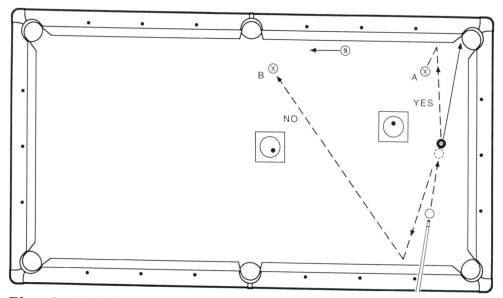

Play the High Percentage Sequence

You could focus your efforts primarily on making balls, with position play as a secondary objective. However, this approach will leave you with too many tough shots. You could also make the mistake of sacrificing the shot to gain unnecessarily perfect position. Ideally, what's best is to strike the proper balance between pocketing the object ball and playing shape. By all means, don't allow one vital component of your shots to suffer because you've overemphasized the other.

In the diagrammed position, you are faced with an absolutely straight-in shot on the 8-ball. The 9-ball is next. The smart choice is to shoot a soft follow shot, sending the cue ball to position A. This gives you a very makeable shot on the 9-ball into the far corner pocket. Let's figure the odds of making this sequence of shots at 80-90%. Now we'll try for position B. This would require a very firm stroke with draw and righthand english. This position play could cause you to easily miss the 8-ball. What's more, you're not even guaranteed that you'll get the position you're after. We'll rate the odds of making this sequence of shots at no better than 50%. We'll conclude this discussion with the table below. Keep it in mind always as you try to balance your shots so you can play the highest percentage sequence possible.

First Shot	Second Shot	
1) Easy	Hard	No
2) Hard	Easy	No
3) Easy/Medium	Easy/Medium	Yes

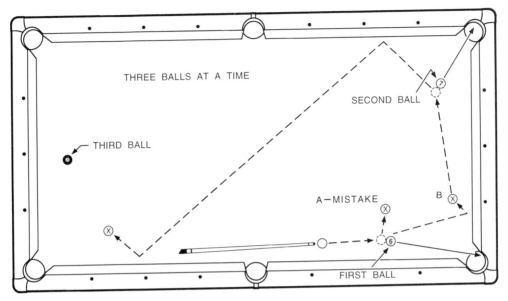

Plan for Three Balls at a Time

Every single professional pool player plans ahead for at least three shots at a time. This is one the main reasons why they make it look so easy to pocket ball after ball and run rack upon rack. You can also use the principle of planning for three balls at a time to greatly improve your game. All you need do is to plug a simple concept into you mental computer and apply it consistently. From now on, take your planning process one step further. Before shooting the first ball, ask yourself:

1) How can I make the first ball and play position on the second ball?
2) What position on the second ball will make it possible to play position on the third ball?

That's all there is to it! Simply make the first ball and at the same time get the correct position on the second ball. Using this principle, note that the key is <u>correct position</u> on the second ball. Let's now take a look at the diagram to see further how this principle works.

The game is Eight Ball. You need only pocket the 6, 7, and 8-balls to win. Position A shows what can happen when you fail to plan ahead. A stop shot pockets the 6 and leaves a straight in shot on the 7-ball. From this position, it will be nearly impossible to get good shape on the 8-ball. Now let's plan for three shots at a time. Number one is to pocket the 6-ball in the corner. Number two is to follow the cue ball to position B for a simple cut shot on the 7-ball. Number three, we can now play for position on the 8-ball because we have an angle on the 7-ball that allows us to easily send the cue ball down the table as diagrammed.

In actual play, you will continue to roll forward with this principle as you run through a rack from beginning to end. After your first shot, the second ball becomes the first, the third ball becomes the second, and you must then add a third ball to the sequence.

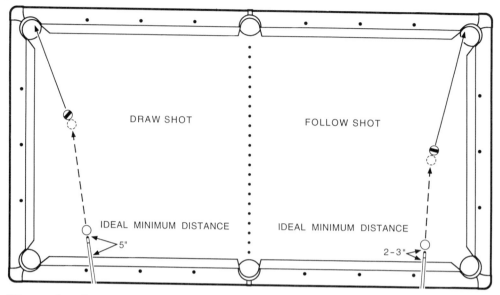

Keep the Cue Ball Away from the Rail

One of the cardinal rules of position plays is to keep the cue ball off the rail. Under pressure even the simplest shots can become tough when the cue ball's snuggled up against the cushion. With the cue ball on the rail you also lose a number of your options for playing shape. Worst of all, draw shots become virtually impossible.

Follow shots require less distance from the rail than draw shots in order for you to stroke the cue ball with your customary accuracy and force. When bridging on the rail, your cue, when held level, is automatically at the proper elevation for a follow shot. With the cue ball 2"-3" off the rail, you should be able to generate near maximum follow to the cue ball.

Draw shots are a different story. That's because the rail forces you to shoot down on the cue ball with an elevated cue to create drawspin. On top of this, a downward stroke restricts your follow through because the bed of the table gets in the way of your cue stick. As a result, the minimum distance that works best for draw shots is at least 5". Even at this distance you'd be hard pressed to draw the cue ball anywhere near as far as when your bridge hand is on the cloth.

Draw shots are somewhat easier to execute with the cue ball close to the cushion provided you are shooting away from the rail at an angle. The reason for this is that the angle increases the actual distance of the cue ball from the point where the cue stick overlaps the rail.

You won't always be able to avoid leaving the cue ball on or near the cushion. However, these rules of thumb should help you keep the cue ball a minimum distance from the rail so that you can play position without having to compensate for using a rail bridge.

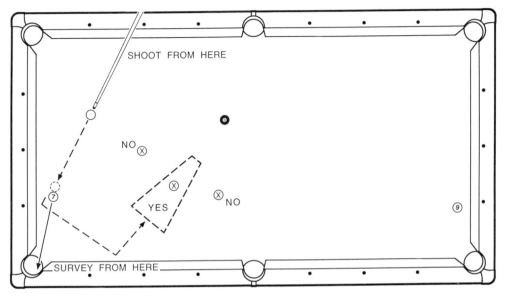

Survey the Table Before Shooting

Sometimes you can execute a shot properly by using only the insights gained from your approach to the table from behind the cue ball. A quick look around the table will tell you all you need to know. Quite often, however, it will pay for you to view your shot from another angle so that you can gain some additional perspective. This can help you to avoid committing a costly blunder.

It is most important for you to walk to where you think you'd like to position the cue ball for the next shot. Your survey could confirm your choice of position. It could also alert you to previously unseen dangers. Armed with the knowledge that your survey has revealed, you should now have total confidence in the shot your are about to play. There are some choice bits of information that you can learn from your survey. They include:

Are you playing shape on a ball that can't be made, or perhaps only has only ½ pocket wide opening?
What's your rail target?
Are other object balls possibly in your way?
Are you sure you are playing to the right side of the next ball?

Balls near the center of the table require an extra measure of precision. The diagram illustrates this point. Your goal is to pocket the 7, 8, and 9-balls, in that order. Your position behind the cue stick gives you one vantage point from which to plot your position for the 8-ball. To improve your odds of making all three balls, however, you should take a moment to walk around to the opposite side of the table. From this angle you can now tell exactly where you'll need the cue ball for the best possible position on the 8-ball. Now you've eliminated the guesswork. Now your position play is firmly etched in your mind. As a reminder, commit this sequence to memory: survey the table first, plan your shot, then execute.

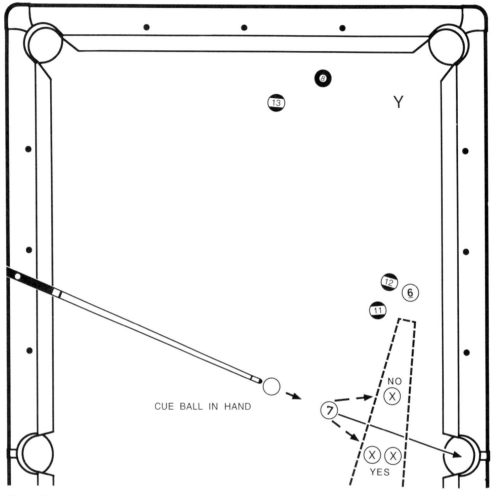

Pay Attention to Details

Good players pay close attention to even the smallest details. That's one reason why they got to be top players in the first place. They know that one seemingly insignificant bit of knowledge, when needed, can spell the difference between victory and defeat.

As your game develops, you'll want to take the same attitude as the players do. Build a strong foundation for your game by getting the basics down pat. Then start piling on the knowledge. You'll want to fill your memory bank as full as possible with all of the details that you can discover.

The diagrammed example is from a game of Eight Ball. You have cue ball in hand on the solids (6 and 7-balls).

It is very important to get the correct angle on the 6-ball so you can then follow the cue ball down to Y for the gamewinning 8-ball. Some players might shoot the 7 in the side and try to get closer to the 6-ball. However, the position zone gets narrower the closer you get to the 6-ball. By paying attention to details, you would instead follow the cue ball to a wider spot in the position zone, giving yourself a larger margin for error. It will also be easier to reach the cue ball from the position labeled Yes.

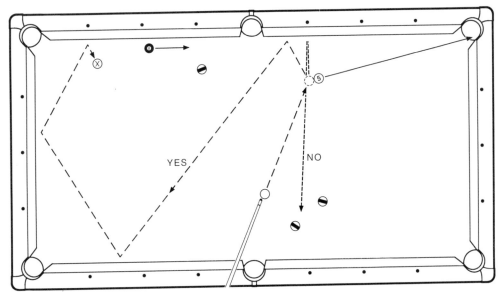

Use Your Imagination

Most of your position plays will consist of basic shots that come up over and over again. However, you will often be called upon to successfully negotiate position plays that require you to exercise you imagination. By keeping your mind open to new position plays, you will begin to turn unusual shots into the ordinary. You will expand your repertoire of possible position plays. You will also discover that a great number of the new position plays that you master will serve as building blocks for still further advancements in your game.

Our example is taken from a game of Eight Ball. You need only pocket the 5-ball and then the 8-ball to win the game. Unfortunately, two of your opponents striped balls prevent you from crossing the table and back for position on the 8. However, you can still gain position on the 8 by exercising your imagination and employing the somewhat unusual position route outlined in the diagram. Not many players would have visualized this four rail position route, and yet the shot is not nearly as difficult as it may appear. The successful execution of this shot only required a medium hard stroke with draw and left english <u>and</u> some creativity.

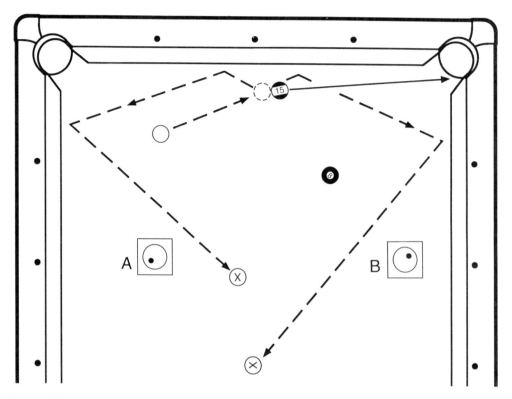

Play Your Game

Keep your own capabilities in mind when playing position. Get to know your game, what you can and can't do. Then play your game, not someone else's. Most games of pool are won by consistently executing a series of high percentage shots and not by off the wall heroics. That doesn't mean you shouldn't stretch your game by trying more difficult shots. But if you regularly play shots under game conditions that you know are way over your head, then don't plan on too many trips to the winners circle. When you come across a position play in competition that's too tough for your game right now, pass on the shot. But make a mental note to work on it at your next practice session.

Most tennis players favor either their forehand or backhand. Similarly, pool players tend to lean towards either draw shots or follow shots. Some players also prefer to use lots of English regularly. In general, its okay if you slightly favor one positional tool. After all, it builds your confidence if you have a shot you can count on in the clutch. Make sure, however that your game does not suffer because you can't draw (or follow) the cue ball, or because the thought of using English scares you to death. Play to your strengths, but also be sure to shore up any glaring deficiencies.

The example is from a game of Eight Ball. It demonstrates the principle of playing your game. The goal is to pocket your last ball, the 15, and then the 8-ball. Those who prefer to draw the cue ball would probably chose route A. Follow shooters would most likely choose Route B.

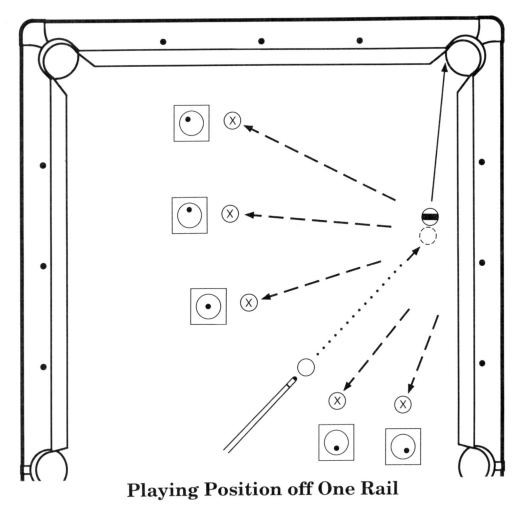

Playing Position off One Rail

The cue ball will contact at least one rail on a very high percentage of your shots after pocketing the object ball. Therefore, it is extremely important for you to have a working knowledge of how the cue ball will react after contacting the rails. Over the next several pages we will discuss how to play position off only one rail. Then we'll move on to the intricacies of multi-rail position play (see next section).

There are a number of factors that can influence the cue balls path after it has struck the rail. The force of your stroke and the speed of the table will largely determine how far the cue ball rolls. Some cushions can act like a soft pillow, while lively rails will propel the cue ball like a pinball. The location of both the object ball and cue ball will also greatly influence the roll of the cue ball. For example, everything else being equal, the closer the object ball is to the rail, the further the cue ball will rebound off the cushion. And finally, where you strike the cue ball has the biggest effect of all. The diagram shows this. The shot is a fairly, simple cut shot into the corner pocket. We'll assume that a medium stroke is being used. Notice the wide variety of possible destinations that results simply from altering the point that is struck on the cue ball.

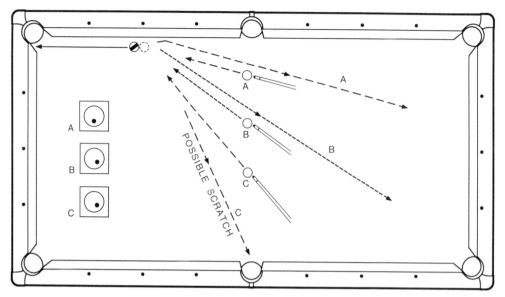

Drawing the Cue Ball Down the Table

The goal of the position play diagrammed above is to bring the cue ball back down the table using a draw stroke. From position A, the shot is not difficult. As the cut angle increases (position B), however, problems arise. If the shot is hit incorrectly, the cue ball will rebound from the cushion at an excessively sharp angle. This could lead to a scratch in the opposite side pocket. There are several things that you can do to minimize your chances of scratching. For starters, add some outside (right) english to the draw. You should use a stroke that's as smooth and easy as possible, but that will still supply the force you need. By hitting the shot easier with lots of spin, you will reduce the cue ball's tendency to bounce directly away from the rail. You can also improve your chances by aiming for the inside part of the pocket (in this example, it's the right side). This slight adjustment in aiming will effectively decrease the cut angle ever so slightly, but possibly just enough to allow you to avoid scratching in the side pocket. Lastly, you should get to know this shot so well that you can tell when the cut angle is so sharp (position C) that a side pocket scratch is practically unavoidable.

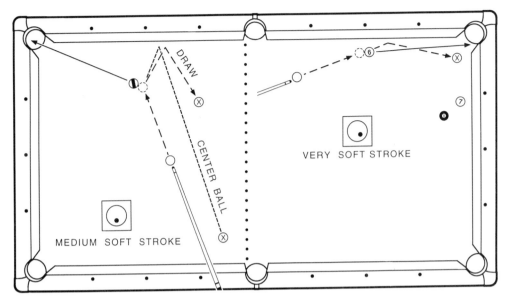

The Kill Shot

On cut shots where the angle's not too severe, the kill shot will enable you to stop the cue ball quickly after it hits the rail. Notice in the left portion of the diagram how the cue ball's roll was checked compared to the resulting position shooting the same shot with centerball. The kill shot is hit with a very slow and smooth stroke at the maximum low point on the cue ball. The kill shot is most effective if the object ball is at least a few inches off the rail.

The Soft Draw Creeper Shot

In the right side of the diagram, position using follow would not work because the 8-ball is in the way. The answer is to apply low right english to the cue ball with a very soft stroke, so soft in fact, that the cue ball will have lost all of its draw by the time that it's reached the object ball. The right english will make the cue ball creep down the table close to the rail for perfect position on the 7-ball.

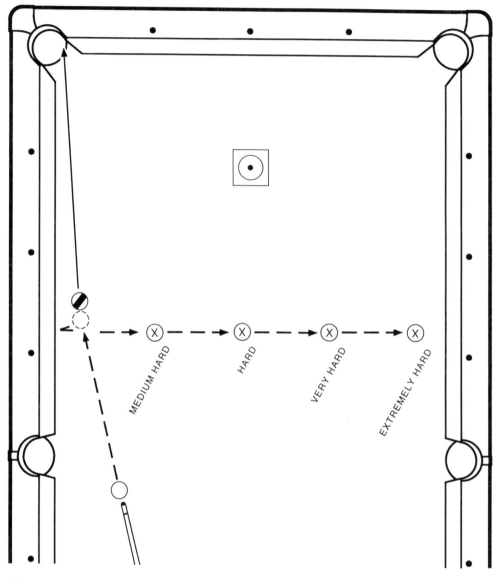

Slight Angle Force Shot

When you have only a slight angle on a ball that's near the rail and you need to send the cue ball across the table, then it's time to employ the slight angle force shot. A couple of modifications in your shooting technique will get the job done. Lengthen your bridge to accommodate the longer power stroke you'll be using, accelerate smoothly but forcefully through the shot and use more wrist action right at the moment of contact with the cue ball. Speed control is tough to gauge on this shot so practice until you can come close to each of the cue ball positions shown in the diagram.

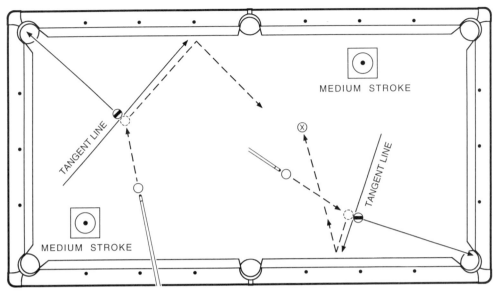

Force Shots Off A Side Rail

By using tangent lines and a medium stroke with centerball, you can play position off the rail with great predictability. The cut angle along with stroke speed will determine just how far the cue ball will travel down the table after contacting the rails. Observe carefully the path of the cue ball in both positions.

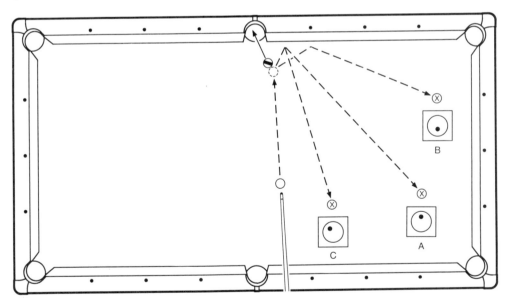

Side Pocket off the Rail Position

There are a number of potential position plays in the side pocket cut shot shown above. Follow with a medium stroke would send the cue ball to position A. A soft draw stroke with a little right hand english would lead to position B.   Follow with left english would narrow the rebound angle, resulting in position C.

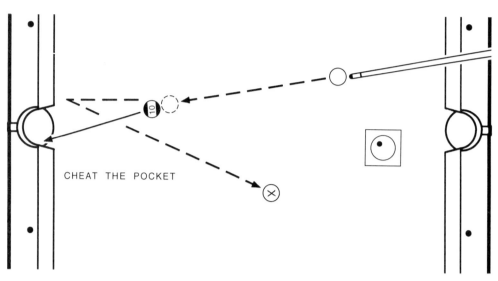

CHEAT THE POCKET

Side Pocket Inside English Follow Shots

Side pockets are large and inviting targets as long as the object ball is out in front of the pocket. This can make it easier for you to play position while using english off the rail. In the diagram, you have a dead straight-in shot. By cheating the pocket to the left side and applying top left english, the cue ball will turn to the left after it contacts the cushion.

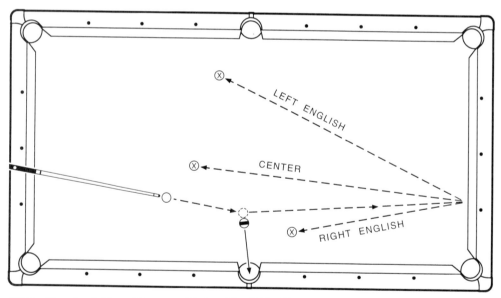

LEFT ENGLISH

CENTER

RIGHT ENGLISH

Side Pocket Cut Shots off the End Rail

Side pocket cut shots give you many options to play shape. Each route shown above uses a different hit on the cue ball. Speed of stroke is crucial because of the distance the cue ball's traveling. Note that you can also influence the cue ball's path by cheating the pocket to either side.

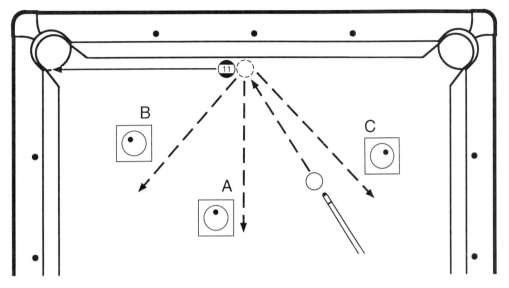

Using English off the Rail

Follow with english gives you a variety of options for position on cut shots down the rail. Line A shows the cue balls direction using only follow. Line B demonstrates the path of the cue ball with left english and follow. Follow with right english (line C) actually will bring the cue ball back up the table in a manner that's similar to how draw would work in this situation.

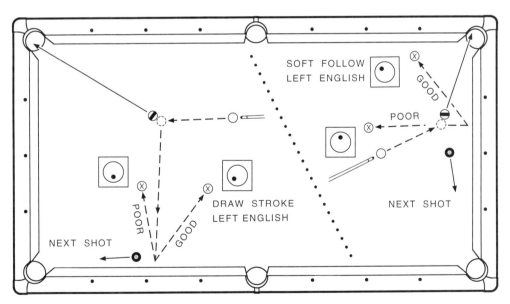

Getting a Better Angle with English

In both examples the cue ball will strike the rail near your next object ball and then rebound, leaving you with a difficult next shot. You can, however, end up with a much easier next shot by simply adding in some english. The english will help pull the cue ball in the opposite direction from the object ball. Be sure to use a soft stroke, which allows the english to work better.

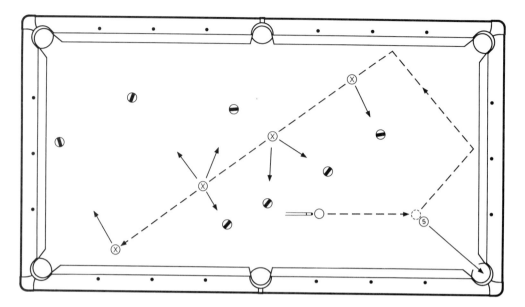

Multi-rail Position

The ability to play position by sending the cue ball off of two or more rails can be very useful in any pool game, but is an absolute must if you want to be a Nine Ball player. Multi-rail position plays require that you understand and make full use of the principles of position discussed earlier in the chapter. Among the key concepts that you'll want to keep in mind are: speed control, planning your route, using rail targets, avoiding scratches, natural shape, and position zones.

As always, speed control rules first, simply because of the vast distances that the cue ball travels on multi-rail shape shots. By controlling the speed of the cue ball effectively, you can give yourself numerous opportunities for shape. The diagram reveals how this works using the most basic of position plays, the two-railer (for more on the two-railer, refer to the principle of natural shape). After cutting the 5-ball into the corner pocket, the cue ball, using centerball, will embark on the pathway indicated. Four possible stopping points are shown, along with a great number of possible shots on the next ball. The position plays that will be covered in the following pages can offer you similar position play possibilities.

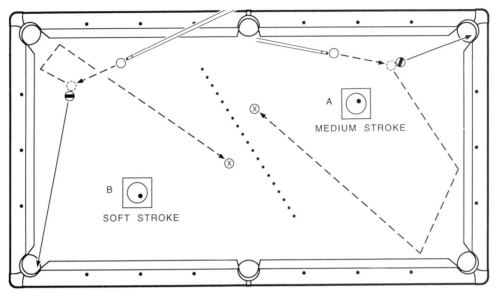

Two More Two-Railers

There are literally countless situations when you will want to use two-rail shape. In position A, a medium-firm follow stroke with high right english will send the cue ball across and out into the middle of the table. A soft draw stroke with right hand english gets the job done in position B.

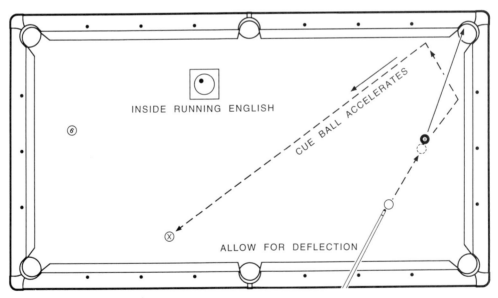

Two Rail Inside English Follow Shot

Even though you are nearly straight in on the 8-ball, you can still send the cue ball to the opposite end of the table for the 9-ball by using follow with inside english (left, in this example). English will accelerate the role of the cue ball off the two cushions. The tough part is aiming this shot correctly. Make sure to allow for plenty of deflection by adjusting your aim, in this example, to the left.

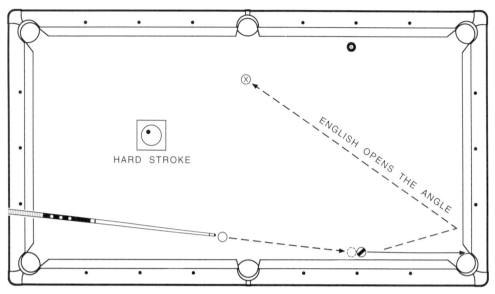

Power Two Rail-Follow

It would be very tough to force the cue ball clear across the table. An alternative is to follow the cue ball two rails using left hand english. The english will cause the cue ball to veer to the left across the width of the table. If the pockets are tight your aim and stroke will need to be nearly perfect on this shot!

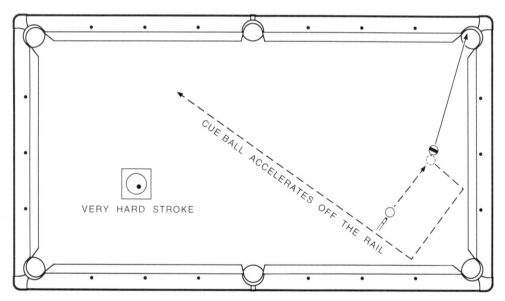

Two Railer with Draw and Force

This shot requires a very firm stroke with low right hand english. Once the cue ball contacts the rail it will pick up plenty of speed, enough in fact, to send the cue ball to the other end of the table if needed. The key is proper stroke speed, as you must first force the cue ball into the first rail.

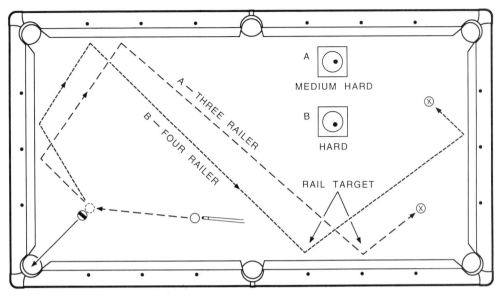

Basic Three-Rail Position

All good Nine Ball players have mastered this shot, perhaps because it's used so often. The idea is to swing the cue ball around the table and down close to the opposite end rail without scratching in the corner. Speed control is less of a problem than you might think as the cue ball will slow down quickly after hitting the third rail. You should plan to hit the third rail at least a diamond or more up from the corner pocket to insure against a scratch. The position of the balls governs where you'll hit the cue ball. The shot in the diagram was hit in the center with a bit of right english and a medium-hard stroke.

Four-Rail Position

This shot is simply an extension of the basic three-railer we just discussed. The object is to have the cue ball land further across the table on the right rail for purposes of position. Use more draw on this shot than you would on the three-railer so that the cue ball will strike further up on the third (side) rail.

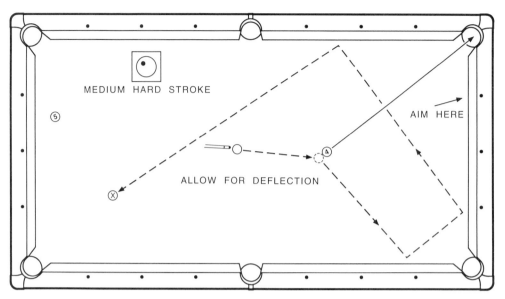

Inside English Three-Railer

A medium-hard stroke with inside running english will propel the cue ball around the table as diagrammed. In this example, the 4-ball should be aimed at the first diamond to allow for a considerable amount of deflection. Adjusting your aim for deflection is the real secret to this shot. Just how much is mostly a matter of judgement.

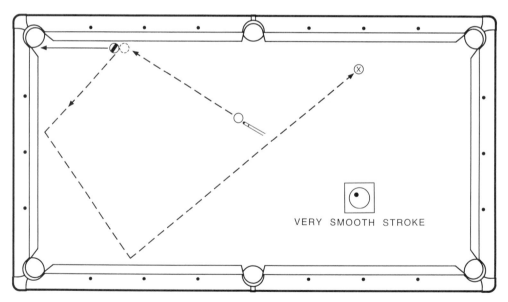

Three-Rails with Inside Follow

Shooting hard down the rail with inside english so that the cue ball will travel completely around the table is not easy, but this shot will win you a lot of games. Use a very smooth stroke with high inside english (left in this example) and be sure, once again, to factor in deflection when aiming.

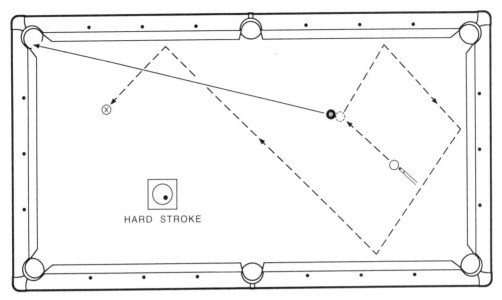

HARD STROKE

Three-Railer with Outside English and Draw

Your goal is to send the cue ball to position X after pocketing the 8 in the far corner pocket. A hard stroke with low right english will send the cue ball along the diagrammed path. There is a tendency to jump too quickly on this shot. Make sure to stay with the shot as long as you can before backing out of the way of the on-rushing cue ball.

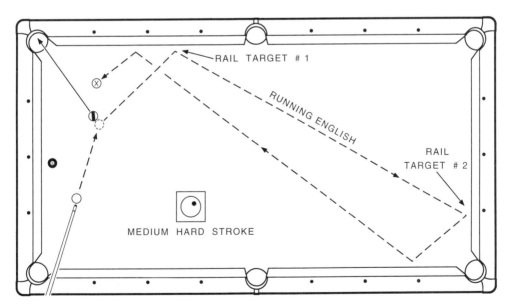

RAIL TARGET # 1

RUNNING ENGLISH

RAIL TARGET # 2

MEDIUM HARD STROKE

Around the Table

You must hit the right spot on the rail fairly close to the side pocket to avoid scratching in the lower right hand corner pocket. Right hand running english and a follow stroke should do the trick. A medium-hard stroke is all that's required to fuel the cue ball's journey around the table of approximately 18-20 feet.

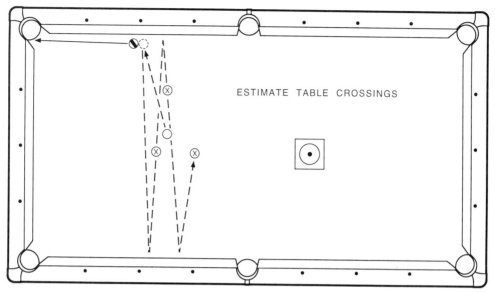

Thin Cut Cross the Table Shot

On thin cut shots you must shoot hard enough to get the ball to the pocket. At the same time you need to estimate how many times the cue ball will bounce back and forth across the table. This takes expert speed control. Depending on the cut angle and the speed of the table, you can expect the cue ball to cross the table anywhere from 1½ to 3 or more times.

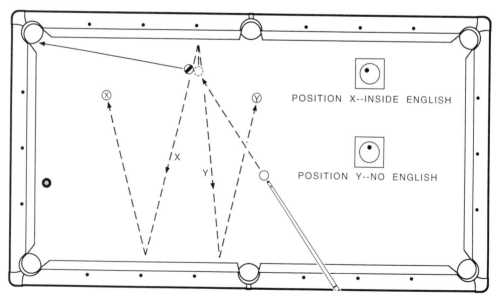

Twice Across with Inside Follow

Many players go wrong on this shot by failing to bring the cue ball further down the table for the 8-ball. All that's required is a medium stroke and some left hand (inside) english. Position X obviously gives you a much better shot on the 8-ball than from position Y.

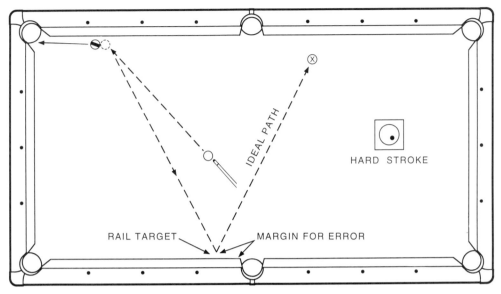

Drawing Across the Table Twice

On medium angle cut shots down the rail, you can easily advance the cue ball up the table. Your rail target is a spot on the opposite rail that's as close to the side pocket as possible. However, you should allow a little room for error. Here's the secret: the closer you can come to the side pocket without scratching, the further you can send the cue ball down the table.

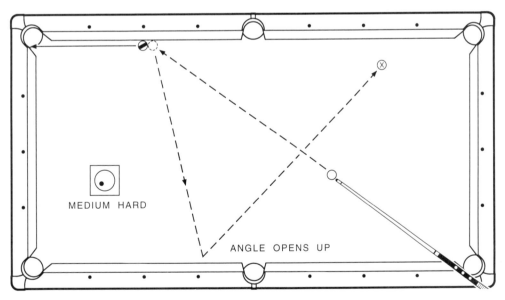

Inside English off the Rail Draw Shot

In the position above the object ball's frozen. You can easily get shape at the opposite end of the table by using low _left_ english with a medium-firm stroke. The cue ball will first come nearly straight across the table. The english will take off the _second_ rail, sending the cue ball rapidly down the table at a sharp angle.

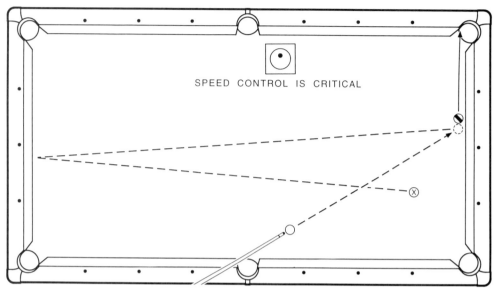

Up and Down the Table

This position play requires great speed control and accuracy. The best results are achieved by using a follow stroke in the center. However, if the object ball is a few inches off the rail, you should use a touch of inside english (left in the example) to help the cue ball go straight up and down the table.

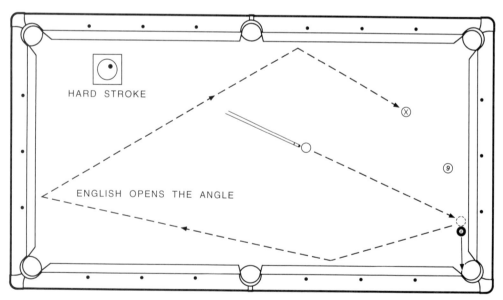

Around the Table Three-Railer

This shot is a better choice than going straight up and down the table when the object ball is near both the rail and the pocket. Apply follow with inside english, (right in the example) using a hard stroke. When stroked correctly the cue ball will spin across the table off the second rail (far left), arriving at position X for excellent position.

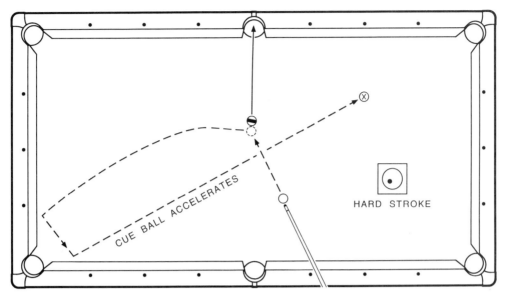

Side Pocket Two-Railer

A hard draw stroke with outside english (left in the diagram) will send the cue ball on the diagrammed path. The cue ball will accelerate sharply upon contact with both the first and second rails. Watch carefully for the arc that the cue ball makes soon after contacting the object ball.

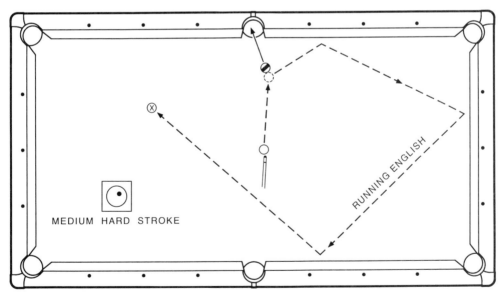

Side Pocket Three-Railer

A medium-hard follow stroke with running english(right english in the example) will send the cue ball three rails around the table for position at point **X**. When the object ball is closer to the pocket, you must guard against a scratch in the opposite corner pocket. Experiment with this shot from several nearby locations, and note the path that the cue ball takes each time.

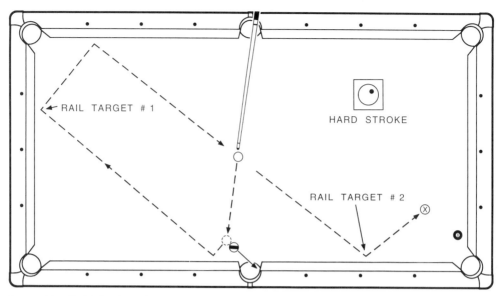

Four Rail Side Pocket Shape

This shot is a variation of the three rail side pocket shot discussed earlier.
You must set your rail targets very carefully, and then hit them just right.
The diagram shows the path of the cue ball that you should be trying to
duplicate. Use a hard stroke with high right english.

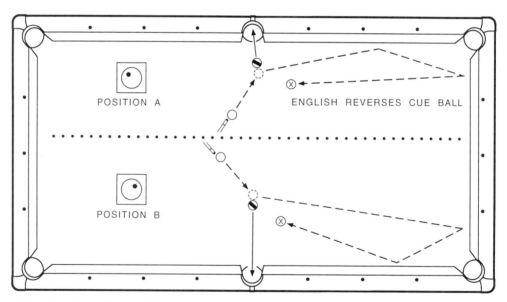

Side Pocket Shape Using Inside English

Inside english can help you to bring the cue ball back up the same side of the
table that the object ball is on. With the ball near the pocket in position A,
you may wish to contact the side rail first. The left english really takes hold
off the second rail, reversing the cue ball's course. With the object ball
further from the rail, as in position B, you should aim to hit the end rail
first.

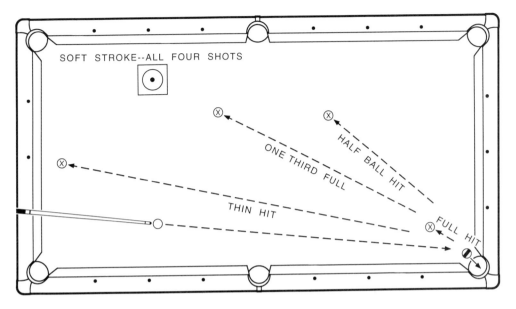

Balls Near the Pocket

Beginners love shooting balls near the pocket. Advanced players, however, have learned to respect these shots because of the special challenges that they present. They know that getting good position on the next ball is no sure thing. On shots such as those shown in the diagram virtually any contact with the cue ball will pocket the object ball. However, that's not a good reason to get sloppy with your aim. On the contrary, you should aim with equal or even greater care on these shots. Keep in mind that one little slip can send the cue ball hurtling out of control to the opposite end of the table.

To play good shape on shots close to the pocket, you will need to pay special attention to the thickness of the hit. In the diagram, all four shots were stroked softly with centerball. You'll immediately notice how the cue balls traveling distance was directly affected by how much contact was made with the object ball. For example, the full hit on the striped ball absorbed much of the cue ball's energy. As a result, the cue ball rebounded but a short distance from the cushion. In sharp contrast, the cue ball gave up little of its momentum as it barely clipped the object ball in passing as a result of a thin hit. Even with a soft stroke, the cue ball still rolled clear to the opposite end of the table. The difficulties encountered when playing position on balls close to the pocket grow as the distance between the cue ball and object ball increases. This happens because a firmer stroke is required in order to control the cue ball. Therefore, any errors in contacting the object ball are further magnified. Your best bet is to practice playing position on these shots with the care and precision that you would give to balls further from the pocket. By all means, resolve not to take these pocket hangers for granted any longer.

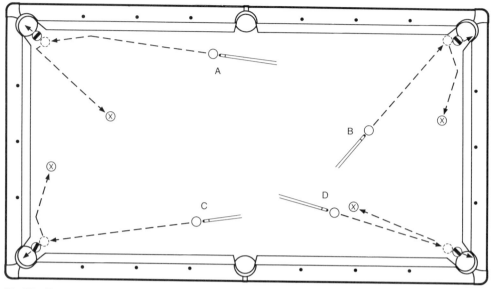

Balls Deep in the Jaws

Balls near the pocket are a cause for concern, but balls deep in the jaws can be downright troublesome. Not only is shape difficult to manage, but it's also possible, strangely enough, to actually miss these sitting ducks. You can also add in the likelihood of scratching on a too full hit with the object ball. Wow! These pocket hangers aren't nearly as much fun as their proximity to the pocket would make them appear at first glance.

Because of the difficulties mentioned above, your goals should be a bit more modest when playing position on these shots. Make your priorities, 1) Pocket the ball without scratching and 2) get some kind of workable position on the next ball. The diagram illustrates a few recommended strategies for playing deep in the pocket position. In position A, your angle of approach is along the rail. Aim to hit the rail a very short distance above the pocket. With a soft stroke the cue ball should continue on as diagrammed. When shooting directly at the object ball, you may wish to employ the more daring approach shown in position B. Aim between the left of the pocket and the object ball. The cue ball will be deflected across the opening of the pocket. Option C is to hit the outside half of the object ball directly with draw. Perhaps the toughest position play in this situation is position D. Your shot here is to make full hit on the object ball with draw. It is not easy to get the cue ball to draw back at precisely the desired direction when object ball deep in the jaws.

Position plays on ball in the jaws should be practiced at very close range so that you can aim the shot with great precision. You should also experiment with different angles of approach using draw and follow, and with both thick and thin hits.

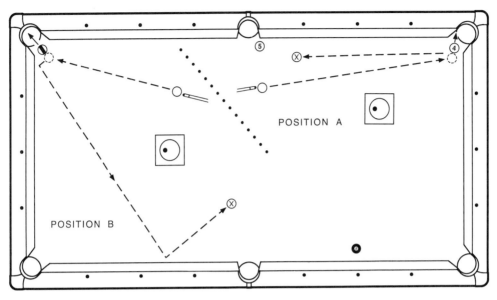

Playing Shape with English

Pocketing balls using english is tougher except for when the object ball is near the pocket. In this situation, english can be used freely to achieve your desired position. In position A, a fairly thin hit on the 4-ball with lots of left english will give you good shape on the 5. A half ball hit with plenty of left english will pull the cue ball across the table for shape in position B.

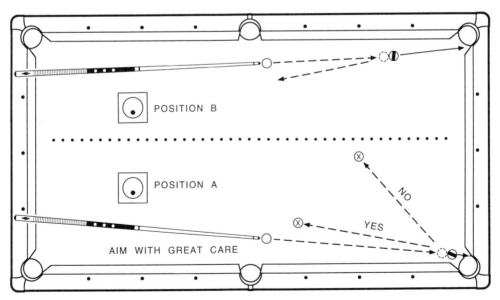

Draw Shots on Balls Near the Pocket

It's much easier to draw the cue ball back straight in position B than position A because balls near the pocket tend to weaken our sense of aim. It is also easier to get a sense of the proper line that you want the cue ball to return on in position B. The lesson: be extra, extra careful when using draw when the object ball is in front of the pocket.

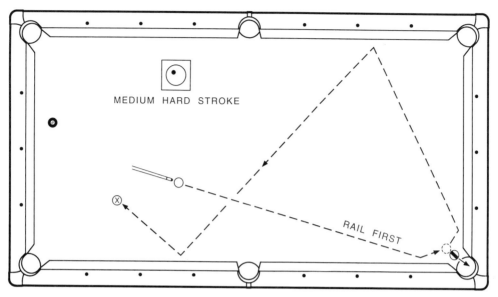

Using Rail First Position on Pocket Hangers

When the object ball is near the pocket and you need to get the cue back down to the other end of the table, you should consider going rail first. It can enable you to control the cue ball's speed better and give you a lower risk shot. The key to this shot is to just barely clip the object ball.

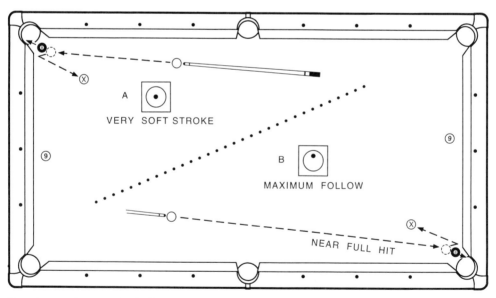

Back to the Rail Follow Shot

From position A, it's easy to hit the right portion of the 8-ball with a very soft stroke for shape on the 9-ball. Position B is a longer version of the same shot. At this distance you should protect against the cue ball rolling off. A medium-hard stroke with maximum follow and a nearly full hit on the 8-ball will cause the cue ball to stop quickly as it rebounds off the cushion.

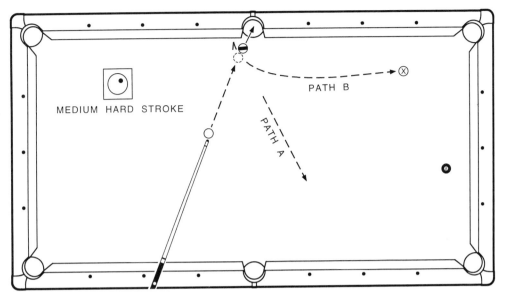

Change of Direction Follow Shot

You can change the cue balls direction to get better position on the 8-ball (path B) because the object ball is again very close to the pocket. You need to use top, right english with a medium-firm stroke. You'll also want to shoot the stripe ball into the left side of the pocket.

Variety of Position Plays

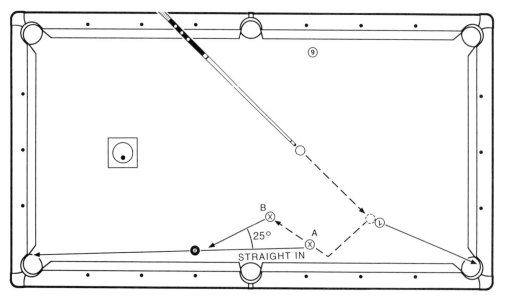

Playing up Close to Get an Angle

Getting close to the object ball can help you create a better angle for playing position on the next ball. At close range you can also make the most of a sharper angle because you can now shoot hard with much greater confidence.

The position in the diagram arises quite frequently in a game of Nine Ball. A soft draw shot on the 7 would leave the cue ball at position A. From this position, the 8-ball is nearly straight-in, making it extremely difficult to then get position on the 9-ball. Now we'll go back to our shot on the 7-ball. This time we're going to apply a little extra draw to the cue ball. As a result the cue ball has come to rest at position B. Notice the vast improvement in our position. Instead of a near straight-in shot, we now have approximately a 25° cut angle on the 8-ball. At this angle, it will be easy to float the cue ball across the table for good position on the 9-ball.

Little things can loom large when playing pool. In our example, a little extra draw created a much better angle that turned a potentially troublesome situation into an easy run out. Pay attention to details, always.

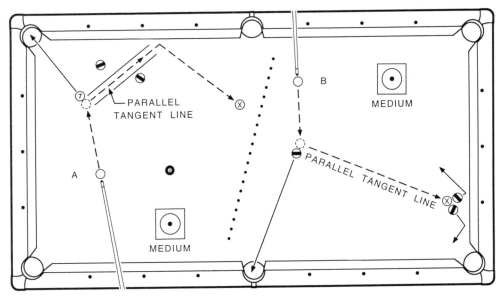

Using Tangent Lines to Control the Cue Ball

You can forecast the cue ball's path with great accuracy by using parallel tangent lines and by stroking the cue ball in the center with at least a medium stroke. After contacting the object ball, the cue ball will roll sideways at a right angle to the point of contact, as the diagram demonstrates. You can use this bit of information to accurately plan your position route, avoid obstructing object balls (A) and to break up clusters.

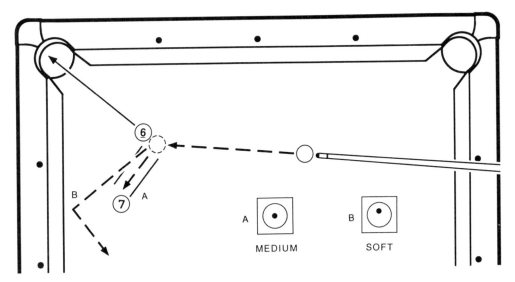

Hit or Miss Using Tangent Lines

Parallel tangent lines can be used to predict trouble in advance. In the diagrammed position, your goal is to pocket the 6-ball and bypass the 7-ball. The tangent line shows that the cue ball will, after contact, smack right into the 7 (A). A soft stoke with follow, in this case, will alter the course of the cue ball slightly (B), allowing it to avoid the 7.

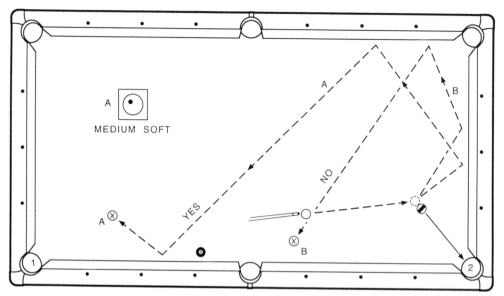

Playing Shape on the Short Side

In this example, a number of players would try for position B, which would leave an easy shot into the corner pocket #1. This approach, however, requires near perfect execution. In addition, there's the danger of a side pocket scratch or of overrunning your position. The high percentage shot is to play position for pocket #2 on the opposite side of the 8-ball. The lesson: don't force your shape unnecessarily to obtain a shorter shot.

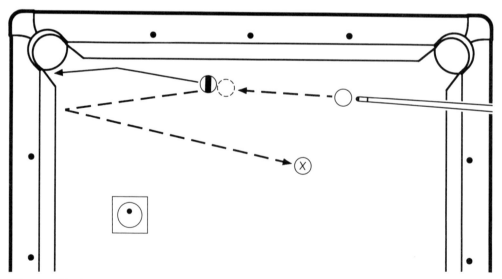

Cheat the Pocket for Shape

This shot works well on most tables except those with tight pockets. The shot is purposefully cut the object ball into the rail slightly before the pocket. This provides you with an angle to work with on a otherwise straight in shot. Note the course of the cue ball.

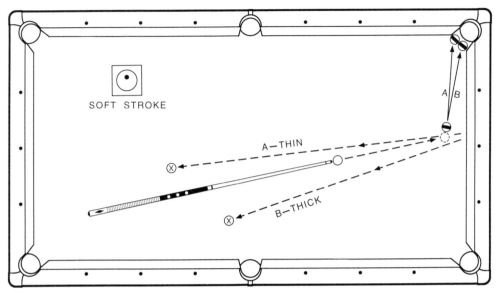

Thick or Thin Will Alter the Cue Ball's Path

Shooting into either side of the pocket on cut shots allows you to alter the path of the cue ball. A thin hit on the stripe into the left side of the pocket will bring the cue ball back along line A. A thicker hit will send the stripe into the right side of the pocket which will result in path B. Be sure to aim with great care when shooting into either side of the pocket.

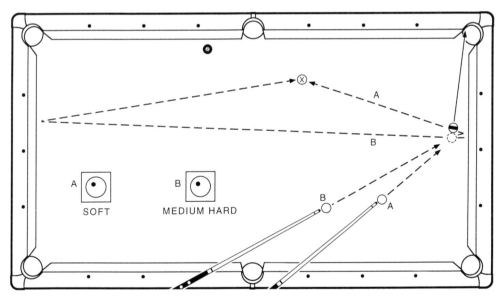

When to Play the Extra Rail

A small difference in the cue ball's location can make a big difference in how you play position. The goal is to arrive at position X. A soft stroke would work from point A. However, from point B you would be unable to stop the cue ball near X without sending the cue ball to the far rail and back as shown.

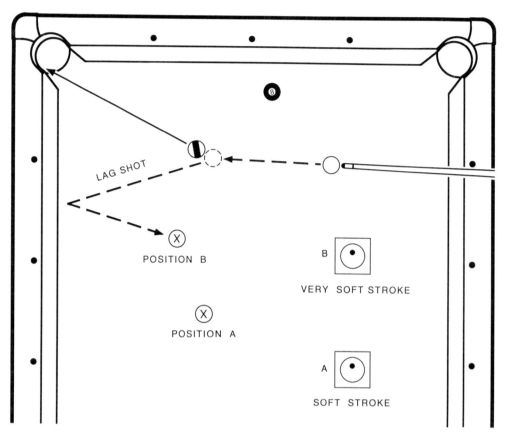

The Lag Shot

The lag shot requires great touch and a very sensitive feel for distance. The object on the lag shot is to die the object ball into the pocket. Lag shots will minimize the cue balls roll. They will also severely limit the initial sideways movement that accompanies all cut shots. The net result is a highly useful position tool.

What's required on lag shots is an extremely soft stroke. Going back to our 1-10 scale of stroke force, lag shots would rate a 1 or 2 at most. You'll only want to use lag shots on reasonably short shots so you won't be victimized by table roll or stroke inaccuracies. It also helps to keep the cut angle to a minimum by favoring one side of the pocket. If you're cutting to the left, aim to the right side of the pocket. Of course, you'll do this opposite when cutting to the right.

The diagram demonstrates the benefits of the lag shot. The challenge is to pocket the stripe ball and at the same time gain good position on the 8-ball. Position A shows what would happen if you pocketed the stripe using a soft stroke. Now take a look at your position using a lag shot (position B). The 8-ball's suddenly become much easier. Although it helps to cheat the pocket, don't make the mistake of undercutting the ball. Make sure you hit the shot with enough speed to get the object ball to the pocket. Don't come up short!

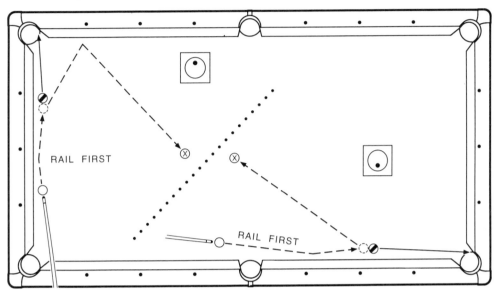

Go Rail First to Gain an Angle

In both examples you are faced with straight in shots. You need to maneuver the cue ball away from the rail for position. The rail first shot can help out. With practice you will learn how far to aim up the rail from the object ball (Note: there's more on this shot in chapter 3).

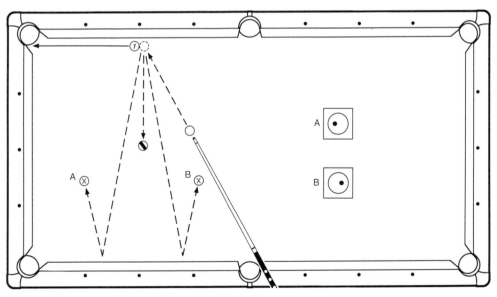

Avoiding Balls Coming Across the Table

Hitting other balls can ruin your position. Altering the cue balls path slightly can help you avoid this mistake. Unwanted contact often happens when a ball is directly across from where the cue ball will be contacting an object ball that's on or near the rail, as shown. In this example, a little left (route A) or right (route B) english will enable you to sidestep the next ball.

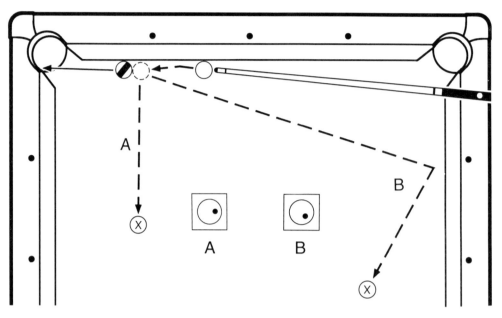

Frozen/Frozen Position Plays

When both the cue ball and the object ball are frozen to the rail, you can still play shape from this difficult position providing both balls are sufficiently close to the pocket as diagrammed. In the example above, you can force the cue ball away from the rail along line A by aiming slightly into the cushion first. Use english on the side of the cue ball that's closest to the rail (right english in this example). You can also bring the cue ball back along line B by using draw with right english. Again, you will want to aim into the rail. On both shots, be sure to shoot with authority. In the diagram below, you goal is to follow the cue ball along the indicated line. Simply shoot straight at the object ball with outside english (right in this example), and don't worry about following the object into the pocket. It won't happen.

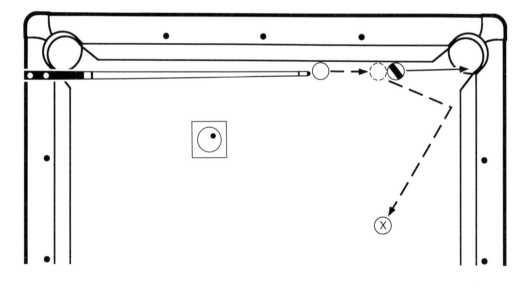

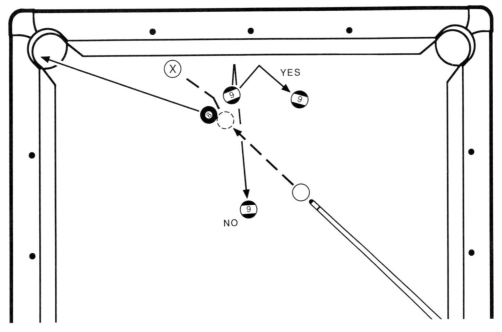

Bumping Your Next Ball into Position

When you can't avoid hitting the next ball, you must then plan for where it will likely end up after contact with the cue ball. As a rule, the second ball usually travels farther than you think it will. For the best results, try to control the next ball by bumping it lightly.

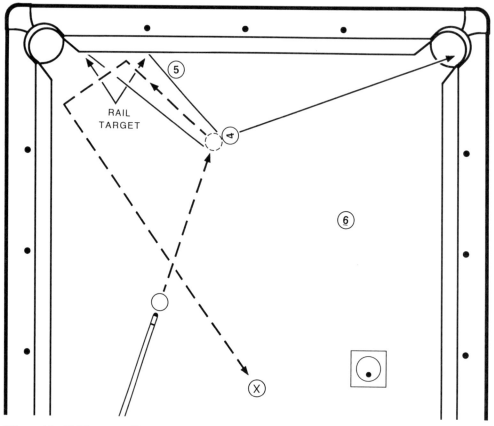

First Rail Target Zones

This position play comes up over and over again. Your only pocket for the object ball is the upper right hand corner pocket. To get position on the 6, you need to send the cue ball two rails and back out to position X in the center of the table. Now here's the rub: the 5 could easily divert the cue ball from its chosen path. On top of this, a scratch in the corner pocket is a distinct possibility. The solution is to plan your shot carefully! Circle the table to gain some additional perspective on the shot. Take a look from the opposite side of the rail you'll first come in contact with. From this angle you can tell the width of your rail target.

In the example, your target zone is approximately three balls wide. Hitting the rail in a zone this size would take great precision, but it can be done. You'll discover most targets are much more inviting. If the rail target is any smaller than that shown above, the shot is too risky for even the most skilled professionals. You'll then have to consider other options.

Now for a pop quiz: What are four principles of position that we put to work on this shot? Answer: Survey the shot, use rail targets, plan your route, and allow for a margin for error. Perhaps you can come up with more. more.

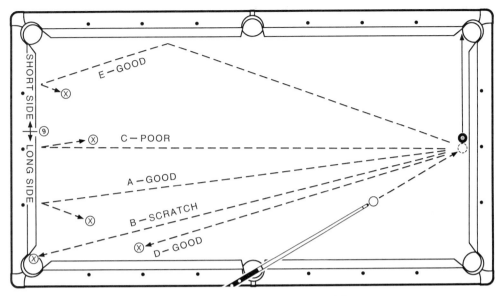

Playing Position Down the Length of the Table

Playing shape down the length of the table is one of the most challenging position plays in the game. The diagram above shows why. Let's say your goal is to cut the 8-ball into the corner pocket and get shape on the 9-ball at the opposite end of the table. At this distance, any cue ball control errors are greatly magnified. If the cue ball were to start off just a few degrees off line A, as in the example, it could be one full diamond off course by the time it arrived at the other end rail. If your target was the first diamond between the 9 and the corner pocket (line A), your miss hit could result in either a scratch (line B) or no shot on the 9 (line C). The alternative is to play it cozy by purposefully coming up short of the end rail (line D). This would help you to avoid the other disasters, and would leave you a thin but makeable cut shot on the 9. It takes great speed control to pull this shot off. Some good players might favor playing to the short side along line E.

This example should give you a good idea of some of the difficulties involved when playing table length shape. On these shots, proper planning, great touch, and near flawless execution are required. So make sure to give them the attention and respect that they deserve.

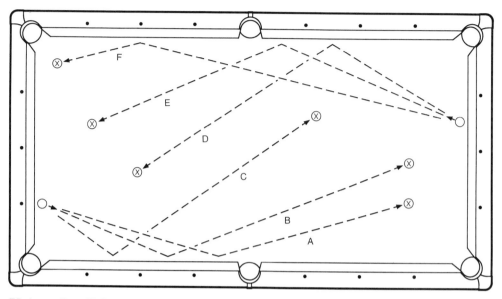

Using the Side Rails for Position

The side rails can be used effectively to help you avoid the pitfalls encountered when playing shape down the length of the table. The side rails offer you a much closer target for the cue ball. It's much easier to visualize hitting a spot on the rail that's, in many cases, only two or three feet away, rather than a spot clear down at the other end of the table. As you'll recall, mistakes are magnified the further the cue ball travels. Using running english off of the side rails helps to solve this problem. With running english, the cue ball will rebound less sharply off the side rail. Narrowing the cue balls pathway gives you a larger margin of error to work with.

One of the big problems that appears when using the side rails for position are the side pockets. It is very frustrating to strike the lip of the side pocket and have the cue ball ricochet back toward you. Scratching in the side pocket is another big problem. The solution lies in first planning your route carefully. This procedure includes choosing the correct side of the side pocket as your rail target. When you are approaching the side rail from a shallow angle (lines A and B), you'll get better results by aiming for the near side rail as indicated. This gives you a large and more inviting target. It also helps to cut down considerably on corner pocket scratches. When your approach angle to the side rail is very sharp, your options increase. Lines C, D, and E show you three possible routes. Again, it's less risky to hit the near side rail first. However, your position play requirements may dictate that you take aim on the far side rail (line F). There are many subtle variations to the basic routes discussed above. Your game will surely benefit form your gaining a complete understanding of how to properly employ the side rails for table length shape.

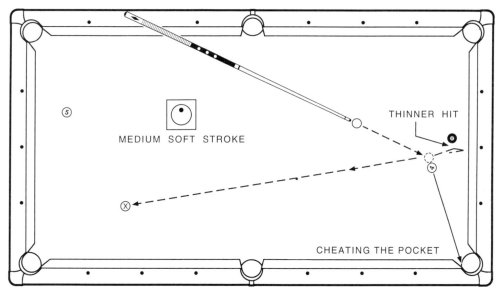

Playing Position off of Other Balls

Sometimes you can't avoid hitting balls that are sitting directly in the path of the cue ball. However, many times you can still play shape even though a collision is unavoidable. It just takes a little know how. Here's one of the keys: you will need to fine tune the direction that the cue ball takes after it contacts the other ball. Your goal is to optimize the cue ball's contact with the second object ball. There are three primary techniques that you can employ to influence the direction of the cue ball; english, speed of stroke, and cheating the pocket. Any of the above alone or in combination can be used to alter the path of the cue ball. As we'll see in a moment, a small change in the direction of the cue ball can make all of the difference in the world.

The diagram gives you a position play that ruins many players hopes for shape. Your shot is to pocket the 4-ball and send the cue ball down the table for position on the 5- ball. Contact with the 8-ball is unavoidable. If you were to employ a normal follow shot at medium speed, you would strike the 8-ball full on. This would kill the cue balls speed, and spoil you chances for position at the same time. Now for plan B. A soft stroke will minimize the sideways drift of the cue ball, resulting in a thinner hit on the 8-ball. In addition, we're going to also cheat the pocket by shooting the 4-ball in the right hand side of the corner pocket. This will lead to an even thinner hit on the 8-ball. By altering the cue balls path ever so slightly, the cue ball will now barely skim the 8-ball. As a result, the cue ball will retain much of its forward momentum, allowing it to rebound off the cushion and out for good shape on the 5-ball.

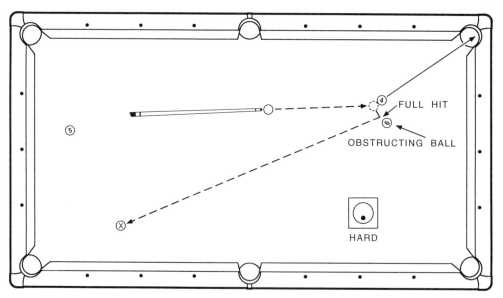

Drawing off an Object Ball for Position

Thanks to the 6-ball it looks like there's no way to get decent position on the 5-ball. However, you can still get good shape by simply shooting a draw shot off the obstructing ball! Incidentally, this shot only works if the ball you're drawing off of is within a few inches of the first ball.

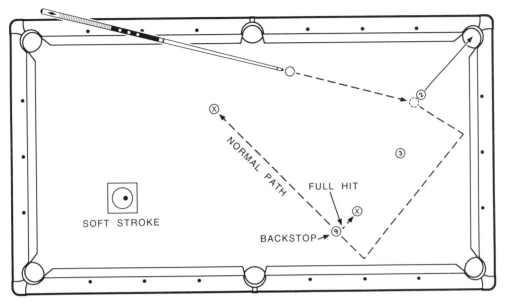

Using Balls as Backstops

In the position above it would normally be impossible to stop the cue in time for an easy shot on the 3-ball because of the force required to pocket the 2-ball. However, in this position there is a way. The 9-ball, which is sitting in the cue balls route, can be used as a backstop. Controlling the cue ball's path so that you get a full hit on the "backstop" is the key to this shot.

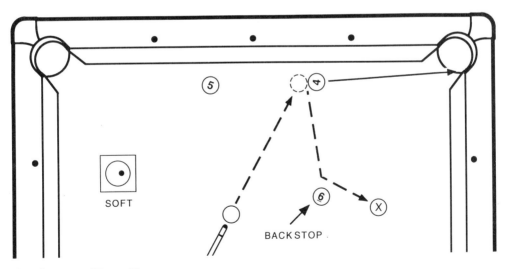

Backstops-Part Two

A thin cut on the 4-ball will cause the cue ball to roll far down the table. However, by using the 6-ball as a backstop, you can still get good position on the 5, which is your next shot. On this shot you must make sure to hit the 6 full or slightly to the side as shown. If you hit the wrong side of the 6-ball, the cue ball will veer to the left, leaving you with a tough cut or a bank shot on the 5.

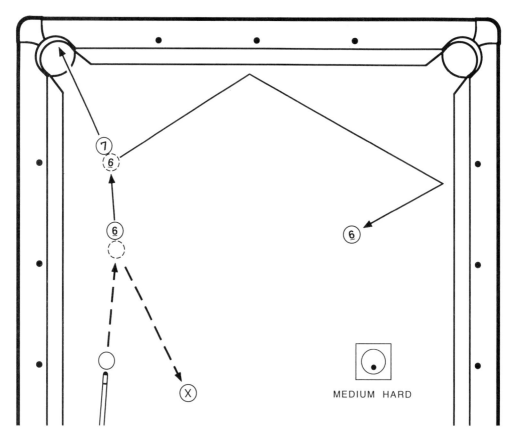

MEDIUM HARD

Playing Shape off Combinations

Most combination shots are tough enough to start with. Now consider the following: when you shoot that combo, the first ball is going to relocate. If that's the ball you need position on next, you are in effect playing position on a moving target. Now you need to gauge accurately the movement of both the cue ball and your next object ball! Sometimes this is easy, sometimes not. It all depends on the initial position of all three balls. There are several key factors involved in estimating what your next shot will be after you've shot the combination. They include: the cut angle on the cue ball to the first object ball; the cut angle on the first object ball to the second object ball; and the speed of stroke. It's not as complicated as it sounds. The diagram should help to explain how this works.

The combination shot shown requires a slight cut to the right side of the 6-ball. With a medium/firm draw stroke, the cue ball would come back to position X. A medium/firm stroke on the cue ball should be enough to power the 6-ball two rails, and out into the middle of the table as diagramed. Under our planned scenario, we would have a highly makeable shot on the 6 after shooting the combo. You may often be surprised by the roll of the balls (particularly the next object ball). Playing position on combos takes great judgement which only comes with experience. But don't give up on this position play and just bang away at combos.

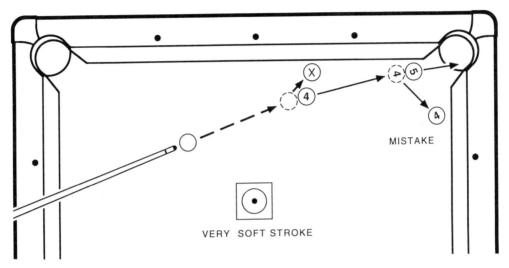

Combos with the Balls Near the Pocket

The position play in the diagram seems easy enough: just combo in the 5-ball and you should be all set for a gimme on the 4-ball. However, unless you're very careful with this shot, the 4-ball can easily wind up on the adjoining rail. You can avoid this unpleasant occurrence with a very soft stroke that sends the first ball <u>directly</u> into the middle of the second ball.

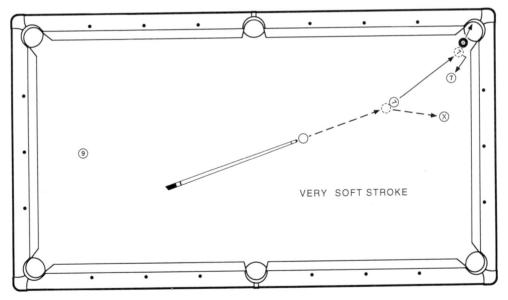

Combos with a Ball in the Jaws

Here's another simple situation that can lead to trouble. Your plan is to combo in the 8-ball in a game of Nine Ball and use the 7-ball to get position on the 9 at the other end of the table. The danger lies in following the 7 in on top of the 8. To avoid this mistake, shoot the combo very softly, avoid using any draw whatsoever, and be sure to cut the 8 in with the 7.

A CHECKLIST OF COMMON MISTAKES

All players make mistakes when playing for position. That's no crime. The real crime, however, comes from repeating the same mistakes over and over again. Below is a checklist of some of the most common mistakes. You are advised to go over the list one by one. Ask yourself if you could be guilty of consistently committing one or more of the mistakes on the list. Be objective. However, if you are in denial about your game, have a friend or knowledgeable observer evaluate your game. Be sure to use the insights gained to improve your game.

Shooting too hard
Shooting too easy
Over use of draw
Don't use enough draw
Over use follow
Don't use follow enough
Improper use of english
Missing balls to get shape
Making the ball, but not playing for shape
Scratching too often
Leaving the cue ball on the rail
Running into other object balls
Leaving long shots
Playing too close to the next shot
Getting the wrong angle
Leaving straight in shots when you need an angle
Trying to play perfect shape, especially when it's not needed
Failure to plan your shot
Taking shape for granted
Choosing the wrong position route
Choosing the wrong position zone
Failure to adapt to the table

CHAPTER 6

EIGHT BALL

Mastering Offensive And Defensive Strategies

Eight Ball has long been the most popular pool game, especially among newcomers to the sport. The rules are simple: each player must first pocket all the balls in his/her group (either the solids, 1-7, or the stripes, 9-15). Once this is accomplished, the shooter then pockets the gamewinning 8-ball.

Eight Ball is unusual in that each player only pockets the balls in his/her group. The opponent's balls are seen as obstructions that effectively prevent a player from easily clearing the table. In effect, each player's balls are like pieces on a chess board. They must be moved and/or pocketed to their best advantage, always keeping in mind the position of the entire table.

Most new players like Eight Ball because the object of the game is easy to learn; just keeping pocketing the balls in your group until it's time to take aim on the 8-ball. This approach works fine for beginning players. Over time, however, it becomes evident that there is much more to the game. At the upper levels of play, Eight Ball is an exquisite blend of offensive and defensive strategy. Runouts must be carefully plotted and executed with great precision. When necessary, defensive maneuvers must be carefully calculated to put your opponent in a stranglehold until the position of the balls favors your chance of running out.

Over the pages ahead you will find a number of practical strategies. These will help speed up your development as an Eight Ball player. Hopefully, each one will serve as the springboard for your learning even more of the nuances and subtleties of this fascinating game.

What can Make you a Winner

There are a number of key elements that go into making up a successful game of Eight Ball. Each skill must be developed, one by one. Each piece of knowledge gained through years of play must be filed away in your memory bank and recalled when needed under game conditions. Below is a blueprint for a winning game of Eight Ball. If you make each element a part of your game, you will be tough to beat.

- **Position and Pattern Play** - Carefully plan your runouts from start to finish (the 8-ball) and execute them precisely. Also learn to allow for changes in your pattern as the run progresses (Plan B).
- **Pick the Best Group** - Carefully assess the table and choose your group according to which offers the easiest runout and/or the best defensive opportunities.
- **Play the Table -** Play the percentages. Take what the table gives you. Don't try to win by playing shots with a low probability of success unless absolutely necessary.
- **Shotmaking Skills -** The congested conditions of an Eight Ball game often necessitates the execution of a variety of specialty shots, including banks and combos. This is especially true on a bar table.
- **Balancing Offensive and Defensive** - Know when to go for a runout and when to purposely turn the table over to your opponent. Don't' pocket a series of balls that won't lead to a makeable shot on the 8-ball.
- **Adjust your Game to the Competition -** You can up your winning percentage by varying your strategy, depending on your opponent's skill level. A key: delay your runouts as long as possible, especially against weaker opponents. Let them clear away all the obstacles to your run.
- **Develop a Strategy but Remain Flexible** - Follow your game plan as closely as possible, but learn to recognize the instant when you must shift gears to plan B.
- **Defensive Play** - Create a storehouse of safeties and strategic maneuvers that will limit your opponent's responses and/or set up the rack for your turn.
- **Know the Rules** - They often play a big part in the outcome of a game. Ball in hand rules can change your strategy significantly (so to can local rules or house rules).
- **Kick Shots** - Skill at kick shots is especially important if you are playing under ball in hand rules. Don't let your opponent's safeties lead to ball in hand.
- **The Break** - A good break can enable a skillful pattern and position player to runout quite often, especially on the big table. Control is the most important feature of a good break shot.

Assessing the Table

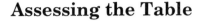

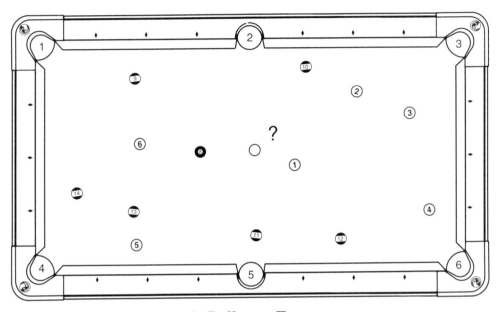

Your and Your Opponent's Balls are Easy

You've just broken the rack. One ball from each group was made on the break. A quick survey reveals that there are no clusters and no balls on the rails. There is an open pocket for each shot. It should be easy to avoid your opponent's balls throughout your run whatever group you choose. Both groups look very tempting. So, which group should you pick?

In this example, your choice is largely a matter of personal choice; both groups are easy. Perhaps you feel the 5 and 6 could give you trouble. If so, then take the stripes. With layouts like these, you have the luxury of choosing the group that looks most like a sure thing.

Once you've decided on a group, analyzed the layout and decided on your sequence, it's time to enter the execution stage. Even though the layout is simple, a win is not guaranteed. It's easy with this type of rack to assume the game is already over; this type of thinking can lose you the game. You need to approach the rack with the singular goal of running out. Your first turn could be your only turn. The lesson: never take a win for granted. Stay focused.

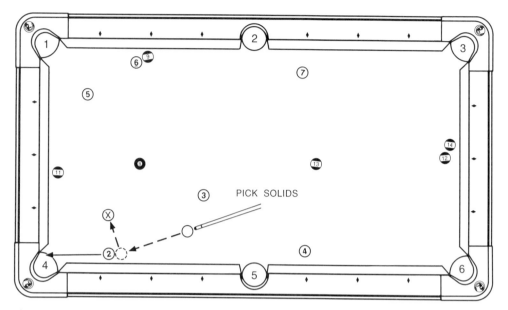

One Group is Easy - The Other is Hard

You've just broken the balls and pocketed one solid and two stripes. Although there are now less stripes to shoot, don't let that influence your choice of groups. It's the position of the balls that counts when deciding which group to play, not the number of balls left on the table. Which group is the better choice?

The stripes will be extremely tough, if not impossible to run. The 9-ball is clustered with the 6 and there is no break ball in the vicinity. The 12/14 cluster at the opposite end of the table also presents a major problem. Finally, your first shot on either the 11 or 13-ball is no bargain.

The solids look pretty inviting even though the 6-ball is presently tied up. A soft follow shot on the 2-ball into pocket #4 will give you an ideal angle to play the 5-ball into pocket #1, breaking the cluster in the process. You should then have a choice of two or three balls to play on your next shot.

When faced with a relatively easy runout like this, don't make the mistake of playing too defensively. The cluster should be broken immediately as described above. This is a layout that says "Go". Don't play conservatively, for example, pocketing a few balls first before breaking up the cluster. You might not get another opportunity like the one you have right now. After you've pocketed a few balls but failed to complete your run, your opponent will then have total control of the game (see The Failed Runout).

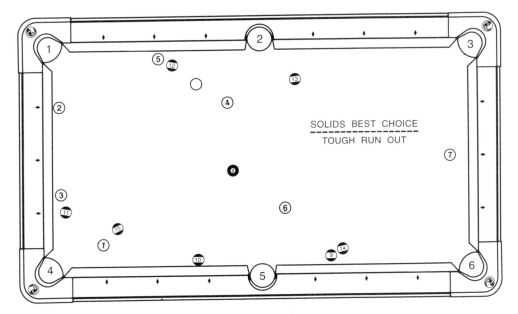

Assessing the Trouble Spots

Before you pick your group and begin your run you need to carefully evaluate the trouble spots. Ask yourself which group looks better? Does one group have clusters or balls on the rail? Are pockets blocked? Which group looks better in the event of a defensive battle? Can you reasonably take care of any trouble balls? Finally, is there a realistic chance of running either group? These are a few of the questions that you'll need to answer before you make an educated choice.

The stripes are a tangled up mess in the diagram. The 15-ball is blocked by the 1. The 9, 11, 12 and 14-balls are clustered in <u>three</u> different locations. Even world champion players would have trouble running this group. If you choose the stripes, you'll have to play a highly strategic and defensive game as the chances of running out are almost nil.

Analyzing the solids, there are a couple minor trouble spots, but nothing like the stripes. The 3-ball is blocked by the 11. It can be broken out, however, by playing the 1-ball into pocket #4. Shooting the 2-ball into pocket #1will free- up the 5-ball.

Although neither group looks very promising, the solids look much better than the stripes. Running out won't be easy. But even if you don't, your chances of winning are above average as your opponent's stripes are so poorly positioned.

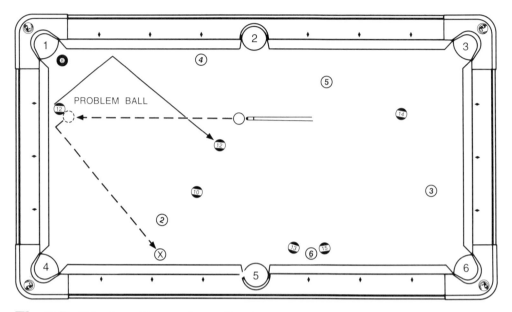

The 8-Ball is in a Precarious Position

It is still early in the rack, you've got the stripes and it's your shot. You could play the 14-ball into pocket #3, but then what? Your opponent's 6-ball is nestled up against your 13 and 15-balls. Worst of all, the 8-ball is blocking the pocket on your 12-ball. It would be extremely difficult to play position on the 12-ball into pocket #4. On top of this, your opponent's 5-ball is preventing you from banking the 12-ball into pocket #3.

At this point, you would be correct in concluding that a runout is impossible as the 12-ball seriously jeopardizes your chances of winning the game. Your thought processes should now be focused on improving your position (i.e., getting the 12-ball away from the 8-ball) and preventing your opponent from running out. Luckily your opponent also has some problems to deal with, such as the 4-ball on the side rail and the 6-ball in a cluster.

It is now time to punt, to willingly give the table back to your opponent in the hopes that he/she does not execute a superior runout. If you are fortunate enough to shoot again, it should be from a position that gives you a shot at winning. That means banking the 12-ball away from the corner pocket as diagrammed. The cue ball has landed at position X. From here your opponent will have to play some exceptional pool to keep you from returning to the table.

Strategy

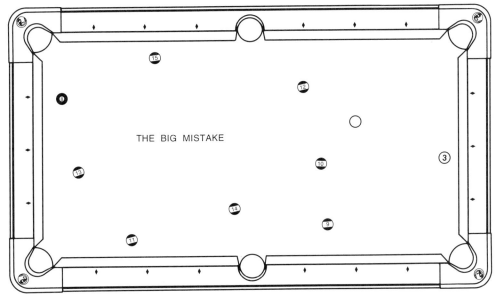

THE BIG MISTAKE

The Big Mistake: The Failed Runout

More has been written about the disastrous consequences of the failed runout than perhaps any other subject regarding the art and science of Eight Ball. A failed runout, by definition, is an unsuccessful attempt to runout, leaving your opponent an open table and an easy win.

Wide open tables, as illustrated above, make it relatively easy for the average player to run out. An expert player would be expected to run the layout above or one of similar difficulty ninety-eight percent of the time. As you can tell, it's most definitely in your best interests to avoid the failed runout as it essentially hands the game over to your opponent.

If you find, upon analyzing your game, that you've been guilty of failed runouts, the following checklist will help you pinpoint the problem. Are you:

Failing to plan the entire rack from the break?
Failing to execute a strategy that is within your skill level?
Trying low percentage shots, breakouts, or position plays?

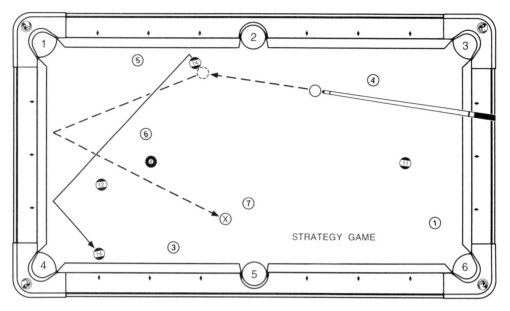

STRATEGY GAME

Winning a Lost Game

You have the stripes and it's your turn. You are clearly in a jam. The 5-ball is blocking the 14-ball, the 8 is in the way of the 12 and you have no shot on the 11-ball. To make matters worse, you are outnumbered six balls to three and your opponent's solids are in a much better position.

Although the game appears lost it's not over until it's over. You can still win by improving your position for your next turn while at the same time making it tougher for your opponent to run out. Here's how. Bank the 14-ball away from the top rail freeing it from the 5-ball. If you hit the 14 with the proper force, it will come to rest on the bottom rail thus blocking your opponent's 3-ball into pocket #4.

The net result is that you've freed the 14 while blocking your opponent's ball thus turning the tide somewhat in your favor. If your opponent can't run out, you've given yourself a much better chance of winning on your next turn. The lesson: even in a game that appears lost, don't give up. Keep plugging away.

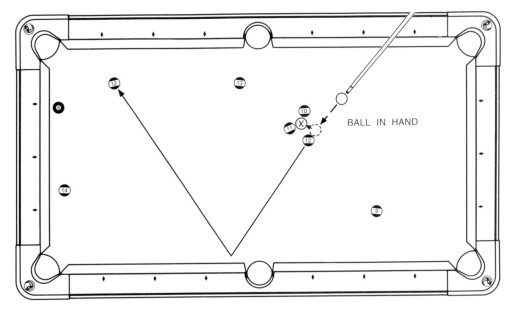

Tightening the Screws

Your opponent has just scratched while pocketing the last solid, giving you ball in hand. You could runout from here as there are no clusters to worry about and your opponent's balls are off the table. At this point, you need not hurry to run out. Take a moment to survey the layout, double checking for possible problems.

The 14-ball is on the same rail as the 8-ball, eliminating it as a key ball (see key ball on pg. 220) for the 8. Further inspection reveals no other suitable key ball is available. Both of these mildly troublesome problems can be solved by playing a safety!

Play a soft bank shot on the 12- ball so it ends up near, but not on the same rail as, the 8-ball. At the same time, slide the cue ball in between your 10 and 11-balls. You've now set up the rack for a very easy runout and left your opponent with virtually no chance of even hitting the 8-ball.

With ball in hand a second time, pocket the 14-ball, then the 9, 10, 11 and 13-balls. Use the 12 as your key ball. It will enable you to easily play position on the 8-ball.

You could have chosen to run the rack the first time with ball in hand; the odds were probably eighty to ninety-five percent in your favor. But by playing safe, you upped your odds of winning to over ninety-five percent. The lesson: don't hesitate to tighten the screws to increase your chances for victory whenever possible by whatever means (within the rules, of course) are available.

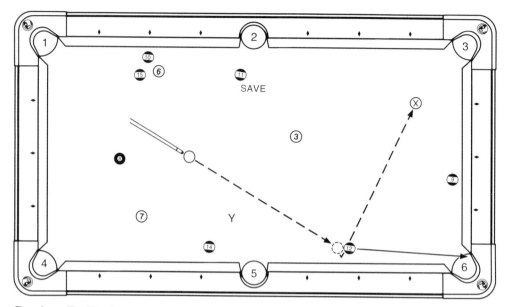

Saving Balls for a Specific Purpose

The 9-ball on the right end rail is a nuisance that must be dealt with sooner or later. It would be easy to get good shape on the 9 by playing the 11 into pocket #2. However, you should pass on this shot as you'll need the 11-ball for a more important purpose later in the run.

Play the 12-ball into pocket #6 with follow so the cue ball stops at position X for the 9-ball. Although the 12 is a tougher shot, it allows you to take care of the pesky 9-ball while preserving the 11 to break the 6/10/15 cluster.

After playing the 9 into pocket #6 and the 14 into pocket #4, the cue ball should wind up at position Y. From this angle, you can play the 11 into pocket #2 driving the cue ball into the cluster on the top rail, freeing up your 10 and 15-balls.

At times each ball is ideally situated for a specific purpose. You will increase your runout percentage by learning to use each ball to its best possible advantage. In this example, that meant recognizing that the 11-ball could serve more than one purpose and saving it for breaking the cluster.

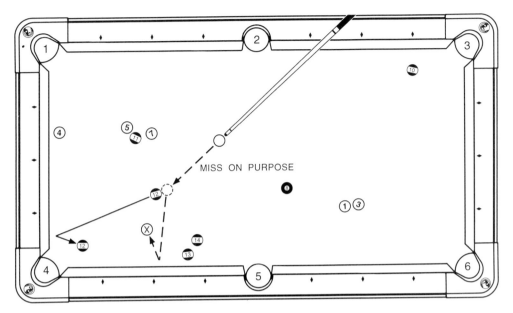

MISS ON PURPOSE

Let Your Opponent do the Dirty Work

You and your opponent share a common goal: to break up the 5/7/11 cluster. But which of you should have that duty? The answer depends on the position of the balls. In this case, why not let your opponent do the dirty work? Your balls are not exactly positioned for the task. And even if your opponent separates the cluster, he/she will still have trouble running out because of the 1/3 cluster.

It's now time to con your opponent into doing you a favor. Put on your actors hat and give the 12-ball your full attention; act surprised when you miss the 12 (as diagrammed). What you will have done is leave the cue ball in perfect position (X) for your opponent to break the cluster by playing the 4 into pocket #1.

Unless he/she gets a roll when breaking the cluster, chances are you'll get another crack at a wide open table, thanks to your con job. This ploy will work on some, but not all, of your opponents. Experienced players will opt to break the 1/3 cluster and play safe, figuring you won't run out. As always, it pays to know who you're playing and to adjust your strategy accordingly.

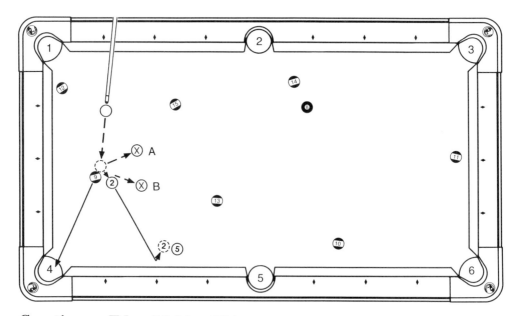

Creating an Edge: Making Things Tougher for Your Opponent

Your opponent's runout attempt has failed, leaving you with the layout above. You could begin your run by playing the 9-ball into pocket #4, drawing the cue to position A. This approach follows an accepted principle which says to leave your opponent's balls alone. However, there is an alternative strategy which can build your advantage by making things tough for your opponent.

With this layout you have an easy run although you must still pocket 8-balls to secure victory. Even with "gimme" racks like this, good players have been known to mess up. This being the case, why not build an edge, just in case you do fail to run out? Simply play a follow shot on the 9-ball. The cue ball will then bump into your opponent's 2-ball, sending it over to the rail next to his/her 5-ball.

What you've done is insure your victory. You still have an easy shot on the 12-ball. In addition, your opponent now has very little chance of winning the game if you fail to run out. You will also have created a mild degree of stress and anguish in your opponent who was thinking he/she would have another shot at the game if you failed in your run out attempt.

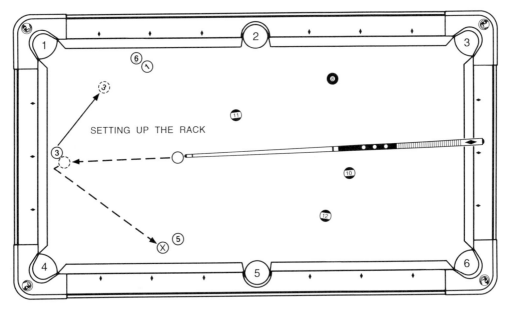

SETTING UP THE RACK

Setting up the Rack

When you don't have a reasonable shot, the best move is to improve the position of your balls and to play safe. In this example, a soft hit on the 3 will send it over near the 1/6 cluster. The 3 can now be used as a break ball. At the same time the cue ball has rolled behind the 5-ball (X), hooking your opponent.

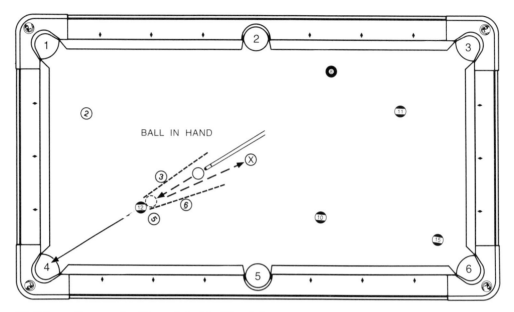

Taking Care of a Trouble Ball with Ball in Hand

Your opponent has just committed a foul, giving you cue ball in hand. You've got several balls to choose from. However, you should start your run with the ball on which it is most difficult to play position. In this case, your choice should be the 12-ball as it is surrounded by several solids. Playing shape into that small position zone will not be easy. So make sure you take maximum advantage of the opportunity ball in hand provides you. In this example, it gave you the ability to dispose of a ball that would otherwise have proven to be quite troublesome.

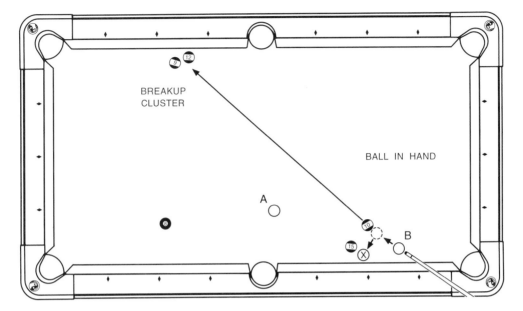

Breaking Balls Open with Ball in Hand

Your opponent has just made his/her last solid and scratched, giving you cue ball in hand. It's now time to plot your strategy, to discover how you can take advantage of being able to place the cue ball anywhere on the table. You could try to run out, but that means that you'll have to separate the 9/12 cluster and get position after the breakout. Because the cue ball will have to travel some distance across and down the table to break the cluster (after pocketing either the 15 or 10 balls), there's a possibility of missing the cluster altogether. Now , if you fail to break the cluster, your opponent will have a shot at the 8-ball.

Fortunately, you have a better choice available. Place the cue ball at position B and shoot the 10-ball directly into the cluster. Use a touch of draw and a soft stroke. The cue ball will float over behind the 15-ball, hooking your opponent. Now you've got all of your group apart for what should prove to be a very easy runout on your next turn at the table.

Some players take exception to giving an opponent another chance, but what you are really doing is greatly improving your odds for a win. Your chance of running out is probably 70%. After playing the safety you've given your opponent perhaps one chance in a hundred of kicking two rails and pocketing the 8 ball into pocket #4. Remember, in Eight Ball your opponent can legally pocket the 8 ball in only one pocket; slop shots lose you the game. After your opponent has kicked for the 8 ball and missed, your chances of running out may now be as much as ninety-five percent.

The lesson to be learned is to keep stacking the odds as heavily as you can in your favor. Don't be impatient and unnecessarily attempt to run out just because you have cue ball in hand. Some observers will accuse you of playing chicken; however, those who know the game and play to win (don't you?) will applaud you for your intelligent strategic maneuvers.

Offensive Play

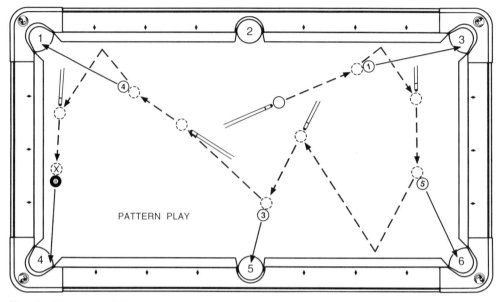

PATTERN PLAY

Basic Pattern Play

Pattern play is defined as the order in which you play the balls. Patterns that are well thought out and executed make it much easier to run out. On the other hand, poor pattern play can bring your efforts to run even the easiest rack to an abrupt halt.

Some players struggle with this part of the game while others seem to have a natural instinct for running the balls in the correct order. Nevertheless, any player who gives some thought and study to this vital phase of the game can improve their overall performance.

It takes time to learn to read a table. You can begin by asking yourself the following questions:

What ball(s) can I make to start the run?

Which ball(s) are easiest and lead to a second shot?

How can I play the entire rack?

With a questioning mind and lots of practice, you will learn to select correct patterns. If you continue to play one shot at a time without a plan for the entire rack, your runouts will be few and far between.

The diagram illustrates basic pattern play. The 1-ball is played into pocket #3 with a soft follow stroke, leaving you on the 5-ball. Play the 5 into pocket #6 with a medium soft follow stroke for an easy shot on the 3-ball. A medium soft draw on the 3-ball leaves you perfect shape on the 4. A soft follow shot gives you position on the 8-ball.

Although this was an easy run, it could have been bungled with poor pattern play. Notice, however, how each shot flowed to the next, the natural order in which the balls were played.

As your pattern play improves, you'll begin to make sense out of the apparent chaos of increasingly complex patterns.

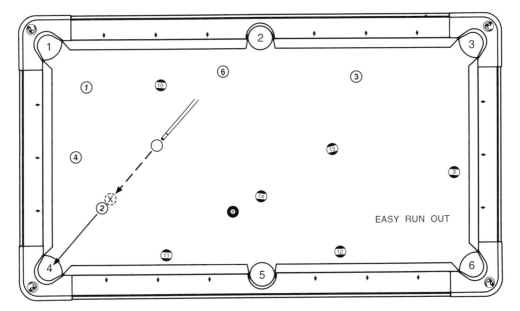

EASY RUN OUT

Simple Patterns

This layout presents you with a fairly routine runout. All of your solids as well as the 8-ball are in the clear. You need only identify your pattern and execute it successfully.

You can begin planning your pattern by using the process of elimination. The 6-ball cut into the side pocket is tricky on a bar table. The 3-ball is a long shot that could be missed under pressure while the 4 is a very low percentage shot (tough cut).

That leaves the 1 or 2-ball, either of which would be acceptable. In this example, the 2-ball was chosen. As you make your decisions and the number of balls remaining decreases, the pattern becomes clearer and clearer. After pocketing the 2-ball, you could play the 1 into pocket #1 and the 4 into pocket #4.

Your position on the 4 should enable you to get shape on the 3 into pocket #3. After the 3 you will want position on the 6-ball into pocket #1. Some players may be tempted to play the 3/6 sequence in reverse order; this will leave you with a tough shot on the 8-ball. Playing a stop shot on the 6 leaves you an easy shot on the 8-ball into pocket #5.

Notice that every shot was easy and how playing position from shot to shot was simple. When you play your patterns correctly you can expect to run routine racks like this nearly every time.

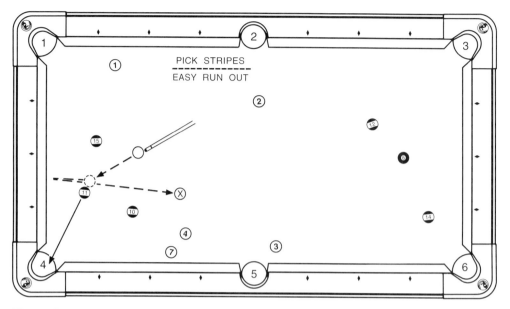

Easy Run Out Pattern

After breaking the balls you must now choose a group. The solids and stripes are well spread out and there are no serious trouble spots. However, as there is no simple opening shot for the solids, and the stripes offer an easy shot on the 11-ball, this is the determining factor for this rack.

After shooting the 11-ball you should remain at this end of the table for the 10 and 15-balls. The diagram shows the ideal position on the 10-ball.

By playing this 3-ball sequence correctly you have accomplished the following objectives:

> Chosen the correct group
> Played the right ball first (11)
> Moved the cue ball easily without getting into trouble
> Cleared one end of the table without leaving stragglers
> Traveled to the opposite end of the table for the 12, 14 and 8

For newer players, this may sound confusing. However, over time, the type of planning and thinking described above will become second nature as a certain consciousness for pattern play develops.

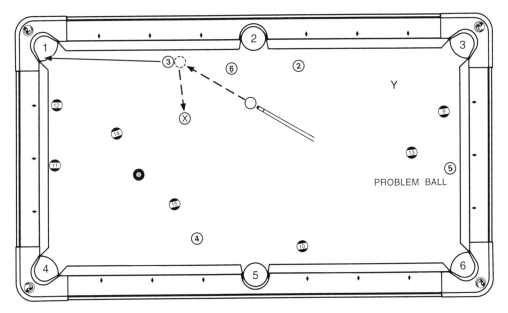

Medium Tough Runouts

This layout is mildly challenging. You have the solids and it's your shot. Your biggest concern should be the 5-ball which is surrounded by two stripes. If you can get good position to play the 5 into pocket #6, you stand an excellent chance of winning the game. Your efforts should be primarily centered on devising a plan to take care of the 5-ball.

Here's how to do it. First identify where you need to place the cue ball to play the 5. Upon surveying the table, you decide that position Y would enable you to pocket the 5 and play shape on the next ball, the 4. Going back to your first ball, the 3, a soft follow shot into pocket #1 will position the cue ball at X.

Now, take a moment to identify the pattern leading to position Y. If you said to shoot the 6-ball into pocket #2 with a stop shot, and then the 2 into pocket #3 with a soft follow stroke to position Y, you were right. The key to this pattern is getting lined up properly on the 2-ball so you can easily get shape on the problem ball, in this case the 5.

In this example it took three shots to get proper position on the 5. This is not uncommon. Before banging away indiscriminately, devise a plan and a pattern for dealing with problem balls. Remember that it is best to have an easy shot to play position to a precise target zone.

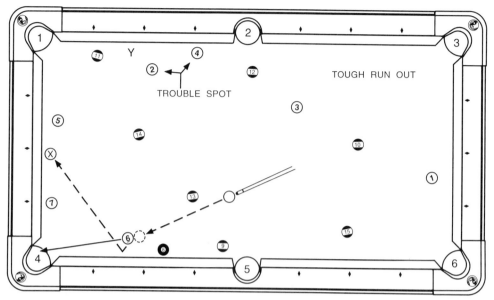

Advanced Pattern Play

You've got the solids and it's your shot. A review of the layout tells you that running out this rack won't be easy. The 2 and 4-balls on the upper side rail are your biggest worry. The 1-ball near the end rail doesn't help matters. And because of your opponent's 9 and 13-balls, you will need to play precision shape on the 8-ball.

You could choose to use stall tactics (such as lagging the 6-ball up to pocket #4, blocking the 8-ball) except that your opponent's balls are so well situated that this probably won't work. Therefore, your best option is to attempt to run this troublesome rack. It will require expert planning and execution.

The 3-ball is a difficult shot that leads nowhere. Therefore, the 6-ball is the logical starting point. A follow shot to position X will give you position on the 5-ball into pocket #1. Next, send the cue ball to the top rail (position Y) for the 4-ball into pocket #3 or the 2-ball into pocket #6. The successful completion of this sequence of shots indicates you're ready for world-class competition. Now let's back up a moment. If you failed to get the correct angle on the 5-ball, you could play the 7 first to get the required angle on the 5. Good pattern play will often allow you the opportunity to take an extra shot to position the cue ball where needed.

If you manage to successfully run the first five balls (as above), take a deep breath; the remaining balls, the 3, 1 and 8, are no picnic. Your reward for running tough racks like this is a great sense of satisfaction for a job well done. Even your opponent will likely applaud your efforts with the sweetest words in pool, "Nice run!".

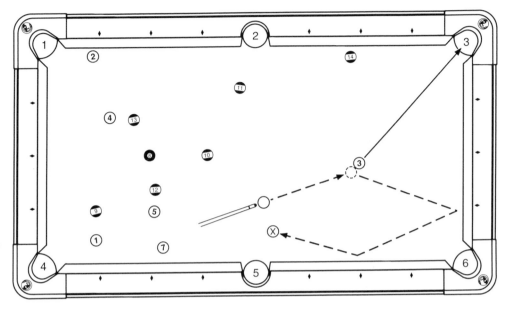

A Tough but Runnable Pattern

Although there are no clusters and the balls are somewhat spread out, this rack will nevertheless put your imagination and execution skills to the test. Plenty of things can go wrong during a run, especially after you've quickly picked off three or four ducks. Don't be in a hurry to start pocketing balls. Take a moment to devise a workable plan that can take you clear to the 8-ball.

You can start your planning by figuring out where and how you're going to play the 8-ball. In other words, begin your strategizing with the end in mind. Even though the 8-ball will go into five of the six pockets, it will be difficult to play shape on due to your opponent's stripes. It's hard to say exactly which ball you should save for the shot before the eight. Whatever your choice, bear in mind that you will need to play position with great care to avoid getting hooked.

Now for the rest of the rack. You could start your run with the 1, 7 or 3-ball. The 3 is probably your best bet as it eliminates the need to pick up this straggler later in the game. With the cue ball at position X, your next shot is the 7 into pocket #4. Next comes the 1 into the same pocket. While playing the 1, you could bump the 9 out of the way, clearing pocket #4 for the 8-ball. One logical sequence for the remaining balls is as follows: 5-ball into pocket #6, 4-ball into pocket #1, 2-ball into pocket #1 and finally, the 8 into either pocket #'s 3,4 or 6. Note that where you play the 8-ball depends entirely on the position you get on the 2. Even though the 8 is surrounded, you still have a number of options for shape. Each requires a well executed shot on the last solid.

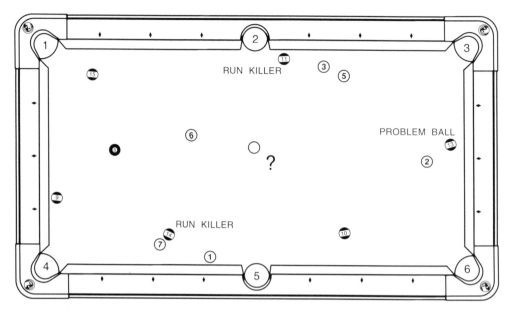

Run Killers - What Could Stop Your Run?

You are playing the stripes. A runout is possible but certainly not guaranteed. The 11-ball near the side pocket will be tough to play shape on while the 14-ball is part of a cluster. Both of these balls could kill your chances for a run out. In addition, the 13-ball is in a tough spot on the end rail.

After considering these trouble spots, the obvious question is what should you do. If you try to run out and fail you'll likely leave the table open for your opponent to run out. Perhaps you should devise a safety and wait for things to loosen up. What you don't want to do is pocket three or four easy balls (such as the 15,9,10 in the example) and worry about the trouble spots when you have no position balls left on the table.

Now is the time to worry about the run killers. It's much better to have some well placed balls still on the table for another possible turn if you are unable to deal successfully with the problem balls on your first attempt. In addition, the more of your balls that remain on the table, the more obstacles your opponent will have to play around during his/her attempt to run out.

Let's now consider our original question, do we run out or play safe? Perhaps the answer is a little of both. Your best play might be to bank the 11-ball into pocket #5 while at the same time sliding the cue ball down the table between the rail and the 3-ball. If you make the 11, you'll also have position on the 13-ball. And if you miss the bank, at least you'll have freed up one of your trouble balls. Plus you'll have left your opponent, thanks to the 7/14 cluster, with a challenging runout. When a runout is uncertain and your opponent has no cinch run either, sometimes it's best to hedge your bet by playing a shot that's half offense, half defense.

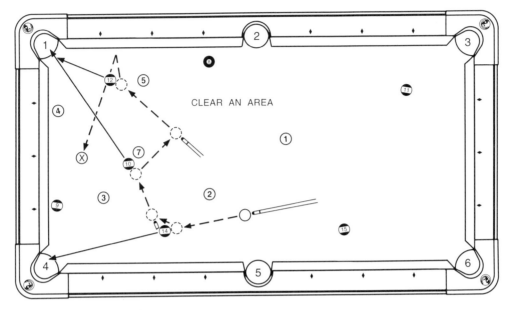

CLEAR AN AREA

Clearing Out an Area

Four of your stripes are mixed in with solids on the left side of the table. The 11 and 15-balls are by themselves at the other end of the table. You can start your run by playing either the 14 or 15-balls. You have perfect position on the 14-ball. By shooting the 14 first, you can get started on clearing up all the stripes on this end of the table. You can pick up the 15-ball later in your run.

While you're at one end of the table, it's often a good idea to play all of your balls in this area before moving on to balls in other areas. This is especially true when your group is mixed up with your opponent's balls. It's much easier to play precision shape for balls like the 10 and 12 when the cue ball needs to travel only a short distance, as in the diagram.

If you were to play the 14 and then the 15, it would be much tougher to come back and clear up the rest of the stripes. When possible you want to finish clearing an area with a shot that makes it easy to send the cue ball down the table. In this example, the 9-ball acts as your escape shot. From position X it will be easy to get good position on the 15-ball. Then the 11, followed by the 8 and the game is yours.

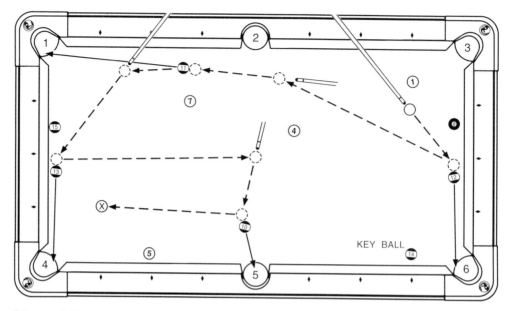

Up and Down the Table

Normally it's easiest to clear one area of the table before moving on to the next ball or group of balls. In doing so you can exert maximum control over the cue ball by keeping its traveling distance to a minimum. There are times you will need to send the cue ball up and down the table due to the layout. In this case, your planning and cue ball control will need to be extra sharp.

In the position above, the 12-ball should be played first into pocket #6. The 11 comes next as it will enable you to then play position on either of the two balls, the 13 or 15, on the end rail (Note: the 14-ball was left for later as a key ball). When two balls are close together on the same rail and either or both are frozen to the cushion, you will nearly always need to leave the area and come back later for the second ball.

In this example, you would then play position for the 10 into side pocket #5. It is now time to go back to the end rail to pick off the 15-ball. From here the rest is easy. The 14 and 8-balls present no problems at all.

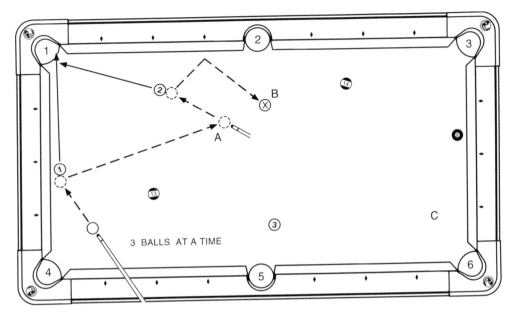

3 BALLS AT A TIME

Three Balls at a Time

You have the freedom to shoot any ball in your group at any time. This does not mean, however, that you should pick off the balls in your group at random. On the contrary, always have a plan in mind. Although it's best if you can establish a plan for the entire rack, at a minimum you should be planning for three balls at a time. Let's see how this works

The 1-ball obviously comes first. But, then what? The 2 or the 3-ball? It will be easiest to play position on the 8-ball using the 3. Therefore, your next shot should be on the 2-ball. If you can get good position on the 2 (A), it will then be easy to play shape on the 3-ball (B). From position B it will be a cinch to send the cue ball to C for the 8-ball.

In this sequence, proper planning insured that this would be an easy run out. And yet, you would be surprised how often average players will fail to get out on a simple rack like this. Improper planning or, worse yet, no planning at all, is often the reason for runout failure. When you are facing a difficult run on a congested table, you simply must have a carefully thought out plan of attack. When the runout looks easy, you should still plan your pattern at least three balls ahead. Take nothing for granted. Seemingly small lapses in concentration can prevent you from finishing off easy tables like the one above.

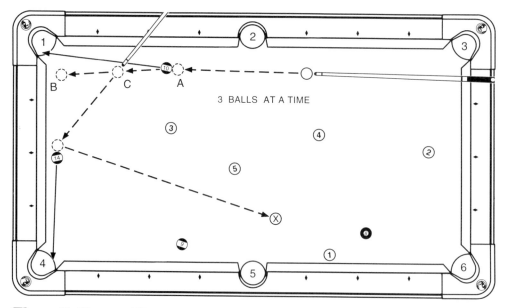

3 BALLS AT A TIME

Three Balls at a Time (II)

Here's another example of the principle of playing three balls ahead. The 10-ball comes first as it's your only open shot. The position of the balls dictates that the 14 should be played next, followed by the 9-ball. Now the sequence has been established. Still, there's the problem of deciding exactly where to leave the cue ball after pocketing the 10-ball.

Option A is to play a stop shot. However, this will leave you with a thin cut on the 14, which will make it difficult to control the cue ball for position on the 9. You could follow the cue ball to position B. Now you would have a straight-in shot which would make it nearly impossible to get good shape on the 9-ball.

Option C is clearly the winner. From this position you can easily send the cue ball to position X for a simple shot on the 9-ball.

It's important to plan at least three balls ahead. Part of the planning process is to establish the proper sequence; what should be shot in what order. Next you need to fine tune your position by determining the best location for the cue ball on each shot. In our example, that means establishing the angle on the 14 that allows you to easily obtain position on the 9-ball. Your runouts will gain consistency and precision when you plan three balls ahead. Choose the sequence. Fine tune the position. Then execute the shot. Plan your work, then work your plan!

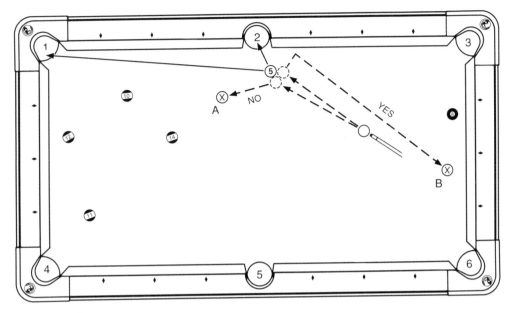

Proper Sequence

All that's left is for you to pocket the 5-ball and the 8 and the game's yours. There are two pockets where you can put the 5, the most obvious being the side pocket. The other is corner pocket #1.

Inexperienced players might make the mistake of automatically playing the easiest shot first. In this example, it would be to pocket the 5-ball in the side, leaving the cue ball at position A. From this spot you would be forced to play a table length bank on the 8 into pocket #1.

The better play is to shoot the 5 into pocket #1 with draw and a little right english. This will bring the cue ball back to position B for an easy shot on the 8. The correct sequence in this example is to play the hard shot first, leaving the easy shot on your game ball. The table below shows why:

Probabilities of Success

Sequence #1		Sequence #2	
5-ball in the side	100%	5-ball in corner	75%
Bank shot on 8-ball	40%	8-ball in corner	100%
Making both balls	40%	Making both balls	75%

Playing sequence #1 your odds of making the 5-ball are quite a bit better. However, when you consider the complete run out, sequence #2 is the winner hands down. It gives you a 75% chance of winning as opposed to 40%. The lesson: Always consider the total picture. Don't just play the easiest shot and hope for the best. Instead play the proper sequence, even if that sometimes means shooting a lower percentage shot.

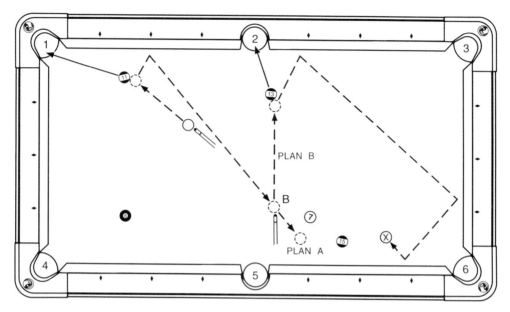

Plan B - Changing a Run Out

You original plan called for playing the 11-ball into pocket #1 and sending the cue ball to position A for shape on the 15. However, we all make mistakes. In this case your cue ball has stopped short at B. Now you must shift gears and switch to plan B, which calls for first playing the 13 into pocket #3 followed by the 15 into pocket #4. The lesson: try to have alternative shots ready and be flexible.

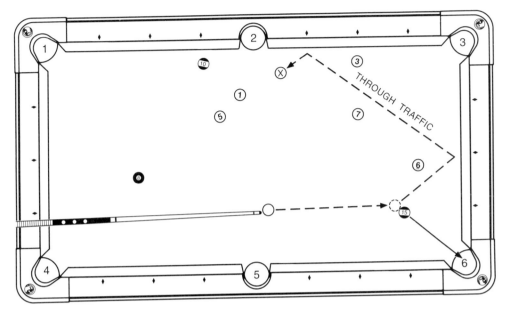

End Game Position: Weaving Through Traffic

All top Eight Ball players are able to move the cue ball through traffic without disturbing other balls. In the example above, you need to sink the 15 and negotiate your way through a labyrinth for position on the 10-ball. This is accomplished by using a soft stroke with a half tip of right english. This will enable you to sidestep the 6-ball and keep you from striking the 3-ball. Good speed control will prevent the cue ball from rolling past position X to behind either the 1 or 5-balls.

This situation comes up repeatedly when you are attempting to run out from the break or when the majority of balls are still on the table. In the early stages of a rack, you often have a choice of several balls to shoot. If you miss position on one ball, you can normally play another ball. Not so at the end of the rack. As you have fewer and fewer balls to choose from and your opponent's balls represent nothing more than a series of potentially troublesome obstacles, the more exacting your position play must become.

You will greatly enhance your ability to work your way through traffic by developing a fine sense of the cue ball's rolling distance, by using english properly off the rails and by planning the cue ball's route carefully. Threading your way through obstacles will enable you to reach the level of a consistent break and run player. Without this skill, you will be limited to finishing off the easy racks after you and your opponent have had one or more cracks at the table.

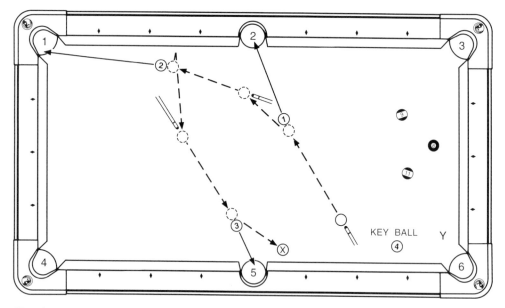

Saving a Key Ball

A key ball is defined as a ball that, when pocketed, allows you to easily get good position on the 8-ball. In the position above, the 8-ball is located behind two of your opponent's stripes. It will still be easy to complete your runout if you save a key ball for the shot before the 8-ball. In the example, the 4-ball is the logical choice.

Even though the 4 is the easiest shot, you should save it for later as your key ball. The 1-ball is played into pocket #2 with a soft follow stroke. This will put you in position to play the 2-ball into pocket #1 and get good shape on the 3-ball. In turn, an easy follow shot on the 3 will set you up for the 4 (the key ball). A soft follow shot will send the cue ball to position Y, giving you a simple shot on the 8-ball.

When playing Eight Ball, take a moment to identify which ball is best suited for playing position on the 8-ball. Now figure out which ball will enable you to get position on the key ball. In many cases, the position of the balls will allow you to plan the entire rack working backwards from the 8. Even if that's not possible, at least try to identify the key ball and a ball before the key ball.

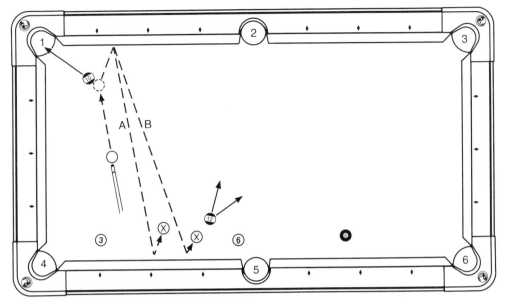

Consider all Six Pockets

Position is not always so obvious, especially when you have few (or only one) balls to play shape on. Matters can be made more difficult when your opponent's balls are blocking one or more pockets. Remember, whenever possible, that you don't want to violate the principle of moving balls around. Most of the time you're better off playing a little tougher shape, rather than knocking balls around and taking potluck.

As part of this philosophy, you will need to stop and consider all six pockets as possible destinations for your next shot. Take the position above. Your must pocket the 10 and then dispose of the 12-ball. But in which pocket? The 3, 6 and 8-balls are all blocking pockets on that side of the table. Don't forget that there are six pockets to choose from. Even though the 12 is less than a diamond from the bottom rail, it can still be made across the table into either pocket #2 or #3.

Line A shows the position route for shape on corner pocket #3, while line B leads to position for the 12 into side pocket #2. As you can see, the position zone for either pocket presents an acceptable target. Good, but not great, speed control will be needed to send the cue ball across the table for position in this area.

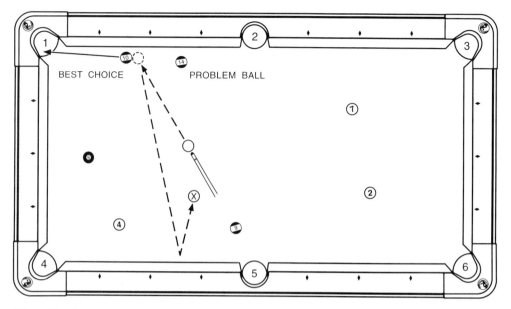

Two Balls to the Same Pocket

It's a good idea to clear pockets for upcoming shots whenever possible. In this diagram, the 10 should be played before the 9-ball. This will clear the pocket for the 14-ball. Failing to clear the shooting lanes can lead to playing combination shots and/or tough, cross table shape, either of which are low percentage shots that lower your odds of winning the game.

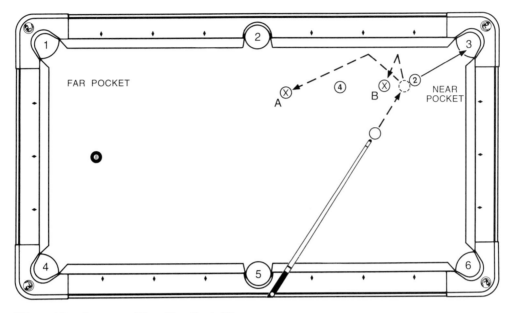

Near Pocket vs. Far Pocket Shape

This 3-ball run looks easy enough. The only question is whether you should play position for the 4-ball into pocket #3 (the same as the 2-ball) or into pocket #1. Although many players prefer to play position for the closer pocket (A), that may not always be the wisest choice. In this example, it should be easy to follow the cue ball softly to position B. From this location you can play the 4 with follow into the far pocket for position on the 8. If you prefer using follow to draw, you'll certainly want to play far pocket shape.

Even players who like to draw may decide to play the 4 into pocket #1. If they get the wrong angle on the 4 while playing shape for pocket #3, it will be very difficult to then play shape on the 8-ball.

On a big table far pocket shape may help you avoid stretching for the cue ball. On a bar table, the distance to the far pocket does not make the shot much more difficult anyway because of the smaller size of the table and the easier pockets.

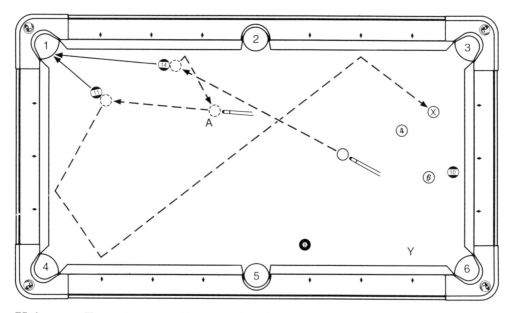

Using an Easy Shot to Play Difficult Shape

To complete your run on the stripes you will need to dispose of the 10-ball which is nestled on the end rail behind two of your opponent's balls. You could shoot the 14 into pocket #1 using draw with right english. This is a tough shot that, if played correctly, would bring the cue ball back to position Y.

A better choice, however, would be to draw the cue back to A for position on the 11. Then play a natural three-railer to position X as diagrammed. This also enables you to achieve your objective of gaining good position on the 10-ball. The big difference, however, is that the 11-ball is a much easier shot than the long draw shot on the 14. By using the 11 to get on the 10 you have greatly reduced the possibility of a missed shot.

Playing tough position requires that you focus heavily on speed control and proper routing of the cue ball. Because of this, your accuracy may suffer. It's a good idea whenever possible (as in our example) to use an easy shot to play more difficult position. Although you must still concentrate on making the ball, the easier shot will permit you to focus on properly executing the remaining components of the shot.

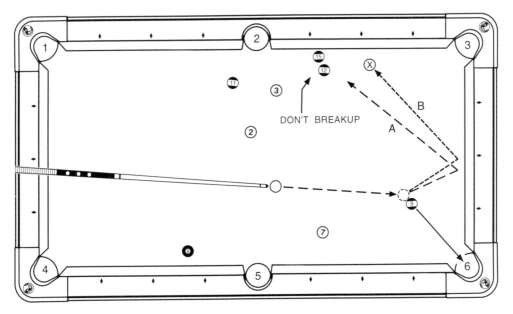

Don't Break up Balls Unnecessarily

Just because two balls are close together does not mean they need to be broken. Some players can't seem to stand the togetherness and opt to put distance between the two balls. This can easily mess up what would otherwise be a simple runout.

The 12 and 15 balls are sitting close together on the side rail. From this position both balls can be made in either pocket #1 or #3. It would be a mistake to pocket the 9 and send the cue ball along line A into the two balls. Although it's possible to marginally improve their position, it's more likely that either or both balls could wind up in a real cluster with your opponent's two balls close by.

A much smarter choice would be to play the balls as they lie. A soft stroke with left english will send the cue ball along line B for ideal position on either ball into the upper left corner pocket.

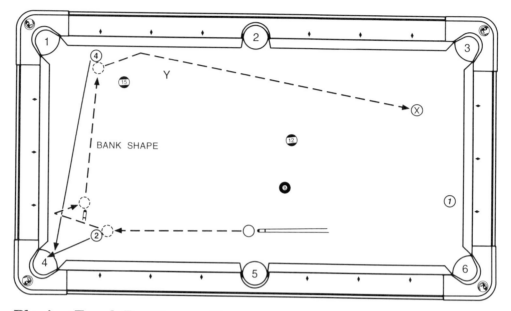

Playing Tough Position on Purpose

Obvious position is, upon further inspection, sometimes obviously wrong. Take the example above. You have the solids and it's your shot.   2-ball is your only open shot, so it comes first. Now for the 4-ball. Many players would make the obvious play; send the cue ball to position Y. While this sets up an easy shot on the 4-ball, it will not be easy to get to the opposite end of the table for the 1-ball. This is especially true if the cue ball and 4-ball are not lined up straight into the pocket or if your draw stroke is weak.

A not so obvious pattern can make this a relatively easy run out. Play the 2-ball with a soft follow stroke to setup a cross corner bank shot on the 4-ball. Now play the 4 with draw and right english. The cue ball will travel down the table as diagrammed for perfect shape on the 1, allowing you to complete the runout.

The bank shot is somewhat tougher than the straight in from position Y. In this case, however, it's worth playing a little tougher shot for perfect position on the 1-ball.

The position in this diagram is but another reminder of the importance of planning three balls ahead. Always consider the total run out, not isolated segments. Remember to look beyond the obvious play when your first choice may not get the job done.

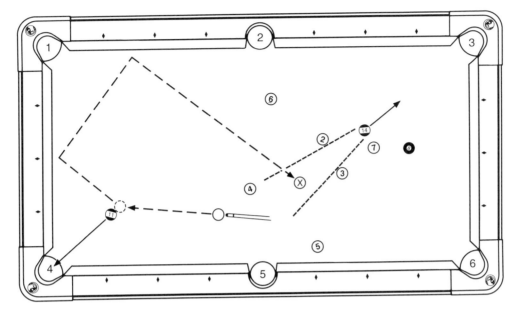

Playing for a Roll and Position

Occasionally you will be faced with a very difficult position play at the end of a game when your opponent still has several balls remaining. In the position above, you will need to stroke the cue ball at near perfect speed in order to stop it in the extremely small position zone indicated. If you hit the cue ball too soft or too hard, you will be left without a shot on the 14-ball.

Should you miss getting position, you will almost certainly spend the rest of the game watching your opponent run out as you sit praying for him/her to commit a blunder.

There's nothing much you can do in the situation above except execute a near perfect shot. In this example, you should carefully observe the location and boundaries of your intended target zone before taking your stance. Imagine the speed you'll need to send the cue ball there, visualize your target and execute your shot. Be sure to follow your regular routine. Don't hurry the shot. Take the time necessary to insure successful execution.

On shots like this, you simply must rise to the occasion. Play the shot with all the skill and confidence you can muster. Remember also that position plays like these are part skill, part luck.

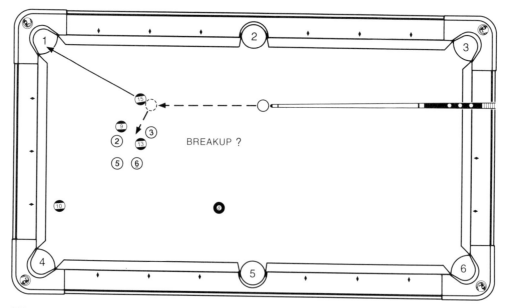

Playing for a Roll on a Breakout

This position appears with some regularity when the balls are not breaking very well. You have a break shot on the 15-ball that should separate both your and your opponent's balls. It's impossible to tell exactly what you'll get from a break shot like this. You could position yourself for a runout, get hooked, recluster the balls elsewhere or worse, set up your opponent's balls for a runout.

Before breaking the cluster, carefully measure the risk versus the possible reward. Also consider the alternative, which is to play safe. Which do you prefer when neither side has a clearcut advantage? An aggressive or defensive strategy? Your opponent's game may also help give you the answer. For example, if he/she is tough to beat in safety battles, you may want to go for the runout.

Just keep in mind that there are no guarantees when you break a cluster like this. Be thankful if things work out as you hope; don't be surprised if they don't.

Defensive Play

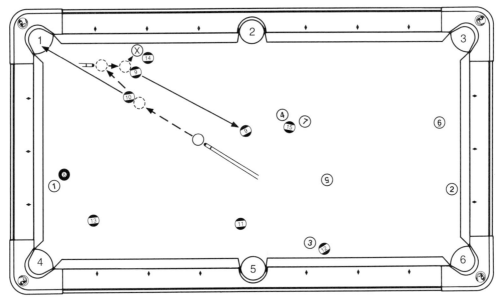

Stake your Claim! - Then Play Safe

Your opponent has failed to make a ball on the break so you now have the choice of solids or stripes. Your assessment of this mess should tell you that a run out is highly unlikely whichever group you select. If you can't run out, what should you do? The first thing should be to determine which group offers the least trouble spots.

The solids look terrible. The 1-ball is tied up with the 8 and the 3 is clustered with the 12. Furthermore, the 2 and 6 are close together on the end rail and the 4 and 7 are clustered with the 15-ball.

Even though the stripes can't be run, they pose far fewer problems. The 12 and 15-balls are clustered with your opponent's balls and the 8 will need to be separated from the 1-ball.

Under these circumstances, you would be wise to choose the stripes. But since you can't run out, your next move is to stake your claim to the stripes. Because a run is not possible you should then play a safety. It would be a mistake to continue pocketing balls that you'll need for various purposes later in the game.

In the position above, a soft follow shot on the 10 gives you the stripes. Now play a safety by sending the cue ball behind the 14-ball. The 9-ball is now in position to serve as a break ball on the 4/7/15 cluster. In addition, you have severely limited your opponent's response. He/she will probably have to kick to hit the 1-ball which will free up the 8, solving one of your problems in the process.

There's no law that states that you must try to run out after making the first ball of your group. If neither group can be run, but one still looks better than the other, stake your claim, then play the best safety you can.

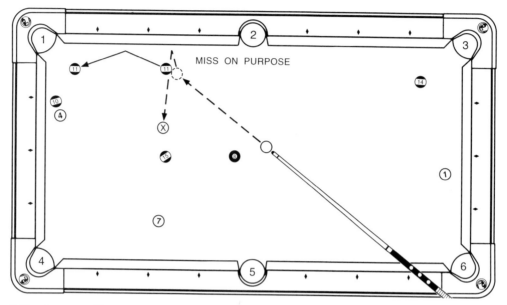

MISS ON PURPOSE

Missing on Purpose

This diagram illustrates a strategy that goes against the grain for many players. Yet, a top player would not hesitate to use this tactic if they thought it gave them their best shot at winning.

Here's the situation: you have the stripes and it's your turn. The 4/10 cluster will keep you from running out unless it's broken. None of your balls is ideally suited for this purpose. The good news is that your opponents's balls are in worse shape.

Because you lack a good break shot, now is the time to manufacture one. You can do this by shooting the 11-ball softly down near the corner pocket. That's right. Your best strategy is to miss the 11 on purpose as it will prove to be much more valuable as a break ball for the 4/10 cluster.

The lesson: if you can't complete a run, do something better with your balls that will increase your chances of running out on another turn.

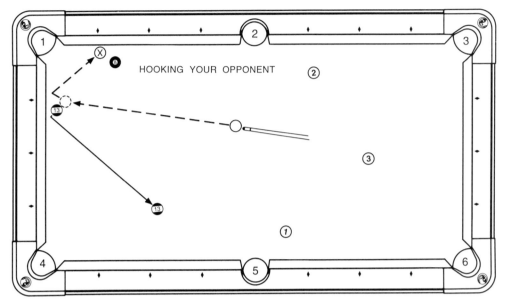

Hooking Your Opponent

The hook shot can be a powerful weapon, even when you are greatly outnumbered. Although you have no reasonable shot and only one remaining ball, you can gain the upper hand by sending the cue ball behind the 8-ball as diagrammed. Even if your opponent makes a good hit on a difficult kick shot, you will probably wind up with a good shot at your 13-ball.

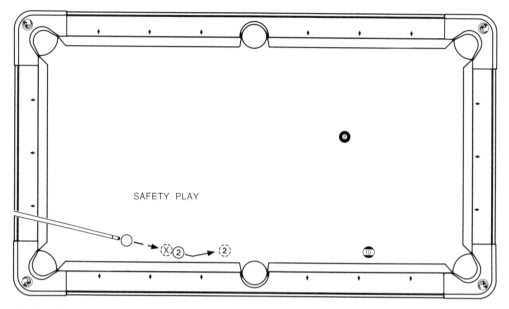

SAFETY PLAY

Soft Hit Safety

In this position, the only shot you have is a very difficult crossover bank to the opposite side pocket. You should pass on this low percentage shot and instead play the devilish little safety shown in the diagram. A very soft hit directly into the 2 will keep your ball in front of the cue ball. And don't mind the comments of less knowledgeable players who might complain about defensive maneuvers like this. It's a legal shot, after all.

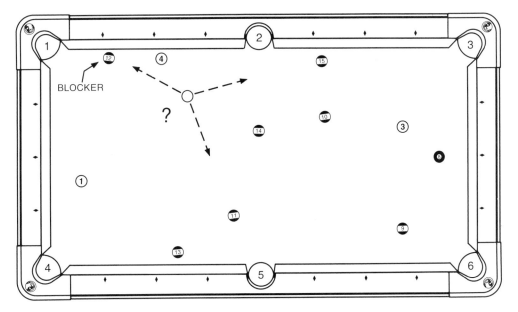

Keeping a Blocker in Place

The pressure sometimes has a way of building up during a run as you get closer and closer to the end of the game. In this position you have your entire group of stripes plus the 8-ball to run.

It would be best to start your run with the 12 ball due to the positioning of the other balls. However, if you are not brimming with confidence, perhaps you could leave the 12-ball for later. You can then begin your run with greater confidence because you know that the 12 will likely keep your opponent from running out should you miss. Then, after getting a rhythm going, you can come back to the 12 when you have only two or three balls left.

The position of the balls gives you the option to play your blocker (the 12-ball) or leave it for later. Your state of mind and the layout can affect your decision making. This example also demonstrates that players of differing abilities may approach a rack with a different pattern or plan for running the balls. A professional player would shoot the 12-ball first. However, a lesser player should not be ashamed to adopt a more defensive approach.

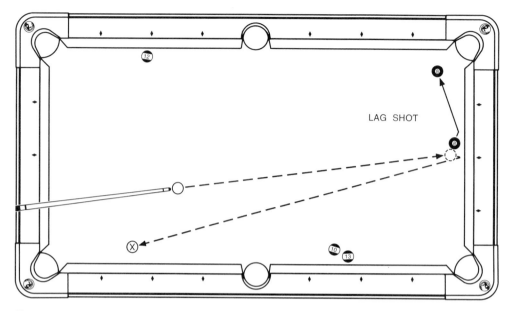

Lagging the Eight Ball on a Tough Shot

You have been left with an extremely difficult cut shot on the 8-ball. Despite your best efforts, a miss is highly probable. So why not purposely miss it, placing it where you can make it on your next turn? Your opponent's cluster should keep him /her from running out.   On top of this, it will be nearly impossible for your opponent to play safe. Keep in mind that even though the 8 is the game ball, you may get more than one crack at it.

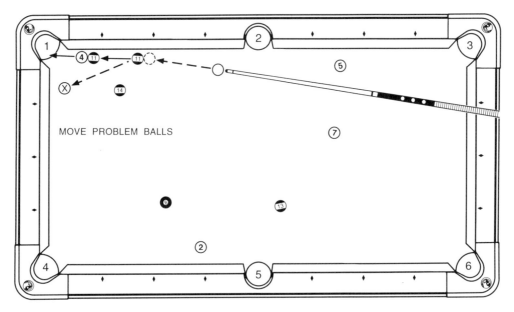

MOVE PROBLEM BALLS

Unblocking Pockets and Playing Safe

You have the stripes in the position above. Although you have a clear shot at the 13-ball, you should pass on this shot as it leads nowhere. Your opponent's 4-ball will keep you from completing your run as it is blocking the pocket on the 11 and 14 balls.

Even though your opponent appears to have the upper hand, you can quickly turn the tables by shooting his/her 4-ball into the pocket with the 11-ball. A soft follow stroke with a half tip of left english will send the cue ball down behind your 14-ball. This diabolical maneuver will enable you to accomplish several objectives at once; removal of the blocker, the 11 is now positioned near the pocket and your opponent is hooked.

Some players may balk at the idea of intentionally making an opponent's ball. However, it is often your best play when a blocker stands in the way of you pocketing your balls. You're heard this message before and you'll hear it again: winning Eight-Ball is largely a matter of playing smart; of playing the exact shot the situation calls for. If you can't bring yourself to play strategically solid shots such as the one above, you will continue to lose games that you could have easily won. Let me emphasize that the strategies and safeties as recommended are all legal shots.

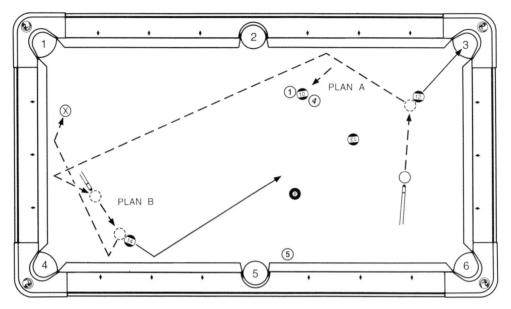

Plan B - Abandoning a Run Out

You must now bite the bullet as your attempt to break out the 10-ball has misfired. Your best bet now is to turn the table over to your opponent rather than attempting some off-the-wall heroic shot that might result in selling out the game. Play safe off the 14 as indicated, leaving your opponent a long tough shot on the 5-ball.

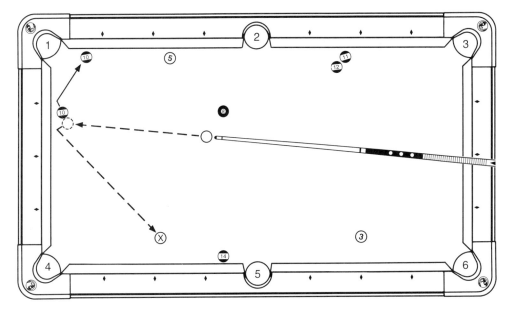

Blocking Pockets

You have no makeable shot in the position above. In addition, your opponent's balls (3 and 5) are in the clear. Now is the time to create some problems for your opponent by blocking access to pocket # 1 for his/her 5-ball. The key to this safety is to lag the 10-ball softly so that it dies near the top rail. The cue ball has ended up at position X. Your opponent has a clear shot at the 3-ball, but it will be nearly impossible for him/her to run both the 3 and 5-balls because of the bock you've established.

Good strategy sometimes dictates leaving your opponent a good shot, as long as he/she will not be in a position to run the rest of the rack. Positive blocking in front of pockets is one of the best ways to implement this strategy.

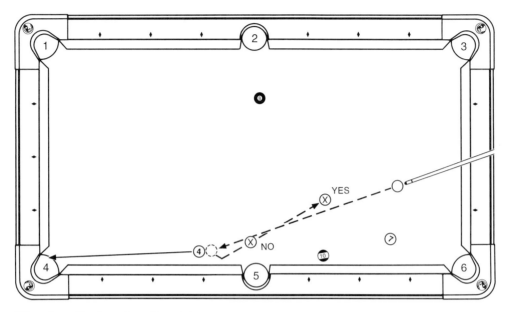

Playing Defensive Position

It's often wise to exercise some cautious optimism on longer shots. In the position above, you have a table length cut shot on the 4-ball, and next comes the 7 and 8. You could play the 4 with a modest amount of draw, leaving the cue ball at the position labeled NO. Notice that if you miss the 4, your opponent will have an easy shot on his/her last ball, the 10. A more defensive approach is to apply a little extra draw, bringing the cue ball back to the position labeled YES. You now have an easy shot on the 7 to complete your run. Furthermore, should you miss the 4, your opponent will not have a reasonable shot on the 10 as the 8-ball is blocking a cross-side bank.

Play each shot with all the confidence you can muster, taking into account the position in which you leave your opponent in the unlikely, but possible, event that you miss the shot.

Shotmaking

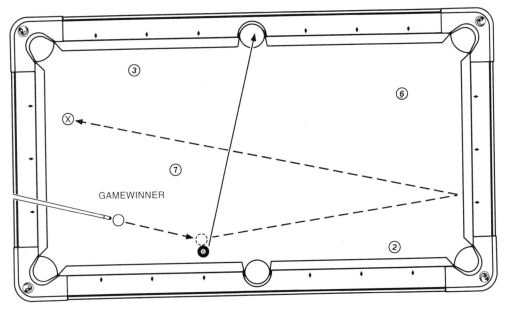

Game-Winning Shots

Eight Ball is normally considered a game of strategy and position play. However, it also pays to be able to successfully execute a wide variety of specialty shots as these can bail you out of tough situations. For example, take the position above. Your opponent has left you with a crossover bank shot into the opposite side pocket. This is not an exceptionally difficult shot. There are players who might make this shot seven times out of ten while others may be successful on only two or three attempts in ten. Obviously your skill at pocketing uncommon shots like this will translate into victories that could swing the outcome of a close match in your favor.

The chapter on shotmaking covers a number of useful shots that can help you win games. Included are sections on combinations, bank shots, billiards and caroms. These shots will enable you to sidestep many of your opponent's safeties and to make up for deficiencies in your position play.

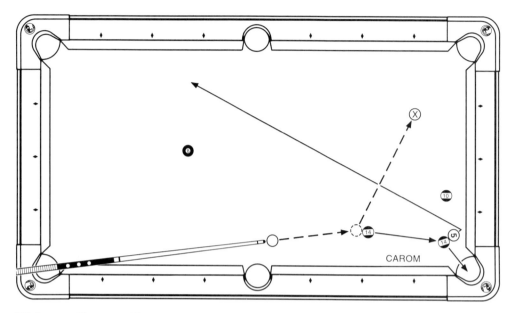

CAROM

Using a Carom Shot to Remove a Blocker

In this position you could easily play the 14-ball directly into the corner pocket. However, you will be left without a shot on the 10-ball, as your opponent's 5-ball is blocking access to the pocket. It's time to get creative. The 14 can be caromed off the 5-ball and into the pocket. This will eliminate the 5-ball, giving you a clear shot on the 10-ball into the same pocket.

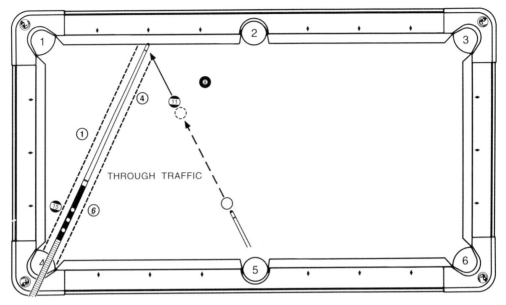

Lining up Banks Through Traffic

The crowded quarters you may encounter during a game of Eight Ball may leave you with nothing but a bank shot. You will need to determine if your proposed bank shot can "go" past one or more of your and/or your opponent's balls.

It's your shot on the stripes in the position above. The 4-ball is blocking the 11 from pocket #1. The 8 is blocking pockets #2 and #5 (a cross side bank). Now is the time to consider banking the 11 into pocket #4. However, it looks as though any of four balls (1,4,6,15) could stand in the way. Before shooting, take the time to plot the exact path of the 11 to see if it will avoid the obstructing balls.

You will recall from our discussion on shotmaking, the section on calculating the contact point on the rail for bank shots. To refresh your memory, the contact point on the first rail is the top side of an isosceles triangle. The two equal sides extend to the target pocket and up to another point up the rail (review How to Measure a Bank Shot-Chapter 3).

Your first step is to calculate the contact point on the top rail (in this diagram, the second diamond). Now place the tip of your cue stick on the rail at the second diamond and hold the butt end over the corner pocket. If the <u>assorted</u> object balls are far enough away from the cue, then you have a channel for the object ball to pass through. The channel must be at least 2½ to 3 inches wide to allow for the full width of the object ball. Therefore, you'd like to have 1 1/4 to 1 3/4 inches on either side of the cue for ample clearance. Don't forget that bank shots are affected by speed, english and the condition of the rails. These must all be factored into your calculations.

Breaking Balls Apart

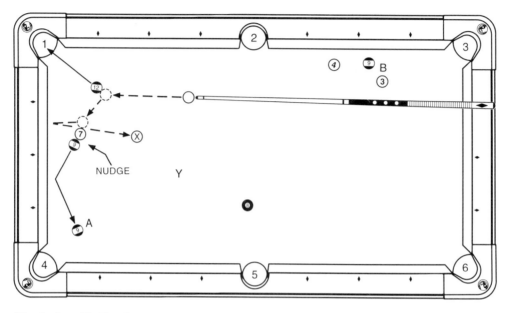

Nudging Balls Apart

Two ball clusters like the 7/9 above need only be tapped lightly to separate the balls. If you can contact the first ball (the 7) thinly, using a soft stroke, the second ball (the 9) will travel only a short distance. In our example the 9 relocated to position A. It will now be an easy shot into pocket #4.

The purpose of a breakshot is to separate the clustered balls in preparation for a subsequent shot. Therefore, you should plan the break keeping the resulting position of the balls in mind. All to often inexperienced players will slam into a cluster, creating new problems in the process. For example, if the 7 had been struck excessively hard (B), the 9-ball may have traveled to the opposite end rail amongst your opponent's balls.

Of course, there are exceptions to the rule. On occasion you may need to apply extra force to a break shot. For example, if your opponent had another ball in front of pocket #4, you would need to send the 9-ball out to position Y to avoid your opponent's blocker. Each break shot must be evaluated on a case by case basis. But keep in mind that most of the time a soft hit will give you the best contact and position on the break out ball.

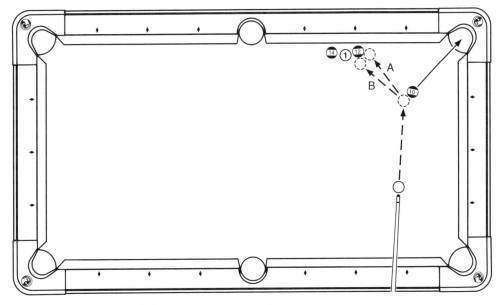

Breaking a Tight Cluster on the Rail

Multiple ball clusters on the rails can be very frustrating. You can set up the perfect break shot, hit the cluster with sufficient force to scatter the balls, and yet have the balls remain clustered. This usually occurs due to the dreaded double kiss, when the cue ball strikes the contact ball at an angle that causes the object ball to bounce off the cushion right back into the cue ball, resulting in a trapped object ball.

The diagram shows an ideally positioned break shot. When breaking a cluster like this some force is required, but the initial point of contact is crucial. In this situation, the cue ball should contact the right half of the 12-ball. This will drive the 12-ball directly into the other two balls, easily separating the cluster.

It would be a mistake to hit the left side of the 12-ball (B). This could create a double kiss and the cluster would probably remain intact.

When a precision hit is needed, it is best to have a break ball that is fairly close to the cluster. When you are close (but not too close) to your work, you can fine tune the cue ball's path to the contact ball by cheating the pocket, using draw, follow or center ball, varying your stroke speed, and by applying english. In our example, you could use any of these techniques (alone or in combination) to allow you to contact the 12-ball precisely where required.

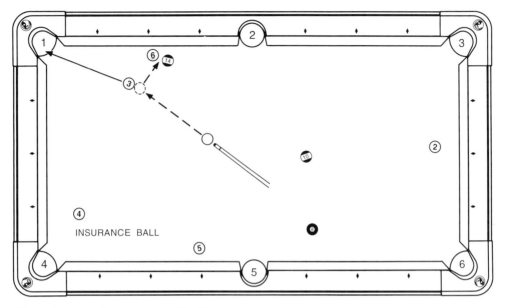

Keeping an Insurance Ball

You have the solids and it's your shot. The 6-ball is tied up with the 14-ball. However, it can be broken apart right now by shooting the 3-ball into pocket #1. It's very possible that you won't have a good shot on the 6-ball immediately following the breakout. In addition, the 2 and 5-balls are not likely candidates for your next shot. Fortunately, the 4-ball is positioned nearby and is out in front of the pocket. Barring a total disaster you should have an easy shot at the 4-ball after the break shot.

In this example, the 4-ball acts as your insurance policy. To insure you have makeable shot after breaking up a cluster, it's always a good idea to have a guaranteed next shot when shooting break shots. When you're making plans to break a cluster, try to locate an insurance ball. And, of course, don't make the common mistake of pocketing that ball prior to the break shot.

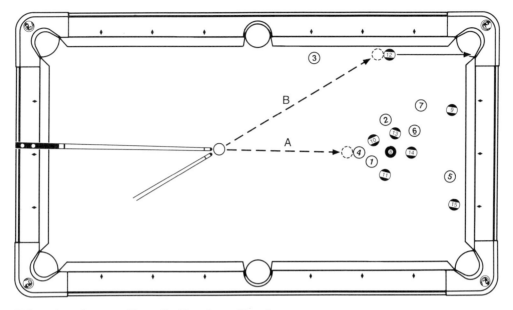

Blasting into a Poorly Broken Rack

The highly congested position above is as a result of a very weak break. Some players like to blast the balls apart (A) in this position, even though they receive no credit for any balls that are slopped into the pockets. The main reason for employing this tactic is to speed up the game when playing a much weaker opponent and to reposition the balls so that a runout is more likely. Another reason for blasting the balls is impatience, a winning player's main enemy.

The big worry, when blasting a rack, is sinking the 8-ball for an automatic loss. Once the balls are in motion a multitude of unimagined collisions could lead directly to this unhappy result. So if you choose to blast a rack when the 8-ball is in the cluster, take great care to evaluate the chances of it squirting out of the cluster and into a pocket.

If there is a break ball available, such as the 12-ball (B), some players will slam it into the corner pocket and try to spread the rack. Using this approach can also lead to pocketing of the 8-ball out of turn. In addition, the ball will often be missed because the player has shot too hard.

When you are faced with a rack like this in competition, your best bet is to play it cozy and wait for an opening to develop. Racks like this are good for testing your patience and honing your safety skills. They can also teach you much about your opponent's reaction to a tense situation.

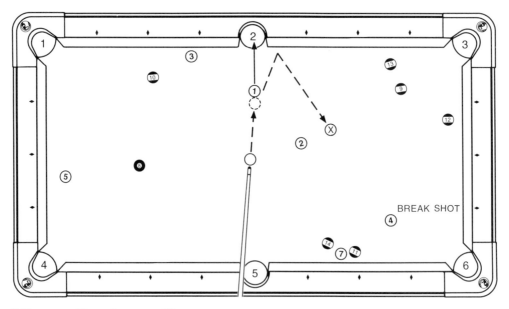

When to Break up a Cluster

Clusters should be broken at the right time, usually as soon as possible. If you wait until later in the rack, you may not have a shot. In the diagram, you are shooting the solids. The 7-ball is clustered with two of your opponent's balls. The 4-ball is the logical choice as a break ball. To start your run, you can use the 1-ball to play position on the mildly troublesome 3-ball. However, your top priority is to break that cluster. A follow shot on the 1-ball can set you up to free your 7-ball as shown.

The beauty of breaking clusters early is that you then have a choice of balls to shoot after the break shot. In this example, your next shot should be the 2-ball into pocket #2. However, the 11-ball may wind up blocking the 2-ball. You could, therefore, wind up playing the 7-ball into pocket #4 or the 3-ball into pocket #1.

On most break shots there is often an element of risk that can't be avoided. However, you can improve your chances of completing your run by following the rule of thumb that says to break out the ball(s) as soon as possible.

Kick Shot Strategy

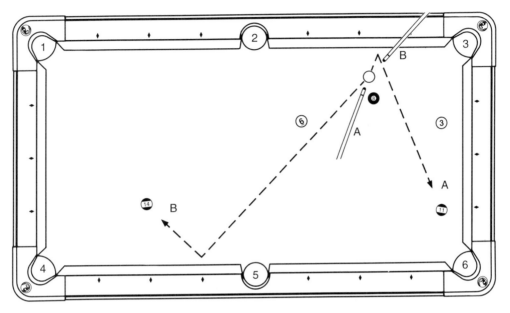

Which Ball to Kick for

It's your turn and you're shooting at the stripes. You must choose between two kick shots. The easiest ball to pocket is the 11 (A). Let's say the odds of hitting the 11 are high while your chances of kicking it into pocket #6 are fairly low. The odds of hitting the 14-ball are not as high as the 11 and the odds of kicking it into pocket #1 are even lower.

The 11-ball is easier to hit and you have a much better chance of making it. Yet the 14-ball is your best shot. The reason is you must always think defense when playing a kick shot. You must consider the outcome if you fail to either make contact with or pocket the ball.

If you fail to pocket the 11, you will leave your opponent an easy shot on the 3-ball. With option B, all you really need to do is hit the 14-ball. This will leave your opponent with a long, thin cut on the 3-ball or, with any luck no shot at all.

When making a choice, don't always shoot the easiest kick shot. Always consider how you can leave your opponent as tough as possible.

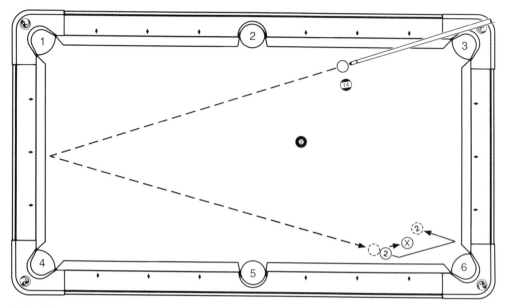

The Lag Kick Shot

It looks like you're in serious trouble in the position above as you are hooked behind the 14-ball. However, you can quickly seize the advantage by successfully executing a lag kick shot. Shoot the cue ball with a soft stroke along the diagrammed pathway. Your objective is to softly hit the 2-ball so that it will come to rest in front of pocket #6. Ideally you will now have an easy shot from just about anywhere on the table. If you are lucky, you might even pocket the 2-ball, and go on to sink the game-winning 8-ball.

Notice in the position above that you have left the cue ball at position X. The 8-ball prevents your opponent from banking the 14 into pocket #5. On top of this, he/she will have a tough time playing a return safety.

The key to this shot was shooting the cue ball softly enough to prevent it from setting your opponent up on his/her 14-ball in the event you missed your 2-ball shot.

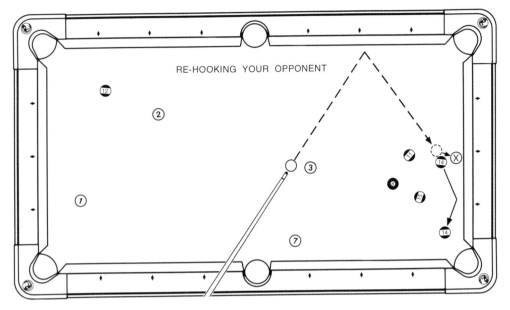

RE-HOOKING YOUR OPPONENT

Soft Kick Safety

In this position you can turn the tables by rehooking your opponent. Use a very soft stroke. Your goals are to gently contact the 14-ball, hit a rail, and leave the cue ball behind a wall of blockers (8,11,15). Don't get greedy in a situation like this and try to pocket a ball. Instead, think soft stroke, accurate hit, and defense. After all, this layout is custom made for hooking your opponent.

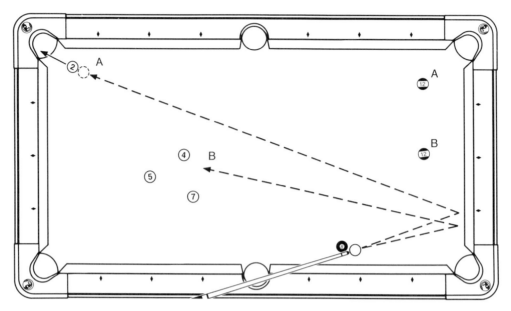

Kicking to a Group

This position is not much fun as you are snookered behind the 8-ball and all of your solids are at the opposite end of the table. The diagram illustrates two possible scenarios, both of which depend on the location of your opponent's 12-ball.

With the 12-ball in front of the pocket at position A, you are forced to go for the 2-ball. No matter which ball you hit in your group, if you don't make it, your opponent will likely have an easy shot on the 12. So, shoot the most makeable ball in your group, the two.

Now let's look at position B. In this case your priorities have changed considerably. Your goal now is to simply make contact with <u>any</u> ball in your group and avoid giving your opponent cue ball in hand. As long as you can meet the requirements of a legal safety and keep the cue ball at the opposite end of the table, your opponent will have an extremely difficult bank or cut shot on the 12. Therefore, in position B you should play to make contact with any of your balls. This is best done by aiming at a group of balls. The 4, 5, and 7-balls provide you with a very wide target that would be awfully tough to miss. Because you are now playing defensively, you are no longer forced into going for the 2-ball as was the case in position A.

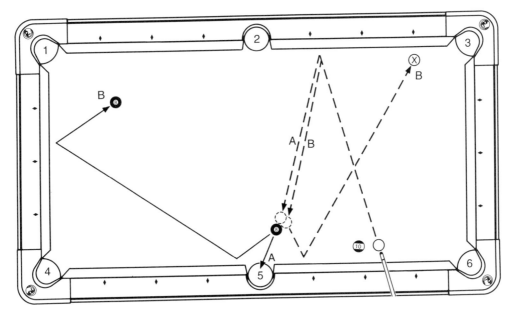

The Forced Kick Shot

Basically it's do or die on this shot as you are forced to kick the 8-ball into pocket #5 as shown by path A. If you can pull this shot off it's great. However, should you miss, it would be best to overcut the 8, sending it to position B. This would, in turn, leave your opponent a bank shot or a difficult safe. This shot demonstrates the principle of missing to a specific side of the target for defensive purposes.

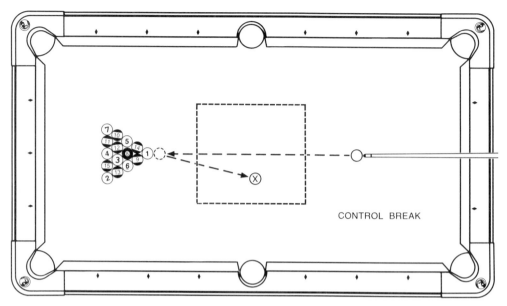

The Control Break Shot

The cue ball is struck slightly below center with a level cue. Use a smooth stroke with a definite snap of the wrist and be sure to follow through. The cue ball is placed on the middle of the head string, although some players prefer to break from off-center. Concentrate on hitting the 1-ball squarely. If executed properly, the cue ball will wind up in the dashed box.

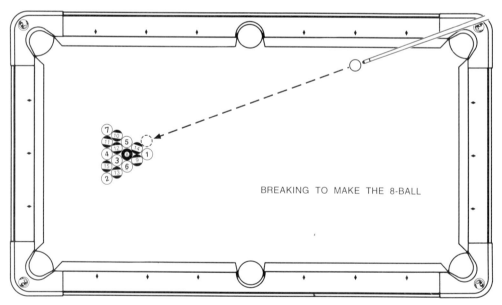

Breaking to Make the 8-Ball

This break creates more movement on the 8-ball, as it will sometimes shoot out of the rack, occasionally into either side pocket. A full, or nearly full hit on the second ball (in this example, the 14) is required. It's harder to control the cue ball on this break.

CHAPTER 7

NINE BALL

Putting Together All Of The Elements Of A Winning Game

Nine ball is pool played at fast forward. Combination shots, caroms, billiards, slop shots and nine balls on the break can all bring the game to a sudden and heart thumping conclusion. Because of this fast-paced action, Nine Ball has become America's second most popular pool game after Eight Ball. Televised pro tournaments (both men and women's) have spurred the game's growth.

Newer players love to "ride the cash" and view nine ball largely as a game of luck. At the other end of the spectrum, Nine Ball, at a professional level, makes extraordinary demands on a player's game. The pros control the cue ball with great precision. In addition, they have powerful breaks, play brutal safeties and are mentally tough. It's no accident that the same players' names appear over and over in the winner's circle.

The rules of the game are very straightforward. The balls are played in chronological order and the player pocketing the 9-ball on a legal shot wins the game. You can win at any time by pocketing the 9 as long as you make contact with the lowest numbered ball first. Unlike 8-ball, the rules of Nine Ball seem to be more uniform. The most popular set of rules, Texas Express, allow ball in hand to a player on any foul committed by an opponent. Three consecutive fouls result in an automatic loss of the game. No balls are respotted after a foul except for the 9-ball. As you may expect, these rules contribute to a fast paced game.

Shotmaking

To succeed at Nine Ball, you must be an excellent shotmaker. Thin cut shots, banks, and long shots are commonplace in any given Nine Ball game and must be part of any player's repertoire. Some critics complain that Nine Ball overemphasizes shotmaking. The truth is that, although you must excel in all areas, position play is undoubtedly the most critical feature to playing the game. Above average shotmaking ability will get you out of trouble spots and occasionally win a game for you but without consistent position play you will never excel at Nine Ball.

It helps to view shotmaking realistically. Your first goal should be to make all your easy shots. You should also expect to make a high percentage of your makeable shots. Lastly, on tough shots, your objective should be to aim and stroke the shot as well as possible. With these goals firmly entrenched, you will learn to concentrate on the easier shots and feel less pressure on the tough shots. It will also help if you are familiar with the percentages for each shot; strategically this will prevent you attempting shots that can set up your opponent for an easy win.

Develop your shotmaking skills through drills and practice as this will increase your confidence on the table. Don't forget, however, that your shotmaking ability will probably vary from day to day. This will assist you in your shot selection. Be sure to pass on sucker shots. These include shots that are too difficult, not just for you, but for anybody, shots that lead nowhere , and shots that lead to certain loss.

Winning Nine Ball

Winning Nine Ball is a blend of a number of essential elements. The list below can serve as your guide to assembling a game that will enable you to compete at a very high level. Unfortunately, there are no short cuts. If you truly wish to master Nine Ball, make each item on this list an integral part of your game.

Position Play

- Executing the basic position plays.
- Learning to play tough position consistently.
- Pattern play - planning your runouts.
- Playing the correct angle.
- Staying on the right side of the cue ball.
- Playing for at least three balls at a time.

Shotmaking

- Basic shotmaking.

- Tough shots you must master: long shots, cut shots, combos, banks, billiards, jump shots, off the rail jacked-up shots.

- Game winning shots under pressure.

- Knowledge of your shot percentages.

The Break

- Power break.

- Controlling the break - consistency, avoiding scratching

- Playing shape off the break.

Push-out Strategy

- Knowing your opponent's skills and tendencies.

- Pushing out to a shot.

- Pushing out to a safety.

- When not to push out.

Safety Play

- Playing tough hook safeties.

- Leaving tough safeties.

- Leaving tough shots.

Kick Shots

- Kicking to hit (the luck factor).

- Kicking to play safe.

- Kicking to make the ball.

Strategy

- How to adjust to the competition.

- Adapting your strategy to your current level of play.

- Adapting to the table.

- Minimizing the impact of mistakes.

- How to maximize ball in hand.

- Finding the proper balance between defense and offense.

- Playing the table - not forcing shots.

- Assessing the rack correctly.

The Intangibles

- Confidence.

- Competitiveness.

- Heart.

- Creativity - Imagination

Adjusting to the Competition

Players of varying skill levels will approach a game of nine ball with many different strategies. A match between two "C" players will probably feature a number of shots at the money ball. These same players will probably attempt a runout only when there are five or less balls left on the table. In contrast, two "A" players will play more safeties and try to runout from the 1-ball.

Certain strategies make sense when two players are competing on more or less even terms. However, you may occasionally find yourself competing against an opponent who is either more or less skilled than yourself. This may dictate a change from your normal strategy. For example, if you are a "C" player who normally competes against "Cs", you'll play one way. However, if you are matched upagainst a "B" player in a tournament, you may wish to play more safeties, especially early in the game. At the same time, if you are a "C" playing a money game against a "B" player who is giving you an extra money ball (or two), you may be wise to ride the money balls at every opportunity.

An "A" player up against a fellow "A" player will try to leave his/her opponent as tough as possible, which usually means hooking the opponent in hopes of getting ball in hand. Furthermore, an "A" player may be reluctant to leave another "A" with anything to work with on a push out. However, when an "A" plays a "C", the strategy changes. Against a "C", the "A" may be able to get away with leaving a tough shot on a push out because he /she knows it is unlikely the "C" player will make the shot, much less runout on the entire rack.

No matter your level of play, try to devise a game plan that's suited to your opponent. This could include more safeties and/or more shots at the money ball. Whatever it takes. By playing smart pool you will increase your winning percentage no matter who you come up against.

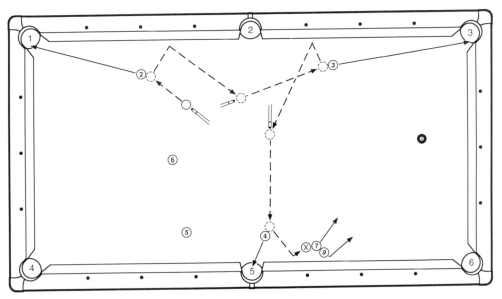

Planning to Break a Cluster

Upon examining the layout above it becomes obvious that the 7/9 cluster could keep you from completing your runout. The time to start planning for this trouble spot is now, before you've pocketed another ball.

The 4-ball is best positioned for the break because it is close to the side pocket and the cluster. That increases your chances of achieving three objectives with one shot:

> Pocket the 4-ball
> Break up the 7/9 cluster
> Get position on the next ball (the 5)

The key to a successful breakout is getting good position on the 4-ball so that you can cut it into the side and have the cue ball proceed into the cluster. The correct positioning of the cue ball is shown in the diagram.

Working backwards, you must now determine what position on the 3-ball will allow you to maneuver the cue ball to the chosen position for the 4. You can best achieve your objective by cutting the 3 into pocket #3 and having the cue ball come off the cushion and back for perfect shape on the 4. Your work would be much tougher, if not impossible, if the cue ball was located on the other side of the 3 over near pocket #2. Now for the 2-ball. The cue ball must be played off the top rail and out far enough to give you the correct angle on the 3-ball.

Now let's execute the run to the breakout. The 2-ball goes into pocket #1 and the cue ball has arrived at the perfect angle for the 3. The 3-ball goes into pocket #3 with the cue ball coming back out for just the right angle on the 4. The 4-ball is played into pocket #5 with just enough force to nudge the 7/9 apart. The cue ball is in good position for the 5-ball into pocket #4.

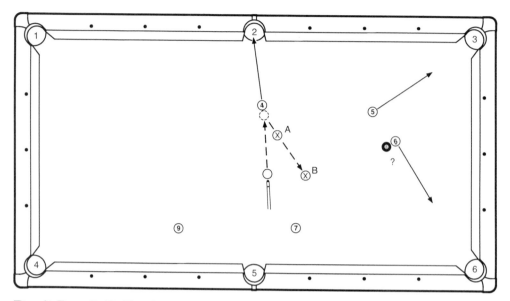

Don't Break Balls that Don't Need to be Broken

It would be a mistake to draw back to position A, even though this would allow you to break up the 6 and 8-ball. You're much better off to draw back to position B and play the 5 in pocket #3 while leaving the cluster alone. The 6 can be made in pocket #6. Therefore, there is no need to send the 6 and 8 to unknown locations that could disrupt your runout.

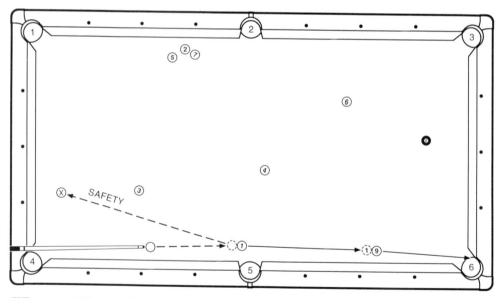

When to Play a Tough Combo

The 1/9 combination is not easy. However, it is your best shot in this position. The 2/5/7 cluster will help prevent your opponent from running out if you miss the 1/9 combination. A defensive strategy is to draw the cue ball back to X behind the 3-ball. If you miss the combo, your opponent may be facing a hook and a cluster that needs separating.

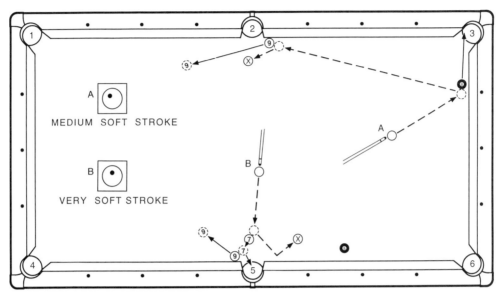

Moving a Trouble Ball

Balls on the rail next to the side pocket can be difficult to pocket and to play good shape on. In position A you can easily control the cue ball's path which enables you to get a better shot on the 9. Don't overlook the chance to carom the 7 into the side pocket, off the 9, in position B so you won't be required to play perfect shape on the 9.

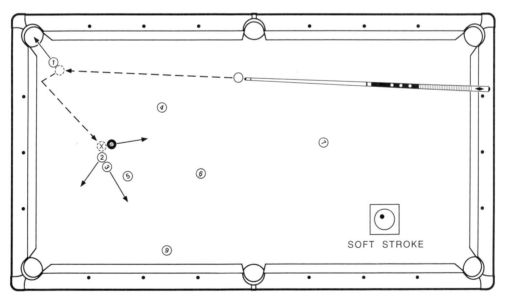

Breaking up a Cluster in Traffic

Sometimes a soft stroke and precision cue ball control can enable you to achieve the best results when breaking apart multiple ball clusters. In the example, if you can hit right between the 2 and 8-balls, the cluster will break apart as indicated. You should be left with a shot on the 2-ball into the lower left corner pocket. Remember, it's precision over power.

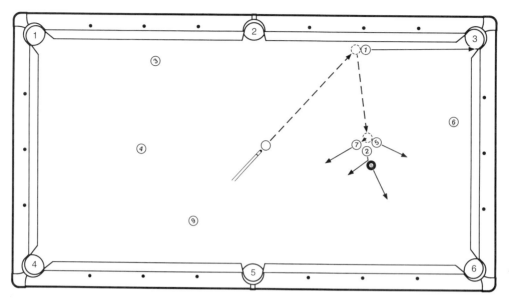

Playing for a Roll on a Breakout

From this position you can shoot the 1-ball into pocket #3 and proceed directly into the 4-ball cluster. At the worst, you should have a safety to play because the 2 will be traveling to an open part of the table. First calculate your odds of getting hooked when playing for a roll on a breakout. If they are high, pass on the breakout and play safe instead.

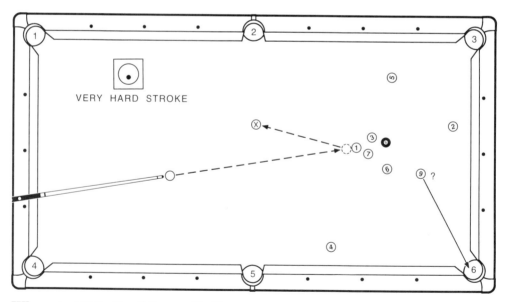

When to Ride the Money Ball

This position can come as a result of a poorly broken rack. If you are playing an opponent who poses little threat of running out, or if you feel like occasionally taking a whack at the balls just to break up the routine, then this is as good a time as any. Use a very hard stroke and draw the cue ball back, almost like you're playing another break shot.

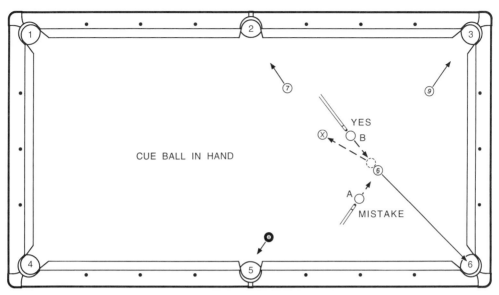

When to Pass on a Combo

With cue ball in hand this four ball runout is about as easy as they come. And yet, some players will get greedy (or lazy) and instead place the cue ball at position A and shoot the 6/9 combo into pocket #3. The lesson: don't be in a hurry to get the game over. Play the percentages (position B), which in this case, <u>heavily</u> favor the runout.

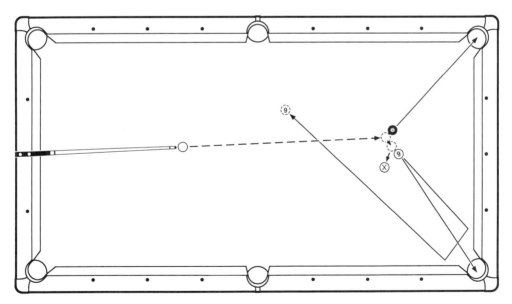

Playing Two Balls at a Time

At this distance it's going to be tough to slow roll the 8 while trying to bump the 9 up next to the lower right corner pocket. Your best bet here is to shoot the 8 firmly with draw. Adjust your aim and/or english as needed, and try to pocket both balls at once! You could make both balls, miss the 8, but make the 9, or make the 8 and get the position shown on the 9.

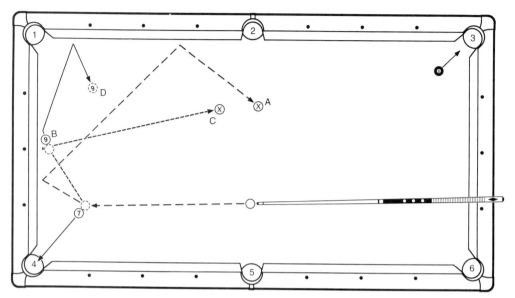

Knocking a Ball Closer to the Pocket

You could play the 7-ball into pocket #4 and send the cue ball to position A. Playing shape from the 8 to the 9, however, won't be very easy. Another approach is to apply some draw so that you can bump the 9-ball from position B to D. The cue ball has ended up at position C. With the 9-ball out in front of the pocket, it will be simple to run the last two balls. The lesson: learn to balance your shots.

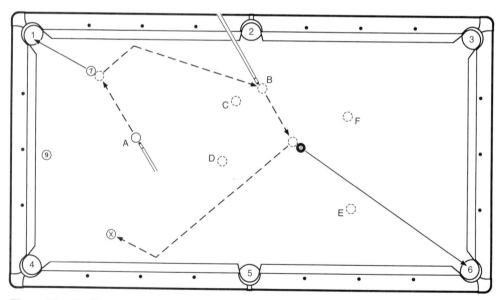

Trouble Balls in the Middle of the Table

It's tough to get the proper angle when a ball is out in the middle of the table. Position B would be okay. Position D is the toughest of the five because it requires four rail shape to get to the 9-ball. Whenever you must send the cue ball to the end rail when the balls in the middle of the table, plan your position with great care.

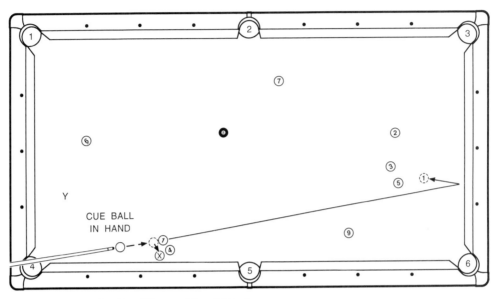

Winning with the Three Foul Rule

Most Nine Ball tournaments today use the three foul rule. If your opponent commits a foul on three consecutive shots, you win the game without having to pocket the 9-ball. Occasionally the position of the balls sets up perfectly for you to take advantage of this rule.

In the diagrammed position your opponent has just scratched on the break giving you ball in hand. That's foul number one. You might consider attempting a runout, but this rack sets up perfectly for a three fouls in a row win. Place the cue ball where shown and shoot the 1-ball softly to the other end of the table behind the 2/3/5 cluster. At the same time, slide the cue ball to X behind the 4-ball. There isn't one player in 10,000 that could hit the 1 and then a rail from this position. Now your opponent has committed foul number two. One more foul and he/she loses! After your opponent has committed his/her second foul you **must** inform them that they are on two fouls if you want to claim a three fouls in a row victory. Don't forget this, and certainly don't expect your opponent to remind you that they are on two fouls.

After your opponent committs the second foul you once again have ball in hand on the 1-ball. Your best move is to send the 1-ball down to position Y and try to snuggle the cue ball in behind the 2/3/5 cluster. Once again your opponent is faced with an incredibly difficult kick shot. If he/she fouls again, that's three fouls in a row. You win the game even though there are still nine balls on the table!

The following tips should alert you to three foul opportunities: 1.) you have ball in hand (which means, of course, that your opponent is on one foul); 2.) the first ball is close to a blocker; 3.) there is a cluster to hide the first behind ball and, 4.) your opponent does not kick very well.

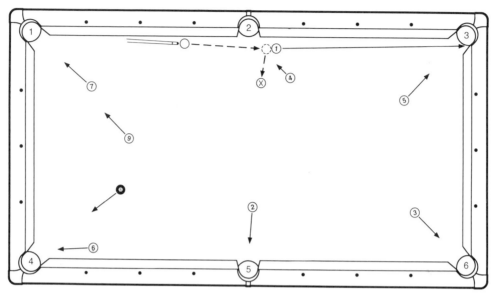

The Easy Run Out

Your assessment of this rack reveals that the balls are well spread and nothing is on the rail. In addition, the 1 through 5 balls are at one end of the table and the 6 through 9 balls at the other. All you need do is shoot the 1 into pocket #3, the 2 in pocket #5, and so forth until the rack is complete. This rack is a custom made runout. Even so, mistakes can ruin easy run outs like this, so maintain your concentration until the end.

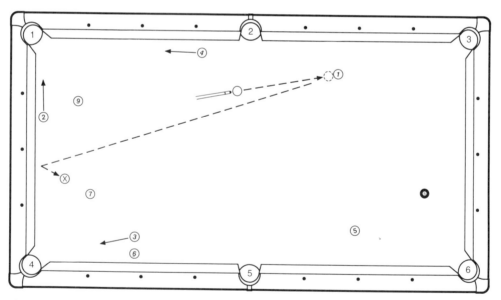

A Tough Rack that Can be Run

You will immediately be challenged to play position on the 2-ball as it requires a long draw shot. The rack does not get much easier the rest of the way. This is the kind of rack that offers no real problems except that your execution must be near flawless from start to finish. Each shot must be thought out carefully and played with great precision.

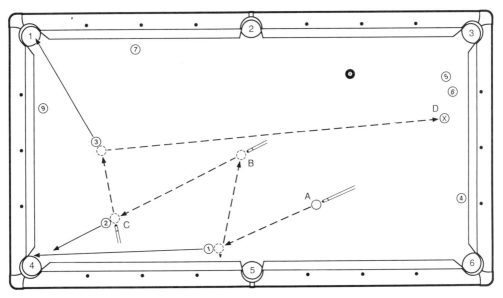

Potential Run Stoppers

Analysis of this rack tells you that it will be easy to pocket the first three balls. However, these balls must be played with a great deal of precision because you will need good shape to get from the 3 to the 4. This position play could easily end your runout if it's not played perfectly. The diagram shows one way to run this sequence.

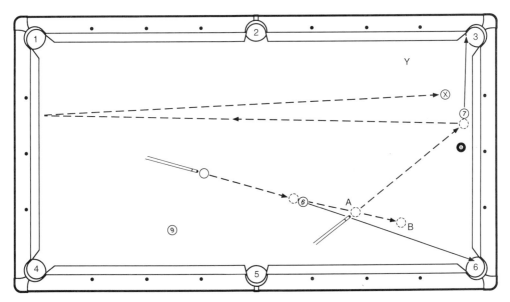

Potential Run Stoppers (2)

This run won't be easy with the next two balls close together on the same rail. You have two choices: play position at A and then send the cue ball two tables lengths to X, or follow to position B and then try to stop the cue ball at Y. Option A assures you of a shot on the 7. With option B, you run the risk of getting hooked behind the 8. Your selection usually depends on the distance between the next two balls.

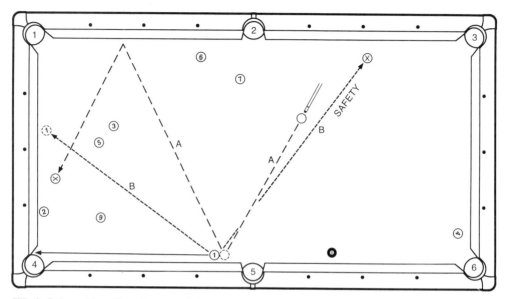

Weighing the Options: Offense vs. Defense

Your analysis tells you that you can seize the initiative by choosing option A, which requires a thin cut shot with excellent speed control. Option B is the more conservative choice. Your decision is largely based on how you are shooting and on whether you tend to play more offense or defense. Interestingly enough, neither option carries with it any guarantees. You could miss the 1 and sell out (A), or your opponent could kick for the 1 and play a return safety.

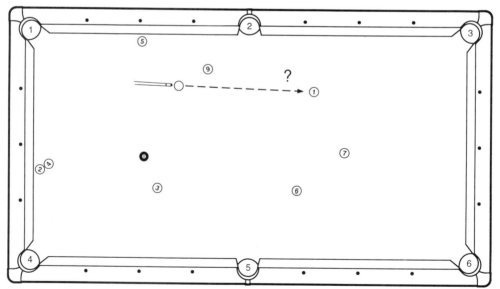

No Possible Runout

Your analysis reveals that you have no chance to run this rack, thanks to the 2/4 cluster. If you shoot the 1 into pocket #3, then you'll be forced to break up the cluster (or give your opponent ball in hand) on your next shot.

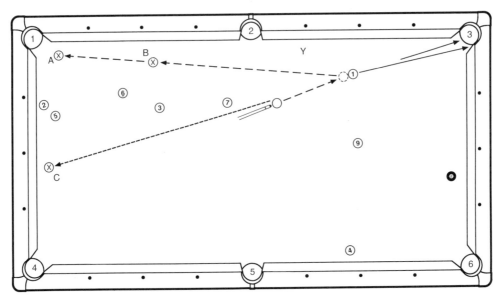

Play the Table, Don't Force the Issue

While you are evaluating the table, be sure to conduct a reality check. Is the shot you're considering within your normal range of capabilities? Is the reward worth the possible risk you're taking? The degree to which you can accurately answer these questions will largely determine the quality of your decision making process. Here's the key question: do you play the table, or do you try to force the issue by playing unrealistic shots? Put your ego aside and answer the question as honestly as possible. Chances are you tend to play shots that are beyond your game as it stands now. I'd say that's the majority of the pool playing populace. If so, learn to use a little more discretion in your choice of shots. Your game will benefit accordingly.

In the diagrammed position you could choose to play a long draw shot to A, which would give you an easy shot on the 2-ball. However, the risk of scratching in pocket #1 is high. In addition, you only have a very small area in which to get good position on the 2-ball. And finally, this draw shot requires flawless speed control. All told, there's a lot of risk for the opportunity of running eight more balls on a fairly difficult layout.

Plan B is to draw the cue ball to position B and then play a safety. A thin hit on the right side of the 2-ball will send the cue ball to the vicinity of position Y. The 6,3, and 7 balls are all potential blockers. This high percentage safety play gives you a much wider margin for error. In addition, it eliminates the possibility of scratching. Players who choose option B are playing what the table gives them. One final note: if you play shape for a safety and overdraw the cue ball, you might wind up with a shot on the 2-ball anyway!

Plan C eliminates the potential for scratching. Now all you have to do is cheat the left side of pocket # 3 and draw the ball back to position C to avoid getting hooked by the 5-ball. Wow! This shot should be labeled for world champions or suckers only. No one else should even think of trying it.

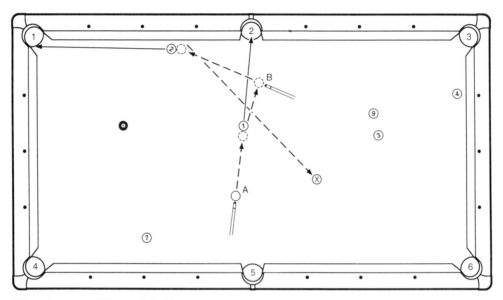

Playing for Three Balls at a Time

Pattern play is the key to running racks of Nine Ball. If you can plan a sensible pattern, and then follow through its execution, the game will become easier than you would have ever imagined. On the other hand, if your patterns are suspect, you will be forever fighting to keep your run alive.

At the heart of pattern play is the principle of playing for three balls at a time, which was introduced in Chapter Five.

Briefly, the principle requires that you play shape on the next ball in such a manner that you can then play position on a third ball. The concept is used throughout the rack until you're down to the last two balls. Once you make the first ball, everything shifts forward as you then add a new third ball to the chain. The table below illustrates this concept as applied to the position in the diagram.

Shot #	1st Ball	2nd Ball	3rd Ball
1	1	2	3
2	2	3	4
3	3	4	7
4	4	7	8
5	7	8	9
6	8	9	
7	9		

Because you are looking at three balls at a time, before you start your run, you need to consider not only how you are going to play the position on the 2, but also how you are going to get shape on the 3. A soft follow shot on the 1 into pocket #2 sends the cue ball to position B. Now you have a cut shot on the 2-ball into pocket #1. With this angle you can now bring the cue ball across the table to position X for an easy shot on the 3-ball. Advance planning and proper execution made this possible. Newer players often make the mistake of following the cue ball to the rail for a straight in shot on the 2. This makes the 2-ball easier. However, it is nearly impossible to get from the 2 to the 3 without leaving a cut shot on the 2-ball.

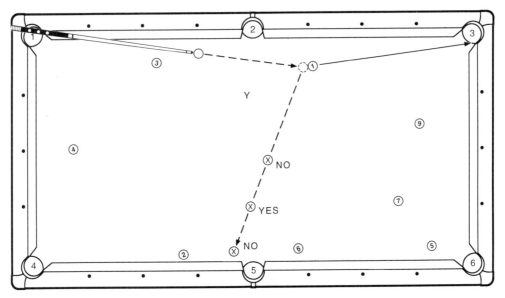

Playing for the Correct Angle

It's important to play for an angle on the majority of your shots in Nine Ball as this makes it much easier to control the cue ball. Your goal is to play position on the 2-ball so that you can then proceed to the 3-ball. An angle on the 2-ball is needed. The cue ball marked "yes" is at the ideal angle for you to then send the cue all to position Y for the 3-ball. The cue ball marked X is too straight, while the first cue marked X is at a difficult angle.

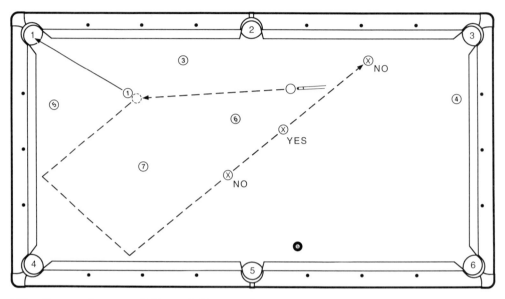

The Importance of Speed Control

On some shots you simply must be able to send the cue ball the exact distance needed to give yourself good position. To do so, you need to be able to feel the force. A link between your hand, eye, and brain must tell you just how hard to stroke the cue ball to have it wind up at the desired location.

When playing Nine Ball the majority of your shots will require a combination of adequate speed control and accurate shotmaking. However, you will often be called upon to execute a position play that requires that little extra something, that heightened sense of feel that will enable you to send the cue ball exactly where needed. At times like this you will either rise to the occasion or your run will end. The ability to consistently execute position plays that require excellent speed control is what separates the best players from the rest.

As you'll recall, you need to be continuously planning for three balls at a time. Therefore, you should be thinking about how to play the 1 to get on the 3 so that you can then play position on the 4-ball. The position labeled "yes" gives you a perfect angle to shoot the 3 into pocket #1 and bring the cue ball across the table to play the 4 into pocket #3.

If you come up 1½' short of the ideal position at the first cue ball labeled "no", you will have a very tough cut shot. Now if you hit the cue ball a couple of feet too far to the position labeled "no" at the top of the table, then you will have a long, tough draw shot to get position on the 4. You continue through the rack without having to pull off a hard recovery shot or without having to turn the table back over to your opponent only by controlling the speed, or rolling distance, of the cue ball.

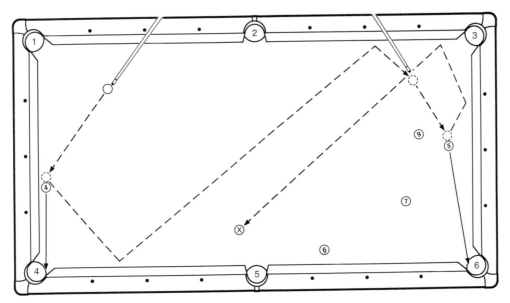

Pattern Play

The diagram illustrates the planning and execution of a basic Nine Ball pattern. It's easiest to get shape on the 5-ball by playing the natural three rail position play diagrammed. This route avoids hitting the 6 or 7 and scratching in pocket #6. The position route from the 5 to the 6 is a natural route that sidesteps any possible contact with the 7-ball.

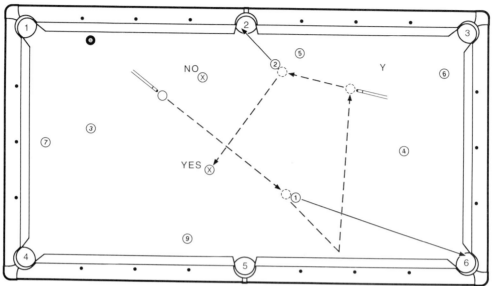

Advanced Pattern Play

Your skill at planning and executing patterns of above average difficulty will be put to the test on this rather demanding layout. Before shooting a single ball you should take a couple of moments to plot your strategy. Your analysis should lead you to the following conclusions:

- The 1-ball is a tough but makeable shot. You will need to apply extra concentration to make the ball and get the proper angle on the 2-ball.
- Running the first three balls should not be too difficult. The key to the rack is getting good position on the 3 so that you can in turn get position on the 4.
- Assuming you obtain good position (at Y) on the 4, the next hurdle is to get from the 6 to the 7-ball at the opposite end of the table.
- With position on the 7, the remaining three balls are of about average difficulty.

With enough experience, and attention to detail, you will learn to evaluate a rack like this in a matter of seconds. Your mind will absorb the information provided by the table, process it quickly, and produce a plan of action. Now let's find out how we can run to the troublesome 4-ball.

Your analysis has revealed that playing position on the 4 is the key to the rack. Therefore, you should decide what position on the 3 will allow you to achieve that objective. The cue ball labeled "yes" is in the ideal position to play natural two rail shape to position Y. It's possible, but not nearly as easy, to play shape on the 4 from the cue ball labeled "no".

A follow stroke with left english will provide you with the correct angle for the 2-ball. You wouldn't want to be on the other side of the 2 because then you would run into the 5-ball. A soft draw stroke on the 2-ball will enable the cue ball to glide into perfect position for the 3-ball (which will be played into pocket #1).

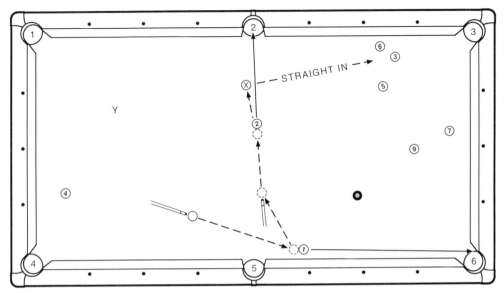

When to Play Straight-In Position

Occasionally you will need to abandon the concept of playing for an angle. A straight in shot on the 3 helps you avoid both the 5 and 6 balls as you draw the cue ball back to Y for position on the 4. Precision shape is a <u>must</u> when playing for straight-in shape. A medium soft draw shot on the 1 brings the cue ball to perfect position on the 2. A soft follow shot on the 2-ball leaves the cue ball at X for ideal position on the 3.

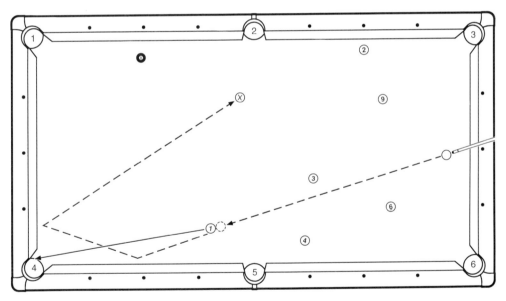

The "Out Shot" - Getting in Line

The 1-ball is the "out shot" in this game. If you can pocket this difficult shot and play position on the 2 (called "getting in line"), then your chances of running out are excellent because the remainder of the rack is fairly routine. Bear down on the "out shot" like it's the game ball because in many cases it's just as important.

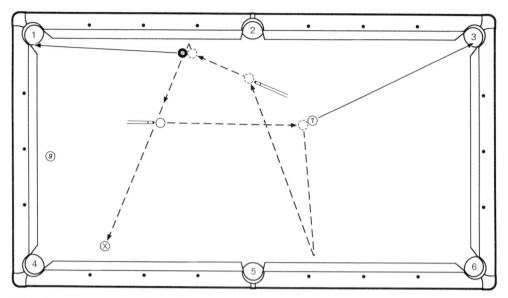

The Importance of the Last Three Balls

This layout looks fairly routine. Shoot the 7 into pocket #3 with a firm draw stroke for position on the 8-ball. Next, a follow shot with a little left english on the 8 will send the cue ball to position X for the 9-ball. That was easy enough, but how many times in 10 tries would you runout from the 7-ball? Two times, five times or a perfect ten out of ten times? You'd be surprised at how often the majority of pool players fail to negotiate the all important last three balls. One reason is simply the numerical odds of pocketing three balls in a row. If you make 70% of your shots, your odds of running three balls are 34%, or about once in three tries. Players who make 80% of their shots have a 51.8% chance of running three balls. Surprisingly enough, those players who pocket 90% of their shots still have only 73% chance of running three balls! Those are the facts. Hopefully they will impress on you the challenge of consistently running the last three balls. Once you can regularly get out from the 7-ball, you'll be beating a lot of players that you thought were pretty good up until now.

Once you gain consistency running out from the 7-ball, you may find yourself running out quite often from the 6, then the 5 and so on. You may eventually progress to where you can run out from the 1-ball on a regular basis. The following pointers may help you to get started towards building a solid run out game: concentrate fully on pocketing each ball, pay careful attention to your position angles, and plan three balls at a time.

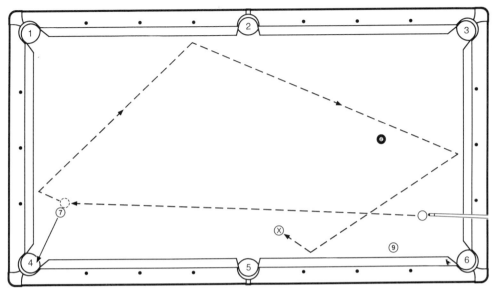

Going the Extra Rail for Position

For the sake of accuracy it is sometimes better to play long shots with a firmer stroke. This is especially true toward the end of the game when there are few, if any, possible obstructions. A firm stroke on the 7 with a half tip of right english will send the cue ball four rails for good shape on the 8-ball. This shot is possible only because the table is wide open.

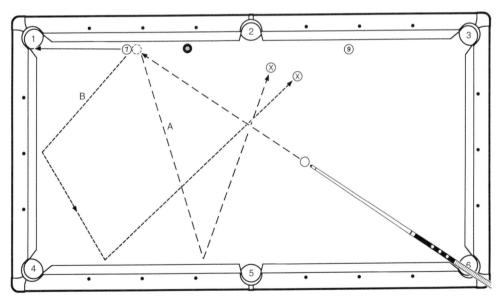

A Difficult Three Ball Run

This layout is tough because all three balls are located on the same rail. The route you choose is a matter of personal preference. When either A or B is executed correctly, the cue ball will wind up at about the same place. A medium hard draw stroke will send the cue ball along route A. A hard stroke with top left english will propel the cue ball along route B.

Push Outs

On the very first shot after the break, the shooter has the option of pushing out. The shooter must first inform their opponent of their intention to push out. The player can then shoot the cue ball anywhere on the table without contacting a ball or hitting a rail. The opponent then has the option of accepting the push out or turning the table back over to the player who pushed out. At this point play proceeds as usual throughout the remainder of the game.

The push out is an important strategic maneuver that can go a long way towards deciding the outcome of the game. It is used when you are hooked after the break or have no reasonable shot at pocketing a ball or playing a safety. The push out often initiates the battle for control of the table. Properly used it gives you the opportunity to put the pressure on your opponent right from the start.

You will need to develop a number of safeties and shots that you can count on. These shots and safeties are more difficult versions of the ones that you normally play throughout the game. You cannot afford the luxury of leaving your opponent easy shots or safeties on a push out because they'll accept the push out and go on to win the game.

You can gain a valuable edge on your opponent by studying their strengths and weaknesses. For example, if you are good at bank shots and your opponent isn't, you would be wise to push out to a bank shot whenever possible. It also will pay for you to study the section on safeties in this chapter, then plan on pushing out to the longer, harder versions of those safeties.

You should work on your speed control on push outs. Often you will want to push the cue ball exactly 2' to a precise location to setup the next shot or safety. In cases like these 1' or 2½' won't do. It's not as easy as it looks to tap a ball a short distance to an exact spot. It takes an extremely soft stroke and expert control of the cue balls rolling distance. When you are pushing out towards a cushion, sometimes it can help your speed control if you hit the cue ball a little harder and have it rebound off the cushion to the desired location.

Be sure not to play the push out in a careless, haphazard manner. Rather, do everything in your power to make the most of this gamewinning maneuver. You should also take notice of the results you are getting when either you or your opponent pushes out. Against players at your level of play, you should be winning the push out battles at least half the time. If not, then you have found a weakness that deserves your attention. Look for tendencies on both your successful and unsuccessful push outs. Are you accepting too many tough shots? Are you pushing out to easy hooks? Are your safeties following push outs effectively hooking your opponent or are they leaving him/her open shots? A little self evaluation can help you pick up the slack in this critical segment of the game. In the pages ahead we will cover a number of principles and strategies that can help you build a solid approach to pushing out.

Push Out Principles

- Don't leave yourself too hard of a shot or safety or your opponent will make you shoot a probable sell out shot.

- Don't leave easy safe shots or your opponent will accept the push out. He/she will then shoot and runout or play a tough safety.

- Make your opponent beat you.

- Master a variety of safeties.

- Master a couple of tough "out" shots - gamewinners.

- Execution is the key - you must be able to execute:
   What you leave yourself.
   What you choose to accept from your opponent.

- The push out is a percentage play - you need to assess your own and your opponent's odds of success- there are few or no guarantees.

- Play to your strengths.

- Take full advantage of your opponents weaknesses.

- Be creative - use your imagination.

- Always ask when considering a push out, "what could my opponent do to beat me from that position?"

- A general rule of thumb:
   -Accept opponents push outs more often than not.
   -Play safeties most of the time on push outs.

Push Out Strategies

- Don't have an automatic response that leads to accepting or rejecting your opponents push outs. Your opponent will pick up on this and take advantage of it.

- Weigh each safety on a case by case basis.

- The shot that you offer your opponent may depend on the run out potential of the rest of the rack.

- Distance is a key strategy - all safes and shots become tougher with distance. Learn to properly gauge the correct distance.

- When a player pushes out to a very tough shot, ask yourself if he/she is going to shoot it, or is there a safety?

- When your opponent pushes to a safety opportunity, ask, "Is it a tough safe or is it a safe that I should shoot?   If I pass, could my opponent lock me up?"

- There's an element of bluffing in safety play. That's where knowing your opponent can allow you to get away with a so-so push out. This can swing the odds in favor of the better player.

- The score of the match and how you are playing may affect your strategy.

- You can use your specialty shot to win the push out battle. Banks, thin cut shots, combinations and jump shots are the most common gamewinners used in the push out battle.

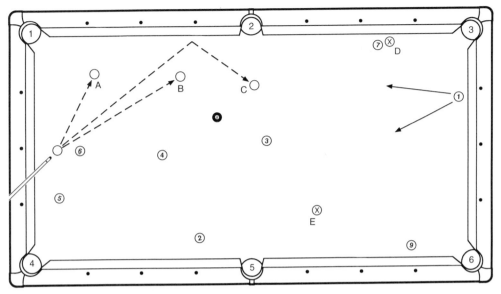

Pushing out to a Shot

The position in the diagram above illustrates basic push out strategy. The rack has just been broken and the incoming player is hooked behind the 6-ball with the 1-ball at the opposite end of the table. Faced with this layout, the shooter has little choice except to push out. But where?

Position A offers a table length bank into pocket #1. If you are an excellent banker and your opponent is not, you might choose this option. The most likely outcome would be for you to make the bank, or for your opponent to accept the push out and miss the shot. In either case, your chances of winning are about average. If you play this shot, the cue ball will end up at position E, giving you a good shot on the 2-ball. If you are going to push out to tough shots like this bank shot, make sure that you will be rewarded with good position on the next ball. Position B makes the bank quite a bit easier. However, if your opponent does not shoot banks very well, it still won't be an easy shot. However, at this shorter distance, the possibility of a safety now enters into the equation. If your opponent plays safe very well, he/she may be able to leave the cue ball behind the 7 (D) while banking the 1-ball down the table along the path indicated by the lower arrow. The various scenarios we've covered so far vividly illustrate the importance of pushing the cue ball the correct distance from the object ball (the 1-ball). It's also important to factor in both your and your opponent's strengths and weaknesses in both shotmaking and safety play.

Position C almost says "I dare you" to your opponent. From this distance he/she will probably seize the initiative and play the shot he/she feels most confident in, be it the bank shot or safety described earlier. Always remember that shots and safeties get easier as the distance to the object ball grows shorter.

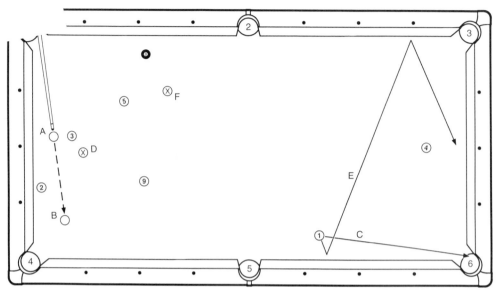

Sucker Shot vs. Smart Safety

After the break the cue ball is hooked behind the 3-ball at position A. If your overly aggressive opponent shoots at everything, then push out to B and offer him/her the shot on the 1 (C) into pocket #6. There is not one chance in a hundred that your opponent will make this tough shot and send the cue ball to D for a good shot on the 2-ball. If he/she doesn't take the bait, play safe by double banking the 1-ball (E) and sending the cue ball to F!

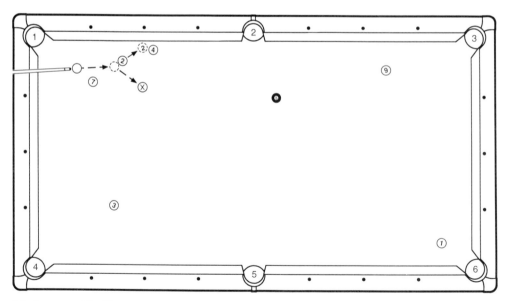

Tying up Balls

There is no way to avoid leaving an easy shot if you push out (unless you want to push out to a kick shot or jump shot). The solution to this predicament is to tie up the rack by easing the 2-ball in behind the 4. Now your opponent has an easy shot that leads nowhere! The end result: if your opponent shoots, he/she will be left with a very tough safety on the 2-ball.

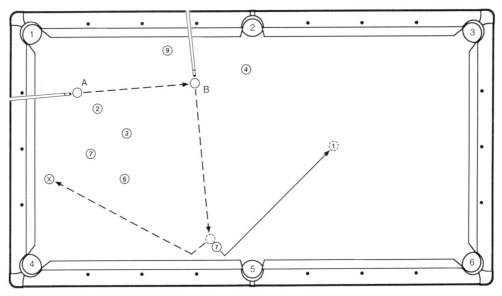

Beware of the Easy Hook

Never push out from A to B as diagrammed because your opponent will almost surely send the cue ball down behind the cluster as shown, leaving you hooked. Of course, should your opponent push out to B, by all means accept the push out and play safe yourself. Only do this, however, after some careful deliberation. After all, you don't want your opponent to think that he/she is playing poor push outs. The lesson: never push out to situations that make it this simple for your opponent to hook you.

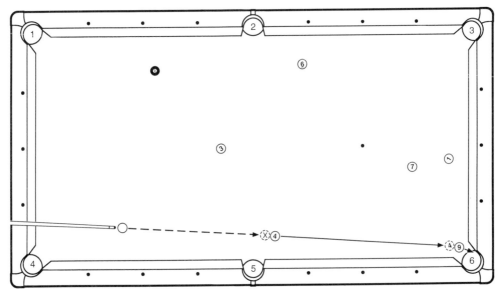

Get the Nine Ball Out of the Pocket

You are hooked and to make matters worse the 1-ball is located near the 9-ball, which is hanging in the jaws! The answer to this problem is to combo in the 9-ball and stop the cue ball dead. The 9-ball is then respotted. Now you or your opponent will be faced with a thin cut or safety on the 1-ball.

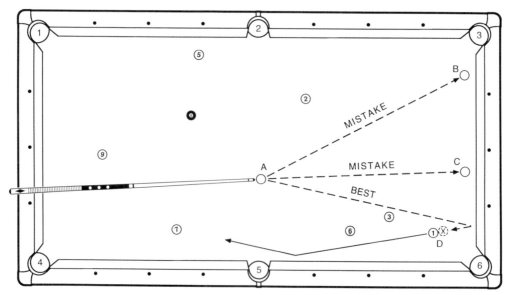

No Good Push Out - The Forced Kick

Sometimes your best choice is to kick for the lowest numbered ball. You could push out from position A to position B as you have no clear shot on the 1-ball. However, this leaves a fairly easy bank into pocket #3. A push out to C is also a mistake because your opponent can now hook you with no trouble at all. In this position your best move is to kick into the 1-ball (D) and hope you can hook your opponent.

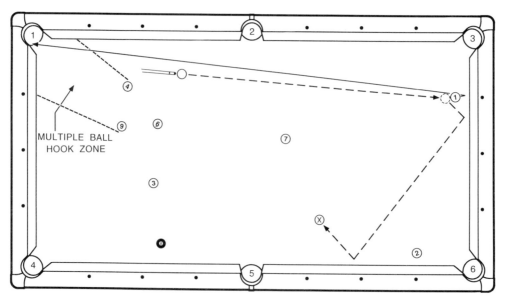

Free Shots - Accepting them

Your opponent has just pushed out to the tough, but makeable long rail bank shot diagrammed above. Should you accept his/her offer? Definitely yes, as you've just been handed a "free shot". If you make the shot, you'll have excellent position on the 2-ball. If you miss, you'll have no penalty to pay as the 1-ball will be down behind the blockers in the hook zone.

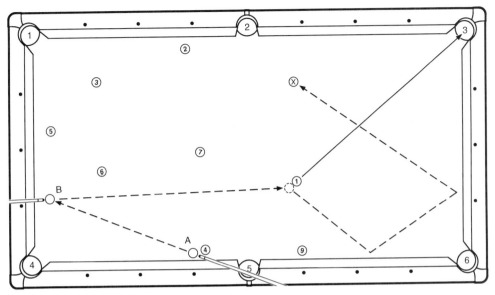

Push Out to a Tough Shot

Let's assume you are shooting extremely well and are very confident in your shotmaking. Furthermore, you know that your opponent is not shooting nearly as straight as you are. In the position above, a push out is in order. Roll the cue ball to B and then play the 1-ball into pocket #3. Since there is not a safety option from this position, you should expect to win or lose the game on this shot. However, if you are in dead stroke, it's worth the gamble.

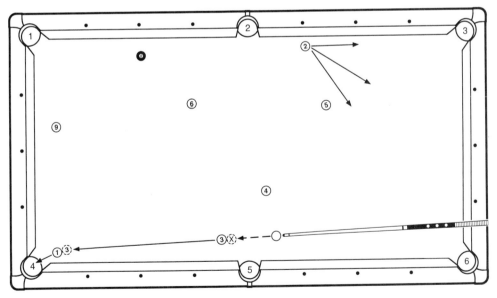

Shoot in an Easy One Ball

The 3-ball is blocking the 1-ball and there's no place to push the cue ball that won't leave an easy shot on the 1. The little known solution is to combo the 1-ball in using a stop shot. Now either you or your opponent will be left with a thin cut shot or safety on the 2-ball on the opposite side of the table.

The Break

The Break

The break is the single most important shot in the game. It is pool's equivalent of the first serve in tennis, the tee shot in golf. A good break gives you the opportunity to run racks. Top pros consistently run out from the break, and on occasion, string several racks together. As you evolve as a Nine Ball player, you will need to move past the one rack mentality; that is, you will need to visualize yourself as a player capable of running several racks. A powerful break is a necessary element of this transition.

A good break will, among other things, boost your confidence. Each time you approach a break shot, eager to watch the balls flying in all directions, you will know there's a good chance a runout table will result. A powerful break can intimidate your opponent. Sitting on the sidelines watching you blast the balls, uncertain as to when, or even if, there will be another opportunity to shoot, it's easy to gauge your opponent's state of mind. He/she is praying to the pool gods, begging for you to make an error. A commanding break can also help you come back from a deficit. The ability to string several racks or break in the game ball a few times can swing the outcome of a match in your favor. At the tour level, many contests are decided on the basis of who is breaking better at that moment.

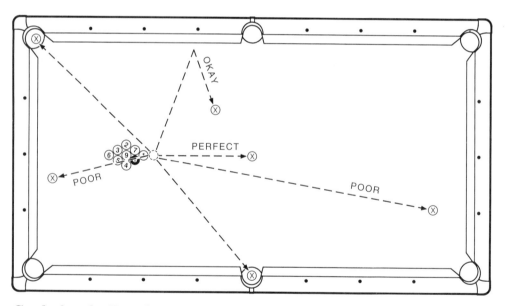

Goals for the Break

The ideal break will pocket the 9-ball without scratching. Obviously, this is every Nine Ball players goal. Just as obvious is the fact that it doesn't seem to happen all that often for the average player. You can, however, increase your odds by focusing more of your energy on your preshot routine; by really bearing down on the one ball, aiming carefully and following through completely, you will be surprised how much more often the 9-ball slips into a pocket.

Although it's wonderful to sink the 9-ball on the break, most players concentrate on pocketing a ball and bringing the cue ball back to the center of the table in preparation for their next shot. With this technique, you'll have, more often than not, a direct shot on the one ball or a possible safety. The diagram shows several possible cue all locations after the break. The position at the far left results from either putting follow on the cue ball or not hitting it squarely at impact. If the cue ball ends up in the vicinity of your original break zone (far right in the illustration), then you've used too much draw. In either case, you have wasted much of the cue ball's energy. Some players prefer to have the cue ball rebound off the side rail and out towards the middle of the table. The scratch shot illustrated, resulted from not contacting the 1-ball squarely. The popular choice of most professionals is the position route on the diagram labeled "perfect", which positions the cue ball in the center of the table.

You should constantly monitor your break by carefully observing the ending location of the cue ball. It will tell you exactly what mistake you are making, if any. Be aware, also, of a tendency to knock the cue ball off the table. If you have this problem, chances are you're hitting down too much on the cue ball. A downward hit causes the cue ball to jump slightly off the table. If the cue ball is slightly airborne and it doesn't hit the 1-ball squarely, it will glance off the 1-ball and fly off the table. This is a fairly easy mistake to correct; if you have this tendency, check your preshot routine to make sure your cue is level throughout your stroke.

Although not pocketing a ball on the break gives the advantage to your opponent, a far bigger mistake is to commit a foul by either scratching or, as discussed above, having the cue ball leave the table. The last thing you want to do, under Texas Express rules, is give your opponent ball in hand after breaking the balls wide open. This essentially hands the game over to your opponent, an advantage you don't want him/her to have at any time. So, take care to exercise control over your cue ball on your break shots.

The Break Stroke

You'll discover that when your regular stroke is working well so too is your break at its best. The break stroke is really a longer, faster version of the smooth and fluid stroke that you use to draw the cue ball the length of the table. Make sure not to tense up and try to overpower the break. Tension will tighten up your muscles and slow down your arm. What you need are relaxed muscles that can whip the cue through at maximum speed. Stroke your break shot fully with an exaggerated follow through. Allow your body to move forward with the shot. Use only as much power as you can control. Let the final position of the cue ball be your guide.

Some players like to line up the break with their head directly over the cue. This makes it necessary to raise up during the stroke to allow the arm to swing forward at top speed. Bear in mind that if you use this approach you will need to learn to time your upper body movement to the forward thrust of your arm. A simpler approach is to set up for the break with your head well above the cue. Now your body is already in position to allow the arm to swing freely through the shot.

Try to keep your cue as level as possible through impact. This will maximize your cue ball control and power. It will also keep the cue ball from flying off the table. Also remember to focus intently on a specific spot on the 1-ball on your final stroke

Despite your best efforts, your break may run in streaks. Sometimes it's working great while at others you can't buy a ball on the break. During the times your break is on the blink, a review of your routine or shift in your technique is in order. For example, you may wish to lengthen your bridge or break closer to the rail . Sometimes your break may not be working due to your playing conditions. For example, the balls do not break as well when the humidity is high. However, if you are in a match and your break is not working, but your opponent's is, then you know that you're doing something wrong. Adjust your break accordingly. You may even want to break from the exact same spot as your opponent. What works for him/her may work for you as well.

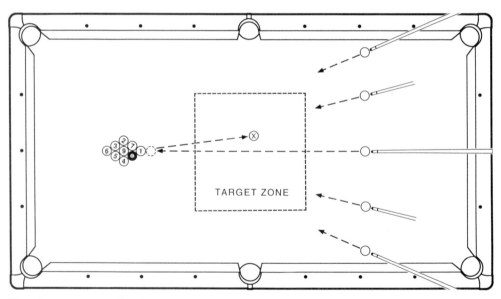

Setting up for the Break

There are several possible cue ball locations for the break shot. The diagram illustrates a few of the most popular spots. Each has its advantages and disadvantages.

The center break gives you a direct line on the 1-ball, which makes it easy to aim the break from this location. In addition, the distance to the 1-ball is the shortest from this position, which makes it easier to control the cue ball. However, it's tougher to make a ball on the break from this position as compared with the other diagrammed positions. For this reason, you very rarely see top players use this break.

The second most popular position is midway between the center of the headstring and the side rail. I refer to this as the 1/4 position. From here the balls seem to scatter better than the with the center break although it is more difficult to line up precisely on the 1-ball from this angle. More balls are pocketed on the break from this position than with the center break. Both the center and 1/4 break position allow you to use the closed bridge, increasing your control.

The favorite break spot of most top players is next to either side rail. The closed rail bridge is used from this position with the cue ball placed two to three inches off the rail. The idea is to force either corner ball (the 4 or the 2) into the corner pocket. Almost all professional players use this break position, despite the fact that the cue ball is 6" further from the 1-ball compared to the center break position. Obviously the increased odds of pocketing a ball on the break are worth the increased distance.

Some players like to break with their bridge on the head rail. From this position you have plenty of room to throw your whole body into the shot. However, any power that may be gained is more than offset by the lack of accuracy that results from shooting the cue ball from such a long distance away from the rack.

If you find, during a match, that your break isn't working, perhaps you should consider changing your setup position. If you normally break from the left rail, try breaking from the right. If that doesn't work, try the 1/4 position. Your goal should be to find a spot as quickly as possible from which you can pocket balls. Remember, each table breaks differently. There may be nothing inherently wrong with your technique, you need only to adjust to a particular table.

Your stroke should provide you with the ideal combination of power and control. You should use a slightly longer bridge than normal as this will enable you to accelerate smoothly. Don't make your bridge so long that you lose control of your ability to strike the cue ball right on the button. Your cue tip should be positioned to strike the cue ball a hair below center. This is all that's needed to bring the cue ball back to the center of the table. The reason for this is that the mass of balls acts as a wall when the cue ball slams into it. Even without draw, the cue ball will rebound off the balls back toward the center as long as the 1-ball is struck squarely.

Be sure to follow your preshot routine when setting up over your break shot. This routine may be somewhat longer and require a little more discipline than your normal routine. The little extra effort that you put into your break shot will show up in your results. Develop your own checklist for your preshot routine.

It is a good idea to check the rack occasionally before you settle into your preshot routine. Ideally all the balls will be frozen together. However, on some tables there are spots where the balls tend to settle that make it difficult to freeze the entire rack. At a minimum, you want to have the first three balls and the 9-ball frozen together. Sometimes it helps to tap the balls lightly with the cue ball to get them to stay in place. Also be sure to notice the location of the rack. The bottom of the 1-ball should sit squarely on the middle of the spot. The rack should not be set at an angle. If your break makes a thudding sound and balls barely scatter across the bottom half of the table, then you may be a victim of the rack move. Your opponent may be taking advantage of the fact that you're not conducting a regular inspection of the rack. If you fall for this trick, you only have yourself to blame.

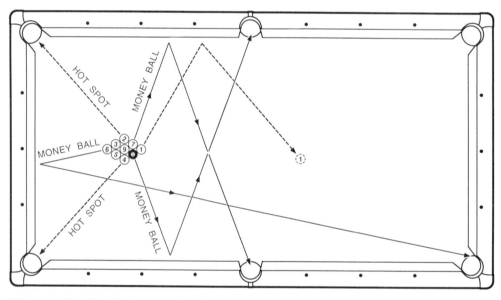

Where the Balls Go on the Break

It's important to know into which pocket the balls are most likely to go especially when you are spotting your opponent (or getting spotted) extra money balls. The diagram shows that the 7-ball and 8-ball are racked up high, right behind the 1-ball. This is the most difficult spot to make a ball from in the rack. If you are spotted the call 8-ball, and your opponent places it in the position shown, you should call it in the opposite side pocket.

Placing two money balls so that they won't go on the break is not too difficult. However, hiding a third money ball is not easy. If you are spotting someone three money balls (for example, the 6, 7 and 8-ball) the best place for the third ball is shown (the 6) in the diagram.

By all means, avoid placing a spot ball in either of the two hot spots as shown in the illustration. It is also not a good idea to place a money ball where either the three or five are located in this diagram.

When the balls are broken properly, the one ball will have a tendency to rebound off the side rail and come back toward the same side of the table from which you broke the balls. The diagram shows one possible outcome.

Safety Play

Introduction

When you are faced with a difficult or nearly impossible shot, your wisest choice may be to play a safety. A safety is simply a defensive maneuver that is designed to leave your opponent in a difficult situation. When faced with 4th and long yardage, football teams will punt the ball to their opponent. Similarity, you must also give up the table to your opponent when the odds of making a shot and getting position are not in your favor. It will help your game if you can quell the hero's impulse that may be driving you to attempt high risk, low probability shots that lead directly to lost games. When you are looking at 4th and long on the pool table, play smart, play the percentages, play the best safety that you can think of that will lock up your opponent tighter than a drum!

Good safety play allows you to win the battle for control of the table. The player who controls the table very often wins the game. Smart safety play can give you ball in hand or an easy shot, either of which translates into victory. This should provide you with incentive enough to develop this not so glamorous but extremely important facet of the game. Also keep in mind that your safeties can frustrate and demoralize your opponent, which of course increases your chances of success.

The best players in the game today all display an ability to run out an open table. What often separates these players is the cat and mouse game called safety play. The best players count on their safeties to win a good percentage of their games. You too would be wise to become highly proficient in recognizing when and how to play safeties. By watching top players, using safeties more often in your games, and by practicing the safeties that appear in this section, you will soon be on your way to playing strong defense. Adopt a positive attitude toward defensive play. It can help counteract many deficiencies in your game as well as help you win many games you might otherwise have lost.

What is a Safety?

Broadly speaking, a safety is a defensive ploy that leaves your opponent a difficult shot, a kick shot, a jump shot, or a return safe. A great safe leaves your opponent absolutely nothing. It is pool's version of checkmate. There are many grades of safeties, which depend on exactly how you leave your opponent.

- The very best safeties lead to ball in hand.

- Very good safeties leave opponents so tough that even though they may avoid a foul, a sell-out usually results.

- Medium grade safeties leaves the games outcome up for grabs. Victory is perhaps a 50/50 proposition.

- Poor safeties are hardly safeties at all as your opponent can turn the tables on you fairly easily, leaving you in a tougher spot than you left him/her.

The very best players have perhaps the most stringent definition of what constitutes a good safety. To them, a good safety occurs when their opponent cannot hit the object ball, either with a kick shot or a jump shot.

Required Skills

Good safety play is a result of the development of a number of skills, just as any other part of the game. The more skills mastered, the deeper the reserve that you can draw from, any one of which can win you a game at any given time. Mastering the following list of skills will help you develop a safety game that will make you a force with which to be reckoned.

- Assessing the table, considering your options, and choosing the best safety play.

- Hitting the object ball with the required thickness.

- Mastering thin hits on the object ball.

- Stopping the cue ball dead in its tracks.

- Floating the cue ball a short distance with a firm stroke.

- A very soft touch.

- Knowledge of where the object ball is going.

- Maneuvering the cue ball through traffic.

- Controlling the use of english off the rail.

- Kick shots and drag draw shots.

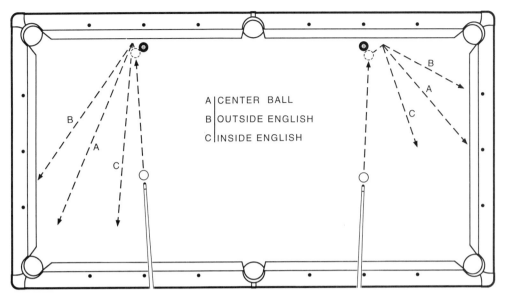

A | CENTER BALL
B | OUTSIDE ENGLISH
C | INSIDE ENGLISH

How Much Ball to Hit

The amount of the object ball that you contact and the english that you use determines the direction of the cue ball. The 8-ball on the left side of the diagram was hit ⅛ full. Notice the different cue ball routes using centerball, outside english and inside english. The 8-ball was hit ½ full on in the example on the right, which greatly altered the cue ball's path off the cushion. To master safety play, you must learn the cue ball's route using various hits with and without english.

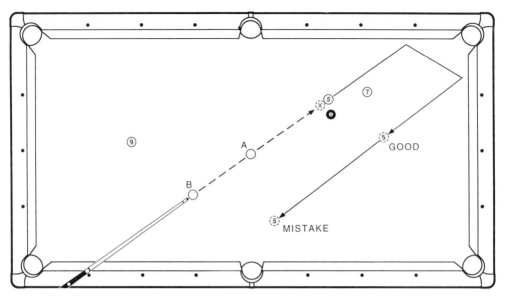

Stopping Distance of the Object Ball

A stop shot on the 5-ball will leave your opponent without a shot, providing the 5 doesn't travel too far. The key is to stop the cue ball dead with minimum stroke speed. From position A, it's fairly simple. From position B, however, the shot is much more difficult as you will need to use a very smooth and slow stroke with a very low hit on the cue ball.

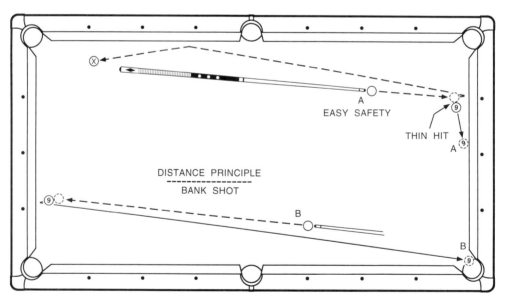

Thin Hit vs. Bank Shot

Thin hit safeties can leave your opponent in a jam, as part A of the diagram demonstrates. When the cue ball is close to the object ball, thin hit safeties are not too difficult. However, they become much more difficult from a distance, as part B shows. Although the cue ball is on the same line to the object ball in part B as in part A, your best choice in B from this distance is to play a bank shot.

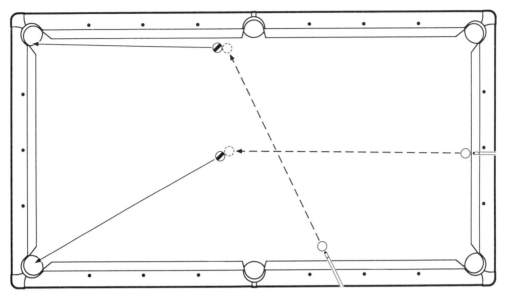

Leaving Tough Shots

Often your best safety play is to leave your opponent a shot that's's tough to pocket or on which to play safe. This defensive tactic comes up regularly during the later stages of the game when there are few, if any, opportunities for a hook. The first diagram presents two makeable, but extremely difficult shots. The shot with the cue ball frozen and the object ball in the middle of the table is tough to aim and stroke accurately. The long thin cut shot is easy to miss, and a sell-out is very likely.

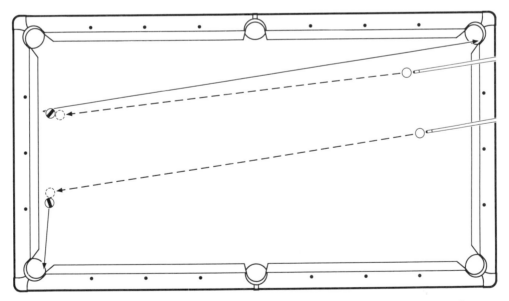

The two shots in the diagram above are also very tough to pocket or play safe. Should your opponent miss either shot, there's a good chance that you will have an easy shot, or at least, a very makeable shot. In all of the examples above, one of the keys was to leave a lot of distance between the cue ball and the object ball.

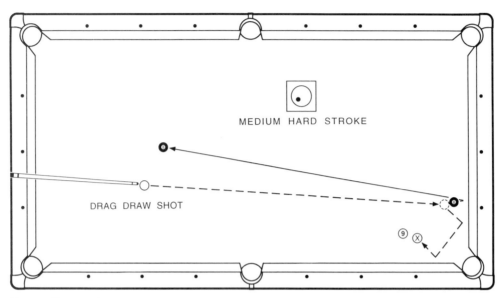

Drag Draw from a Distance

The 8-ball is a tough bank shot. At the same time, the 9-ball gives you the opportunity to play a safety. The 8-ball must be hit accurately over a long distance. This requires a firmer stroke to avoid a table roll. Use draw with a touch of inside (left) english. The idea is to have a minimal amount of draw on the cue ball by the time it contacts the 8.

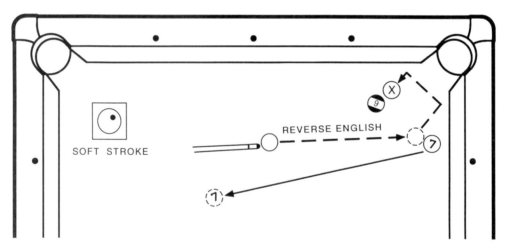

Inside English Kill Shot

Inside english can be used from a short range to put the brakes on the cue ball. In the position above your objective is to bank the 7-ball across the table and hide the cue ball behind the 9-ball. Inside english makes this easy. With right english and a soft stroke, the cue ball will grab hold of both the first and second rails, enabling it to stop quickly behind the 9-ball.

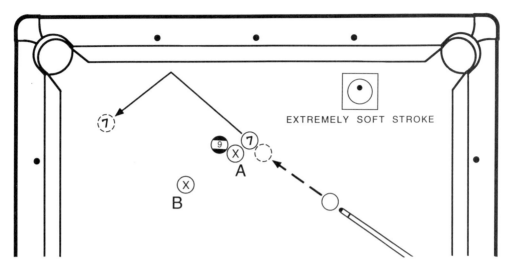

Soft Follow Hook Shot

This safety requires a soft touch and a precise hit on the object ball. The cue ball at position A shows what the shot looks like when executed correctly. The most common error is to overcut the 7-ball, which results in position B. This leaves your opponent a simple shot. Because of the very delicate nature of this safety, it should only be attempted at short range.

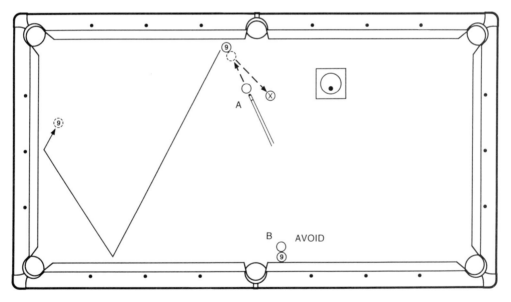

A Situation to Avoid

You must hit a rail after contact with either the cue ball or object ball. Position A shows you a legal safety from a potentially sticky situation. From position A, some players will bunt the object ball hoping to arrive at position B ahead of their opponent. The trouble comes when your opponent beats you to the punch. The lesson: try to avoid this bit of warfare by first playing a safe such as the one shown in position A.

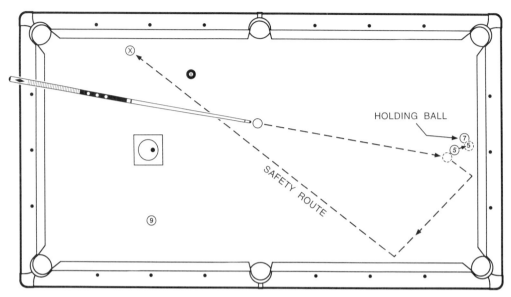

Using a Holding Ball

On longer safety plays where you need to hit the cue ball with a firm stroke, controlling the final placement of the object ball is often a problem. What you don't want to do is relocate the object ball to where your opponent will have an easy shot or safety. The diagram shows you how the 7-ball will check the roll of the 5, holding it in place.

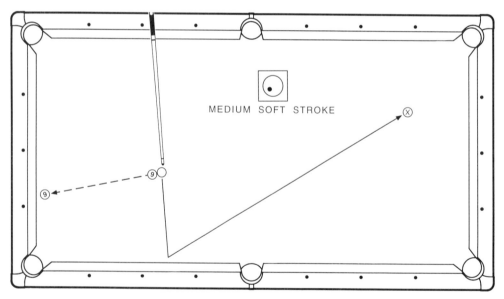

No Shot Thin Hit Safety

In this position you are without a reasonable shot at the 9-ball. Use a draw stroke and hit down on the cue ball. This will increase the english, which will cause the cue ball to rebound sharply off the rail sending it to the opposite end of the table. Be sure to aim away from the 9-ball so that you only graze it in passing.

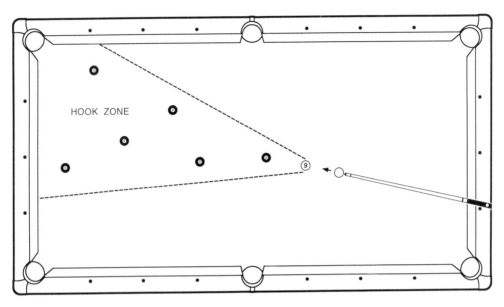

Hook Zones

The objective of safety play is to make it as difficult as possible for your opponent to pocket a ball or play a return safety. The best safes are those that leave one or more balls between the cue ball and the ball your opponent is required to contact. When your opponent is shielded from direct contact with the next ball, he/she is said to be hooked. When hooked your opponent is forced to shoot a kick shot, jump shot or curve shot. Failure to hit the next ball is, of course, a foul which gives you ball in hand.

A solitary ball can be very effective in preventing your opponent from contacting the next ball. The diagram shows that the 9-ball, which is only six inches in front of the cue ball, is blocking a direct hit on all of the 8-balls in the area labeled "hook zone". Hook zones become even larger as the cue ball gets closer and closer to the obstructing ball (the 9-ball in our example).

The effectiveness of your hook safeties depends on several factors, among them your opponent's ability to jump, curve and kick effectively. In the example, a pro would not have much problem hitting any of the six 8-balls within the hook zone. And yet, their chances of winning the game would be uncertain. On the other hand, an average player may only make contact with the 8- ball on perhaps half of their attempts. Every kick shot where they failed to hit the 8-ball would almost surely spell defeat.

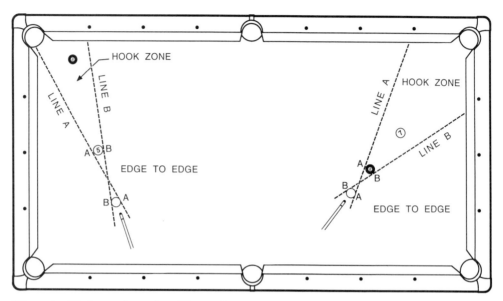

How to Determine the Size of a Hook Zone

You can improve your safety play greatly by learning to recognize potential hook zones. Run a line across each edge of the cue ball to the opposite edge of the blocking ball and extend those lines all the way to the rail. The area inside the lines is the hook zone. Notice that the hook zone is larger in the position on the right because the cue ball is closer to the blocker.

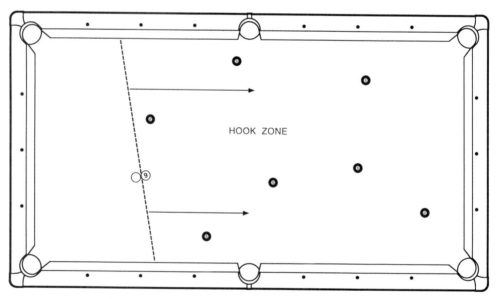

Frozen Hook Zones

The best hooks of all are formed by freezing the cue ball up against the blocker. In the diagrammed position, any ball that's to the right of the dashed line is in the hook zone. That is, it is shielded from a direct hit. Frozen hooks may force your opponent into jacking up and/or playing a difficult multi-rail kick shot that has a very low success rate.

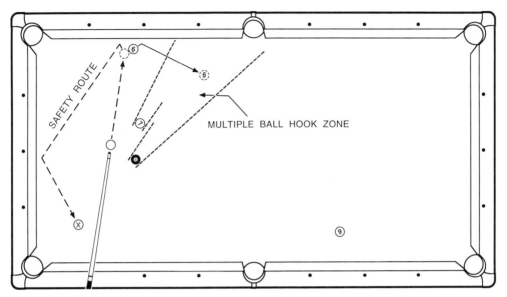

Multiple Ball Hook Zones

When two or more balls are in reasonably close proximity, you have the makings of a large multiple ball hook zone. In our example, the smart play is to hit the 6-ball thinly and send the cue ball two rails to position X. In doing so, the 7 and 8 are now working together to form a rather large hook zone which is blocking a direct hit on the 6-ball.

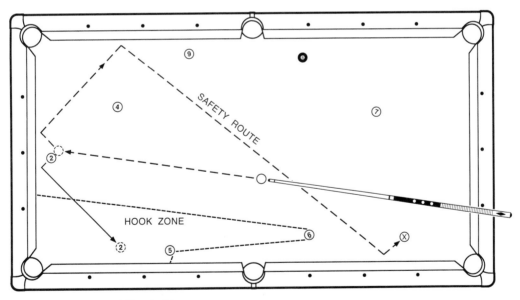

Two Rails to a Hook Zone

This is a safety that appears over and over again, especially early in the rack. The key is to contact just the right amount of the 2-ball so you don't scratch in the lower righthand corner pocket. A touch of outside (right) english helps to control the cue ball. Notice the sizeable multiple ball hook zone that's formed by the 5 and 6 balls.

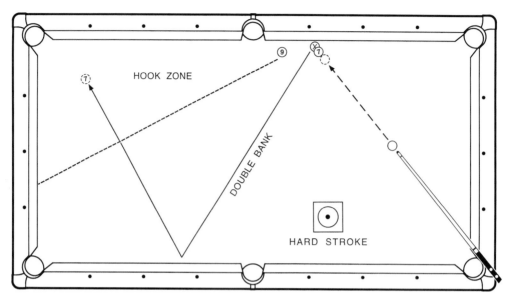

Double Bank Hook Shot

The approach angle on the 7-ball prevents you from banking it into the opposite side pocket. However, the 9-ball is in perfect position for a hook safety. Bank the 7-ball across the table twice as shown using a hard stroke and centerball. The key is to float the cue ball slightly forward to position X. Make sure to hit the 7-ball square in the middle.

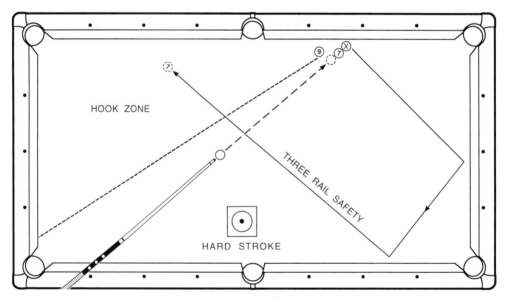

Three Rail Hook Shot

The 9-ball prevents you from cutting the 7-ball into the upper righthand corner pocket. You can, however, play a diabolical safety that will lock your opponent up tight. Use centerball and a hard stroke and hit the 7-ball fully. The cue ball will float to point X while the 7-ball travels three rails, leaving your opponent with a tough kick shot off the rail.

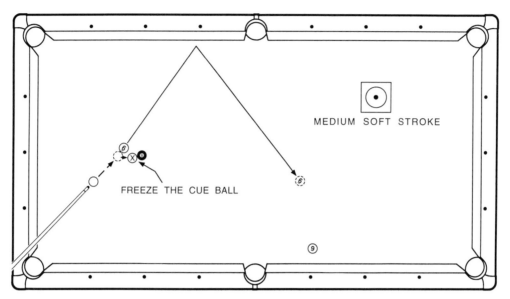

FREEZE THE CUE BALL

MEDIUM SOFT STROKE

Freeze Against the Object Ball

You could elect to bank the 6-ball into the opposite side pocket. A smarter shot is to bank the 6 down the table and pin the cue ball up against the 8-ball. To execute this shot, use a medium soft stroke in the center of the cue ball. The secret is to contact the 6 slightly right of center so that the cue ball floats to the right and up against the 8-ball. Your opponent is now forced into shooting a jacked up two rail kick shot!

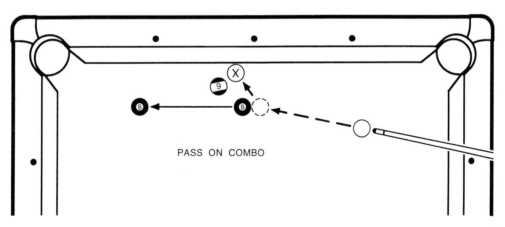

PASS ON COMBO

Pass on a Tough Combo

The 8/9 combination is an extremely difficult shot. Your best bet in this situation is to pass on the combo and instead shoot the 8-ball softly while sending the cue ball up against the rail. From this position it will be next to impossible for your opponent to even make contact with the 8-ball.

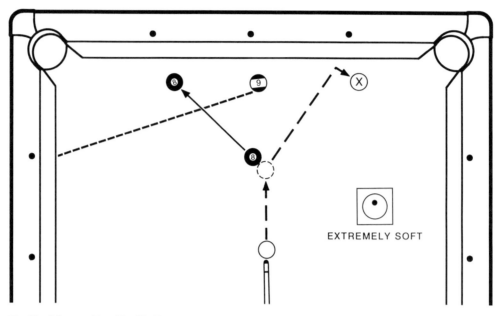

Balls Near the Rail Create Large Hook Zones

The 9-ball is less than the diameter of the cue ball away from the rail. Because of this, it would be impossible to shoot the cue ball between the 9 and the rail. When a potential blocker is in this position it gives you an excellent opportunity to play a hook safety. In the example, it would be very difficult to make the 8-ball and get good position on the 9. The safety is a cinch, however, because of the large hook zone.

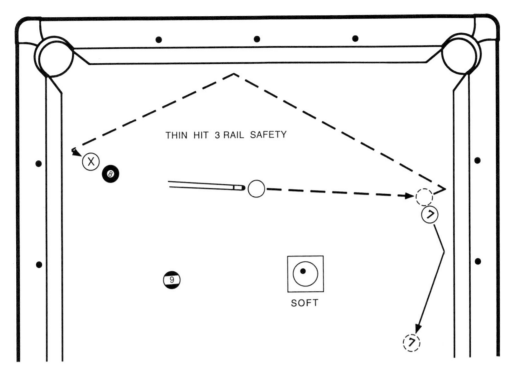

THIN HIT 3 RAIL SAFETY

SOFT

Three Rail Thin Hit Safety

Your skills will be fully tested with this demanding safety. It requires proper routing of the cue ball, just the right amount of english, a thin hit on the 7-ball, and excellent speed control. If you can meet the challenge, you'll have your opponent in a jam!

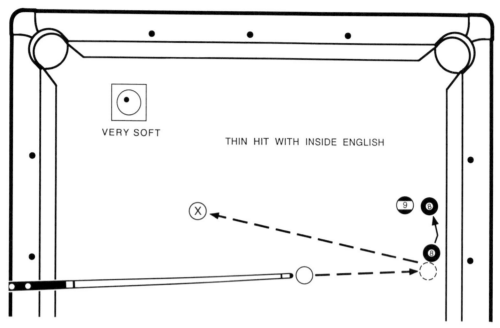

VERY SOFT

THIN HIT WITH INSIDE ENGLISH

Thin Hit Hook Behind a Ball

This safety requires a very thin hit on the 8-ball with inside (left) english. The key is in knowing just how hard to hit the 8 so that it ends up completely behind the 9-ball. If you can leave the 8 as diagrammed, your opponent will be forced into shooting a kick shot.

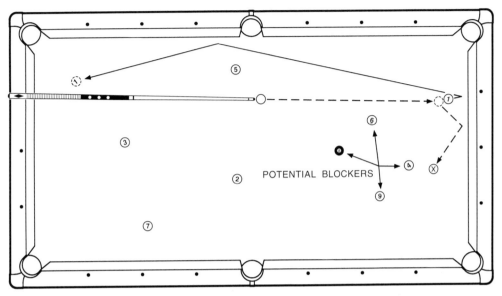

Cluster Racks Offer Hook Shots

Early in the game you will often encounter a group of balls that are near the 1-ball. This may offer you a low risk safety with a high probability of hooking your opponent. The four balls identified as potential blockers provide a fortress for the cue ball. Your opponent will need to weave the cue ball through a maze of obstructing balls in order to make contact with the 1-ball!

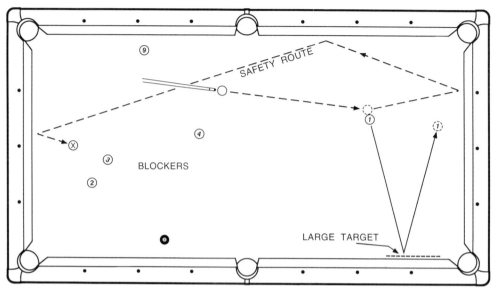

Large target Safety Plays

Sometimes when your shooting is a little off and/or you are faced with a difficult position play, as in the diagram above, you may be wise to play a large target safety. The corner pocket gives you a 43/4" wide target. Notice the 12"-15" target zone for a safety as indicated. If you can place the cue ball as shown, your opponent will have a long kick shot at the 1-ball. Worst case scenario, you leave him/her a very tough cut shot.

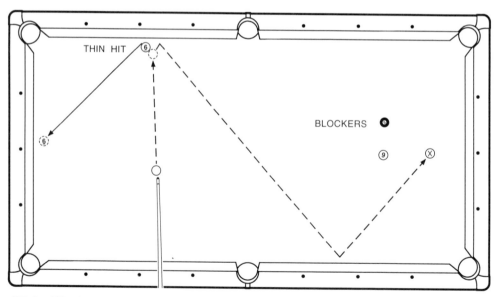

Thin Hit Double Cross Safety

You could play a tough bank shot on the 6-ball into the opposite corner or side pocket. In this situation, the high percentage play is to hit the 6-ball thinly with right english. You'll want to send the 6 to the middle diamond on the end rail which, at the same time, brings the cue ball to rest behind either of the two blockers at the opposite end of the table.

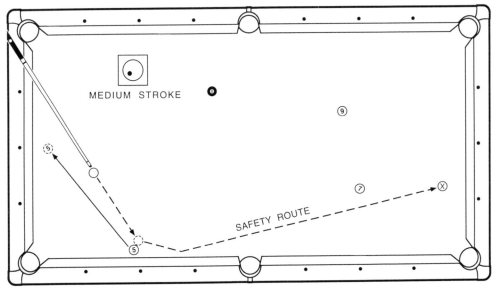

Down the Side Rail Safety

The 8-ball is blocking a bank shot on the 5-ball. As a result, a down the side rail safety will put the odds in your favor. Apply low outside running english to the cue ball. The english will open up the rebound angle, sending the cue ball down the table behind the 7-ball. The secret is to contact the 5-ball properly. In this case, a 1/4 full hit is required.

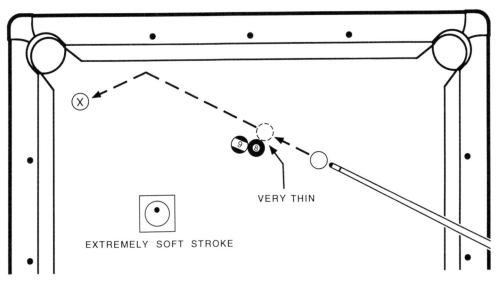

Thin Hit with a Soft Touch

You could shoot a combination bank shot on the 9-ball into the upper righthand corner pocket. A more conservative play is to hit the edge of the 8-ball while sending the cue ball to position X. Your goal is to disturb the 8 and 9 as little as possible. If successful, the best your opponent can do is to play a power kick shot into the 8-ball and pray.

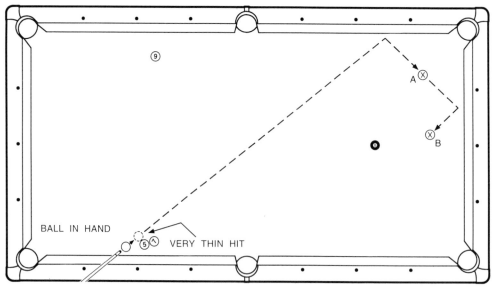

Thin Hit With Ball in Hand

In the diagrammed position you have cue ball in hand but no makeable shot on the 5-ball. A thin hit on the 5-ball will send the cue ball down the table possibly to position A, or even better yet, to position B. Your objective is to force your opponent to break the balls apart on a kick shot. You may also wish to separate the 5 and 7 slightly, hook your opponent, and wind up with ball in hand. Another ploy is to maneuver the 5 and 7 apart enough to where you can play a devastating safety with ball in hand should your opponent fail to hit the 5 on a kick shot. If your opponent gives you ball in hand (rather than opening up the balls with a kick shot), you may want to repeat the first safety over again. Remember to be patient in this situation as you are most definitely in the driver's seat.

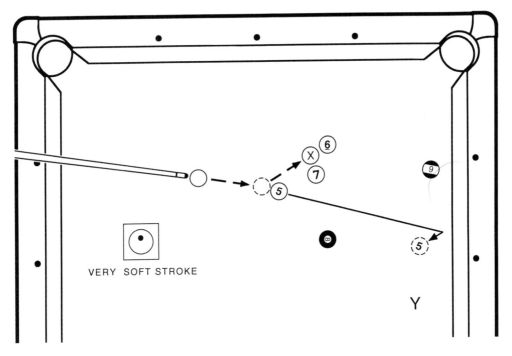

VERY SOFT STROKE

Y

Setting up a Combination

There's no makeable shot on the 5-ball but there is a safety play that can result in an easy victory. Use a soft follow stroke and cut the 5-ball just a little bit to the right. The cue ball will snuggle in behind the 6 and 7 balls. Meanwhile the 5 has come to rest close to and in line with, the 9-ball. If your opponent misses hitting a tough jacked up kick shot, you'll have ball in hand (position Y) for an easy gamewinning combo!

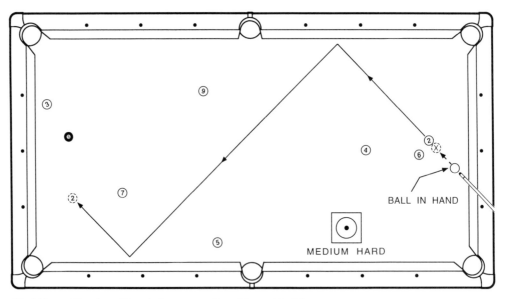

Getting Easier Position on the Next Ball

Even with ball in hand, it still won't be easy to pocket the 2 <u>and</u> get good position on the 3-ball because of all the interference. The solution is to <u>delay running out</u> for one turn. Instead, shoot the 2 down the table close to the 3-ball. When your opponent misses hitting the 2-ball, you'll have no problem making the 2 and getting position on the 3.

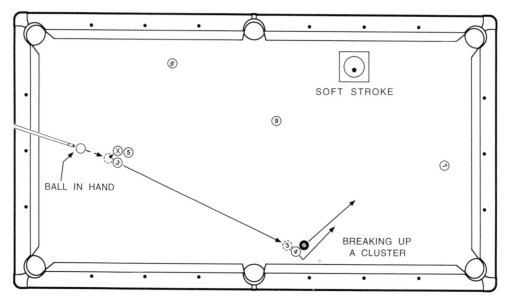

Breaking up Clusters

With cue ball in hand you could try to pocket the 3-ball and break up the 4/8 cluster. A better choice is to shoot the 3 directly into the cluster while freezing the cue ball up against the 5-ball. A soft stroke is all that's necessary to break the balls apart. Furthermore it's your insurance against accidentally pocketing a ball and hooking yourself.

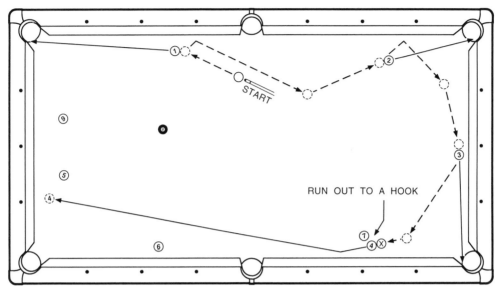

RUN OUT TO A HOOK

Running Out to a Hook

It's not a problem at all to run the first three balls of this rack, as the diagram demonstrates. The 4-ball is another matter as there is no place to shoot it in it's present location next to the 7-ball. You have two choices as you plot your strategy. Option A is to try to break up the cluster when shooting the 3-ball. This approach brings in the element of luck, because you can't be entirely sure what kind of shot, if any, you'll have on the 4. Plan B is to play position on the 4 for a hook shot, as diagrammed. With this choice you are eliminating the luck factor. In addition, your opponent will have a tough time kicking to hit the 4 from position X. Finally, the 4 will be next to the 5-ball, which greatly simplifies the run out.

There's no harm in running to a hook and then taking a breather while your opponent's frustration builds as he sweats out a tough safety. Then with ball in hand, you finish your business by completing the runout.

There's no harm in running to a hook and then taking a breather while your opponent's frustration builds as he sweats out a tough safety. Then with ball in hand, you finish your business by completing the runout.

Sometimes you will want to go ahead and break a cluster during a run. However, if your odds of success are, let's say, under 80%, you might want to consider the run to a hook shot strategy, especially if this increases your chances for victory to 90-100%. Don't forget, winning pool is largely a game of playing the percentages. Consider your options carefully and proceed with the plan that gives you the best chance of winning.

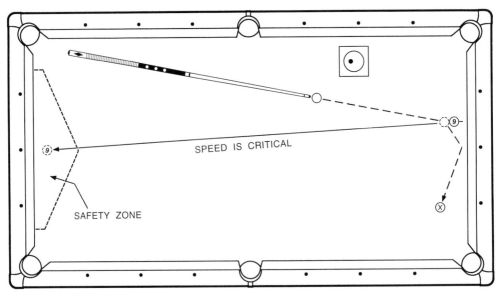

SPEED IS CRITICAL

SAFETY ZONE

Pass on a Bank Shot

Your best bet in this situation is to pass on the bank shot and play safe as diagrammed. Play a crossover bank from this position with a touch of inside english. Speed control is a must! When you send a ball down the table to purposely leave your opponent a tough cut or bank, the widest area of the safety zone is midway between the two corner pockets. As the object ball gets closer to the corner pocket it must be closer to the rail for an effective safety.

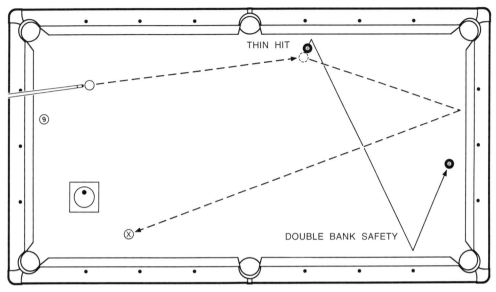

Thin Hit Double Bank Safety

Pocketing the 8-ball and drawing back for good position on the 9-ball is a challenge. If you have any doubts about your ability to pull off this shot, you should strongly consider playing safe. The key is to contact the 8-ball so it follows the indicated path. Take notice of the difficult situation with which your opponent is now stuck!

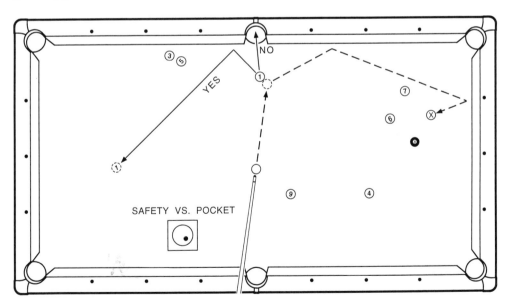

Pass on an Easy Shot that Leads Nowhere

Always ask yourself what comes next when you pocket a ball. If the answer is nothing, your best choice may be to pass on the shot and play a safety. In the position above you could easily pocket the 1-ball in the side. You would then be stuck without a shot on the 3-ball. The 6,7 and 8 balls offer a hiding place for the cue ball. Play your safe accordingly. If your opponent fails to hit the 1, you will be in a much better position to win the game.

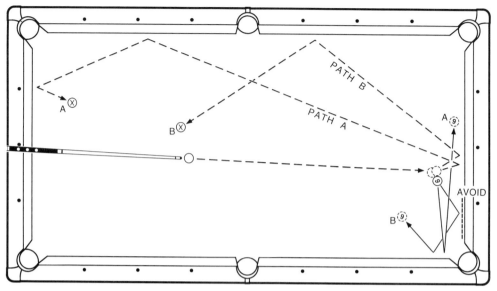

Thin Cut Shot Safeties

Your only choice is to shoot the 9-ball into the lower right corner pocket. On tough shots like this learn to miss on the pro side. If you overcut the shot, you'll send the cue ball down path A while leaving the 9 near the opposite end rail! Do not undercut this shot (see area marked "avoid") because this would likely result in a sell-out as position B indicates.

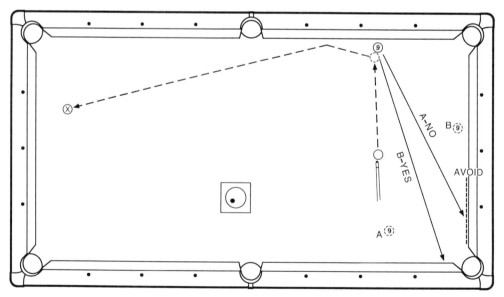

Safety Cross Corner Bank Shots

Safety first should be your guiding principle when shooting tough bank shots on the 9-ball. If your bank hits the end rail in the zone labeled "avoid", you will most likely leave your opponent a makeable shot (see position A). The smart play is to err towards the side rail by banking the 9 along path B. Should you miss on this side of the pocket, your opponent will be faced with a table length bank shot.

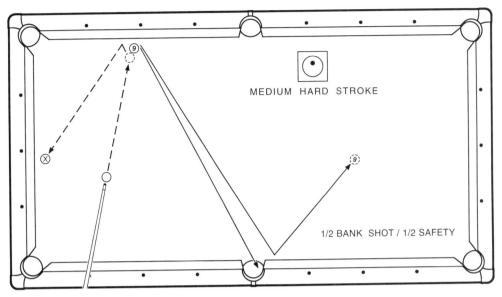

MEDIUM HARD STROKE

1/2 BANK SHOT / 1/2 SAFETY

Cross Side Bank Safeties

You should try to pocket the 9-ball cross side from this position but be sure to leave your opponent as tough a shot as possible just in case you miss. A medium hard stroke with ½ tip of follow will send the cue ball down near the end rail. Your opponent will then be forced into playing a long, tough shot.

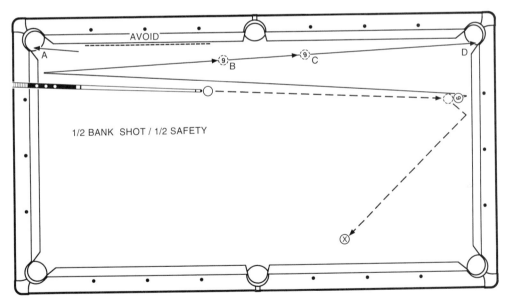

AVOID

1/2 BANK SHOT / 1/2 SAFETY

Long Rail Bank Safeties

There are several possible outcomes to this shot. Hitting the side rail will most likely result in a loss. You could bank the ball directly into the opposite corner pocket (A). If you miss, be sure to hit the end rail first. You could leave your opponent a tough shot at position B or C. You might even double bank the ball into the upper righthand corner pocket.

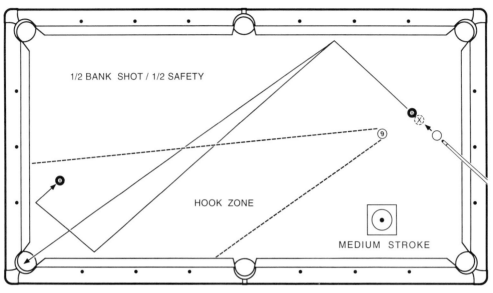

Cross Table Bank/Hook Shot

Your knowledge of potential hook zones will come in handy on this 1/2 bank, 1/2 safety. It would be very tough to pocket the 8-ball in either the side pocket or upper lefthand corner pocket and get good position on the 9. Consider what the hook zone would be if the cue ball stopped next to the 9-ball. You can see that it offers you a large hook zone. The net result is a successful bank or a safety.

How to Play Kick Shots

A kick shot, by definition, occurs when you are forced to play the cue ball off one or more cushions into the object ball. Kick shots happen when your opponent has left the cue ball in a position where you cannot shoot directly at the lowest numbered ball.

Most players view kick shots with about as much fun as a trip to the dentist. Nevertheless, they must be mastered if you hope to rise in the ranks as a Nine Ball player. Kick shots are tough to pocket, but there can be some positive results. You might luck a ball in, leave your opponent a hard shot, or put him/her in a tougher spot than you were left. The worst thing that can happen is to fail to make contact with the ball that you're supposed to hit, giving your opponent ball in hand. The first lesson, therefore, is to at least make contact with the object ball.

When it comes to kick shots, the luck factor is especially prominent. In spite of this, your goal should be to reduce the luck factor as much as you can so that your kicking skills will become a powerful weapon in your game. And who knows, you just might come to enjoy extricating yourself from difficult situtations. You might even become a Houdini of the green felt!

Notes and Strategies on the Kicking Game

- Learn the basic kick routes first and then build on that base of knowledge.

- There are many variables that affect the cue balls path as it rebounds off the first rail - speed of the cue ball, angle of approach, english, and condition of the rails (hard, soft). These must be factored into your calculations - this comes with experience.

- Kick systems can give you a reference point to work from - then you must make the appropriate adjustments to fine tune your aim.

- Kick safety battles often take place early in the game when blockers are plentiful. Don't be surprised if you are hooked by your opponents kick shots one or more times. Keep fighting until the battle for control of the table has been resolved.

- Your kick strategy may change as the rack progresses and you have less places to rehook your opponent.

- Kicking skills have improved greatly in recent years - the best players can purposely hit one side of the object ball or the other with good speed control! In other words, they know where both the cue ball and object ball are going to end on kick shots!

- Goals for each kick shot (safety, hit the ball, pocket the ball) vary with the difficulty factor.

- Good kickers always play the percentages.

- The better you play safe, the more you limit your opponents ability to kick successfully.

- Running english seems to make some kicks easier.

- To kick or jump is often the choice - an advantage of kicking is that you won't knock the cue ball and/or object ball off the table.

- Beware of scratching on kick shots.

- If you can't hit a kick shot, then consider other options (tie up the rack, etc.), don't just give away ball in hand.

- Jacked up kick shots are extremely difficult - use a short stroke and avoid any english.

- Balls that are frozen to the rail are extremely difficult to kick in, even when they are only a few inches from the pocket.

- Balls near the rail offer two chances to pocket - by direct hit or by going rail first.

- As a rule of thumb, most safety kicks are hit softly.

- Try to avoid kicking the object ball to the open end of the table where there are no blockers.

- Your main goal, the majority of the time, will be to play a return safety, not pocket the ball.

- Try to pocket kick shots only when the object ball is near the pocket or you have no other choice.

- Learn to recognize the kick shots that are ½ shot/½ safety.

Improve Your Skills with Kick Pool

You can rapidly develop your "eye" and your sense of aim for any required skill in pool by simply spending enough time practicing the thing that you want to learn. A fun way to reduce the drudgery of practicing kick shots (by the way, how many of you have ever practiced kicking?) is to play a game called kick pool with a friend. Below is a set of rules for the game. They can be modified as needed. The main objective of the game, however, remains the same: to give you an enjoyable and effective method for improving your kicking skills so that you'll feel encouraged to work on this very important part of the game.

- Rack the balls as you would for Nine Ball. (However, you can shoot at any ball in the rack at any time).

- Break the rack wide open. If a ball is made on the break, then it is re-spotted and the breaker continues to shoot.

- The objective is to pocket balls only on kick shots. The first player to five wins the game.

- Kick shots must be shot into a designated pocket.

- There is no loss of a point for failure to hit the called ball, but your opponent gets ball in hand.

- There is a one point penalty for scratching. On scratches your opponent gets ball in hand. A ball is also re-spotted.

- All balls made in the wrong pocket are re-spotted.

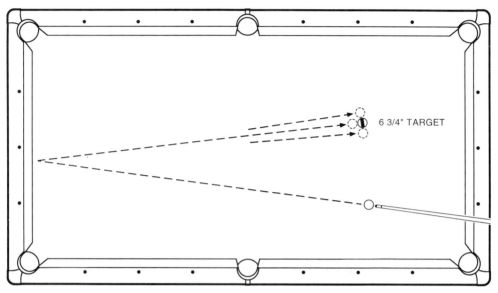

Kick Shot Target Size

If you dislike the idea of playing kick shots, then perhaps you will benefit from a confidence booster. It's true that the object ball is only 2¼" wide. However, you need only brush the edge and then hit a rail to play a legal shot. Because of that, your effective <u>target size is really 6¾" wide</u> as the diagram demonstrates.

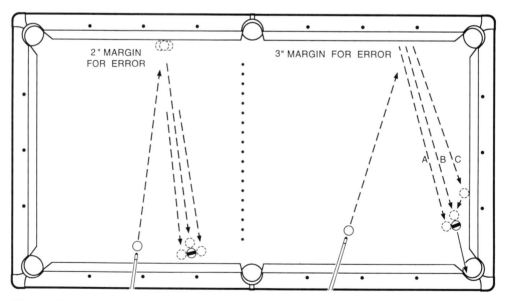

Short Rail Kick Shot Target Size

The short rail kick shot on the left side of the diagram is relatively easy to hit because your rebound angle is very sharp. Notice the large (2") margin for error. You have an even wider margin for error in the right hand position because you can skim the ball (A), hit it fully (B) or contact the rail several inches up from the stripe (C) and still make a good hit.

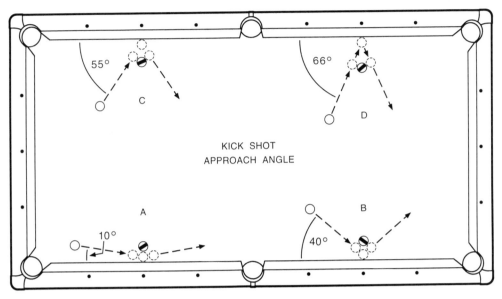

KICK SHOT
APPROACH ANGLE

Kick Shot Approach Angle

When you are planning your kick shots it can be very helpful to know if the cue ball can possibly squeeze between the rail and an object ball that's relatively close to the rail. There are two things that you need to know to make these calculations: the distance of the object ball from the rail and the cue ball's angle of approach. The illustrations above should help to explain this concept.

In position A, the object ball is just a hair over 2¼" (a ball's width) from the rail. As the diagram shows, you could concievably miss hitting the stripe if your approach angle was 10° or <u>less</u>. If your approach angle was <u>over</u> 10°, you couldn't miss hitting the stripe ball on a kick shot because the cue ball couldn't sneak behind and around it.

The stripe ball is 3" from the rail in position B. As a result, you must now approach the rail from over a 40° angle to insure that you'll make contact with the object ball. As the approach angle decreases from 40°, it becomes easier and easier to fit the cue ball between the rail and the stripe. Should this happen, you would have committed a foul, giving your opponent cue ball in hand. It's important to know these approach angles!

In position C the stripe is nearly 4" (or 1¾ ball widths) away from the rail. Now it takes an approach angle of over 55° to guarantee contact with the stripe ball. The cue ball must approach the rail at a sharp angle (60°) in position D when the object ball is a little over 5½" from the rail if you want to be sure of contacting the object ball.

Perhaps when you've played a kick shot you've been surprised to see the cue ball miss your intended target as it squeezed between the object ball and the rail. Hopefully this discussion of approach angles will help you plan more accurately so you can increase your percentage of successful kick shots.

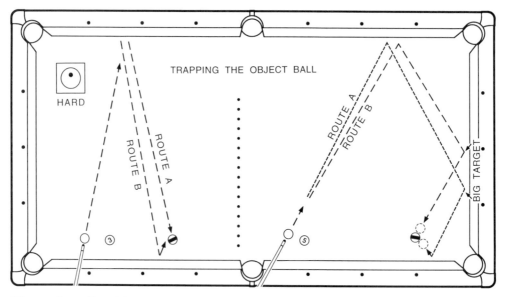

Trapping the Object Ball

You can increase your odds of making contact on kick shots by learning to trap the object ball. A trap shot essentially gives you two or more high percentage chances of contacting the object ball on a kick shot.

You are faced with a one rail kick shot in the position on the left. You could choose route A, which is a direct hit on the stripe ball. Route B involves contacting the second rail first before hitting the stripe. Either route may be acceptable. However, you can increase your odds by aiming between the two contact points on the first rail at the top of the diagram. This allows you to trap the object ball. Now you can either hit the object ball directly or by rebounding off the second rail and into the stripe. Use a hard stroke just in case you hit the second rail as this will help drive the object ball to another rail, thus completing the requirements for a safety.

You could shoot directly across into the stripe in the position on the right. Many players are surprised to learn that you can increase your odds of success in this situation by playing a multi-rail trap shot. Route A is a three rail kick shot. Route B covers two rails. Once again, you can maximize your chances of contacting the stripe by aiming between the two contact points at the top of the diagram. Because of the angle of approach, it will be impossible to circle around behind the stripe without hitting it. No matter what your level of play, your first priority on a kick shot is always to at least hit the ball you're kicking at. Only on rare occasions will you want to intentionally give your opponent ball in hand. A two way kick shot or trap shot, gives you the best shot at meeting your primary objective as they provide you with the largest margin for error.

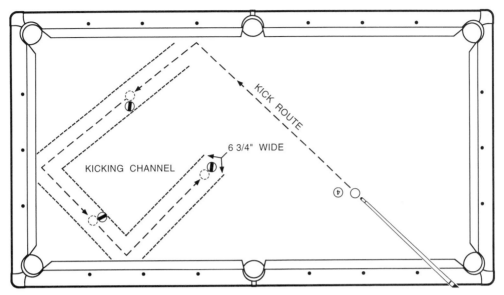

Size of Kicking Channels

This diagram will help build your confidence in your ability to make contact with the object ball on kick shots. First take notice of the kick route. As you'll recall, the cue ball is 2¼" wide. It will therefore make contact with any ball that's within a pathway that's 6¾" wide (3x2¼"). The diagram demonstrates your margin for error on kick shots as the cue ball will contact any ball that's within the 6¾" wide channel.

Kick Routes

You can avoid giving your opponent cue ball in hand by learning as many kick routes as possible. There are a number of basic kick shots that appear over and over again. These would include the one rail kick shot that appears in the diagram below to the left. Some common two rail kick routes appear in the diagram below to the right. Other kick shots that deserve your attention are presented on the next page.

You should first learn the various kick routes using centerball. Mark the beginning and ending position of the cue ball. The next step is to aim at the same place on the rail, only this time apply ½ tip of running english, then a full tip. Again mark the ending position of the cue ball and take careful note of how the cue ball's route is altered by using english.

The cue ball normally picks up a bit of running english when it contacts the rail at an angle. This effect is most pronounced at approach angles of about 25° - 50°. Therefore, it follows that kicking with reverse english is not easy because you are, in effect causing the cue ball to go against the grain. Nevertheless, it pays to learn not only the various kick routes in the diagrams but others that require reverse english.

Once you've got a good grip on the basic kick routes, it's time to use your imagination. Don't give up when faced with a kick shot you've never shot before. Exercise a little creativity and you just might come up with a game saving kick shot that you can add to your repertoire.

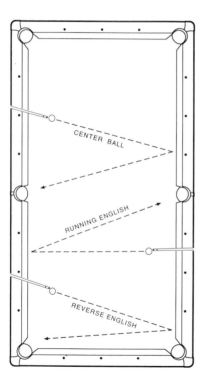

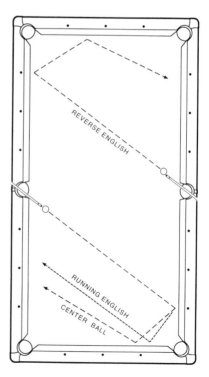

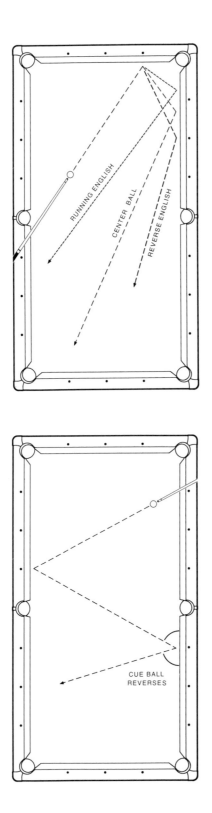

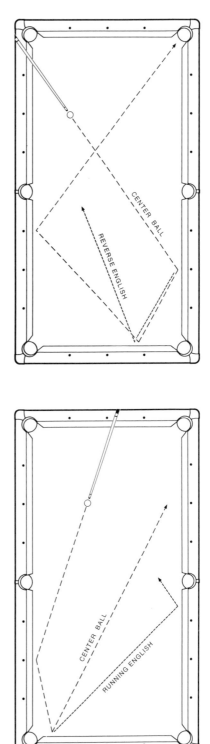

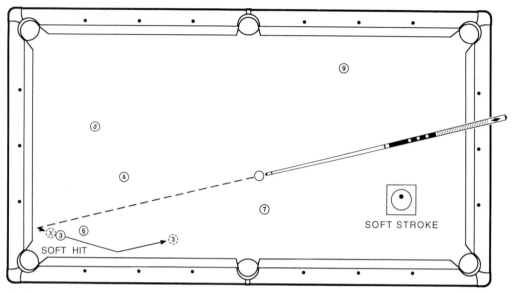

SOFT STROKE

SOFT HIT

Soft Hit Kick Safety

Some players make the mistake of always hitting kick shots hard in the hopes that they can luck a ball into one of the six pockets. And yet, the primary goal of most kick shots should be to play a safety. A soft and accurate kick shot on the 3-ball has re-hooked your opponent as the 6-ball now stands between the cue ball and the 3. Safety kicks using a soft stroke are highly effective when blockers surround the object ball.

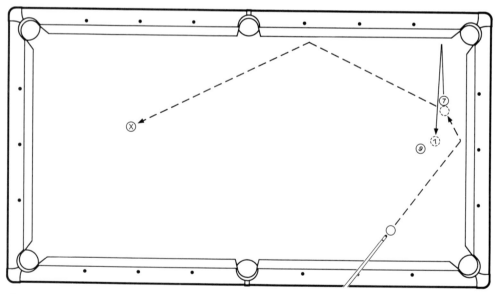

One Rail Safety Kick

The 9-ball is blocking the 7-ball from a direct hit. In addition, it would be very difficult to pocket the 7 in the corner going rail first. However, your best bet is to try to make the 7 rail first. The tendency on this shot is to undercut the 7-ball coming off the cushion. This could very easily result in the safety that's shown above!

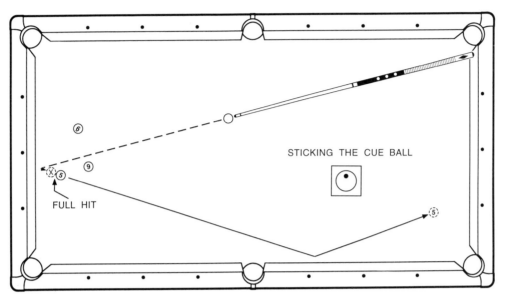

Sticking the Cue Ball with Follow

When the ball you must hit is within a few inches of the rail, it's possible to make the cue ball stop dead in it's tracks. In the position above, your goal is to send the 5-ball down the table and re-hook your opponent. Use at least a medium hard stroke and one tip of <u>follow</u>. The follow will act as draw when it rebounds from the cushion, allowing the cue ball to stop dead. Another key is to hit the object ball full.

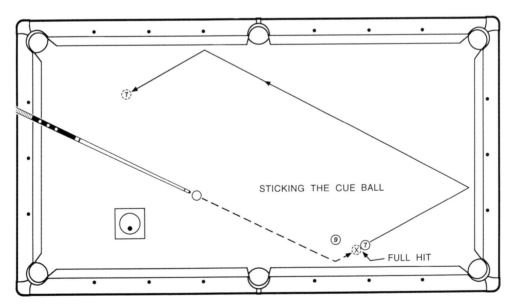

Sticking the Cue Ball with Draw

Once again your goal is to stick the cue ball behind a blocker (9-ball) and counter your opponent's hook with one of your own. This time you will need to use a sharp draw stroke to stop the cue ball because of the cue ball's shallow angle of approach. The real secret to this kick safety is to make full contact with the 7-ball.

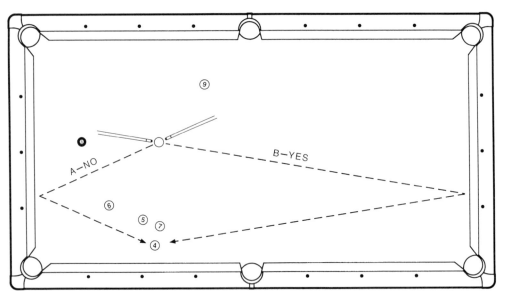

Avoid the Open End of the Table

You have two choices on this kick shot. Route A is much shorter to the 4-ball. However, there is a major drawback. Both the cue ball and the 4-ball will be heading toward the open end of the table which contains no blockers. Route B makes it a little tougher to hit the 4, but you have a better chance of hooking your opponent because of all the potential blockers in the area.

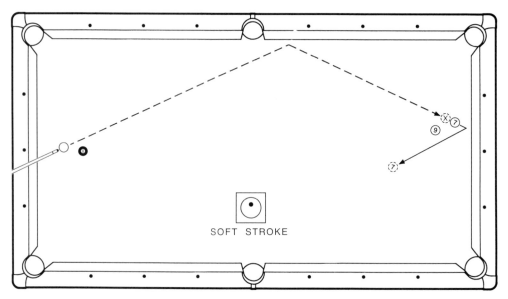

Kicking with Speed and Accuracy

The keys to this kick shot are near perfect accuracy and speed control. The plan is to softly contact the 7-ball in the center. The goal is to knock the 7 away from the rail and leave the cue ball behind the 9-ball! If you can approach this kind of touch and accuracy, you can compete with the best players in the world.

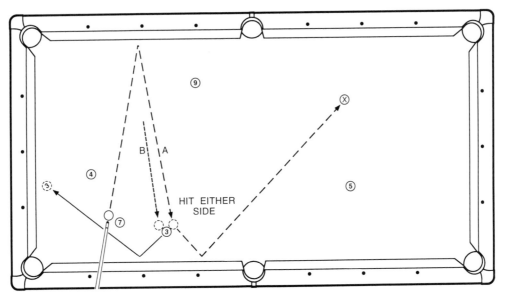

Splitting the Cue Ball and the Object Ball

When playing a kick safety you'll often want to split the cue ball and object ball apart, sending each ball to the opposite side of the table. In doing so you will likely either hook your opponent or leave him/her a tough shot. In the diagram the cue ball (line A) has knocked the 3-ball to the end rail while the cue ball is well down the table. This created a counter hook. If you had hit the other side of the 3 (line B) you could have achieved a similar objective, only this time the cue ball would be behind the cluster and the 3 would be at the right side of the table.

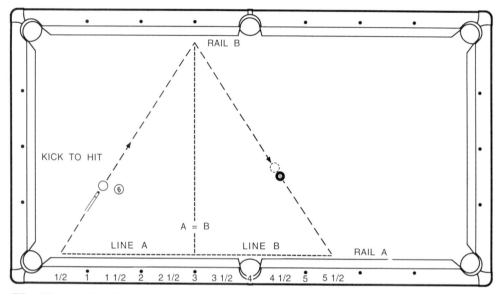

The Triangle Method

A little knowledge of geometry helps in explaining some of the wonders of pool. Perhaps you'll recall that an Isosceles triangle has two sides that are equal in length. We're going to use an Isoceles triangle to demonstrate how you can accurately execute kick shots.

In the diagram the two sides of the triangle that extend across the table from rail A to rail B are equal in length. When you combine these two sides with the heavy dashed line that runs along rail A, then you have a complete Isosceles triangle.

Notice that the cue ball and the 8-ball are located on opposite sides of the triangle. If you were to shoot the cue ball to the apex of the triangle on rail B, then it would rebound from that point and proceed directly into the 8-ball as diagrammed.

The tough part of this shot is to locate the position of the triangle so that you can then identify the point of aim, in other words, the apex of the triangle. Here's how it's done using the diamonds on the side rail. The first step is to estimate where you think you should aim the cue ball on rail B. In the example, a point of aim was chosen on rail B that's three diamonds up from the corner pocket. Now extend a line from the estimated contact point back through the cue ball to rail A. Notice that it contacts the rail ½ diamond up from the corner pocket. Now draw a line straight across the table from the contact point. It hits rail A at the third diamond. The difference between the two contact points is 2½ diamonds (3-½= 2½). This area forms line A. Now extend the bottom line of the triangle another 2½ diamonds so that line A equals line B. The base of the triangle now extends 5½ diamonds up the rail. Now for the acid test. Draw a line from the bottom right end of the triangle (that's located 5½ diamonds up from the corner) across the table to the estimated contact point on rail B. If the object ball is positioned on that line, as in the example, then you have estimated the contact point on rail B correctly! If the 8-ball were slightly left or right of the line, you would simply adjust your contact point a notch or two to the left or right on rail B.

Remember also that your stroke speed and the condition of the cushions affect the rebound angle. Also keep in mind that on wide approach angles the cue ball tends to rebound at a slightly wider angle. These factors can help you fine tune your calculations.

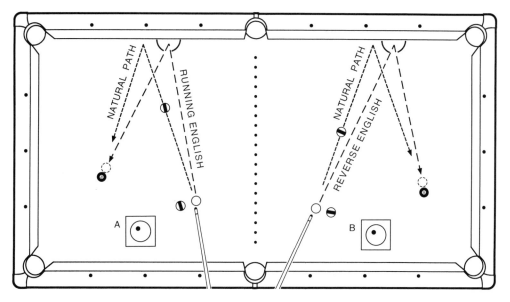

Using English to Avoid Other Balls

The natural path to the 8-ball is being blocked in positions A and B. You can still hit the 8-ball in both cases by using english because it changes the rebound angle of the cue ball. In position A running english (left) will widen the rebound angle, sending the cue ball into the 8. Notice how reverse english (left) sharpens the rebound angle in position B, which enables you to make contact with the 8-ball.

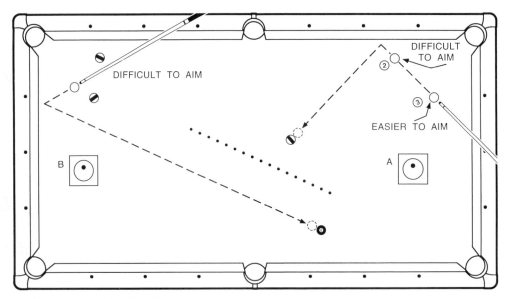

Difficult to Aim Kick Shots

Kick shots are surprisingly difficult to aim correctly when the cue ball is close to the rail you must hit, as in positions A and B. Therefore you should try to avoid using any english. The kick shot is much easier to aim in position A with the cue ball that's next to the 3. It may help to try visualizing a longer line of approach to the first rail.

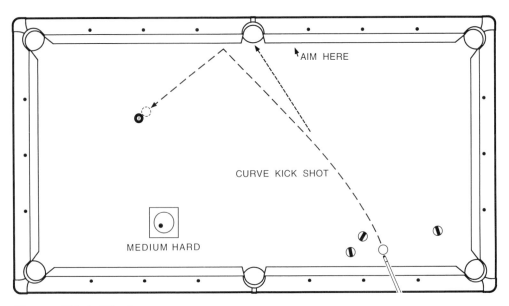

Curve Kick Shots

At first glance it appears as if the cluster of stripe balls is blocking all possible kick shots to the eight ball. You can solve this dilemma, however, by playing a curve kick shot. Aim to the right of the side pocket as indicated. Use a medium hard stroke, elevate your cue, and strike the cue ball with ½ tip of draw. The cue ball will then follow the diagrammed path to the 8-ball.

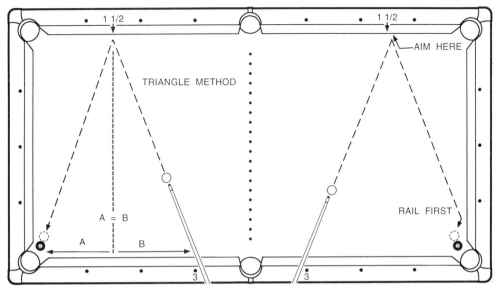

Kicking Balls in Using the Triangle Method

On most kick shots your main objectives are to hit the object ball and play safe. It is very difficult to purposefully make a kick shot when the object ball is more than a few inches from the pocket. On the other hand, you can reasonably expect to make a very high percentage of your kick shots when the object ball is in front of the pocket, as in the diagram above.

In the left hand portion of the diagram you can pocket the 8-ball by shooting a kick shot along a path that would cause the cue ball to scratch if the 8-ball was not in the way. You can find the point of aim on the top rail by using the triangle method once again. Pick out a spot on the top rail that you think is about where you should be aiming. Now draw a line from that point through the cue ball to the bottom rail. You can see that it contacts the rail at the third diamond up from the lower lefthand corner pocket. Your aiming point on the top rail should be half the distance from the upper lefthand corner pocket. In our example the contact point is indeed 1½ diamonds (half the distance) up the rail from the corner pocket. Therefore, if we aim to hit the rail at this point, the cue ball will follow a path directly into the 8-ball as indicated. A word of caution is in order. If you hit the 8-ball perfectly square and with enough force, you may follow the object ball in for a scratch. There are three solutions to this potential problem. One is to shoot so softly that the cue ball dies short of the pocket. The second solution is to depend on luck, to count on not being so unfortunate as to strike the 8-ball square in the middle. The best way to avoid scratching, however, is presented in the right hand portion of the diagram which shows the identical shot.

Using the triangle method our point of aim is the same, or 1½ diamonds from the upper righthand corner pocket. This time we're going to aim an inch or two to the right of our original point of aim. This will cause the cue ball to cut the 8-ball in <u>after</u> contacting the end rail first. By going rail first we've virtually eliminated the possibility of scratching.

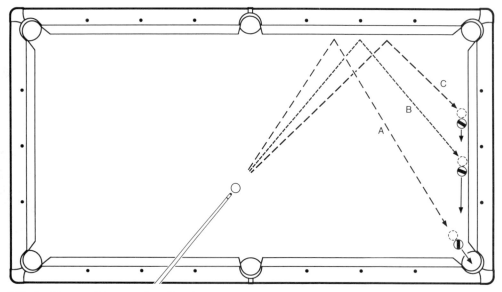

Kick Shots Along the Rail

Your goal is to pocket each of the stripe balls in the lower righthand corner pocket. The cue ball will be shot from the same location on each shot. Your point of aim is 2½ diamonds from the upper righthand corner pocket in shot A. Observe how your point of aim moves down the rail on B and C as the stripe ball is located further from the pocket. Kick shots B and C can be pocketed quite often when the ball is close to, but not touching the rail.

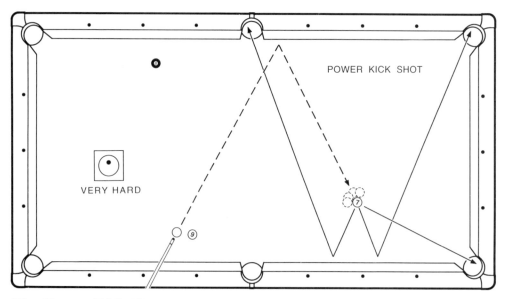

The Power Ride Kick Shot

Late in the game there are few, if any, balls you can use to rehook your opponent. In this situation you might as well go for broke and try to get lucky by playing a power kick shot. Your objective is to hit the object ball as hard as possible so that it can reach as many pockets as possible. The diagram shows only three potential results on this shot.

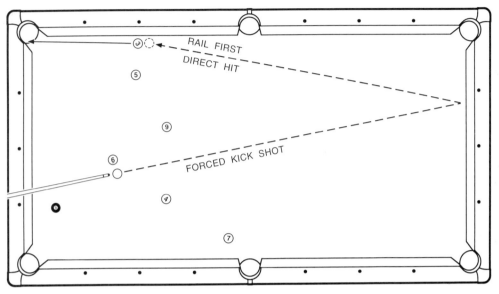

The Forced Kick Shot

You really have no choice but to shoot a kick shot at the 3-ball off the far end rail. When forced to shoot a difficult kick, be sure to give it your best shot. Don't just bemoan the fact that you're hooked and bang away halfheartedly. Aim as carefully as possible. Remember that you have two chances to make this shot, by either a direct hit or by going rail first. Even if you miss the shot, you may re-hook your opponent.

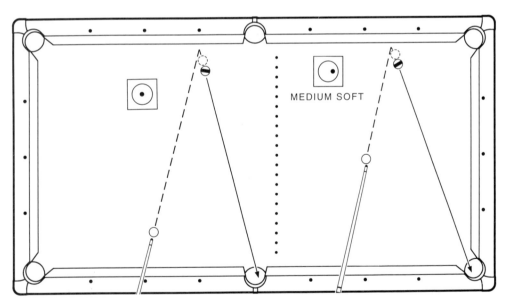

Short Rail Kick Shots

When the object ball is fairly close to the opposite rail and within a diamond or so of the opposite pocket, it can be kicked in fairly often. The closeness of the ball to the rail helps you judge the proper angle of approach. Use centerball whenever possible. In the position on the right, right english is needed to make proper contact. Use a medium soft stroke.

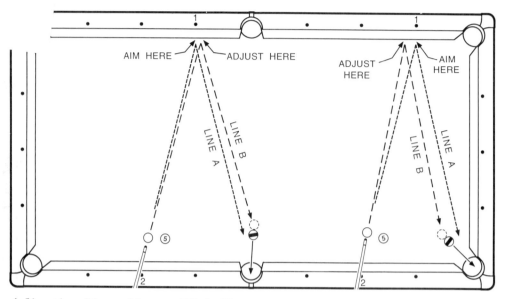

Adjusting Your Aim on Kick Shots

We discussed earlier how you can make shots that are in front of the pocket using the triangle method. You can also use this technique if the kicking angle is fairly sharp and the object ball is on or near the line to the pocket. The diagram will help to illustrate this concept.

In the position on the left, the cue ball will contact the first diamond from the side pocket at the top of the table using the triangle method. It will then proceed towards the center or the side pocket at the bottom of the table. If you shoot the cue ball along line A, you would miss the stripe ball to the right of the pocket. However, so far we have only used the triangle to give us a point of reference. Now we know that a small adjustment in aim is in order. Because the stripe is located a couple of inches to the right of line A, we must adjust our aim on the top rail slightly to the right as shown. If we compensate correctly, the cue ball will travel along line B and pocket the stripe in the side. In a worst case scenario, this method should nearly guarantee that we make contact with the stripe, thereby avoiding a foul that would give our opponent ball in hand.

The position on the right provides you with another example of how to use the triangle method. Line A shows the path that the cue ball would take if it were to travel along the triangle. Notice that the stripe ball is to the left of line A. You must therefore adjust your aim on the top rail a few inches to the left to complete the aiming process.

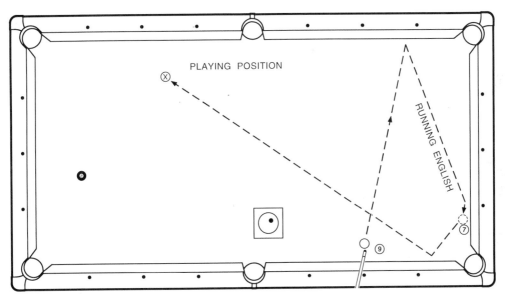

Playing Position of Kick Shots

Your goal on kick shots when the ball is near the pocket, should be to make the ball and to play position on the next ball if possible. You have no choice except to try to pocket the 7-ball in the lower righthand corner pocket. A touch of running english (right) will help to send the cue ball down the table for good position on the 8-ball.

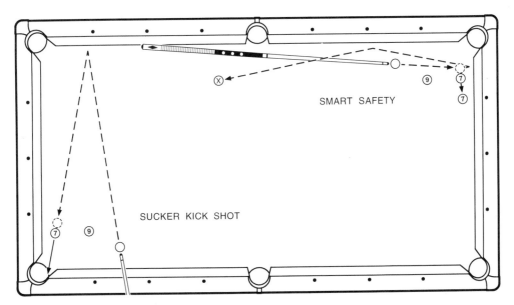

Sucker Kick Shots

The kick shot on the left side of the diagram looks easy to some players, but it's not. In fact, this shot should be labeled for suckers only. The position at the top right portion of the diagram is <u>exactly</u> the same. There is room to shoot past the 9-ball, skim the 7 and send the cue ball down the table. The lesson: don't shoot low percentage kick shots when you have the option of playing a high percentage safety.

CHAPTER 8

THE MENTAL GAME

Realizing Your Full Potential

As long as you can view pool as a <u>game</u>, you will derive great enjoyment both from competing and playing the game well. Learn to love the game for the challenges it presents and for what it can teach you about yourself. Always keep an open mind. Accept new ideas and information that can improve your game. With these principles firmly entrenched, you are well on your way to mastering the mental game.

In the early stages of a pool player's development, the physical side of the game is emphasized. This is a necessity. You must develop some competence in the fundamentals before you are ready to embrace the psychological aspects of pool. The mental side comes into play soon enough; a slump, or some difficulty grasping a particular type of shot, will definitely test your resolve and patience. A positive attitude will always help you; consider it as a type of funda<u>mental</u>. It will also give you an advantage when it comes time to tackle the more advanced features of the mental game.

You should embrace obstacles as opportunities presented that test your game and your mental strength. This is what the game of pool is really about; playing your best pool when it means the most to you. Don't downplay the significance of the mental game. As you work to develop both your physical and mental games, you ensure more rapid progress. You can look forward to beating a better player, competing successfully in your pool league or winning a local tournament. Whatever your goals might be, you will attain them far more quickly by working on your total game.

As stated, pool is primarily a physical game in the beginning stages. As you rise through the ranks, you will discover just how important the mental game becomes. At the professional level, pool becomes primarily a mental game. Often the difference between winning and losing is one minor mental error. Learn to appreciate the power of the mental game and how it affects your performance as a pool player.

There are basically three types of pool; practice pool, fun pool and pressure pool. Everybody, without exception, feels the heat at one time or another. The best players learn how to deal with the pressure and to make it work for them. When it comes to playing in competition, don't expect miracles or a quick fix. Remember, experience really is the best teacher. It takes time to develop all facets of your game, including the ability to play under pressure.

In the pages ahead, we'll discuss some ideas that can help you improve your mental game. Try them out. Put them to the test, just as you would a new stance or stroke.

Realizing Your Potential with a Positive Attitude

Your attitude will make or break you as a pool player. How you feel about your game, about practice, your opponent or the conditions under which you are playing will greatly determine your success. If you are playing in a tournament on slow tables with tight pockets, you must convince yourself that you love to play under these conditions. The same thing holds true when playing on fast tables with easy pockets. Whatever the conditions, you must find a reason to like them. The fact that it will help your game should be reason enough.

Try to look for the good in all situations. Choose the attitude that will help you play your best, not the one that gives you an excuse for losing. You must fill up your mental computer with as many positive attitudes as possible while eliminating the negatives. Your mind acts like a computer. It can only deliver what you put into your program. Garbage in, garbage out. Why not instead reprogram your computer as follows: winning attitude in, winning pool out. Make no mistake, correct thinking will help your game. You can't always be in dead stroke. You can, however, be in dead think the majority of the time. When your thinking is good and your attitude is positive, your play will reach a higher level of consistency. This will enable you to win even when your "A" game is on vacation. You can learn to win ugly.

All players feel fear at one time or another; fear of blowing a key shot in front of your teammates, losing a money match or ending a long run at the table. It's what you do about these fears that counts. You can overcome choking with effort and patience. During an important match and especially at critical moments, you can learn to employ techniques, new ways of thinking, that will help you counteract your fears. One of these techniques is to concentrate on your performance without worrying about the outcome. Give it your best shot. That's all you can do. The victories will come when they come. Sometimes you will play well and still lose. Other times you will win when you least expect to. Play each shot individually as well as you can and don't be too hard on yourself if things don't work out as planned.

At times you will play over your head. Your attitude towards these times of exceptional play can influence your development as a player. If you think your good shooting was a fluke, then that's what it was. On the other hand, you could view the experience as an example of your true potential. After all, it was you who made those incredible shots and position plays, not some stranger. Try to become more familiar with the person (you) who played pool at that peak level. As you do, it will enable you to turn that isolated performance into a regular event. Your belief in yourself, your attitude towards your game and your commitment to improvement means everything. Winning attitude in, winning pool out.

Confidence

When a pool player's confidence is high, they know they're going to hit the center of the pocket. This frees the mind to concentrate on strategy and position. When a pool player is shooting effortlessly with unerring accuracy, they are said to be in "the zone", in "dead stroke", "dead punch", shooting the lights out, or unconscious. There's nothing like playing with confidence. Confidence is different from overconfidence or cockiness, both of which can lead to carelessness and poor shot selection.

Success breeds success... and confidence. As your play improves, your confidence level grows proportionately. You enter into an upward spiral where improved play builds your confidence and your more confident demeanor leads to better play. In other words, your mental and physical games feed off each other, creating your optimal game.

It's difficult to say which comes first, confidence or physical skill. Some new players who are confident people by nature may begin the upward spiral with confidence while others may need to achieve a certain level of physical skill before they feel some confidence in their game. Whether the chicken comes before the egg or vice versa, the important thing to remember is the link between confidence and skill. Your confidence level should grow in direct proportion to your skills as a player. If not, then you're not giving yourself enough credit. You'll be like the beauty who thinks she's a wallflower. Your belief in your game must rise with your level of play. After all, if you don't believe in your game, who will?

Your desire to improve and your belief that it's within you to be a better player tomorrow than you are today are vital to your progress. And yet, for most of us, it's a challenge to always be confident. The game, by it's very nature, will continually test your confidence and resolve. You will occasionally be plagued by doubt, no matter what your level of play. These lapses are to be expected. What's important is how long you stay in a negative state. Make every effort to pull your mental game back on line to avoid a prolonged slump.

Confident thinking usually produces positive results. When you are down over a shot and you're sure you're going to make it, how often do you? When good players feel right over a shot, it usually goes in. How often do you make the shot when you're thinking negatively? When that little voice tells me I'm going to miss, I generally miss. Fortunately, that little voice doesn't speak to me very often anymore. But when it does, I'm in trouble. The shot is doomed. You've probably had similar experiences. When something tells you you're going to miss, you miss. Interestingly enough, those misses often come on routine shots we expect to make, and would most definitely make if we were confident. Positive or negative. Confidence or doubt. It's your choice. To play your best pool, you need to develop the habit of thinking confidently about your game.

When you're competing and you're not playing at your top speed, your confidence will be tested. What helps is to keep your spirits up, to tell yourself that your top game will reappear at any moment. When you do have those special moments of shooting great pool, let them feed on themselves. Give yourself a pat on the back. As a true pool player who experiences the highs and lows, you deserve the boost to your confidence when you're playing the game well. Why wouldn't you? Yet, there are some players who start to think negatively. They wonder when it will end. Why cut it short? Sometimes a hot streak is really a launching pad to a whole new level of play. Don't doubt that it can happen for you. Have confidence in your game and your ability to improve. You can if you think you can. In the final analysis, when it's down to the deciding game of an important match, and it's your turn to shine, it's your confidence, your belief in your ability in your heart of hearts that will spell the difference between winning and losing.

Concentration

When you are totally focused on the game, a large and noisy crowd doesn't exist. The amount of the wager, the title that's on the line, these things cease to matter. When you are at one with the game, it's just you, your cue, the table and the balls. You're in your own private world. In this altered state, the game is played one shot at a time, one game at a time. The zone of peak performance is everyone's dream. If you have never experienced it, you have something truly wondrous to look forward to. If you've been in the zone, there is no place you'd rather be!

When you are concentrating well, your opponent does not matter.

His/her skill level may be intimidating. You may have lost to him/her in the past, but none of this matters. While you are at the table, your opponent is sitting on the sidelines. As long as have your mind on the business at hand, you are giving yourself your best chance of playing great pool. You may even surprise yourself with your performance.

The ability to insulate oneself from all extraneous matters and play pool with a singleminded purpose is what makes a champion. Important matches have a way of bringing the game into focus. When the pressure is on, players either rise to the occasion or fold. It's unusual to maintain the status quo under competitive pressure. Will you play better or worse? Will you concentrate like a demon possessed or will you be distracted by a whisper in the crowd? The answer is probably both. At times your game will soar. At other times, you will be easily distracted and your mind will be on everything but the game.

Realistically, the goal is to enter a state of complete concentration as often as possible. There are plenty of valid reasons why some circumstances, some real life events, could override your ability to concentrate. But, if you make it your goal to concentrate fully on your game, it will happen.

Some players are able to turn on the concentration like a light switch while others need to summon the powers that be to enter the same state. Trying to concentrate is not always the answer. It can result in wasting energy better spent on playing the game. Don't try. Just play pool. Think about your game plan. Follow your preshot routine. Execute the shot. Again and again. Consider this your mantra. By focusing your energy on playing the game, you have a better chance of entering the zone. It only makes sense. When you're in the zone, there is nothing but the game. Therefore, entering the zone requires that you do what you're going to do when you're there; think and play pool. That's all.

Self Image

Noted psychologist and plastic surgeon Dr. Maxwell Maltz was curious as to why many of his patients still felt poorly about themselves even after reconstructive surgery had transformed their appearance. The answer, he discovered, lay in their self image. Although these patients looked fine, they couldn't accept the change. They would cling tenaciously to their belief, however inaccurate, that their faces were still flawed. The physical scars were removed but their mental and emotional scars remained, hidden below the surface, altering their perception of reality.

How you feel about your talent and your game will largely determine your progress as a pool player. You can have a world of potential but if you see yourself as only an average player, that's what you'll be. You will be limited by your inaccurate perception of your talent and ability. There's nothing wrong with playing at any level as long as you enjoy the game and are satisfied with your play. But if your goal is to play the best pool you are capable of, you'll need to shed inappropriate labels you may have placed on yourself.

You can start by making an honest appraisal of your game. Have you been holding back? Do you quickly revert back to your regular game every time you find yourself playing better than normal? Do you have trouble accepting compliments about your play? Do you enjoy playing familiar opponents while avoiding matches with players who you feel, perhaps incorrectly, are better than you? If you answered yes to any of these questions, then perhaps you need to overhaul you self image as a pool player. You play better than you think you do. You could be on the threshold of a quantum leap in your game. The only thing holding you back is your self image. Give yourself the opportunity to fulfill your potential. Don't give in to false beliefs about yourself. Be honest and give yourself the benefit of the doubt. Chances are you play a lot better than you think you can.

Mental Toughness

Mental toughness will win you a lot of matches, even against superior players. It is a necessary ingredient for playing top caliber pool. When it gets down to crunch time, you've got to have the inner strength to come through with the winning shot. The players refer to mental toughness as "heart". A player who can win against tough competition, win the cash in a money game or stage a comeback in the face of defeat is said to have heart. This individual is a clutch player who enjoys the game most when the pressure's really on.

There are many good players with beautiful strokes whose games fall apart under pressure. They simply don't have the mental toughness that will allow them to perform at their usual level of play. Don't feel too bad if you've blown a shot or two in the clutch. I know I've dogged my share. In fact, every player has succumbed to the pressure at one time or another in their careers. You either develop a thick hide that shields you from the pressure or you choose to be a recreational player. No shame should be attached to the latter choice; each person knows his or her strengths and motivations. This section is devoted to those players who have the desire and/or traits to withstand pressure play, to take their games to the highest level possible.

Those players who have become mentally tough competitors or who seem to have a natural disposition to withstand pressure are the toughest players to beat. Consider yourself fortunate if you are mentally strong to begin with. If not, take heart, for mental toughness can be acquired. Experience really is the best teacher. If you want to be league champion, you join a league and keep playing until you become accustomed to the pressure. If your goal is to become a tournament player, play in as many tournaments as you can. When you begin, expect to feel a little nervous. Don't be too surprised if you blow a few matches. It's all part of the learning process. You'll start coming through in situations that once caused you to fall apart.

Build on these positive experiences and the memories of your successful outings. They represent you at your best, as a player who can come through when the chips are down.

No matter how much heart you develop, there will still be times you blow a match that was in your grasp. This happens to everyone at every level of play. Just don't let a mistake or two in a crucial situation do permanent damage to your game. It takes a lot of work to develop mental toughness. Don't give it away. When you miss a shot, admit it, tell yourself that's not like you, and let it go. Leads that you blow and shots that you miss are really just further tests of your mental toughness, your heart. In fact, how quickly you recover from a missed shot and move on to the next shot is one of the most obvious indications of mental toughness.

The next time you're in the heat of battle, tell yourself that you're the kind of player that comes through under pressure. Rise to the occasion. Make that winning shot. Execute what you know you can. Do this often enough and other players may start talking about your game in glowing terms. They may even pay you one of the highest compliments a pool player can receive, "You've got heart!".

Excuses

In a famous line from the movie, "The Hustler", big time stakehorse Bert Gordon (played by George C. Scott) counsels the hustler, Fast Eddy Felson (played by Paul Newman) that, "Excuses are a loser's best friend". This timeless bit of advice is offered after Fast Eddy has been outsmarted by Minnesota Fats (played by Jackie Gleason).

Of course, there are always valid reasons why we lose at pool. These reasons are not excuses. Wrong. The real reason we lose most games is that we are outplayed, or we played less than our best game of pool.

Fast Eddy was the better pool player, but still lost the contest. He drank too much or he would have won. Did he have a valid reason for losing? No. What he had was an excuse. When a match is over, it's easy to come up with a hundred "reasons" why you lost. None of them really matters. The results are the same. On the scoreboard they don't put an asterisk that says, "This player would have won if he'd gotten his share of the breaks". After the game is over, you can probably find solace in telling your tale of woe to whoever will listen (most likely someone who also uses excuses). You can convince yourself that you could have won and should have won. But, as long as you make excuses you will deny yourself the great gift that losing offers you; the chance to learn more about yourself and your game.

Try a new approach for a change. The next time you lose a match, forget about the excuses and the bad breaks. Take a closer look at how you really played. Let's say you lost a match 9-6. Your opponent made the nine on the break three times to your none. He was "lucky", you were not. Let's say you handed over four games that you could easily have won. If you had played better shape, taken more time over your shots, you could have won a few of those games. Take two wins off your opponent's score and add them to yours. Now it's 8-7, your favor. Furthermore, one of your opponent's winning break shots came after you blew a relatively easy shot on the 9-ball in the previous game. Take one more game off his score. Now it's 8-6, in your favor. Despite your opponent's "good luck", you were the cause of your own defeat. The outcome could have been different had you taken greater advantage of your opportunities.

Occasionally you will lose because you were outplayed. You played your best, but your opponent played better. You will probably discover upon closer analysis, however, that you could have won many more matches by simply playing better. Take a closer look at how you played. Be one hundred percent accountable for your game and for your mistakes. An honest appraisal of your play will only help you improve your game. And that is what every pool player wants.

There are a million excuses for losing, but only one reason; you played less than your best. The following list shares some of the most popular and widely used excuses out there today.

> I was out of stroke
> My opponent was in dead stroke
> I got terrible rolls
> My opponent got all the rolls
> The table was too fast
> The table was too slow
> The pockets were too tight
> My opponent sharked me
> The crowd was too noisy
> The room was too crowded
> The bet was too high (I choked)
> The bet was too low (no interest in the game)
> I had too much too drink
> They didn't serve alcohol
> My mind was on work, my wife, etc.
> I argued with the wife, etc.
> The place was too hot
> The place was too cold
> My tip needs repairing

As you can see, the list could go on and on. Once you become aware of excuse-making, you can cut it out of your game. When you do, all that's left is the game. Good or bad, let your game speak for itself. Be responsible for your game. This will speed up your learning, make you a better competitor and allow you to focus better on the task at hand.

The Luck Factor

When you smash open a rack of Nine Ball, you never know exactly what you're going to get. A 9 on the break, an easy run out, a scratch. Nothing is certain. The luck factor enters into every game of pool. The roll of the balls is what makes pool so fascinating and, at times, infuriating. We love it when the rolls are going our way. We can't stand it when our opponent is getting more than his/her share of the breaks. When the match is over, the conversation inevitably centers on how each person played and who got the rolls.

In the long run, which could be days, weeks, even months, the rolls always even out, unless you've created bad karma for yourself. As an example, when a touring pro is tearing up the circuit, winning five or six tournaments in a year, excellent play is primarily responsible. Interestingly enough, that same player can go the whole next season with no wins to his credit. How can a player's performance vary that much? Chances are he got some good breaks during his big year and none the following year. The rolls always even out.

The bad news is that poor rolls can keep you from winning when you've played great pool. The good news is that they will sometimes help you win even when your game is off track.

It will increase your peace of mind if you can accept the rolls and the breaks of the game philosophically. Each and every tournament or league match you'll ever be involved in is contested over the short run where the luck factor exerts it's greatest influence. In a race to eleven, the rolls will often determine the outcome. Perhaps you've seen one player knock another into the loser's bracket by a lopsided score. Later in the tournament, the two players meet again, only this time the score is reversed. A shift in the rolls is usually the reason.

The next time you are agonizing over the rolls, stop and remember that the deck is also stacked in your favor. Accept the luck factor as part of the game because it's never going to change. Adopt a fatalistic attitude toward the rolls. Enjoy and appreciate the good breaks and accept the bad, perhaps with a certain amusement. Watching the roll of the balls, good or bad, is one of the true joys of the game.

Opponents

Your attitude towards your opponent will go a long way toward determining your success as a pool player. If you are fearful because you believe that your opponent is much better than you are, then you are beat from the start. The same is true of the player who is a jinx, who has your number. If you are easily intimidated, there are a number of forceful personalities with which you will have trouble. Losses can also result from not respecting an opponent who then surprises you with the quality of his/her play.

No matter what the competition, learn to enjoy the opportunity to do battle with a worthy opponent. Without an opponent, pool wouldn't be the same game. Relish the chance to play in your own version of the World Championship. Put your fears aside no matter who you are up against. Learn to play the table, not your opponent. This is easier said than done. But if you can learn to play your game, to perform at your optimal level, then you will give yourself your best shot at winning. Enough experience and a strong belief in your game will bring you to the point where you can play your game no matter the competition.

Some players believe you should hate your opponent. These players need to be motivated by external stimuli. And while it might work for some players, it diverts mental energy away from your game, energy that could be better used to play at your optimal level. Most high level players prefer to simply compete hard, remaining detached from their opponent.

Opponents must be dealt with on occasion, such as when their behavior slips over the line of acceptability. But, for the most part, your mind should be focused on playing your game. Although you may not hate your opponent, don't sympathize with them either. In fact, you should show no mercy. Win by as wide as margin as possible. Don't let up. It's your best defense against sloppy play or a sudden turn of fortune. Concentrate fully to ensure your victory.

When you are playing against an opponent of equal or greater ability, you will spend at least half your time awaiting your turn. Your thought processes during this time can definitely contribute to the outcome of the match. You can sit in your chair hoping your opponent will miss. Or you can use your waiting time productively. You can watch for weaknesses in your opponent's game. You can look for ways to play around his/her strengths. Look for signs that tell you "I can beat this person". It will build your confidence when you see your opponent make mistakes. You should also spend time marshalling your strengths, and thinking positive thoughts about your game. When you get a shot be ready to make the most of it, no matter what miraculous feats your opponent may have just performed.

When competing against someone whose game you really respect, learn all you can from watching them play. But don't be in awe of their game, as you still have a match to play. You need all your positive energy to focus on playing your game.

When the match is over, don't be crushed by your defeats. Feel proud that you gave it your best effort, that you directed your energy to playing the best game you could. Shake hands with your opponent, smile and congratulate him/her. Remember that your opponent is a fellow competitor who has fought a good fight. They also deserve to win. And if you care at all about your reputation, you'll realize there's no point in playing the role of the poor loser. Be a good sport both during and after the competition.

Self Talk

Your mind never rests. Even while you're playing pool you are constantly in a dialogue with yourself. You're engaging in self talk. This seemingly harmless pastime can greatly influence your game. In fact, it may even determine your success as a player. Fortunately, you have a choice in the matter. You can choose to build yourself up or tear yourself down. Your self talk can prepare you to bounce back from a poor shot. It can also turn a poor shot into a string of missed balls. You engage in self talk whether you are aware of it or not. So you might as well make it work for you instead of against you.

There are two kinds of self talk: positive or negative. You can deliver messages that will either improve your game or harm it. Take for example your reaction to missing an easy ball. Do you say, "I'm a lousy player, I stink!", or do you say, "I've got to get into my routine so I can eliminate these mental errors". The first response reinforces the negative outcome. In the second, you are taking steps to solve a problem and improve your play. There's a huge difference. Let's move onto your next shot. Are you still kicking yourself for missing the last shot or are you mentally prepared to give your next shot your best effort? I don't have to tell you which response maximizes your chances for victory.

Listed below are a number of common thoughts and events that take place during a match. I've listed a positive and negative response to each one. No doubt you've experienced these events before. How did you respond? How did your response affect your play and the outcome of the game?

Event	Positive	Negative
Miss an easy nine ball	I'll sharpen up my routine.	I'm a loser!
Out of stroke	I'll find other ways to win until my best (" A") game returns.	I'm a goner, I've no chance now.
Skillful opponent	I'm going to do my best and with a couple breaks I can beat this guy.	There's no way I can beat this guy.
Pockets are too tight	The table is tough so I'll play more safeties. My opponent will also miss.	I can't make a ball under these conditions.
Getting no rolls	I'll wait for my turn. The rolls always even out.	I'm so unlucky. Why is this happening to me?

It's tough enough to beat your opponent, why would you want to have to also beat yourself? The next time you are in the heat of battle, take notice of your self talk. If you are engaging in negative dialogue, then it's time to reprogram your mental computer. Substitute negative dialogue with positive dialogue about yourself and your game. Resolve to forever break the bad habit of negative self talk. Be patient with yourself, as it will probably take some time. Bad habits die hard. By making positive self talk a way of life, you will also reap another important benefit: you will have the best support system a person could have when the going gets tough. Yourself!

Goals and Hurdles

Without goals and dreams your game is like a ship without a rudder. Your destination will be unknown. In contrast, a goal that you feel strongly about can provide the emotional fuel needed to take you wherever you choose to go. It all begins by making a commitment to yourself and your game. Once you make a commitment and establish goals, you will have a purpose and a destination. Your play will take on new meaning. You will begin your personal journey toward pool excellence.

Put aside some time to think seriously about your game. What is it you really want to accomplish? And in what time frame? Make your goals realistic. They should present a definite challenge, but also be attainable. A realistic goal encourages you to improve, but is not so difficult that it causes you to give up in despair. Goals should be specific and measurable. For instance, your goal might be to make a tough shot eight out of ten times in practice. Or to win sixty percent of your league games. Some goals can be realized in a day or a week. Others may take months or years. Establish a list of goals covering a variety of time frames, ideally each building on the next. The example below illustrates the process.

Time Frame	Goal
Daily	Work on specific shots in practice
Monthly	Incorporate a new technique into your stroke
Yearly	Raise overall game from "C" to "B"
Five year	Become a local champion and a semi-pro
Lifetime	Always learn. Derive satisfaction and joy from pool

You goal seeking will be most effective when you write them down. By involving your senses in the process, you strengthen your commitment. There's something about seeing your goals on paper. Pursue your goals in a relaxed and confident manner. If you put too much pressure on yourself to reach your goals, you'll take some of the fun out of learning. Make sure you review your goals regularly. As you reach certain goals, replace them with new ones. Along the way you will be creating a higher standard of play.

Certain goals may also appear as roadblocks. You may bump up against them several times, only to fall back each time. Let's say your goal is to win the Friday night Eight Ball tournament at your favorite pool room. So far the pattern has been that once you reach the finals, you blow your chance of winning. You know you're physically capable or you wouldn't get as far as you do. The missing element is the mental readiness. This is something every player at every level goes through at some point in their career. Your failure should be looked upon as another learning experience; as another step toward realizing your goal. You could ask yourself what you could do differently the next time you're in a similar position. But be content that you are working on your goal every time you play that Friday night tournament and lose. Know that if you keep banging on the door, you'll eventually break it down. You are simply facing a psychological hurdle not unlike other hurdles you've cleared in the past or will encounter in the future.

When you clear a significant hurdle, take a moment to enjoy the experience. You've just won your personal Super Bowl. Bask in the warmth and good feelings that come from a job well done. Then prepare to move forward with confidence towards your next objective. Understand also the cumulative effect of your successes. Every hurdle you jump, each goal you realize, will build your confidence and the belief that you can scale the next. You're on your way!

Dealing with a Slump

You can't always expect to be playing your "A" game. All players experience slumps. It's your reaction to a slump that makes the difference. If you employ the proper techniques, slumps may do little damage. They can even serve a useful purpose. The trouble comes when a slump sinks its teeth into your game and you allow it to perpetuate itself.

Slumps come in several sizes and shapes. During a physical slump, your stroke may be off kilter. Even so, your attitude and thinking may remain at peak levels. Under these conditions, you can still play a very solid game. Sometimes a good mental game can even carry you into the winners circle.

During a slump in your mental game, you are lacking that certain something that will put you over the hump. Your stroke may feel fine. You may even be in dead stroke. However, there is a missing piece or two in the mental game. Slumps like these can be frustrating. You know you've got the game to win, but you keep getting in your own way.

The worst slump, of course, occurs when both your mental and physical games are off. Poor physical play can lead to mental deterioration. A negative attitude leads to even poorer play. Each part of your game feeds off the other. This kind of slump can last an indeterminate amount of time.

If you learn to recognize the early signs of a slump and move quickly, you can greatly reduce the time spent in a slump.

If you find yourself in a slump, keep your spirits up. Don't give up on yourself. Instead, take the time to learn something now that can help your game. Before the slump you were playing well despite a flaw in your technique that you knew would need your attention sooner or later. Now may be the time to solve that problem. Once you get used to shooting with your new, improved stroke, you may go on to play better then ever. While in a mental slump you may discover a technique that will improve your ability to concentrate. Perhaps a new set of goals will motivate you to higher levels of achievement.

Whatever the cause of your slump, you should take constructive steps to pull yourself from its grasp within a reasonable period of time. Above all, don't wallow in a slump wondering whether you're ever going to play well again. A slump is really nothing more than a test of your resolve and a learning experience. Keep the faith. It may take awhile for your best game to reappear. But, on the other hand, something may click into place and you may suddenly find yourself playing better than ever.

Your development as a player will most likely follow a pattern of two steps forward, one back. Your game will be a series of higher highs and higher lows. Once your game reaches a certain level, you may discover that your slumps are less frequent and of shorter duration. You will achieve a certain level of consistency. You will have a game that you can count on almost every time you play. When you reach this stage, you are truly a player.

The Mental Side to Pocketing Balls

To play your best pool you've got to love the game. You've got to accept and relish the challenge that each and every shot presents. It also helps to enjoy the process of playing, practicing and learning the game.

Each shot begins with the planning process. Once you've selected your shot, it's time to go into your preshot routine. Make it a habit to use your routine on every shot. This will help build your confidence, concentration and consistency. Remember the three C's. When your routine begins, you enter into a beautiful place called pool where it's just you and the game. You are totally focused on the shot at hand.

When you are in your routine, let nothing disturb you or shake your confidence. If you question what you are doing, or don't feel quite right over the shot, get up and start your routine again. To do this takes great discipline. You will be rewarded by a decrease in the amount of balls you miss.

Most of your shots will be familiar to you. You've made most of them before, some shots hundreds, even thousands of times. This should give you confidence. In fact, playing pool well is largely a matter of executing what you already know. So call upon your previous successes under pressure.

They will tell you that you can handle the situation. Give yourself credit for your skill and ability to play the shot and play it well. Learn to play one shot at a time. When the crowd's stirring, the league championship is on the line or some other worthy goal is within your grasp, it's easy for your mind to go off in a thousand directions. However, you must train yourself to focus totally if your goal is to play well in the heat of competition. Forget about the trophy or the big check you're about to win. Thinking about these things is what causes players to choke. Don't get ahead of yourself. When you're under pressure it's all about execution. Step into your routine, give it your best aim and trust your stroke. Don't steer the shot. Just let it go with trust and complete confidence. That's the best you can do. You will maximize your chances by believing that a shot will go in, but not being overly concerned if it doesn't. Build relaxation into your game and this will reduce your fear and anxiety.

Your warm-up strokes should leave you feeling relaxed, comfortable and decisive. Once you are stroking the shot, your eyes should be fixed on the target. You stroke will work best when its linked to the target. Stay as natural as possible. Now is not the time to get technical with your grip, stance or follow through. It's best if you can simply let the stroke happen. If you must think about something, hopefully your thoughts are on making a smooth stroke.

If you are confident in your aim and your stroke is smooth and straight, then you've done everything that you can to make the shot. Accept the results, positive or negative. After making the shot, summon your concentration and go through your routine again from start to finish. Leave nothing out. Play this way, shot after shot, until the game is over or you must give up the table. If you miss, don't get angry. Anger will tighten your muscles and severely affect your performance. Try to learn something from the errant shot so you don't make the same mistake again. Don't let one bad shot affect your confidence for the shots that will follow. After analyzing your mistake, get your mind set for your next turn.

Difficult shots require a little something extra. Don't necessarily try harder on them, just pay a little more attention. Increase your focus. Perhaps a couple extra practice strokes will help you zero in on the target better. On hard shots you can take a little pressure off by adopting this line of thought: you know you can't be expected to make every hard shot. Certainly the spectators don't expect you to. Therefore, lighten up on yourself. Tell yourself that the best you can do is give it your best shot. If you make it, great. If you miss, so what! Nobody's perfect. With this attitude you won't miss because you choked. You'll miss because you missed.

After making a great shot, a mini celebration is in order. Let your self-congratulatory glow fade before playing your next shot. Take a sip of water, rub your shaft clean and chalk your tip. Allow yourself a few moments to come back down to earth before attempting the next shot. Emotionally, you need to be on an even keel to address your next shot. Your attitude towards each shot is key. Don't take routine shots for granted. Take pride in how you execute each shot, no matter how easy. If the shot is quite simple, focus on playing the best position possible. Find something to spark your interest in each and every shot. On tough shots, learn to rise to the occasion in a confident and relaxed manner. We all have our trouble shots. These shots teach us that we have more to learn about this great game so don't let them upset you. Put them on your "to do" list for your next practice session.

In the final analysis, you know you'll have truly mastered the game when you can play each shot to the best of your ability, no matter the occasion. You will have earned your black belt in pool. As you will, or may have already, discovered, the game is not about banging balls into the pocket. It's all about your mind and how well you can let it work for you. Remember this equation:

Your potential - mental disturbance = Your ultimate performance

How to Make Pressure Shots

The next time you are facing a shot for all the marbles, perhaps it will help you to use a couple techniques on this list. They will ease the pressure by boosting your confidence and by giving you something positive to focus on.

1) Stick with your normal preshot routine. Don't rush the shot. Take your usual time to settle in and shoot.

2) Take a couple of deep breaths, hold and exhale slowly. This will help relax you.

3) Tell yourself you've made this shot thousand's of times before. It's no big deal.

4) Downplay the significance of the shot. Remember, first and foremost, pool is a game.

5) Keep your focus on the here and now. Don't get ahead of yourself by thinking about what the shot means.

6) Enjoy the moment. Tell yourself this is the kind of situation you love to be in. Pressure shots are why you play pool.

7) Tell yourself the last shot is the easiest shot. You don't have to worry about playing position. Make the shot and keep the cue ball from scratching.

8) Under pressure most players tend to shoot a little harder. Give yourself the luxury of giving the shot a good firm stroke. Don't baby it.

9) Know your options for playing safe. Maybe you can play a partial safety.

10) Concentrate on using a firm bridge. It gives you something positive to focus on.

11) When you're down in your stance, if you have any doubts about your shot, get up and start your preshot routine again.

12) Prepare for the competition so that you feel confident in your game.

Spiritual Pool

Pool is a religion for many players. It is a way of life. These players recognize the spiritual aspect of pool. They know their actions and behaviors create both positive and negative consequences. Furthermore, they know the importance of having the pool gods on their side. I know from my experience that certain actions can lead to an immediate and negative response. For example, if I get a little lackadaisical with my position play, I'll wind up hooking myself or scratching. The lesson here is that the pool gods don't reward sloppy play. Perhaps you've had a similar experience.

The game of pool is tough enough as it is without incurring the wrath of the pool gods. If you want to create good karma, follow their ten commandments of pool, listed below.

1.) Love pool for the great game it is.
2.) Be a good winner and an even better loser.
3.) Learn to accept good and bad rolls.
4.) Respect your opponent.
5.) Respect the rules and tradition of the game.
6.) Never take any shot for granted.
7.) Learn from your mistakes and be a lifelong student of the game.
8.) Share your knowledge and love of pool with others.
9.) Make no excuses for poor play.
10.) Never give up during a match or any other time.

COMPETITIVE PLAY

How To Prepare For Tournaments, Money Games & League Play

By it's nature, pool brings out the competitive instinct in most participants. That helps to explain the popularity of the three most popular forms of competition: tournament pool, money games and league play. In this chapter we'll discuss how you can gain greater enjoyment from your favorite form(s) of competition and how you can improve your play.

Tournaments are a very popular training ground for new players as witnessed by the proliferation of weekly tournaments at most pool rooms and taverns. A friendly money game for a couple of bucks can sharpen your skills under pressure and program you for tournament play. Social players and serious types alike both enjoy the chance to compete weekly with their teammates in league competition. A number of major associations end their year with championships for big prize money and trophies.

No matter what your flavor, you will find a number of competitive options available in your area. You will find that playing a variety of opponents under all sorts of conditions is one of the best ways to learn the game.

Furthermore, nothing can replace the lessons that come from playing under the heat. They will reveal much about your game and, more importantly, about yourself. Play competitively as much as possible and you will soon learn to enjoy the pressure. With enough experience you will learn to play even better when the heat is on. In turn, your victories against worthy opponents will help produce some of your fondest memories.

Opponents

Your opponent will most likely exert some influence on the quality of your play despite your efforts to remain 100% focused on your game. Because of this, you should be prepared to do what you can to minimize that impact. Being aware and keeping your perspective are the most effective tools you can use to combat the impact. When two players compete there is always an unspoken battle for psychological dominance. Both players may compete on more or less equal terms. They are both respectful of each other's game but are not intimidated. In some cases, both players may be somewhat afraid of each other. As a result, both their games suffer. Finally, one player may simply intimidate the other into virtual submission.

Each of the three scenarios above may evolve during a match. One player's good play may cause his/her opponent to dog shots. Often this effect will snowball. Perhaps both players will feed off each other's play as they take their games to new heights. And lastly, both players may be so intimidated that neither can make a ball. Under these circumstances, whoever can right their ship first wins the match.

Sometimes dominance is established before the match even begins. One player may be used to tournament play or high stakes action while the other is not. One player may also be a known and respected name with a reputation for playing under pressure. These players are tough to beat. Nevertheless, you can still beat a name player despite prematch jitters. Your experience and belief in your ability to play the game plus a few breaks can enable you to upset name players. It happens more often than you think. Here's the winning formula:

A few rolls + Exceptional play + Your opponent has an off day = Victory

When you're up against a superior player, try to stay as relaxed as possible. Play loose. And, as always, stay in your routine and think positive. Your opponent may feel some added pressure because he/she is expected to beat you.

It helps if you can believe that you play better as this will build your confidence. Find something(s) about your opponent's game that you think you do better. Maybe he/she takes too many chances, or you play better safeties. If you are playing particularly well, ask yourself if you'd like to play you when you're in peak form. Remember, your best game is also pretty darn good. Your opponent may not like your action.

Your actual performance, physically speaking, may be most affected by the tempo of your opponent's play. As a rule of thumb, fast players feel the negative effects of slow play much more than slow players feel any negative effects of playing with a fast player. Fast players who slow their game down will lose their rhythm. Slow players who speed up will miss balls because of carelessness. So, whatever you do, don't fall into the trap of playing the game at your opponent's tempo.

I would say that fast players are the easiest to play as long as you don't speed up your game. A fast player gets the job over in a hurry. As a result, you retain possession of the table for much longer periods of time (assuming it's an even game). This enables you to take time with your shots while your opponent fidgets on the sidelines. As you might expect, extremely slow players drive fast players crazy and very slow players make it hard to maintain your level of concentration. The ultimate tempo is the one that allows you to play your best game, regardless of your opponent. The majority of the very best players seem to move along at a very measured and steady pace that gives them enough time to complete their routine without paralyzing themselves over a shot.

The knowledge you gain from observing your opponent's play can be put to good use. For example, you may wish to play more safeties if your opponent kicks poorly or is having trouble figuring out how the cue ball reacts off the table's cushions. You would also not be wise to leave bank shots if your opponent is an expert in that area.

The psychological dominance we spoke of earlier may become highly visible as a match progresses. When one player's game begins to fall apart it is said that he/she is "breaking down". The breakdown happens in all sports. It is that moment when your opponent mentally throws in the towel before the contest is over. They have admitted defeat. The remainder of the contest is a mere formality. Signs to watch for include: your opponent slumps in the chair, misses easy shots, whines and pouts and stops trying.

All players have experienced breaking down at one time or another. The very best learn to overcome this tendency, which is just another reason why they are so tough to beat. The best antidote is to build your will power and develop a fighting spirit. When you are down, but not out, continue to play hard. Play for your own sense of self respect. Keep fighting and your opponent will respect you. Once this becomes a habit, you will be far less likely to break down in the future, under any circumstances.

All players adopt a certain demeanor during competition. Each has a distinctive pool personality that could possibly exert an influence on your play. No doubt you enjoy playing with some people while others get under your skin. Sometimes the effects are very subtle. You may find yourself easing up slightly because you genuinely like your opponent and can't stand the thought of seeing them in any more pain. Whatever the circumstances, be advised that your opponent's personality can worm its way into your psyche, undermining your play in the process. Resolve not to let your opponent's personality have any effect on your play, because in nine cases out of ten it will hurt your game.

Listed below are a number of common personality traits along with the possible ruinous effects on your game. In each case the antidote is the same: play your game and ignore them to the best of your ability.

Personality Trait	Effect on your game
The Nice Guy	You hate hurting him/her. Loss of competitive edge.
The Jerk	Your anger makes you try too hard.
The Crybaby	You feel sorry for him/her. You feel guilty for getting the rolls.
The Talker	Distracts you from your routine.
The Gamesman	Plants seeds in your mind that eat away at your concentration.
The Clown	You start to think the game's not worth playing.
The Professor	Continually offers advice. Tends to undermine your confidence.
The Serious type	He puts your nerves on edge. Unspoken criticism? No humor.
The Silent type	Psychological warfare at its best. You wonder what he/she is thinking.
The Showboater	Their antics are designed to make you believe they play better than they really do.
The Professional	This player is a role model for your behavior. Imitate, but don't be intimidated.

Sharking

There are a number of techniques that your opponent may use to break your concentration. This is referred to as sharking. In an ideal world, of course, no player would deliberately shark another. Every match would be a test of each player's skill. However, since sharking probably dates back to the birth of the sport, don't expect it to stop in your lifetime. It's as simple as that. Whether you like it or not, it's part of the game. Therefore, it's in your best interests to learn how to effectively combat shark attacks.

There are two broad categories of sharking tactics: obvious physical distractions and the more subtle mental games. Some of the more common physical sharks would include:

Jingling change
Constant coughing
Waving the cue stick
Tapping the cue tip
Moving while in the players line of sight
Standing too close to the table
Wriggling a foot
Breaking down the cue as if to signify the end of the game
Talking while you're shooting

Obviously this list could be greatly expanded. A physical shark is a deliberate attempt to distract you while you are in the act of shooting. When your opponents shark you in this manner, they are depriving you of your right to play the shot uncontested. This kind of sharking should not be tolerated, especially if it disturbs you to the point that you miss your shot. There are a number of countermeasures that can be effective. During a tournament you can call your opponent's behavior to the attention of an official. You may be awarded ball in hand or, possibly, the match. You could refuse to play or quit altogether until the sharking stops. It may even help to embarrass your opponent by making a remark to the crowd. As a last resort, you could turn the match into a sharkfest. Fight fire with fire. However, this is not highly recommended as it puts you on your opponent's level. It may even backfire by distracting you from playing your game.

Physical sharks can be very damaging to your play if you succumb easily to distractions. As your game develops and your concentration grows, you will become less affected by this type of sharking. I've found that most players who use these tactics don't play very well anyway. To me, these attempts are really a sign of weakness. These players know they aren't good enough to win with their play alone, so they resort to shark tactics. Imagine their frustration when you calmly go about your business, totally oblivious to their childish attempts to knock you off your game.

Pool requires intense concentration, as we've discussed many times before. Knowing this, many players will try to distract you from your mission with comments and suggestions that are designed to get inside your head. The idea is to get you to think about anything except the proper execution of your next shot. This form of sharking can be very subtle and very potent. You will need a thick hide to repel your opponent's attempts to get your mind off track. The best defense is a total belief in your game and total control of your thought processes.

Let's assume that you're leading in a match, you've gotten a couple of breaks, but you're also playing well. Your opponent whispers to a friend, but loud enough for you to hear, that you can't play, that you're just lucky.

What would you think? Would you be angry or amused? Would you let his comment upset you to the point you missed your next shot? A seasoned player who's shark-proof would recognize that this was a weak attempt to distract him/her, and go on to pocket his/her next ball and play perfect position, ignoring the comment altogether. A beginning player will probably let it affect him/her, not being familiar with the practice of sharking and/or not confident enough in his/her game to ignore it.

Psychological sharking is only as damaging as you let it be. You will encounter sharking untold times during your career as a pool player. Again, I advise that you take an amused and detached view of your opponent's attempts to erode your confidence. Recognize that when opponents apply the subtle shark, they are really only testing your mental strength. Are you strong enough to withstand it? Are you confident of your game and yourself, or are you at the mercy of your opponent? If these questions upset you, then I accomplished what a shark artist could. Toughen up! Don't let your opponent invade the sanctuary of your mind.

Now let's turn to the other side of the coin: should you use shark moves? Should you engage in psychological warfare? I believe the answer lies in your ability to concentrate and your feelings about the ethics of invading an opponent's personal space. I will say this, if sharking takes away from your game and/or makes you feel guilty, then it's probably not for you. Let your cue do the talking. On the other hand, if you view it as merely another way to test your opponent's game, then it's probably okay. It's your decision.

Tournaments

Tournaments cater to all levels of expertise from the local to the national scene. No matter how you play I would encourage you to participate in as many tournaments as is practical for you. Tournaments are an excellent way to gain experience and knowledge at a relatively low cost.

For a flat entry fee, unlike a money game, you can challenge yourself on any level you wish. Many local tournaments charge as little as five dollars ($5) per entry and many add to the pot to make it more attractive to entrants. As you gain more experience and move up the ladder, the tournaments increase, of course, in price. A local semi-pro tournament may cost between $35 and $75. Choose according to your skill level as well as your comfort level and you'll perform better. Remember, you'll have plenty of time to move up to tougher competition.

In most locations there are a number of Eight Ball tournaments that cater specifically to the beginner/intermediate player. I would suggest starting at this level if you've never played competitively before. As your game progresses, you may find yourself playing in local tournaments that are open to pros and amateurs alike. You may find yourself competing against a local champion or tour player for a nominal entry fee.

Whatever your level, be sure to take advantage of the opportunity provided by the tournaments in your area as they offer you the chance to play a variety of opponents under different conditions.

Preparing for a Tournament

There are a number of practical steps that you can take to prepare yourself physically and mentally to compete in important tournaments. These suggestions are designed to put you in stroke and to put your mind at ease so you can focus on playing your best pool.

- Begin your preparations several days or weeks in advance.
- Practice at the tournament site, if possible, or on similar equipment.
- Play easy opponents to build your run out power.
- Play tough games to sharpen your competitive focus.
- Compete in local tournaments to build your tolerance to pressure.
- Get plenty of rest, eat nutritiously and don't abuse alcohol.
- Make sure you have all your equipment with you -shapers, tappers, shaft cleaners, etc.
- Allow yourself plenty of time to get to the tournament so you won't feel pressured before the tournament even starts.
- Observe your opponent's strengths and weaknesses whenever possible. Develop a game plan for each one.
- Warm up at the tournament site, if possible on the table on which you'll be playing. Test the table for rolls, speed, pocket tightness and how the cue ball reacts off the cushions.
- Consider all possible distractions and eliminate them from your mind. You won't need any excuses for losing.
- Don't be overly concerned with anxiety before your matches. All players feel it. Learn to make it work for you (see mental game).

Winning Tournaments

One of the first things you'll discover about tournament pool is that justice is not always served. That's the brutal nature of the game. You can play great and get knocked out in the first round. You can play at 80% of your top game and win the tournament. There are a number of variables that can swing the outcome for or against you in any given match. None of these necessarily has anything to do with how you are playing. You may get a couple of bad breaks, your opponent may get all the rolls or might play incredible pool. Any or all of these can lead to a tough loss.

Most tournaments use the blind draw method to pair opponents. Each tournament board is composed of two main brackets: the top half and the bottom half. Within each bracket is a number of smaller brackets. You could conceivably start with a string of easy matches that puts you in the money and allows you to build momentum for the tougher opponents whom you'll eventually run up against. On the other hand, you could draw the #1 player your first match. While this may not mean you'll lose, it certainly changes the odds. Before you've even hit your first ball, the element of luck is already working for or against you. Winning tournaments comes from playing well <u>and</u> from getting some breaks along the way. The best player does not always win. Once you realize this, your tournament experiences will be more enjoyable. You will be thankful for your good fortune and more accepting of "bad" fortune. Remember, if you play in enough tournaments, the breaks will even out. In the long run it's the quality of your game that matters most.

The tournament format greatly influences the outcome of each match. On the pro tour, the races are long enough so that the winner will most likely have played the best pool. Shorter matches increase the luck factor disproportionately. In a single game Eight Ball tournament format, it is easy to see how the breaks might favor the poorer player. As a rule of thumb, average players prefer shorter races as they increase the element of luck. Top level players have learned that a longer race, as mentioned previously, generally ensures victory for the better player.

Winning is an acquired skill. It takes time to learn to win, especially against top flight competition. You've no doubt witnessed up-and-coming players, in a variety of sports, lead into the finals and then blow the match. They had the physical game to win, but their mental games weren't seasoned enough to withstand the pressure.

If you are new to tournament competition, be patient. It sometimes takes champions years to learn how to win under pressure. Although some players mature faster than others, some never quite get the hang of winning. This type of player continues to get in his/her own way; he/she may need to pay special attention to the mental game.

Your will to win is one of your most valuable assets. Try to develop a sense of purpose and the feeling you can't be beaten. This strong belief in yourself will communicate itself against whomever you're competing. This is not sharking by any stretch of the imagination. When the will to win is strong, you are more focused. You'll make tougher shots, play smarter safeties. You'll be motivated to play your best pool possible.

When you are playing well and are motivated to win, you may enter that altered state where you can't miss, where nothing exists but you, your cue and the balls. The breaks will be going your way. You may feel destined to win. When this happens, stay out of your own way for as long as you can and let it take you as far as it can. Go with the flow, enjoy the experience of fulfilling your dreams and your potential as a tournament player.

The Score

The score of a match should have no effect on your play. However, because you are only human the score does matter. It's hard to block it out completely.   In fact, your ability to win could be impaired by the extent to which you focus on and agonize over the score.

Should you forget about the score and just play pool? That would probably work best, especially in pressure situations. However, I don't expect one reader in ten thousand to be able to follow that advice. Since you will want to follow the score, you must make sure that watching the scoreboard will not hurt your game. You could start by telling yourself that how you play matters most. Yes, the score is important, but, sometimes, the score can be out of your control. The breaks and your opponent's play will see to that.

At the beginning of a match you have hopefully achieved a state of relaxation and anticipation about the contest. Unfortunately, it is easy to lose that frame of mind when things start to go against you. Once you lose focus, it's an easy step to letting the match get away from you. The score can have an immediate and substantial impact on your play if you let it. Let's discuss a couple of possible scenarios as examples.

We'll assume you're playing a race to 9 in Nine Ball (first player to win nine games wins the match). Certainly you'll want to get off to a good start as this will greatly improve your chances of victory. This being the case, what would you begin to think if your opponent broke and ran the first rack perfectly? In the second game you make an unnecessary mental error. Your opponent wins, then breaks in the 9-ball. You're down 0-3. Has anything changed in your attitude from the start of the match? You might be thinking anything from your opponent's playing well to you can't make a ball. You may even start to wonder if you'll ever win a game. Notice that none of your thoughts have anything to do with playing pool well. You're mostly aware that the score is lopsided in your opponent's favor and you're starting to feel a little panicked. This is normal. But, with experience comes knowledge. You'll soon learn to counteract the negative impact of a poor start. You can use the score as a means of motivating yourself to play better.

Bad starts and big leads can be overcome by playing one game at a time, one shot at a time. Coming from behind is only accomplished by playing good pool. The score will not magically turn in your favor. Tell yourself you're not going down without a fight. Tell yourself you have nothing to lose...but the match. Build your competitive spirit. As the great New York Yankee catcher, Yogi Berra, once said, "It ain't over 'til it's over!".

The rolls often dictate who jumps out in front. Remind yourself that your turn will come. And when it does, plan to make the most of it. Try to maintain your eagerness to play, no matter what happens in the early part of the match. In our example the race was to nine, not three. Even though your opponent was graced with the early lead, there still remains plenty of pool to be played.

Back to our example. The score is now 2-6. You're down, but not out. It would be easy to give up and some players make a habit of it. Don't you. Anything's possible, so remain optimistic. It's your turn and you run out. The score is now 3-6. Now is the time to be aggressive. If you can break and run or employ some of the other defensive maneuvers illustrated in this book you will have narrowed your opponent's lead to only two games (4-6). You may say to yourself, "The game is on, I can still win this match. I feel things turning in my favor". Thoughts like these will only reinforce your play. At the same time, your opponent will feel the momentum shifting toward you. What looked an easy win a few moments ago has turned into a contest. Your opponent might even start to fold under the pressure that you are now applying.

As you can see, each player's thinking is subject to the ebb and flow of the score, the breaks and how each player is performing. Now that you've turned things around, be prepared to play your heart out to the finish. Keep the pressure on until you've beaten the odds with your come- from- behind victory. The matches you win from overcoming big deficits will be among your sweetest victories. However, they'll never happen if you don't give them a chance to. Never give up!

In our second scenario we'll assume that you've jumped off to a 4-0 lead. You're playing well and the rolls are going in your favor. Under these conditions, how could your awareness of the score possibly affect you? As we discussed earlier, getting off to a good start and wining are two separate issues. A 4-0 lead is no guarantee of a victory. The momentum can shift at any time on any shot. One mental error can ignite your opponent's game and put you in your seat for several racks. It happens all the time. You will occasionally lose a big lead. Make sure you learn not to blow a big lead. There's a big difference between the two. In our example, with your 4-0 lead, you need to keep the pressure on. Stick to your game plan, which should include aggressive shotmaking and defensive play (safeties) whenever called for. And by all means, don't fritter away your lead by taking unnecessary chances. Make your opponent work for everything.

When it comes to the score, pool players fall into three categories: the front runners, who play best with a big lead, comebackers who play best when their backs are against the wall and those players who play their best no matter what the score. I suggest you plan on becoming a member of the latter, the elite group.

When one basketball team badly outscores another in a short period of time, it is called a run. One team is hot and is probably a little lucky at the same time. Pool is no different. The rolls are not doled out one at a time to each player. Remember this when you fall behind in the early going. All that's at work is the natural ebb and flow of the rolls and breaks of the game. Get used to this phenomenon and your system will suffer less shock when you're playing competitively.

In close matches there is often a pivotal game. A pivotal game usually comes in the later stages and has a direct bearing on the final outcome. When the match is analyzed at the end, both players will likely be able to pinpoint the exact moment the match turned in the victor's favor. As an example, in a race to seven with the score tied 5-5, the eleventh game would be pivotal. The winner would have a 6-5 lead, the break and at least two games to win one. The loser would be facing worse than 3-1 odds at this point of winning the match.

Now let's assume that you're ahead 5-4 in a race to seven. If you runout you'll be leading 6-4 and be breaking to win the match. Should you miss and your opponent win, the score would be tied 5-5. Missing one shot cost you, in effect, two games, and the break! You can see why each game gets increasingly important toward the end of a match when you have less time to make up a deficit. Each "turnover" that costs you a game really costs you two games and the break. Further, if you value the break at half a game, then each loss now costs you three games!

Hill-Hill

When a player needs only one more game to win a match, he/she is said to be on the hill. When the score is tied with only one game remaining, the match is at hill-hill. There's no pressure in pool quite like the final game with the score tied. It's do or die. At this point, the champion takes his/her game up a notch and rises to the occasion. This can be anything from making a spectacular shot, running a difficult rack perfectly, or running a routine rack with no errors. In crunch time, certain players will almost never beat themselves. Your attitude toward the hill-hill game is critical. Tell yourself that you enjoy competing, that you live for moments like this. Win or lose, you're going to give it your best shot. Visualize yourself as a steely-eyed competitor who can come through when the match is on the line. And, as always, concentrate on each shot, follow your routine and see yourself as a winner.

Tactics

Before play begins, you should have a game plan for the match. The plan will be largely based on how you are playing, the conditions and your opponent. Your warm-up session should tell you how your stroke is working. This will affect your shot selection. You may also learn that the table is very fast, so you will need to shoot with a more delicate touch. And finally, your scouting report and/or knowledge of your opponent may include information on how to combat his/her strengths while taking advantage of his/her weaknesses.

A well-thought out plan of attack will enable you to enter the contest with greater confidence. It will also help you avoid any unpleasant surprises during the match. Once the match is underway, you should try to stick to your plan and have faith that it will work for you. For example, in the post game analysis at the 1994 World Championships, Earl Strickland, the winner, revealed that he followed an offensive game plan as he didn't want to get into a defensive battle with Efren Reyes, who is a master of safety play.

As play progresses, you should monitor the effectiveness of your plan and your shot selection. If everything is going fine, leave well enough alone. However, if you are having trouble with tight pockets, for example, you may be wise to play more safeties. You may also wish to gamble on a tough shot if you feel that it's necessary to break your opponent's momentum and/or build your own momentum. Have confidence in your plan, but remain flexible.

During a match you may find that you are losing your composure. Your opponent has the momentum and the lead, and perhaps you are starting to question your ability to hang in there. Under these conditions, in some sports, teams will call a time out. Similarly, you should call time. Do something that will break the negative state into which you are sliding.

The length of a race may also influence your decision making. A long race enables you to play more offensively because you have more time to recover from your mistakes. On the other hand, defense must be emphasized in short races as each game and every shot is crucial. In either case, there is no place for sloppy play. Your best game plan of all is to play every shot as well as possible. Keep the pressure on by sending a message to your opponent that you are going to take full advantage of every opportunity.

Once you get near the end of a match, turn on the afterburners. Be a closer. Learn how to play the final game at 110% of your normal speed. Tell yourself that you can finish what you've started. You'll be surprised what this can do for your game. A great many matches are decided in the final game or two when the player with the most heart emerges victorious.

Money Games

Every player has his own reasons for playing. Some like the social benefits of league play, others prefer the excitement of tournament competition. And then there are those who seek the thrill of a money game. Gambling, in addition to other factors, has contributed to the tawdry image pool has been fighting over the last half century. Yet, when you stop to think about it, many other respectable sports encourage betting; horse racing jumps immediately to mind. Betting on baseball, football, and basketball are certainly, to many people, as American as apple pie. Articles have been written about golf champions wagering during practice rounds. The problems with gambling remain the same no matter the sport. As long as each player can exercise the moderation necessary to enjoy the benefits of wagering, there should be no negatives associated with the practice.

There are definite levels of betting in pool. These range from a friendly bet between buddies at practice sessions to those who live on the road and make their living from playing pool. Most of the readers of this book will probably fall into the former category. I would offer a word of caution when entering into a money game with someone you don't know; he or she may be a road player and thus have all the shark and hustle moves down.

A friendly wager can accomplish a number of things. The biggest benefit is it can help you learn to play under pressure, readying you for tournament competition. As you learn, your confidence level will increase, thus improving your game. As a practical matter, most of you are going to develop your own philosophy and approach to betting on yourselves. Some of you may even refrain from the practice altogether. But for those that have an interest in playing for money, I'll pass along some advice that may help.

Money Management

A friendly bet that adds a little zip to the contest is appropriate for most players. The amount of the wager should have a direct correlation to an individual's financial resources. Losing should sting just a little, not cause undue hardship. You will have, most likely, a built-in comfort zone that will let you know when you are getting into dangerous territory. You shouldn't let a large wager get in the way of your enjoyment of the game. Don't feel bad about what you are willing to lose. You are the best judge of what your pocketbook can afford and your heart can handle. Not everyone likes to bet or was born with the nerves of a riverboat gambler.

There will always be those who play for the thrill of the action. The bigger the bet, the better. Many of these players make their living from betting large sums. They're used to the pressure. Still others are purely gamblers. They'll bet their entire bankroll on one game and don't mind sleeping in their cars when they lose. These types are in the minority and are exceptions to the rule.

You can keep your losses within reason by determining your maximum loss before play begins. The amount you choose to wager per game or set should represent only a portion of your bankroll. In other words, don't play until you go broke. Let's assume you've allocated $50 for a Nine Ball game. Unless you're a true gambler, you won't want to bet it all on one game. A good rule of thumb is to divide your betting cash by ten to derive the amount you should play for. In our example, that would be $5 per game. Each betting unit ($5) is known in pool talk as a barrel. You would have ten barrels, or shots, at your opponent. If you're playing a set, a race to 7, for example, divide your stake into a minimum of two sets. By dividing your stake into smaller units you ensure that you can ride out a poor start or some excellent early play by your opponent. The number of barrels can be decreased to 5 or 6 if you are the odds-on favorite. Similarly, you may wish to divide your funds by 15 or more against a particularly tough opponent.

Once play begins, try to stick to your money game plan. In our example, if you lose $50, swallow your pride and call it quits for the night. If your opponent wants to lose $200 or $300 to you, that's his choice. He's set his own limit. Remember, in eight out of ten cases, you'll be better off resisting the temptation to chase after the cash.

When you are ahead, your opponents may wish to double the bet in an attempt to recoup their losses. Should you accept their offer, you could see your lead quickly disappear. Of course, you could also end up winning a bundle. At this point, it's strictly a judgment call. If you feel you can continue your good play for more money and you don't sense any change in momentum, you should accept the offer. You can always quit if the game gets back to to even. Be advised that some players will give you some difficulty if you do quit even.   If you feel that the tide is starting to turn, however, keep the bet where it's at.   Force your opponent to win as many games as you have won to get even. This will give your opponent time to cool off until you start winning position.

Shrewd money management is no substitute for playing well. It can, however, enable you to stay in the game long enough for your "A" game to appear and/or to weather a series of bad rolls or excellent play by your opponent. It will also help you to minimize your losses and maximize your winnings.

Format

Paying after every game gives you the greatest flexibility. You can adjust the bet at any time. This format can also help to limit your losses. After a few games you can quit if you feel you're up against a superior opponent or your game is off. It also ensures that you'll get paid if you win. This becomes especially important if you're playing a stranger or playing for high stakes. Keeping score "on the wire", as it's referred to, can result in not getting paid. I've seen cases where the loser will head to the bathroom, never to be seen again. By keeping score, accumulating losses and wins, you are extending credit to your opponent. Be sure your opponent is creditworthy.

Top players like to "freeze up the cash", that is they like to play by the game with a set amount put up in advance. As an example, the players may compete for $500 a game, each putting up $5,000. The winner is the first to get ten games ahead. This format virtually guarantees that the better player (at least on that occasion) will get the cash. Be advised that under this format, if the match is evenly contested, it can last for several hours.

A great many players prefer the excitement of playing races. This format is exactly the same as that used in tournaments. The first player to win a set amount of games wins the set. For some reason, most sets are played to an odd number of games. Newer players seem to prefer races to 5 or 7 games. Short races like these greatly elevate the luck factor. More experienced players like to test their skills with longer races to 9, 11 or more.

Races are favored by those players who like fast action. A race to 7, for example, can last a maximum of 13 games. This is not a time-consuming proposition for more experienced players. The disadvantage of races is that a player does not necessarily receive credit for every win. A player could win the first set 9-0, lose the second 8-9 and be even despite that the fact he/she won nearly twice as many games.

Spotting

Most pool games lend themselves to handicapping or spotting as it is called in pool lingo. Spots allow players of differing abilities to compete on fairly equal terms. As a rule of thumb however, it seems like the better player wins more often than not despite the spot. Newer players should not let this prevent them from playing tougher competition. As long as the bet is reasonably low, these games should be viewed as playing lessons. As a word of caution for newer players, avoid becoming dependent on large spots as this will slow down your rate of progress.

Nine Ball is known as the money game. This is partially due to the large number of spots that can be given. One example of this is spotting the breaks. No matter who wins the game, the player getting spotted breaks the rack, eliminating the better player's chances of running several racks. Players can also be spotted additional money balls. Of course each player wins on the Nine Ball, but a player spotted the "wild 8" would also win anytime the 8- ball is legally pocketed. The 8-ball is a common spot for two players of fairly equal ability. Conversely, when one player has an overwhelming advantage, the spot may be several balls; for instance, the 6, 7, and 8-balls. This is referred to as the 6-out.

The players may agree that the spot ball be called. This eliminates slop shots on the money ball. A player getting the call 7 would have to designate where the 7 will be pocketed. If the player sinks the 7 without calling the shot, he/she continues shooting but does not get credit for a win unless he/she pockets the 9-ball.

Another popular spot is called the last-two. This is one of the smallest handicaps in Nine Ball. A player receiving this spot wins when they make the ball before the 9, whatever it happens to be. This spot eliminates slop shots on the extra money ball. The last three is simply an extension of the last two. Very good players have been known to give up as much as the last 6 to players of much lesser ability.

Another form of weight is to receive games on the wire. In a race to seven, one player may begin the set with a two game spot. This player needs only five games to win whereas his opponent needs to win seven. Finally, one player may give the other odds on the money.

As you can see, the potential combinations are truly mind boggling. Let's see, "I'll give you the call 7, wild 8 and the breaks and two games on the wire in a race to 7." If you can make sense of this jargon then you may be ready to play some Nine Ball for the cash.

Two players discussing a spot are said to be making a game. Their conversation is not unlike that of a used car salesman pitching a deal or a defense attorney at work. Often the best talker wins, in which case the game may be over before it even starts.

A typical conversation may go as follows:

Player A: How can we match up?
Player B: I need at least the 7 and the breaks.
Player A: There's no way I can give you that. I haven't picked up a cue in a month.
Player B: How come you're always in dead stroke?
Player A: Tell you what, I'll give you the 7, winner breaks.
Player B: Race to 7 for fifty?
Player A: Make it 9 for a C-note.
Player B: You're on.

Conversations like the one above take place thousands of times a day in pool rooms across the country. If you're going to play Nine Ball for money, be prepared to sharpen your negotiating skills. You should obviously avoid getting into a game where you have little chance of winning (except for a playing lesson against a superior player). Games like these are called a "lock-up". If you play enough, you will inevitably come across a situation where you have been outnegotiated or have underestimated your opponent's game. This happens to everyone at least once. Learn from it and move on.

As your game and/or conversational ability improves, you will find that you can actually make a little extra money playing pool. But don't quit your day job!

One basic negotiating strategy you'll encounter involves your potential adversary building up your game as much as possible with a barrage of cheap compliments. At the same time, he/she will be tearing down his/her game. Another popular ploy is what I call the intimidation move, which is designed to destroy your confidence. Your adversary tears your game down, telling you can't play a lick. They will offer to give you a huge spot and it still won't even be a contest. Below is a sampling of some common negotiating ploys you'll be sure to hear if you play money pool.

"I'm in a slump, I can't beat anybody."
"You beat Joe and he gives me weight."
"I hardly slept last night."
"You robbed me last time we played."
"There's no way I can give that much weight."
"You're playing too good."
"I haven't been playing at all."

Backers

Backers or stakehorses, are willing to put up the money for a pool game in exchange for a percentage of the profits. Winnings are typically split fifty-fifty, although sometimes a player accepts a lesser share in a really big money game. Backers have long been a part of pool and have contributed much to the game's colorful history. They are an integral and vital part of the money game economy.

Backers are typically gentlemen gamblers. They like the action as much, if not more, than the winning. The characteristics you should look for in a backer include, obviously, ample cash, a carefree attitude toward money, nerves of steel and faith in the player(s) they back. A good backer will leave you alone to play your game, offer encouragement when they see you need it, and handle all side bets. In other words, they're in your corner, much like a boxer's manager.

A good stakehorse must be treated with respect. Always play your heart out no matter what the situation or how far you may be behind. Treat their money as if it were your own. Don't make games where your chances of winning are less than half just because you feel like some action or need the money. You don't want them to feel you sold them a losing proposition. Remember, it's their belief in you that causes them to back you; mess with that belief and you may lose that stakehorse.

The worst thing a player can do to his stakehorse is lose on purpose and split the winnings later with his opponent. This is known as dumping or doing business. Not only does this create bad karma, it damages the players' reputations with any future backers whose support they may try to enlist.

As this book is being written, a large number of skilled players are without the sponsorship of major organizations. This makes it impossible for these players to live solely on their tournament earnings as athletes in other sports are able to do. As a result, players who are in the top 200 in the country, but are not quite good enough to play the tour full time, are forced to supplement their tournament earnings by playing money pool sponsored by backers.

Playing Conditions

You have great flexibility regarding playing conditions in a money match. Make sure you are comfortable with all the external conditions of the playing environment, the rules specific to that match, the agreed-upon handicapping, or anything else that you feel will affect your performance. You don't want an excuse for losing should it come to that.

For example, if you are traveling to another player's room, be aware of the home court advantage. The table your opponent has selected may be the one he/she practices on six hours a day. He/she will obviously know every roll and quirk of that table. In some cases you may elect to play your match at a neutral site. Of course, if you are playing the match in your own room, you would be motivated to select the table you know best. It is only natural to try to gain every advantage you can.

Check for unusual conditions. Lighting is a good example; you'll want to avoid the glare from daylight coming through an uncovered window. A dead rail may affect certain shots as will a pillar that's close to the table.

You really have no reason to play under unsuitable conditions unless you're a glutton for punishment.

It's mandatory that the rules be established before play begins. You have no recourse for disputing an infraction of a rule if it has not been discussed prior to play. This is especially true if you are playing in a strange environment. Despite the standard rules that govern Eight Ball tournament play, most taverns seem to have a separate set of house rules.

Nine Ball is a different story. Although most games are now played under what are referred to as Texas Express rules, it is still a good idea to clarify certain points. If you play cue ball fouls only and re-spot only the money ball, make sure your opponent is aware of, and agrees with, this ruling. Iron out your differences prior to play. It's also a good idea to have a neutral third party available for decisions on disputed hits.

Before play begins, you should establish a time frame for the match and stick to it. Don't let your opponent pressure you into extending play. Some players will insist that you follow an unwritten code that says you won't quit a winner. It can be aggravating if one party jumps out to an early lead, pockets the cash and takes off, giving you no opportunity to win it back. However, neither player should have a problem with ending play as long as they stick to their original time limit.

Hustles and Shark Moves

There will always be a few players who will use questionable tactics to separate you from your (or your stakehorse's) cash. These shenanigans should cause you little or no concern as long as you know what to look out for and exercise a little common sense. It also helps to remember that your two biggest enemies, in relation to the hustler, are greed and ego. I've compiled a list of some of the more common hustles I've come across during my pool career. Perhaps you can add to the list.

- Stalling to raise the bet - The ageless con. Your opponent loses a few games, creating a false sense of security, then wants to raise the bet, appealing to your greed.
- Proposition games - A common example in Eight Ball would be for your opponent to allow you to remove all your balls at the start of the game, leaving only the 8-ball. The result is you never get a shot on the 8 because your opponent's balls are in the way.
- Proposition shots - These are pool's equivalent of three-card monty. The hustler knows the precise odds of pocketing a seemingly impossible shot because he's practiced it a thousand times.
- Assaulting the ego - This is a rather crude hustle that raises your anger, due to goading, to a level where you end up betting several times more than you normally do or can afford.

- Pretending to be lucky - Hustler wins with their "B" game, an assortment of seemingly lucky shots on the 9-ball. You figure they can't keep winning, so you keep betting; the hustler then brings out his "A" game and starts to run racks.
- The tag team - The weaker member of a hustle team plays you first to build your confidence while the better player awaits his turn.
- The drunk routine - This shark pretends to be an easy mark, loaded with cash, who can barely stand at the table. Note: Some players actually perform best while intoxicated.
- The rich businessman - This appeals to those who believe that no one who wears a suit and works for a living can shoot pool. Appeals also to greed.
- The pretty girl shark - This hustle depends on the shark's girl friend acting as a distraction to throw you off your game.
- Firing air barrels - Your opponent assures you it's okay for you to keep score and pay at the end, the reason being he has no money.

Leagues

One of the most popular forms of amateur competition is league pool. Teams are typically comprised of four or five members who pay a set amount each week to play in a series of matches with other teams in their division. The vast majority of league play is conducted on bar tables, although there has been an increase in play on regulation sized tables. Eight Ball is the predominant game although Nine Ball leagues are gaining in popularity. An average league season may last anywhere from ten to thirty weeks. Matches are generally played once a week either at home or a host tavern according to a pre-set schedule. Matches can last anywhere from two to three hours. There are leagues for both men and women. Although co-ed teams do exist they are not as common and are usually played in a partners format. The primary difference between some male and female leagues are in the number of games played, men's leagues playing more games per match.

There are a number of associations that sponsor league play nationwide. Each of these holds an annual tournament in Las Vegas that attracts contestants from across the country. They compete for substantial prize money in a number of different divisions. There are team tournaments as well as competitions for individual honors. In some areas leagues are run by local operators. By necessity, the scale of these leagues' tournaments are much smaller, although not any less valuable to the players.

Competition

Leagues offer you the opportunity to enjoy competitive pool on a regular basis no matter your level of play. If you are new to the game, leagues can help you in a variety of ways. League play offers its own unique brand of pressure in that team members may feel they're letting the team down when they lose a game. It also exposes players to the arena of spectator pool. It can be intimidating at first to have twenty pairs of eyes watching your every shot. New players especially feel the pressure. Most adjust with time and the support of their fellow team members to where they actually enjoy playing and winning under pressure.

League operators keep a detailed series of records on each team and each individual's performance. Newsletters and bulletins may typically list team standings, individual win/loss records and runouts from the break. These statistics tell you exactly how you and your team stack up against the rest of the league. These can be used both to keep your team motivated and as incentive for team members to improve their individual games. This information can also be used to set goals for both the team and team members. Goals might include any or all of the following:

> Improve your game
> Play better under pressure
> Have the best record on your team and/or league
> Win the league tournament
> Compete successfully in a national tournament
> Help your teammates with their games
> Help your team move up in the standings

Getting Involved

When you form a team and/or join a league you are making a long-term commitment to play each week with a certain group of people. It would be in your best interests, therefore, to make every effort to ensure that your league experience is as enjoyable and rewarding as possible. Making sure you are compatible with your team members, that you share a love and enthusiasm for the game, that you are all committed to the team are all factors that help guarantee a successful season.

Each team needs a captain to handle the team's affairs. These may include record keeping, collecting money, setting the line-up, and arranging for substitute players (subs) if needed. Most teams have a co-captain to pick up the slack, but the job is time consuming and, depending on the team, can be a great source of pressure. The team members can help by being on time, giving enough notice when not able to play so a sub can be found and generally acting in as considerate a manner as possible. For those who can't guarantee weekly attendance but like league play, perhaps signing on as a substitute would be a good compromise.

League play is most fun when you are on fairly equal terms with the other players in the league. Matching the skills of your team to the league you're considering joining is probably a good idea. It certainly wouldn't be very challenging for a "B" team to join a "C" league although some leagues do handicap their matches for just that reason. To derive as much satisfaction and challenge as you can from league pool, it pays to find as perfect a match as possible between you and your league. Check out the caliber of players (the skill level), the format, number of weeks, number of games per match, prize money in relation to the cost per week to play, tournament schedule, the size of the league operation (national or local sponsor) and how you fit with the other players in the league. And, most important, have fun!

CHAPTER 10

HOW TO IMPROVE

Taking Your Game To The Next Level

Learning to play pool and improving your game is like embarking on an endless journey. There is so much to learn that even the very best players in the world are constantly seeking knowledge that can give them the critical edge. So should you.

The knowledge and skills that go into creating a top caliber game of pool are not learned overnight. There are no magic formulas or secrets that alone will guarantee your success. Instead, the foundation of pool is built brick by brick, until your game is a wall that few opponents care to run up against. The main thing for you to remember as you progress along your individual journey is that patience is indeed a virtue.

The journey from point A to point B, from beginner to accomplished player takes time. Sometimes perhaps the journey feels like it's taking more time than you'd like. But don't forget, it takes as long as it takes. You will go as far as your time, talent and tenacity allows.

Your progression should be one step at a time as you build a solid foundation for your game. Fundamentals come first, then aiming, basic position play, etc., etc. Make sure not to rush things by skipping over any part of the learning process. If you try to get ahead of the process, you'll only cheat yourself out of developing the most solid foundation possible for your game.

Webster's dictionary defines denial as "a refusal to believe or accept." This definition could be completed by adding "the truth about your pool game." Many players find it difficult to accept responsibility for deficiencies in their game. Never forget, however, that the balls don't lie, that results speak for themselves. If you are missing shots that you know you shouldn't, if you are failing to beat players you feel you should be beating, then it's time for a change. You will need to break bad habits, learn new techniques, and add constantly to your body of knowledge. Hone and refine and work on improving your game, always.

Pool is fun to play at any level of skill, as it should be. I've seen beginners have as much fun as anybody when playing the game. Having fun, enjoying pool for the great game that it is, should always be a top priority. Realize, however, that there are different kinds of fun. I hope that you'll learn to enjoy the serious kind of fun that comes with the realization that you are making significant progress with your game.

The journey that we alluded to earlier takes you through many peaks and valleys. Sometimes your game will be clicking on all cylinders, while at other times you'll be mired in a slump. That's only natural. It happens to all players. Keep in mind that you can learn when you are playing well. Take notice of what you are doing right and try to solidify good habits. At the same time, remember that when your game is suffering, it may be time to consider a change or two that could catapult your game to new levels of play. So don't give up on yourself when your game has temporarily gone sour. It may only be a lull before you scale new heights.

The Learning Curve

There is a well-defined learning curve that describes the development of virtually all pool players. Your understanding of the learning curve will help you recognize the various stages of progress in your game. We'll go through the stages one at a time.

The beginning stage is probably the most fun and exciting. This stage could be called the rapid development phase. Starting from ground zero, progress tends to come quickly and in spurts. Improvements in fundamentals most often leads to immediate and sizable gains in the quality of your play. Hot streaks will pop up occasionally that will whet your appetite for the game even further. A game that was once an occasional pastime may turn into an obsession. As certain goals are reached, the excitement grows. Important milestones might include making a tough shot for the first time, beating a friend you've always wanted to beat, or running your first rack of Eight Ball.

The speed with which you move through the first phase of the curve depends largely on how much time you spend playing and practicing the game. From my experience, I've noticed that most new players who tend to get bitten by the bug find themselves playing significantly more pool.

The graph illustrates a typical example of the learning curve. The vertical axis shows the percentage of a player's capability that they have

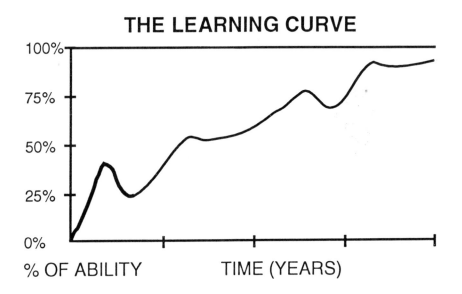

THE LEARNING CURVE

100% ⊤
75% ⊢
50% ⊢
25% ⊢
0%

% OF ABILITY   TIME (YEARS)

achieved. The horizontal axis demonstrates the progress of the curve over time, measured in years. Notice that a new player may, within a period of less than a year, reach a point where they have realized 40% of their talent for the game. After a fast start, it's not uncommon for a beginner to experience an unpleasant slump, depicted on the graph as a down-turn. This is a critical juncture for many new players. Some get disgusted or disillusioned with the game, perhaps because of its difficulty, and reduce their play or even quit playing altogether. The great joy that the game can provide lies ahead, however, for those who stick with it and resolve to improve their game.

The next phase in a player's development takes them through the intermediate stage of the learning curve. After gaining some proficiency at the game and possibly experiencing a slump, many players are set to make rapid progress. In fact, those who really work hard and/or have a certain knack for the game will experience a quantum leap in their skills. Refinements in fundamental technique, an understanding of position and strategy may all come together to cause their game to jump forward. At this stage, pool is still a lot of fun, but for different reasons. What was once an occasional pastime is now a big part of the players recreational life.

Goals are now being met and reset at higher levels. The player may now be enjoying and learning from their participation in leagues and local tournaments. Perhaps a rack of Eight Ball is being run every so often. In short, the player now has a respectable game that regularly features some exciting shotmaking. In addition, the struggle to make even the simplest shots is history. Referring to the curve, the second phase of development may last a couple of more years as they progress to about 75% of their potential.

As the intermediate phase comes to a conclusion, many enthusiasts will find that their game has leveled off, that progress is limited or even halted.   The player may then enter into another down cycle as disappointment sets in because they are no longer getting better. At this stage, the majority of players have "hit the wall". They have reached a plateau from which further gains, if any, in their play will come at a much slower pace. Plateau's are often thought of negatively because all players always want to keep getting better. But just remember that even when a plateau has been reached, it comes only after much learning has taken place. Players on a plateau should not necessarily be unhappy with their game. After all, they have now attained a level of expertise in a great game that will provide them with enjoyment for many years to come.

"Play Your Best Pool" was written to help players at any stage of their game continue to push forward, to achieve the goal of playing the best that they can, whatever their level of skill or stage of development. The plateau phase concludes with a player reaching perhaps 80% to 90% of his/her potential. Beyond the plateau is the land of the true enthusiast and the championship level players.   Progress now comes in small, almost imperceptible increments, but is very real nevertheless.   Further refinements in technique, and the accumulation of bits and pieces of knowledge in all aspects of the game enable the player to continue to inch forward towards that mythical goal of 100% realization of their potential. Even though progress may appear to be limited, better players can and do feel real excitement about the progress of their game. For example, a new approach to breaking the balls could take a player to the next level. Perhaps a refinement in their mental approach or preshot routine could eliminate a tendency to miss balls in the later stages of a tough match. Either of these developments could catapult a local champion onto the Professional Billiards Tour.

From beginner to champion and all levels in between, there is much to be learned and much enjoyment to be derived from pool. I hope that all readers will enjoy the challenge of learning and perfecting their game to the best of their ability, during the never ending journey to play your best pool possible.

The Learning Sequence

You will maximize your chances for success by learning the various skills of the game in the proper sequence. In other words, you must learn to walk before you can run.   That means becoming well grounded in the fundamentals. These would include the bridge, stance, grip, and stroke.

Next comes aiming and then basic shotmaking. Start with short shots that are straight in or at a slight angle. As your stroke and eye develop, you can then move on to cut shots, gradually increasing the cut angle as your progress dictates. In the early stages you should stroke the cue ball only on the center axis. Avoid using any english whatsoever. Be patient. There will be plenty of time later on to learn english, bank shots, combinations and everything else that goes into making a solid, well-rounded game. First things first.

When you feel comfortable with your stroke and can pocket easy and medium difficult shots regularly, then it's time to learn basic position. This would include stop shots, draw, and follow. Again, refrain from using english. I'll repeat, take the time necessary to learn the fundamentals, elementary shotmaking, and basic position before tackling more difficult elements of the game. You will find that when you learn each element in the proper sequence, then you will be much better prepared to learn the tougher skills when the time is right.

Mastering Change

Change is necessary to improve your game. You must not be afraid to risk giving up the known for the unknown if you wish to play better. Changing your game is not easy. It takes real commitment. You must be dedicated to working on the changes until they pass through the awkward stage and become comfortable to you. There is a common tendency to slip back into the old way of doing things. Let's say you've been gripping the cue too tightly and you'd like to employ a looser grip to increase the action on the cue ball. In the long run, you know that this change will help your game. Two weeks after making the change, the new grip may still feel funny to you. Furthermore, you might not be playing as well as you did with the tight grip. At this point, many players will give up and revert back to their old behavior. This is the moment of truth. When you are in the process of changing old habits, and adopting new methods, you need to stick with the change until it begins to feel comfortable. As a rule of thumb, you should expect it to take 30 days for the old habits to die off and for the new changes to effectively take hold. If you give up before that, you're cheating yourself out of the opportunity to improve your game.

What feels good to you now may be due only to habit, not because it works. When making a change, you should prepare yourself for the awkward period we discussed above. However, consider this: the new change could feel great sooner, rather than later, maybe even right away. Furthermore, you could possibly reap big rewards right away! That's a possibility that can make change an exciting part of your development as a player.

When making changes, it often helps to have someone watch your practice sessions. They can see things you can't. They can confirm that you're on the right track and detect any backsliding toward your old habits. One change often leads to another. The second change is often necessary to compensate for the first change. For example, we talked earlier about the player who wanted to lighten up on his grip pressure. With a lighter grip the player will get more action on the cue ball. Therefore, the player can now use a softer stroke (change #2) to achieve the same cue ball movement.

There's an old saying that goes "If it ain't broke, don't fix it". Don't change just for the sake of change. Don't make the mistake of tinkering constantly with your stroke. But do always keep an open mind to the possibility of fundamentally sound changes that can have a positive impact on your game.

Setting Goals

You can use goals to improve your game. Goals will give you something to work for and a time table for reaching your goal. The following suggestions should be helpful in establishing and maintaining a successful program for improvement that effectively makes us of the goal setting process:

- Establish your goals for your game, not someone else's.
- Have specific goals that are measurable.
- Make your goals realistic.
- Use short-term, intermediate, and long-term goals.
- Update your goals regularly.
- Have a well-defined plan of action.

There are several techniques that you can use to measure your progress. For example, during each practice session set up 10 different shots and shoot them each 10 times apiece. That's a total of 100 shots. Set up the exact same shots at each session and keep a record of your successful attempts. Hopefully this will reveal a positive trend. Other methods that will help you recognize your improvement include:

- Making shots that you've always missed before.
- Beating friends that you've never beaten before.
- Running your first rack of Eight Ball or Nine Ball.
- Having the best winning percentage on your team.
- Getting barred from competing at one level of competition.
- The local tournament official ups your handicap rating.
- Players you've beaten start asking for a spot (handicap).
- You run 25 or 50 balls at straight pool for a new high run.

Working with an Instructor

You can give your game a real boost and cut years off the learning process by working with a qualified instructor. In addition, they can teach you things you might possibly never learn on your own. A regular program is highly recommended in the early stages to get new players off to a good start. This is important because bad habits that become ingrained due to poor fundamentals become harder and harder to break as time goes by. A good instructor can help to avoid having to re-learn the game later on.

Experienced players can also benefit from formal instruction. A good instructor can help spot a flaw or offer some suggestions on the fine points of the game that can help long time players end a slump or breakout above a plateau. Good players can also use an instructor who knows their game well to give them an occasional tune-up when needed.

You should choose your instructor carefully, as a poor one may do more harm than good. A good teacher does not need to play like a touring professional. They should, however, be able to play a reasonably good game as you should learn from demonstrations by your instructor. Perhaps you are wondering whether a certain instructor is right for you. Consider giving them a try, and come back for more if you are satisfied with their approach. You should pay special attention to how you are being taught when you are evaluating an instructor. A good instructor will show interest in your game. They will ask you questions about what you are doing, and how and why you play the way you do. A Q & A session allows them to tailor their instruction precisely to your game. A word of caution: be extremely wary of method instructors who insist that their way of stroking the cue ball is the only way. These instructors can be especially harmful if their techniques are somewhat offbeat and require that you totally change your approach to the game.

The only way to really get your money's worth is to listen to your instructor and to trust his judgment. When you don't understand something, ask questions. It's important for you to know what to do and why. Be sure to practice what you learn while it's still fresh in your mind. A good teacher can help bring out the best in your game, but don't expect miracles. You must always remember to accept responsibility for your game.

The Pyramid of Excellence

The pyramid of excellence provides you with a visual demonstration of the various levels of play from beginner (D) through touring professional (A+). I'll take a moment to describe them briefly:

D A beginner or someone who plays so infrequently that their game remains in the beginner category.

C- A below average player - this denotes a player with some recognizable skills who has definitely risen from the ranks of the beginners. This is the first major milestone.

C An average player - describes a large section of pool enthusiasts with experience whose games perhaps have leveled off, or that only play occasionally.

C+ Above average player - this group plays a very acceptable game of pool. They tend to dominate their level of competition.

B- This is perhaps the biggest hurdle, as a good number of players peak at the C+ level. A B- is a good player who is quite capable of running a rack of Eight Ball or Nine Ball. However, they usually lack consistency.

B A solid, advanced player - these players can run out fairly regularly, but lack a little consistency.

B+ Players at this level are often mistaken for lower level A players when they are playing well because they play a very tough, well-rounded game. They can run out from nearly anywhere at anytime.

A- Another big jump is required to break through to the "A" level. This group of players could be classified as semi-pros or top amateurs. They are very skilled in nearly all facets of the game. They run out easily and very often.

A A professional quality player who can compete with and occasionally beat all but the best players. Very skilled, solid, and consistent. Runs multiple racks quite often. Tough to beat.

A+ Touring Pro - the best. Skilled in every area of the game. Breaks and runs out multiple racks regularly. Definitely in a class by themselves.

I'd like to emphasize that there is nothing wrong with being on any segment of the pyramid. There will always be players both above and below you on the pyramid. The main thing is to enjoy the game. The pyramid can, however, serve as a motivational tool for those players with a true desire to improve their games and to rise in the rankings. Where do you see yourself at present in the pyramid? What are your goals? Are you a relatively new player who in a couple of years hopes to rise into the advanced level of the pyramid? Whatever your current level of play, I hope that you decide to play your best pool possible and rise in the rankings as far as you can.

In the final analysis, the results you achieve in competitive play are the best indicator of your game, and of the progress that you are making toward your goals. Where are you now in the ranks of the pool players in your area? Where would you like to be? Look at the rankings constructively, and let them spur you on to even greater levels of accomplishment.

THE PYRAMID OF EXCELLENCE

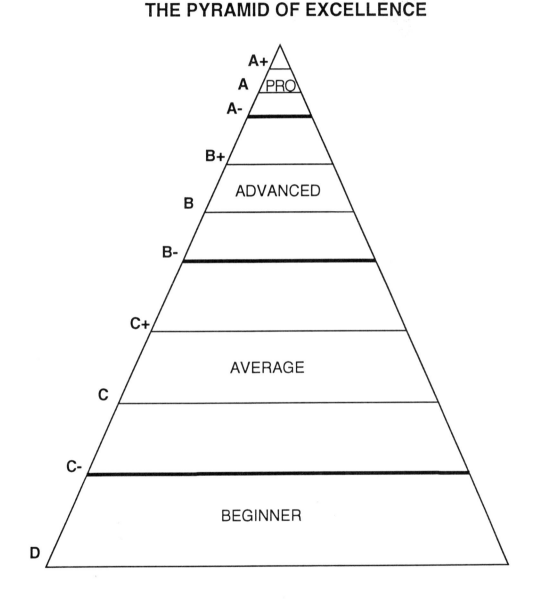

The Champion's Checklist

One of the main reasons top players are so tough to beat is that they seem to do everything well. They have many strengths, and very few, if any, weaknesses. The list below presents you with just about every skill and mental quality that's needed to play at the upper levels of the game.

Don't be intimidated by the list. It takes many years for even the most devoted players to master the items on this list. Use the checklist as a guide. Rate yourself in each category using the 1-10 scale. Be objective. Once you've completed your evaluation, you can use this information to improve your game. Perhaps you're good at safety play, but you don't use them enough in competition. You may want to start taking advantage of this strength in you game. Your analysis might also show that you are weak on combinations. If that's the case, then you have an important shot to work on at your next practice session. Newer players should emphasize the basics (identified with an asterisk).

Fundamentals
* Grip
* Stance
* Bridge
* Stroke
* Aiming
* Preshot routine

Shotmaking
* Basic shotmaking
  Cut shots
  Long shots
  Frozen to the Rail
  Combinations
  Banks
  Caroms
  Billiards
  Kick Shots
  Jump Shots
  Jacked up over a ball
  Curve Shots
  The break
  (power/control)

Position Play
* Basic position
* Stop Shots
* Draw Shots
* Follow Shots
* Speed of stroke
  Pattern recognition
  Inside english
  Outside english
  Multi-rail position
  Imagination

Strategy
  Table Assessment
  Controlling the table
  Offensive vs. defensive
  Push-out strategy
  Reading opponents games
  Adapting to conditions
  Experience (the know-how)
  Knowledge of the rules

Mental Qualities
    Confidence
    Desire to compete
    Heart
*   Concentration
    Memory-recall
*   Patience
    Judgment
    Playing with a lead
    Coming from behind
    Creativity
*   Love for the game
    Discipline

Safety Play
    Knowledge of the safeties
    Ability to execute
    Imagination

Sources of Knowledge

One of the keys to playing your best pool is to build up as large a store house of knowledge as possible and to be able to recall that information as needed. It is very important, therefore, to always keep an open mind to learning all you can about this fascinating game.

In the past it was often thought that the best players possessed secrets to the game that they were reluctant to share under any circumstance, possibly for fear that the competition might catch up to them. You've no doubt heard the phrase "I've taught you everything you know, but not everything that I know". Fortunately, things have changed as pool is now becoming part of the information age. Today there are many sources of information that can help both new and experienced players alike improve their games and cut years off the learning curve. Listed below are a number of sources of information. Take advantage of them and your game will benefit accordingly.

- Watch good players on TV - this is a great way to learn the game. Pay special attention to their fundamentals, position play, and strategy.

- Attend tournaments in your area - the pro tours combined (men's and ladies) now total over 30 events annually. The McDermott Tour is now comprised of over 150 events. If the tour comes to your area don't miss this opportunity to watch and learn from the best. Check the schedules in the pool magazines. Most major metropolitan areas now conduct numerous tournaments that feature the best players in the region. The play is excellent, and much can be learned from these professional caliber players. Also, keep an eye out for clinics and exhibitions in your area.

- Ask questions - some good players are willing to share some of their knowledge with you, just for the asking. If you sense that a player is approachable, you may want to take a chance and see what you can learn. Nothing ventured, nothing gained. Don't forget to watch older players whose games have fallen off somewhat with age, but that have a wealth of knowledge to offer.

- Pool magazines and periodicals - there are several fine publications that offer instructional columns and articles, tips on equipment, interviews and articles on top players and other information that can improve your play. These publications are inexpensive and well worth the price of a subscription.

- Books on pool - after a couple of days of banging balls into the rails I purchased a copy of Willie Mosconi's red book (he wrote two books) and followed his advice on the fundamentals of the game. It helped get my game off to a good start. There are a number of fine books on the game. All of them have something to offer.

- Video tapes - tapes have grown tremendously popular in recent years. They offer the advantage of observing the instructor demonstrating his/her techniques. Some tapes are excellent; some not.

- Play better players - one of the best ways to learn is to play better players. The lessons you acquire from experiencing defeat at the hands of a master have a way of making a strong impression on your game. If they won't play you for nothing, try to get off as cheaply as possible. Consider your loss a price you'll gladly pay for learning the game.

- Cassette Tapes - there are a number of cassette tapes that can be quite useful in helping you master the mental side of the game.

PRACTICING POOL

Drills And Routines For Developing Your Skills

Pool is best learned in the beginning stages by long, closely spaced practice sessions. These sessions are required to build muscle memory and to develop and retain a sense of aim and proper stroke speed. Virtually all great players have put in long hours at the practice table over a concentrated period of time. It's not unusual for them to have spent 4-10 hours a day at the table for the first 2-5 years of their career in order to build a solid foundation for their game. You may not have the time or inclination to practice that much, although regular, disciplined practice sessions will help your game tremendously. In fact, your rate of improvement is <u>directly</u> related to the time you spend practicing. So if you are a beginner who wishes to enjoy the heady experience of a jump in your play, plan to put in the necessary hours of practice.

As your game progresses, long hours of practice are not nearly as crucial. At this stage, practice is for refining your skills or at least maintaining your current level of play.

The quality of your practice sessions is at least as important as the number of hours you spend at the table. Practice doesn't make perfect, perfect practice makes perfect. Keep in mind the next time you work on your game. You're trying to build good habits and proper techniques that will hold up under game conditions. Sloppy, halfhearted practice is not nearly as likely to produce the desired results. In fact, poor practice can become a breeding round for bad habits that can severely undermine your progress. Your attitude towards practicing will go a long way towards determining your success. Hopefully you will learn to love practicing pool nearly as much as playing in competition. After all, it's the next best thing to playing. Look forward to your practice sessions. Set goals for each session and chart your progress. When you catch yourself doing something right, jot down your findings in a notebook. You can also make a game of practicing. Set up certain shots and shoot them 5-10 times each. You can purchase stick-on labels to mark the position of the balls so you can shoot the same shot, over and over again. Keep score and compare your results to previous practices. Imagine you're like a basketball player shooting free throws in practice while trying to up your percentage from perhaps 70% to 80%, as an example.

The majority of your practice time should be alone in the early stages so you can maximize the number of shots taken. It also helps to practice under the watchful eye of a knowledgeable observer who can spot flaws in your technique. You may also want to spend a part of your practice time with friends who have a similar desire to improve their game. Don't allow yourself to get distracted from working on the things you need to improve your game.

There are a very wide variety of skills you'll need to master for a complete game of pool. Each skill is best learned if dealt with separately. That's how you build muscle memory. Perhaps you'll want to devote a whole session to perfecting just one or two things such as aiming cut shots and/or improving your draw stroke. As you develop a number of separate skills, they will gradually come together piece by piece to form a solid, well-rounded game of pool.

The Stroke

The stroke is the heart and soul of every player's game. Because of its importance to your game, the stroke must be worked on constantly until it has been honed to a razor's edge. The following practice routines should help you develop your stroke and get you back on track if you find yourself in a shooting slump. You should, first of all, conduct a periodic review of the basic fundamentals. If you are having trouble with your stroke, there's a good chance you may be committing one of the following fundamental errors. Perhaps you may find it difficult to stay down over the shot until your follow through is complete. Jumping up after the cue strikes the cue ball won't necessarily ruin a shot. However, if you develop a tendency to jump up it could start happening just <u>prior</u> to contact. The consequences of this, as you might expect, are disastrous. Lack of confidence is the primary reason for jumping up. Some players who stand very low to the ball are also prone to jumping up because they are unable to swing their arm freely from a cramped position. If you find you are jumping up, concentrate on stroking with only your arm. This will cure the problem and give you a heightened sense of awareness of your stroke at the same time.

Arm and/or wrist twisting on both the backstroke and the forward stroke is another major stroke flaw. You can detect this error by putting a small piece of tape on the top of the joint of your cue. Now take some practice strokes and watch the tape carefully. If it revolves back and forth (as opposed to staying on top of the cue), that's a sign you are twisting your arm and/or wrist.

The so called death grip has destroyed a number of otherwise picture perfect strokes. If your grip starts out tight at address, chances are it will only get tighter by the time the cue tip contacts the cue ball. A rigid grip promotes a jerky poke and it reduces the action on the cue ball. When you address a shot during practice, stop for a moment and observe the tension (if any) from your shoulder to the tip of your fingers. If you feel tension anywhere, try to relax that part of your body as you prepare to shoot your practice shots. See if it's possible for you to "let go" of this effort to control the cue. You may be pleasantly surprised at the results you get by loosening up, letting go, and trusting your stroke.

Poor tempo can also ruin your stroke. It is often connected to an overly tight grip on the cue. The obvious symptom of poor tempo is a hurried forward stroke. Tension develops as the shooter attempts to muscle the cue ball. If you have this problem, try to slow your stroke down, especially as you make the transition from backstroke to forward stroke. It's in the transition phase of the stroke this problem usually occurs. Make sure to stay down and to concentrate on a smooth follow through.

Lastly, don't forget to review your preshot routine as many shots are missed before the warm up stroking has even begun. Ask yourself if you are planning the shot thoroughly and are making a final decision on how you're going to play the shot before you assume your stance. Make sure also you are settling properly into your stance and are taking an appropriate number of warm-up strokes prior to pulling the trigger.

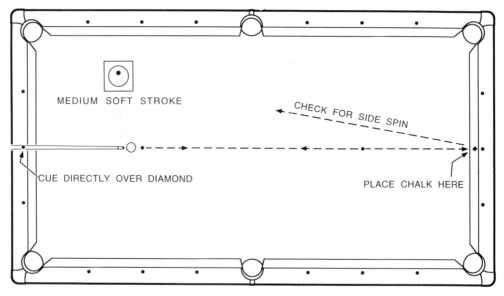

Perfecting Your Stroke

This drill will go a long way toward smoothing out and perfecting your stroke. The first step is to place a piece of chalk at a 45° angle, on the edge of the rail opposite the middle diamond. Now place the cue ball next to the spot exactly in line with the middle diamonds on each end rail as diagrammed. You may also want to check the rail next to the chalk just to make sure that it's in good condition.

Now you are ready to execute the shot. As you prepare to shoot, make sure that your cue is directly over the middle diamond. Take dead aim on the middle of the chalk. Use a medium soft stroke with your cue ½ tip above center. Hold your cue in position on the follow through. Your objective is to have the cue ball rebound back into the middle of your tip. Nothing less than a perfect stroke will do. If you are inadvertently applying sidespin on the cue ball it will miss your cue tip when it returns back down the table. If the side of the cue ball hits your cue, that's not too bad. However, if the cue ball is striking the rail on either side of your cue ½ diamond or more off target, then you have some serious flaws to correct. This drill gives you immediate, unbiased feedback on the accuracy and quality of your setup and stroke. If you are missing the mark, check your follow through. Your cue tip should be pointing directly at the center of the chalk. If it's pointing to the left, and the cue ball's returning down the left side of the table, then you're putting unwanted left english on the cue ball. The opposite holds true if the cue ball's returning down the right side of the table. Your problem may lie in your stroke. You could also be setting up to the cue ball slightly off center. Worst of all, you might be setting up incorrectly and have a flaw in your stroke.

Examine your setup and follow through. You may need to adjust your address position slightly to the left or right. Another possibility is you're twisting your arm and/or wrist through impact. Continue the corrective process until the cue ball's contacting the tip as it returns back down the table.

Once you feel confident stroking the shot above center, try the same drill hitting the cue ball dead center. Next proceed to the draw stroke. This is the toughest of all as any errors will be magnified due to the slightly downward hit on the cue ball. If you can make the cue ball return dead center with draw, congratulations are in order. Your stroke is near perfect! You can also use this drill to test the consistency of your stroke using english. Pick a stroke speed and the amount (i.e., ½ tip center left/medium stroke) you want to hit the cue ball off center. Mark where the cue ball strikes either the side rail or end rail on its return. Use the same english and stroke speed on several consecutive shots. This will tell you a lot about your sense of touch and how consistently you apply english.

One of the beauties of this drill is that you can stroke freely without worrying about pocketing a ball. After about 15-20 minutes of practice with the first version of the drill, you may be pleasantly surprised at your results when you resume shooting balls again. Try switching back and forth between drills and shooting. About five each works well.

This drill takes some discipline, but is well worth the effort. So, whenever you suspect your stroke is off the mark, give this drill a try at your next practice session. It could work wonders for your game.

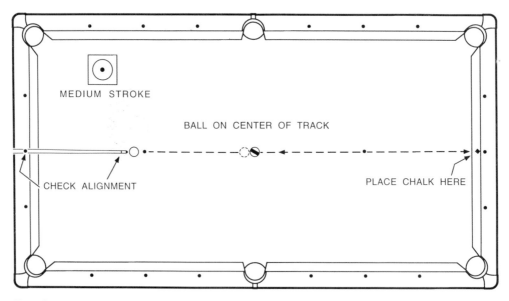

Perfecting Your Stroke (II)

This drill is an extension of the previous routine. Once again place the chalk at the edge of the rail opposite the middle diamond. The cue ball is put in line with the two middle diamonds near or on the spot. Your goal is to have the cue ball return to the tip of your cue stick. What you're especially looking to correct on this drill are both your alignment and your stroke.

At address, pay specific attention to where your cue is pointing. The tip should be pointed directly at the center of the chalk. At the same time your cue should be directly over the middle diamond. In fact, if the butt of your cue is lined up correctly when you look down at your cue the diamond will be obscured from vision! If you can see any part of the diamond at address, then you are not setting up square to the shot.

Let's assume you are lined up squarely. Now take some practice strokes. If the diamond (or part of it) appears on your backstroke, then you are twisting your cue off line during the stroke. Keep taking practice strokes until you can no longer see the diamond. This will help you groove a straight stroke.

To add precision to this drill, you can tape a piece of paper over the diamond. Draw a bright, colored stripe that's the same width as your cue on the paper. If either side of the stripe appears during your stroke, then you are twisting your cue. When you can stroke back and forth without seeing any part of the stripe, your stroke will be perfectly straight.

After shooting up and back at the chalk for a while you'll notice a slight groove in the felt. The second part of the drill consists of placing a ball exactly in the middle of the table on the track you've worn into the felt. Your objective is to shoot a stop shot straight at the object ball. If done correctly, the object ball will rebound off the far rail and return smack into the middle of the cue ball. This drill will test the accuracy of your stroke while shooting at an object ball.

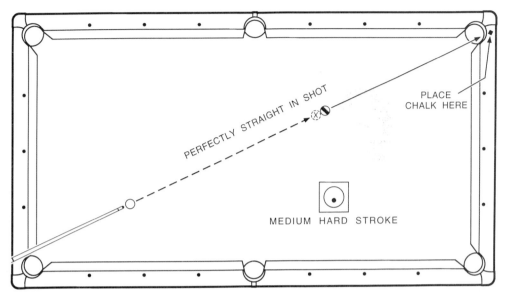

Straight-In Shot Stroke Check

Here's a practice shot that's great for testing the fundamental soundness of your stroke. Set up the cue ball and object ball in a perfectly straight line to the corner pocket. Place a piece of chalk directly in line with the balls over the back of the pocket as shown above. Now you're ready to test you stroke. Use a medium hard stroke and hit the cue ball a half tip below center. Your goal is to pocket the object ball in the center of the pocket and have the cue ball stop precisely in its tracks. In addition, you'll want to hold your follow through as if posing for a picture. Your tip should be pointed straight at the chalk. If it's not, you have a flaw that needs correcting.

If you hit this shot perfectly you will reap great satisfaction at the sight of the ball entering the middle of the pocket as the cue ball stops dead. However, you can still make this shot into either side of the pocket if your stroke is only slightly off track. At the distance shown in the diagram, that's not too bad. Notice, however, the cue ball will drift sideways on a less than perfect shot.

On shots that miss the pocket, and especially those that miss by a wide margin, you will learn to sense when something doesn't feel quite right. Hopefully with enough practice you will detect the flaw(s) in your stroke as you start to hone in on the pocket. Because this shot can be so valuable to developing and maintaining your stroke, you should consider shooting it 10-20 times each practice session. Keep track of how many you make each session and chart your progress. Nine out of ten would be outstanding!

One of the good things about this shot is it eliminates one variable. Most likely any errors you make are because of your stroke. Be aware, however, even on a straight-in shot, your problem could also be the result of faulty aiming.

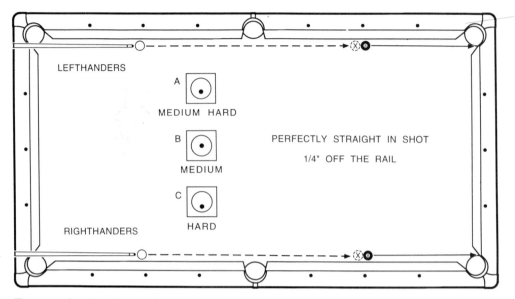

Down the Rail Straight-In Shot Drill

This drill will detect any sideways movement in your stroke. It will also help you grove your stroke. The cue ball and object ball are to be placed ¼" off the rail at the locations in the diagram. Righthanders and lefthanders should shoot this shot at opposite sides of the table so that each can make a bridge that's unobstructed by the rail.

Once you've settled into your stance, check the alignment of your cue stick. Look down at your cue. It should be lined up parallel to the rail. Make any necessary adjustments to straighten out your alignment.

Address the cue ball ½ tip below center. Start out by shooting with a medium hard stroke. Your goal is to make the cue ball stop dead. Stay down on your follow through and check the position of your cue. The tip should be pointing straight at the pocket. In addition, your cue should be parallel to the rail. If it's not, then you have some work to do. The cue ball's position will also provide valuable feedback. It should come to rest exactly ¼" off the rail at the point of contact.

Once you've mastered the first phase of this drill, it's time to move on to step B. Use a medium stroke and strike the cue ball ½ tip above the center. When the shot's hit perfectly, the cue ball will follow the object ball into the corner pocket!

The final phase of this drill is the toughest of all. This time use a hard draw stroke. Try to bring the cue ball back further and further. The ultimate would be to pocket the ball and draw the cue ball all the way back into the opposite corner pocket! Give yourself a perfect "10" if you can pull off this shot. (You can increase the degree of difficulty factor by practicing this shot on tables with tight pockets.)

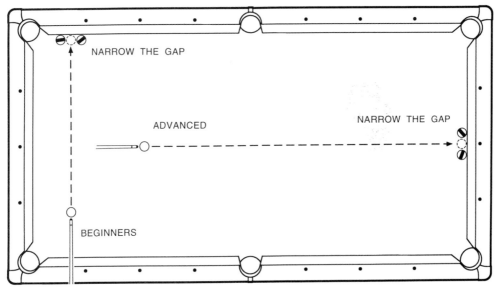

The Field Goal Drill

The field goal drill can improve your stroke and sharpen your sense of aim. Place two object balls on the rail about 2¾" apart. You can approximate this distance by placing a third ball between the two balls. As you'll recall, a ball is 2¼" in diameter. The next step is to move either or both outside balls so the gap between them is 2¾" for starters. Finally, remove the middle ball and position the cue ball as diagrammed. Beginning players should first try this drill shooting across the width of the table. Experienced players should shoot this down the length of the table.

   Your objective is to shoot the cue ball between the two balls without touching either one. Use enough stroke speed so the cue ball returns to its original position. This will help with your accuracy. After you've made a few successful passes at 2¾" (which gave you a ½" margin for error), move the two balls closer together and test your skill with the "goal posts" perhaps only 2½" apart.

   Look for tendencies with your unsuccessful attempts. Are you consistently missing to the left or right? You may very well discover you are habitually aiming slightly to the left or right of the target. This could help to explain why you may be constantly missing balls to the same side of the pocket over and over again.

   Beyond discovering any flaws in your aim and/or stroke you can expect to reap a couple of additional benefits from this drill. Your ability to roll the cue ball long distances down an exact line should help you to feather in thin cut shots and to play those safeties where you must clip only a very small part of the object ball. In addition, the drill helps promote a smooth stroke as you are rolling the cue ball, not hitting it forcefully, at the object ball.

Shotmaking Practice

All players can benefit from devoting a good portion of each practice session to working on their shotmaking. For newer players it's an absolute must. Choose a few shots to work on at each practice. These would include: relatively easy shots that build your confidence, shots that have been giving you trouble, and new shots such as billiards or caroms that you need to master to round out your game. Set up the cue ball and object ball in exactly the same positions and keep shooting the shot until you get it right. If however, you start to get too frustrated, move on to something else. Work on the troublesome shot at a later date, perhaps after getting some advice on how to shoot it properly.

Look for tendencies in your missed shots. Are you primarily missing to the left or right of the pocket? Force yourself to make the necessary compensations. Perhaps you'll even want to over compensate for a persistent error. Eventually you'll find the happy medium as your shots begin to find the pocket. Remember, most missed shots come from not cutting the ball enough.

When you do start making shots consistently, internalize the successful process immediately. Ask yourself: "How did it feel?, How did it look? What was the position of my grip, arm, and stroke before, during and after the shot?" It's also a good idea to have a friend observe your winning form. Be sure to video tape yourself if possible when you're on top of your game. Some of the biggest improvements in your game will come from these magic moments when your awareness of what you are doing correctly goes on to become a part of your game.

When you are having a particularly poor session, try shooting using centerball only. This should improve the accuracy of your shotmaking immediately. When you feel you're back on track, you can begin to use side english once again.

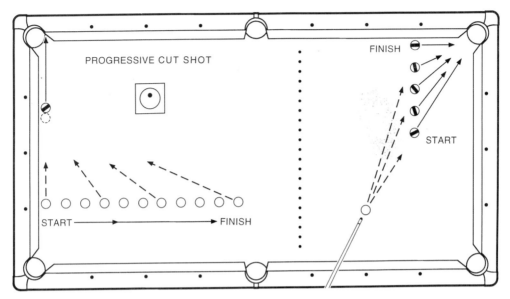

Progressive Cut Shot Drill

In each drill, start out with a straight-in shot and then progress to a series of increasingly difficult cut shots. Progressive drills allow you to raise the bar in manageable increments. Before you know it, you're cutting in shots that might have appeared way beyond your capabilities. You can make a game with these drills by going back one step each time you miss. Keep score of how many shots that it takes you to complete the drill.

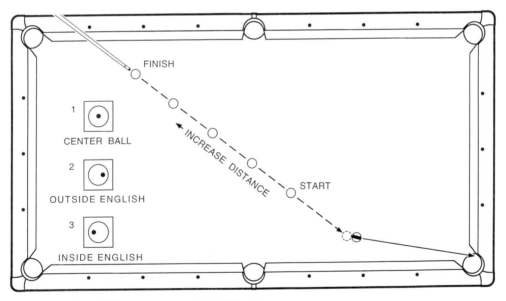

Progressive Distance on Cut Shots

Choose a cut shot such as the one in the diagram and begin to shoot it using centerball. Keep moving the cue ball further away in increments of about one foot each. Now repeat the drill, only this time use outside english. Complete the drill by using inside english, which is by far the toughest part of the drill. Concentrate on the adjustments necessary to pocket the balls.

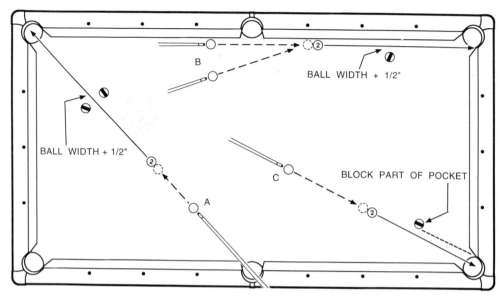

Blocking Part of the Pocket

You can improve your accuracy by reducing the effective opening to the pocket using other balls. In position A, you have a total clearance of 2¾", or ½" more than the width of the 2-ball. Position B demonstrates a couple of rail shots that are partially blocked by the stripe ball. Position C shows you a shot to a partially blocked pocket that comes up over and over again.

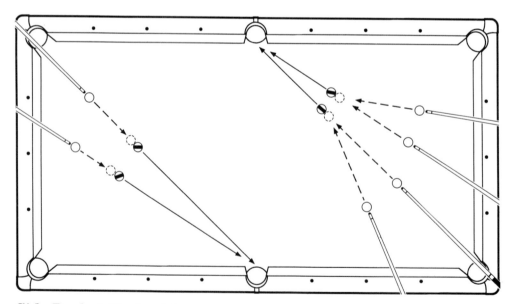

Side Pocket Shotmaking

Far too many players ignore the side pockets, but you can get a leg up on the competition by practicing shots into the side pocket from various distances and angles of approach as diagrammed. As you'll recall from the chapter on shotmaking, the effective opening of the side pockets gets smaller and smaller as the approach angle decreases. Take advantage of these naturally small targets to improve your accuracy.

Position Play Practice

There are a number of highly effective drills and practice routines that can do wonders for your cue ball control. One good place to start is by shooting straight-in shots using the same speed of stroke each time. First use centerball, draw, and then follow. Keep the cue ball in the same place, but move the object ball a couple of inches to the side so you have a slight cut angle. Repeat the drill using centerball, follow, and draw. Take careful notice of how the cue ball reacts after cutting the object ball in at a small angle. This will provide you with a valuable lesson in position play. Continue with the drill by moving the object ball a couple of inches further to the side each time until you've completed the drill from 3-4 locations.

A soft stroke is vital to good position play. One way to develop a delicate touch is to practice shots using such a soft stroke that the object ball literally topples into the pocket just as it's about to run completely out of steam. This drill will also come in handy when you need to use the lag shot to gain good position. Remember, however, that this drill is primarily for practice only. When playing in competition, an overly soft stroke could lead to missed shots because of a bad table roll.

The power stroke enables you to move the cue ball across the table even when you have only a small angle go work with. This shot requires near perfect technique in order to send the cue ball from a few inches to several feet across the table to the desired location.

You can significantly change the movement of the cue ball by altering the length of your bridge. For example, set up a follow shot at a slight cue angle (perhaps 5°). Try using different length bridges measuring 6", 8", and 10" or more. Use a medium speed of stroke from each location and observe carefully where the cue ball comes to rest. Next, setup the same shot and repeat the drill again, but this time using a firmer stroke. Once again, take careful notice where the cue ball winds up. This routine will teach you how to control the cue ball's rolling distance by altering your bridge.

You can add great precision to your game by using a second object ball as a target. Set up the cue ball, object ball, and a second object ball. Your objective is to pocket the first ball and have the cue ball roll gently into the second ball. The key to the shot is to set up common position plays that you'll use regularly in competition. The reason for the soft hit on the second ball is to develop your speed control.

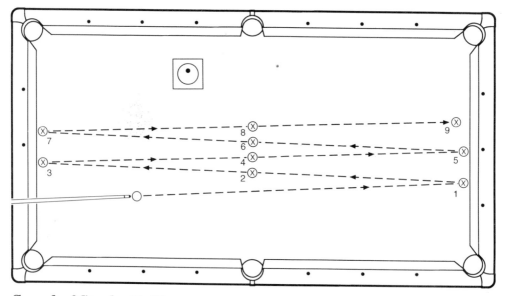

Speed of Stroke Drill

You simply must learn to accurately judge the traveling distance of the cue ball if you ever hope to play position well. To do this, you must learn to feel the force that's required on each and every shot. Here's a simple drill that can help you develop your feel and heighten your sense of touch.

Place the cue ball opposite the second diamond and aim straight at the far end of the table. (Note that for illustration purposes only, the shot is taken at a slight angle.) Now roll the cue ball gently down the table using an extremely soft stroke so that it comes to rest at position # 1. Next, apply a very soft stroke and try to have the cue ball stop at position # 2. Continue to add a measurable increment of force to each successive stroke as you work your way through the drill. Your goal, as the diagram illustrates, is to add ½ table length to the cue ball's traveling distance on each attempt.

It's not easy to land the cue ball precisely at each designated spot. At first, your goal should be to have the cue ball travel further on each shot, and to wind up within a couple of feet of each target. Always be conscious of the feel of your stroke and the force you're applying to each and every stroke. By building a sense of awareness of your stroke force, you'll soon develop a feel for distance that will work wonders for your game. You may also want to pay special attention to position # 3 of the drill, as that's the place you're shooting for when you lag for the opening break in tournament play.

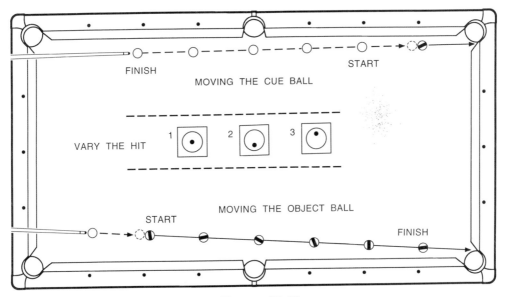

Progressive Distance - Stop, Draw, Follow

A complete mastery of basic position play will go a long way toward improving your game. The two drills in the diagram above provide you with a wide variety of position plays using stop, draw, and follow.

Start with the cue ball one diamond up the rail from the stripe ball, in the drill at the top of the diagram (lefthanders should do this first exercise on the opposite side of the table). Use centerball and observe the reaction of the cue ball as you move it further away from the object ball on successive shots. Once the cue ball has been moved back to even with the side pocket, centerball stroking will no longer stop the cue ball. After completing the first phase of the drill, place the cue ball back at its original position and continue using draw and then follow.

In the second drill at the bottom of the diagram the position of the cue ball remains constant while the object ball is moved closer to the pocket as the drill progresses. Once again, you should begin using centerball and then switch to draw and then follow.

Both drills will teach you plenty about basic cue ball control that will provide you with a solid foundation for playing position.

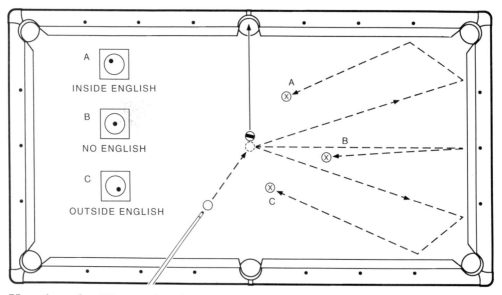

Varying the Hit on the Cue Ball

One of the best ways to teach yourself position is to set up shots such as the one presented in the diagram. Before shooting it's a good idea to mark the position of both balls. That way you can replace them at the exact same location for subsequent shots. In our example, the side pocket cut shot was first hit with follow and inside english (path A). Centerball stroking resulted in bath B while draw with outside english propelled the cue ball along path C. Take note of the variety of ending positions of the cue ball.

Under game conditions it pays to be able to move the cue ball around the table with different combinations of draw, follow, and english. This will enable you to weave your way through traffic and play the position each shot requires. Set up a number of different shots and play them at different speeds of stroke while varying the spot at which you strike the cue ball. Observe carefully where the cue ball stops on each attempt. You may even wish to place another object ball(s) at the spot where the cue ball comes to rest. This will make the comparisons even easier to visualize and remember.

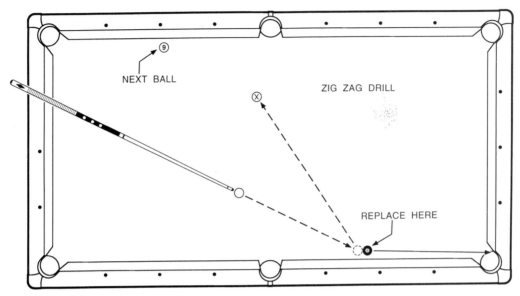

Zig Zag Drill

Place two balls a couple of inches off the rail on opposite sides of the table. After pocketing the first ball, replace it in its original position. Now pocket the second ball while playing shape on the first ball. Replace the second ball in its original position and continue to cross the table from side to side replacing the balls as you go. This drill teach you speed control and how to avoid side pocket scratches.

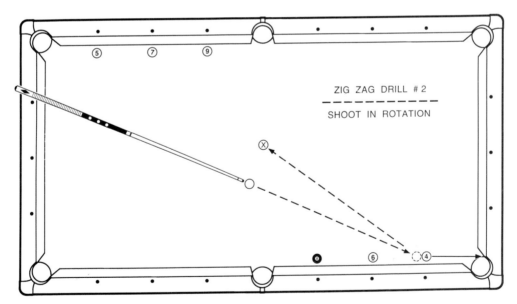

Zig Zag Drill (II)

Set up the last six balls from a rack of Nine Ball as shown above and try to clear the table while shooting the balls in rotation. This drill will thoroughly test your ability to control the cue ball as it travels back and forth across the table. For best results, try to position the cue ball on each shot at about the same angle as the first shot on the 4-ball.

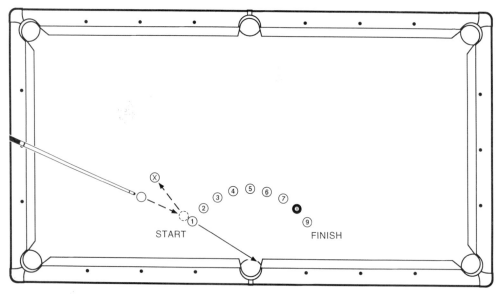

Side Pocket Circle Drill

Place a number of balls in front of the side pocket in a semi-circle and proceed to pocket them in order, all in the side pocket. This drill will improve the sensitive touch needed for short distance position using draw. The secret is to maintain the correct angle on each ball. Therefore, you always want to be shooting cut shots to the <u>right</u>! Of course, if you start at the other side, you'll be cutting to the left.

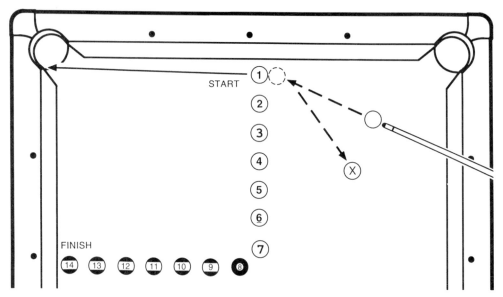

One Corner Pocket Drill

Give yourself a big pat on the back if you can pocket all fourteen balls in order from the position in the diagram. This difficult drill will help you refine your position play. You'll need expert control of the cue ball as you will be called upon to use follow, english, and draw to complete the drill.

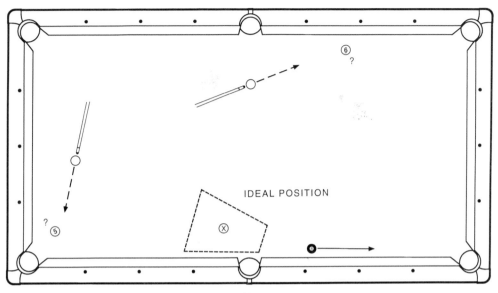

Ball in Hand Runouts - Eight Ball

Randomly scatter two balls from either the stripes or solids and the 8-ball on the table, as in the diagram. Now give yourself ball in hand. You can play either ball from your group first. Plan your run wisely. In the example, it's easiest to get ideal position on the 8-ball by shooting the 5-ball. In this sequence your first shot, therefore, should be on the 6-ball. As your skill rises, start the drill with additional balls from your group.

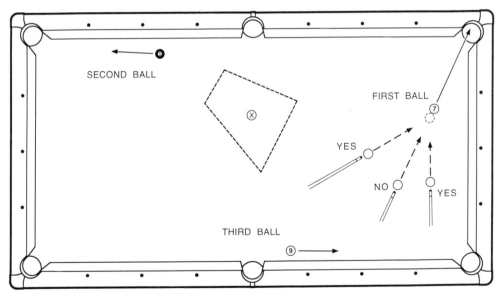

Ball in Hand Runouts - The Nine Ball

Spread the last three balls from the Nine Ball rack, give yourself ball in hand and try to run out. Take time to plan your strategy. The diagram shows one possible three ball sequence. The two positions labeled "yes" will enable you to easily send the cue ball into the position zone for the 8-ball.

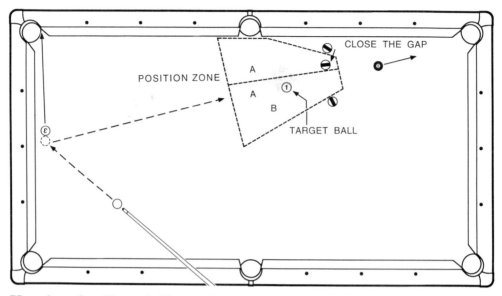

Varying the Size of Shape Zones

Put the 8-ball and 1-ball from the solids on the table at random. Now place a couple of stripe balls near the 8 so the size of your position zone is reduced significantly. Now shoot the solid and try to get good shape on the 8-ball. The position zone in the example is identified by the two A's. You can increase the challenge by shooting the same shot over again. This time, reduce the size of the position zone (to B in the example) by moving one of the stripe balls. You can also add a target ball to the position zone. If you hit it gently, consider it a bullseye!

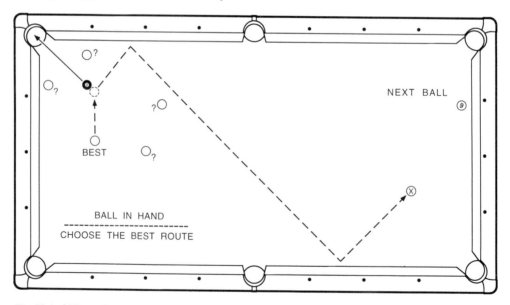

Ball in Hand - Choose the Best Route

Place two balls on the table at random and give yourself ball in hand. Your objective is to discover the best possible route from point A to point B. This is an excellent drill for teaching newer players basic position play.

Safety Practice

Winning at pool comes largely from gaining control of the table with killer safety play. Yet, strangely enough, not one player in perhaps twenty takes the time to practice this crucial aspect of the game. Perhaps safety practice is ignored because it is boring to those who neglect it. Now if you can be that one player in the crowd who can muster the discipline to practice safeties, then you can gain an important edge over the competition.

The section on safety play in the chapter on Nine Ball can provide you with a number of important safety plays to work on in your practice sessions. If you resolve to work diligently to master these safeties and others, you will discover you will be rewarded with cue ball in hand on a much more regular basis. I need not remind you, ball in hand equals victory more often than not.

There are a few points to keep in mind as you practice safeties. Pay special attention to how much of the object ball you hit with the cue ball. One of the big keys is to be able to hit 2/3, 1/2, 1/4, or just the edge of the object ball when needed. You'll also want to concentrate on the roll of the cue ball <u>after</u> it makes contact with the object ball. If you can control the speed and route of the cue ball, you can hook your opponent almost at will! One final pep talk is in order: never forget, successful people do what others don't. Practice your safeties!

English

Pocketing balls using english takes lots of practice to learn how to aim properly, which compensates for throw, deflection, and curve. It's best to start with fairly simple shots using centerball. After you've secured your aim by shooting a given shot with centerball, you're ready to begin applying english to the cue ball. Use ½ tip of outside english at first (you may be wise to confine your side english to this amount for the vast majority of shots that require english). Use a soft stroke. This will teach you the effects of throw. Then begin to gradually increase your stroke speed. As your speed of stroke increases you'll find you will need to compensate more for deflection and less for throw.

As your skill with english grows, you can begin to shoot longer shots and apply as much as one tip of side spin. Nearly all players find it much easier to use outside english, so you should concentrate on mastering it first. When you begin to feel comfortable using outside english you can begin to run through the drills discussed above using inside english.

Pool Games That Can Improve Your Play

A variety of pool games can provide excellent training for the game or games you play most often. The games discussed below can all be played by yourself (or, of course, with a friend). We'll provide some suggestions for using each game to develop your skills.

Eight Ball

Break the balls open, choose solids or stripes, and then try to run out if possible. Also, take time to consider what defensive strategy you would adopt if a runout is not possible. Although it takes some mental shifting of gears, try to pursue the best strategy when it's your "opponent's" turn (this is kind of like playing chess by yourself). Continue in this fashion back and forth until the game is over. If you are practicing on a coin operated table, here's a money saving tip: once you've run off either the stripes or solids, switch over to the remaining balls in the other group and run them out prior to pocketing the 8-ball.

After breaking the balls, remove all of the stripes or solids. Then try to runout. By reducing the congestion, you can simulate actual game conditions when your opponent has failed to complete a runout. This routine will also improve your basic position play. Don't forget to identify the key ball (the ball that you want to shoot before the 8-ball) before starting your run.

Nine Ball

One way to practice Nine Ball is to break open the rack and proceed as if you were playing an opponent, except your opponent is yourself. By practicing under simulated game conditions you will have to use all of the skills that normally come up in a game, including pushouts, kick shots, and safeties. Another good approach is to give yourself ball in hand after the break. If you want to emphasize running out, you may even choose to separate any clusters by hand after the break shot.

Many newer players often have trouble running all nine balls in order. These players may wish to build up to a rack of Nine Ball by first practicing a game called Six Ball. The balls are run in rotation just like Nine Ball. The 6-ball is the money ball. The balls are racked in three rows of one, two, and three balls. The 6-ball is racked in the middle of the third row.

Rotation

Advanced players who wish to hone their position play skills should consider practicing rotation. All fifteen balls are racked and then broken apart. The rack is then run in order, 1 through 15. In the early stages of the rack, the congestion factor makes position play extremely challenging. You can simplify this exercise somewhat by simply scattering the balls by hand across the length of the table.

Bank Pool

This game can help you develop your banking skills. The game is commonly played with a Nine Ball rack. The balls are broken wide open. If whoever is breaking makes a ball, he/she continues to shoot, but is not given credit for the ball(s) made on the break. The first player to make five bank shots wins. However, one point is subtracted for each foul.

Straight Pool

An entire book could be written about the virtues of this wonderful, but often neglected game. Straight pool was, for many years, the game that decided world championships. In today's fast paced world, however, it now ranks far behind both Eight Ball and Nine Ball in popularity. Nevertheless, the game can provide you with a solid foundation for virtually all other games of pool.

All fifteen balls are racked together at the start. You must designate which ball you are going to pocket, and where you plan to shoot it. You can shoot any ball in any pocket. One point is scored for each ball you make. One point is deducted for each foul. Should you foul three times in a row, you lose three points plus an additional fifteen points. All fifteen balls are then re-racked and your opponent has the option of breaking or having you break. Most players play safe on the opening break because it's very difficult to call and pocket a ball out of the rack. Unlike the other games, should your opponent scratch, you get ball in hand behind the head string. For a complete discussion of the rules, I refer you to the Billiard Congress of America's Rule Book.

Straight pool is often referred to as 14.1 Continuous. That's because you clear all the balls but one from the table. The remaining fourteen balls are then racked. The open spot in the rack is at the top of the triangle. The objective is to position the cue ball and the fifteenth ball from the previous rack so that when you pocket this ball, the cue ball will then contact, and open up the new rack of fourteen balls, enabling you to continue your run.

Straight pool is normally played to 50, 75, 100, 125, or 150 points. Experts at the game can run a hundred or more balls. A hundred ball run is the equivalent of running a little over seven racks (7 racks x 14 balls per rack = 98)!

You must concentrate on every single shot if you wish to achieve high runs. High runs are perhaps the greatest joy the game provides. Single minded concentration will help you to focus in any game. Straight pool is great for teaching you pattern play, which is a must if your goal is to play a championship game of Eight Ball. Straight pool demands precision shape, which improves your play in all other games. In addition, the safety play you learn while playing straight pool can be especially useful in both Eight Ball and Nine Ball. Finally, straight pool is a great game to practice by yourself, as it provides you with a concrete method of testing yourself. It's fun to establish new high runs. Naturally, once you set a new high run for yourself, whether it's 10, 20, 50, 100 or more balls, your next goal is to obviously exceed your new record! This requires great concentration, which is good for any game. Enjoy!

One Pocket

One pocket has been gaining in popularity in recent years among the more dedicated pool players, perhaps because the game is an exquisite blend of both offensive and defensive plays. To play one pocket well, you need to be skilled at position play, safeties, kick shots, bank shots and reading the table. As the name suggests, you have one designated pocket into which you shoot your balls. All fifteen balls are racked. Before the game begins, the breaker chooses one of the corner pockets behind the rack as his designated pocket. The opponent then shoots to the other pocket. The first player to pocket eight balls in his/her pocket wins the game. A point is deducted and a ball is spotted for each foul. After a foul, the opponent has cue ball in hand behind the head string. Any ball that is pocketed in other than the two designated corner pockets is re-spotted. The break is perhaps the most important shot as it sets the tone for the entire game. Good players normally break from the rail on the side of the table opposite their designated pocket. The break is hit with a medium soft stroke while hitting part of the head ball, but mostly the second ball behind it. You'll know that your position play is approaching expert status when you can run eight consecutive balls into the same pocket!

HOW TO BUY EQUIPMENT

Acquiring The Tools
Of The Trade

There is an exciting world of products available to the billiard enthusiast including tables, cues and cases, as well as a wide variety of accessories. In addition, there are now a number a highly useful training aids to help you with your game. In this chapter we'll sort through the available maze of offerings and give you some solid advice on how to purchase the table, cue and other items that are right for your game and pocketbook.

Tables

There is a pool table to fit most budgets. In addition, they come in several sizes to accommodate available space. A quality pool table will last a lifetime, allowing for occasional maintenance items such as replacing the cloth. Therefore, I would advise that you spend at least enough to get a table that will last. You should plan on spending upwards of $1,000. A top quality regulation size table will run between $3,000 and $5,000. Figure on spending $1,500 to $2,000 for a good 3½' x 7' table.

Once you get past this range, you are starting to pay for fancy ornamentation and exotic materials, just as you would for an expensive cue. For example, the legs come in a variety of styles, including turned and fluted oak legs and carved, solid oak. The pockets also come in a variety of styles which include specially crafted leather fringe pockets.

As a rule, the thicker the bed of the table, the higher the quality. The playing surface of most good tables is thick slate that is imported from Italy. The slate is leveled and cut precisely to the table dimensions.

Pockets vary in size and depth. On a regulation table, the corner pockets are 4 3/4" wide at the edges. The side pockets measure 5¼". On a bar table, the corner pockets are the same, but the side pockets are smaller, measuring 4 3/4" Some pool rooms, and individual owners as well, take some liberties with those dimensions by decreasing the opening of the pockets to make the table play tougher. You will need to decide if your table is for fun and recreation, in which case you should stick with the standard size pockets. However, if your table is to be used to sharpen your skills for competition, you may wish to tighten up the pockets.

The depth of the pocket will also affect the playability of the table. Regulation size tables tend to have deeper pockets than bar tables. This, of course, makes it easier to miss balls in the jaws on the big table.

The quality of the cushions (or rails) also affects playability of the table. Ideally, the cushions will be consistent and lively. You can really see the english take hold when the cue ball hits the rail on a table with lively rails. What you want to avoid are dead cushions that absorb much of the cue ball's energy at contact. Under these conditions, you must continually power stroke the cue ball to achieve your position. The cushion should be replaced every few years when they no longer deliver the required playing characteristics.

Quality cloth makes all the difference. The best cloth tends to roll faster and truer because the nap is finer. You could compare this to putting on fast greens that have just been moved versus those that have long and uneven blades of grass. On top of this, you won't have to replace a good quality cloth nearly as often. The best cloth is worsted woolen. You may have up to 30 or colors from which to choose, depending on the manufacturer. Every so often, you will need to recover your table unless you like playing on a discolored and uneven surface that rolls forever. It pays to shop around for someone in your area that does quality work at a reasonable price. Be sure to inquire about the cloth your repairman uses before signing him up for the job.

One of the prime considerations in choosing a table is available space. Hopefully, your table will fit comfortably in your recreation room, so you won't have to keep reaching for a sawed-off cue stick when the cue ball's close to the rails. The ideal measurements for your home pool room should allow for the width of the playing surface, the length of your cue and for an adequately long backstroke. The table below shows you the minimum spaced requirement for a pool table, assuming of course, that you do not wish to use a short cue. The calculations assume a maximum back stroke of 6".

Room Size Requirements

Size of Table	Playing Surface	Width of Room	Length of Room
3½' x 7'	40" x 80"	14'	17', 4 "
4' x 8'	44" x 88"	14', 4"	18'
4½' x 9'	50" x 100"	14', 10"	19'

If you have your heart set on a regulation table but your room comes up a few inches short, remember that there are a number of different lengths of shorter cues for shots when the walls get in the way. Also, keep in mind that there won't be all that many shots where the cue ball is on the rail and you are shooting across the table at a 90 degree angle.

When setting up your table, be sure that the legs are positioned on a solid surface (ie., not a carpet). If you must place your table on a rug, it's a good idea to put wooden shims underneath each leg. These can also be useful in leveling the table. The idea is to have your table roll as true as possible. Some models also come with self leveling legs that make it fairly easy to get the table perfectly level. After your table has settled, you may be wise to check it for levelness every so often. You can test the table with a carpenter's level and/or by slowly rolling a ball down the table and watching it's path closely as it slows down. Remember to check the roll both across and down the length of the table.

Colorful lamps with a billiard theme are available to light your table and add to the ambiance. Traditional lamps of green glass and brass in turn-of-the-century styling are also very popular. No matter what style you choose, make sure the light is spread evenly across the length of the table. What don't want are dark and/or long shadows from the balls or dark shadows underneath the rails.

Items for Your Home Pool Room:

- Cue rack for storing your house cues
- Chairs and/or stools that sit high for easy viewing
- A rack for the balls
- Chalk
- Table cover to protect your investment
- A brush for cleaning the table
- A mechanical bridge
- Some sort of scoring device (often they are built into the table)
- Pictures to decorate your walls
- A powder tray
- A tray for the balls.
- A good quality set of balls

Table Care

Dust and pool chalk will eventually accumulate on your table, which requires that you brush the table occasionally. Be sure to brush consistently in the same direction, using a special brush that's made just for a pool table. You may also use a light hand vacuum cleaner. The rails can be cleaned using a damp cloth. You may also wish to clean the bottom of the pockets and/or the ball return.

Cue Stick

Most new players start out using cues provided by the billiard room or tavern. Soon after the pool bug hits, it's time to buy your own cue. There are a wide variety of makes and models to fit any player's needs, tastes and pocketbook. We'll start our discussion by identifying the broad categories of cues now available. This should serve as a basis for establishing your selection criteria.

One Piece House Cue - These are one solid piece of wood. They vary in quality. Some house cues play reasonably well. If you're not ready to spend big bucks on a custom cue, you might offer to buy a house cue that you like from your friendly billiards room. I did this at a cost of $10. You can have a joint put in for another $25-$35. This will give you a low cost starter cue.

Inexpensive and Colorful Designs - For about $10-$50 you can buy a colorful cue with a joint. These are for beginners and casual players. Cues in this category are also ideal for home recreation rooms. You get what you pay for in this category, so don't expect to get a great playing cue in this price range.

Sneaky Pete - These cues look nearly identical to a house cue, however, they have a joint that's visually hard to detect (hence the name). Many hustlers like to use these cues because it makes them look like they are using a house cue. Sneaky Petes are often made by locals who are getting into cue manufacturing as well as by more experienced craftsman. Expect to pay $60-$150 or more for one of these. A good Sneaky Pete will provide excellent playability at a modest price.

Production Cues - This is the real starting point for the semi-serious level players and higher level players. Production cues are made by a number of well respected manufacturers who have perfected their techniques over 10-20 years or longer. Most use the latest technology to assure consistently high quality. In addition, they age the wood properly to insure against warping. The cues in this category all play well and are attractively designed. The price that you pay is directly related to the intricacy of the design work on the butt end of the cue. Expect to pay between $130-$160 for the lower priced models. The fancy cues may cost $500-$1,000 or more.

Custom/Production Cues - These cues are normally associated with the name of a well respected craftsman who is very involved in the manufacturing of the cue. Prices normally start at between $300-$500 for the basic models (little or no extra design work). The more expensive models may cost upwards of $2,000. Cues in this price range are often the choice of many top players as they are of excellent quality and are very playable.

Custom Cues - Master craftsman, many of whose names are folklore in the billiard industry, produce these cues step by step from start to finish. The best known cue makers have been plying their trade for 10-20 years. You can expect to pay $400-$500 for the basic models and up to $3,000 (or higher) depending on the time spent designing and making the cue, and on materials used. You can also count on waiting 2-6 months or longer for your cue as the top names often are booked well in advance. Be assured, however, that the wait will be worth it when your custom cue finally arrives at your door. Needless to say, these cues provide a very satisfactory "hit" on the cue ball. One word of warning: If your purchase a very expensive cue secondhand, make sure that it's the real McCoy. Some unscrupulous operators have been known to make counterfeits. Also, be sure to pay a fair price, and don't expect to make a quick killing reselling your cues.

Selection Criteria

Plan to spend a little time deciding just exactly what you want in a new cue and what price you are willing to pay. A basic model production cue is an ideal starting point for both new and serious players alike. Players with experience who are looking for a particular feel may wish to try several different manufacturers. Finally, collectors who are spending several thousand dollars buying cues for practical reasons and/or as an investment, will need to carefully consider things like price, resale value, design work and authenticity. The following list gives you some of the most basic criteria in selecting a quality cue that conforms to your requirements.

- **Price** - What is in your budget? How often you play and how serious you are about your game (and hence your environment).How does the cue feel when you shoot with it - How's the hit?
- **Tip Size** - 13 mm. is standard. The normal range is 12 mm. to 14 mm. Players who like to use a lot of english will favor a smaller tip. Those who typically play closer to center will use the standard 13 mm. Tip size, of course, is in correlation to the thickness of the shaft. Additionally, those with shorter fingers prefer a thinner shaft.
- **Taper** - This is a matter of personal preference. A shaft with a regular taper will steadily increase in diameter from tip to joint. The highly popular pro taper stays constant until 13"-15" from the tip. From there the shaft gets steadily wider.

- **Balance**- It's very important for the cue to feel properly balanced. The main thing to avoid is a cue that feels too heavy in the butt end (cues like this are referred to as butt heavy).
- **The Butt** - There are different thicknesses in the grip area of the cue. Make sure the thickness conforms to the size of your hand.
- **Wrap** - The grip area is typically covered in irish linen or leather. Different grip materials will enable the cue to stick in place in your hand to varying degrees. What you want to avoid is slippage in your hand.
- **Length** - 58" is now the standard length. Some players prefer an extra inch or two which can help you to easily reach some shots. Very few players opt for a shorter cue.
- **Weight** - This is one of the most important factors. The standard range of weights is 18-21 ounces. With some experience you can feel the difference in weight to within ½ ounce or less. Aim accuracy and speed control are affected by the weight of the cue. If you use a soft stroke, you should consider using a heavier cue. Conversely, if you use a hard stroke, you may get your best result with a lighter cue. The pros, according to a study done by Pool & Billiard Magazine, on average, use a 19½ ounce cue.

Choosing a House Cue

On occasion, you may find the need to play with a house cue. Some upscale rooms will provide you with a nice production cue, often for a nominal fee. However, if you must select a cue off the wall, keep these points in mind:

- Check the tip
- Look at the weight, which is stamped on the side
- Give it the roll test for straightness
- Take a couple of practice shots

Parts of a Cuestick

The shaft is traditionally made of wood. Finer grained wood is of a higher quality. All quality cue makers select only the finest woods and then age and dry them to prevent warping. A good number of custom cues come with two shafts. It's always a good idea to have an extra shaft on hand in case your tip suddenly becomes unplayable. If your cue comes with only one shaft, you can usually order an extra one for about $50-175, depending on the manufacturer.

There are now a number of manufacturers that are making cues out of composite materials. One manufacturer covers maple with fiberglass while others use graphite and titanium.

The butt end of the cue contains all of the fancy ornamentation. Some of the materials that make up the inlays include: black ebony, mother of pearl, bone ivory and abalone. The body of the butt is most typically made from birds-eye maple. There are a wide variety of stains that can be applied including natural stain and cherry. There are a number of exotic woods that make beautiful cues including rosewood, cocobollo, zircote, tulipwood, karinwood and sonokeling wood, to name a few.

At the end of the butt a rubber bumper protects the cue from possible damage. The wrap on more expensive cues is made from pressed and sealed irish linen. This material absorbs perspiration very well. Less costly cues typically use durable nylon for the wrapping.

The joint holds the butt and shaft together. This is a very important part of the cue as it contributes greatly to the feel of the hit. Good players often develop a preference for a particular type of material that goes into the joint. Among the most common today are: micro polished stainless steel, brass, phenolic, plastic implex (imitation ivory) and german nickel/silver. Many players also like a wood-to-wood joint. In any case, what you should be concerned with is playability and durability, and of course, appearance.

The ferrule is the round, hard, white item that goes on the end of the shaft and that holds the tip. Ivory was the traditional material for ferrules, but has long since given way to a variety of durable plastics. A ferrule absorbs much of the shock of impact, preventing damage to the shaft. If your ferrule becomes cracked, you should replace it immediately. This will run you about $30-$35.

Maintaining your Cue

A dirty and/or sticky shaft can have a negative affect on your play, therefore, the primary requirement for maintaining your shaft is that is be kept clean so that it can slide smoothly through your fingers.

For the most part, you will want to avoid using sandpaper as it will slowly erode the thickness of the shaft. Baby powder has long been a popular choice for creating a smooth playing surface. However, after playing for awhile you will need to clean it, as chalk, perspiration and anything else on the surface reduces the slickness of the shaft. There are a number of cleaners and conditioners that are designed specifically for maintaining the shaft of your cue. Many are made out of natural substances such as silk that do not damage your shaft and may, in fact, provide some protection against the elements.

Once you purchase your cue, you may find that the taper is not exactly to your liking. For a nominal fee, you can have the shaft turned down exactly to your specifications.

Once you're done playing, you should take your cue apart and store it in an upright position. Avoid leaning your cue up against the wall at an angle. And by all means, avoid storing your cue in the trunk of your car or otherwise subjecting it to radical changes in temperature.

The Tip

The most important part of the cue is the only part that comes in contact with the cue ball - the tip. A poorly maintained tip can ruin the playability of a $1,000 custom cue. On the other hand, good players can get excellent results from a $10 house cue with a well maintained tip. Miscues, improper feel and loss of english are just some of the penalties you will pay for letting your tip slip into a state of disrepair.

Leather is the material of choice for all top quality cue tips. It sticks to the cue ball when properly chalked and conforms nicely to the roundness of the cue ball. All good quality cues come with a leather tip. However, tips don't last forever. If you are practicing and playing several times a week for hours at a time, you may need to re-tip your shaft every 4-6 months. My suggestion is to find someone locally with an excellent reputation for tip work. They have all the tools and the experience to do the job correctly. In addition, they may recommend a new style of tip that helps your game. The cost is nominal, usually anywhere between $5 to $10.

There is an assortment of equipment for the do-it-yourselfers who prefer to do their own work. The first step is to remove the tip with a knife. Make sure not to cut too close to the ferrule. Next, you should sand off the rest of the tip that is still glued to the ferrule. There are special hand operated sanders that attach to the ferrule and shaft that ensure the tip is removed evenly. You should end up with a flat surface at the end of the ferrule for the new tip. There are a number of fast drying glues which you can use to apply your new tip. Be sure to place the tip precisely on the ferrule. If your ferrule is 13 mm in diameter, be sure to use a tip of equal or larger diameter. You can always trim off the excess. There are devices available for measuring the diameter of the ferrule.

The most distinguishing characteristic between good quality tips is the hardness of the tip. Soft tips tend to grab the cue ball a little better and are favored by some players that like to use a lot of english, however, soft tips wear out faster than a hard tip. Hard tips last longer and retain their shape better. Most top players use a medium-hard or hard tip. You can test a tip for hardness by pressing your fingertip into the top of the tip. There will be some give on a soft tip, but little or none on a hard tip.

It is very important that your tip be shaped properly. The most commonly preferred radius conforms to a dime or a nickel. As a rule of thumb, the further you tend to hit the cue ball off center, the more curve you should have on your tip. A bigger tip (ie., 14 mm) will also need a greater degree of curvature than a smaller tip (ie., 12 mm). 13 mm is the standard size that most new cues come in.

There are a number of products that are designed to bring your tip to the desired degree of curvature. The traditional shaper is a curved piece of plastic with grips that hold a curved piece of sandpaper. The many modern versions are round and made of metal. They have a curved and gnarly surface that conforms to the shape of the tip.

When you first buy your cue or when you replace a tip, don't assume that the curve is exactly as you'd like it. Chances are you only need to apply a shaper to bring it to the proper roundness. You can test your tip for roundness at any time by using the following method: Remove all the chalk and then give the tip a couple of light turns with the shaper. If the pores on the top of the tip start to open up, the tip is too round and needs to be re-shaped. Conversely, if the sides open up but the top doesn't, your tip is too flat and will also need to be shaped. Remember however, the top will always be a little flat due to constant contact with the cue ball. If your shaper test shows that pores are opening evenly across the entire tip, then your tip is in good shape. Another good test for roundness is to simply eyeball the tip. A well trained eye can quickly detect if a tip is too flat or is lopsided.

After initial application of the tip, it is necessary to shape it occasionally during its lifetime. Even the hardest of tips will go through a break-in period when it flattens out after initial use. This is to be expected. What you don't want is to have your tip spread beyond its original size. When this happens, the tip is said to have mushroomed. You can prevent this by applying a small amount of moisture evenly around the edge of the tip. The next step is to rub the tip vigorously with a dollar bill. This will harden the sides of the tip and hopefully reduce or eliminate any mushrooming.

If your tip does mushroom, you can use what's called a shaver to remove the part that overhangs the ferrule. The shaver is placed flush with the ferrule. You then slide the cutting edge toward the tip, cutting off any excess material.

Occasionally you may have a tip separate. When this happens, you can see between the layers of leather. A separated tip feels like you are hitting the cue ball with a sponge. You can test for separation by placing your fingernail in the side of the tip and pulling upward away from the shaft. The separation will then expose itself. Once a tip begins to separate, you should plan on replacing it as soon as possible. You should also use your other shaft.

While playing, you should make it a habit to chalk up before nearly every shot. This rule should be amended to absolutely before every draw shot or shot where you're going to hit the cue ball very far off center. Chalk should be applied evenly across the entire surface of the tip using a series of light brush-like strokes. Remember, more is not necessarily better. Don't use just any chalk either. Brand new chalk is harder to apply and may not spread evenly. You can solve this problem by grinding the edge of a quarter into the center of the chalk until you have worn a smooth curved edge across the chalk. You'll also want to avoid well-worn chalk cubes that have a big hole in them and wet chalk. Some players use handy chalk holders that attach to their belt. These insure they will have just the right chalk for every shot.

Chalking up regularly is important to your game. Be sure not to omit this necessary procedure just because you are playing a thoughtless or unscrupulous opponent who removes the chalk from the table or always seems to have the only piece in his/her hand.

During play, you should check your tip regularly for smoothness. This is done by running your fingertip or a napkin across the tip to remove the excess chalk. If the surface is dark and shiny, the tip will not hold chalk very well. We all know to what this can lead to. A shiny, dark tip should be scuffed immediately. I've been using a handy little tool called the tip tapper that's specifically designed for this purpose.

I like to work the entire top of the tip, starting at the edges while lightly pressing the tapper against the tip. The tapper is held in position while the cue is turned in a circular fashion until I've worked my way to the top. A couple of light strokes will remove any excess leather that may have been pulled up. The final step is to gently tap the entire playing surface of the tip. I estimate that you will need to scuff your tip after a few hours of play. Check your tip regularly, but only rough it up as often as necessary. Otherwise, you'll be making unnecessary trips to the tip repairman.

When you're done playing, you can take one final step to maintain your tip. Wipe the chalk off the tip and this will keep the top of the tip from drying out.

Cue Cases

Between league play and Nine Ball tournaments your cue will spend considerable time resting in its case. If you have purchased a relatively inexpensive starter cue, you may be able to get by with a $10 to $15 soft cue made of vinyl. On the other hand, if you are now the proud owner of a $1,000+ custom cue, you will want to buy a sturdy, top of the line case to protect your substantial investment. In any event, a case should protect your cue from rubbing and nicking and from the elements.

Cue cases come in all sizes, shapes and colors and are made from a wide variety of materials. Soft cases are generally the least expensive. They are sufficient for less expensive cues. If you are not overly concerned about the long term health of your $50 beginner cue, then a $15 vinyl soft case will work just fine. I would suggest, however, that your case at least have some padding and a separation for the shaft and the butt. A velcro pouch to store your shapers, tappers and other accessory items also comes in handy.

The box case also has been around forever and continues to be a popular choice among serious players with cues that need solid protection. A good quality box case may cost between $40 and $100+ The box case opens and closes like a suitcase and has a handle for carrying. The more expensive models may be decorated with silver or brass clasps and corner protectors. Box cases are generally covered with vinyl although some of the fancier models are made of wood. Some models are now extra long with a compartment at the end to hold your accessories so that they don't damage your cue.

Probably the most popular cases today are what might be called tube cases. They run in price from $40 to $200+. The shaft and butt slip down through the end of the case into individualized compartments that are foam formed for maximum protection. These cases are so strong that one manufacturer shows a car sitting on top of the case! (I'm not recommending, however, that you try this experiment). Tube cases are constructed from a variety of materials including; vinyl, suede leather, ostrich, cordura, and heavy gauge nylon. When you factor in the handiwork on the exterior, you can wind up with a case that will make any fashion statement that you wish to make. The cases are also very functional. Most models have one or more pouches running down the side. The larger models have some to resemble golf bags with extra large pockets and shoulder straps.

Today's player, more than ever, makes use of a variety of cue sticks. It's not uncommon for players of nearly all levels to use a jump cue and a break cue along with their regular stick. My research shows some cases now offer compartments for as many as three butts and four shafts.
(Note: Collector cases can exceed these specifications). Before plunking down a lot of money on a fancy case, you should stop to evaluate what size will best suit your needs, both present and future. That way you won't wind up carrying your jump cue in one hand while your regular cue sits comfortably in its case.

Accessory Items

There are a number of accessories that can help to improve your play and aid in the maintenance of your equipment. Below are just a few of the ones I feel are most helpful.

Jump Cue - Jumping over obstructing balls can be made easier by using a cue that's specifically designed for this purpose. Jump cues are generally shorter and lighter than a regular cue. Jump cues help you to achieve maximum speed while using a short, wristy stroke which allows the cue ball to become airborne easily. Some jump cues come as part of a break cue, which is then broken down to a shorter cue for jump shots. Typically a jump cue is about 2/3 to 3/4 the length of a regular cue.

Break Cue - It's a good idea to carry a stick with you for break shots only. This will save a lot of wear and tear on your regular stick. Studies have shown that pros now use a break stick that's of equal weight to their regular cue. They have discovered that it's important to have a cue that's light enough it can be whipped through the cue ball at the highest possible speed. On break shots you will hit the cue ball very close to center. As a result, you should consider using a flatter tip as this will ensure a consistent hit on the cue ball. You'll also want to use a hard tip as it will produce maximum cue ball speed and will last longer.

Tip Maintenance - Your tip should be scuffed regularly as we've mentioned before, to help avoid costly miscues. My favorite tool is the Tip Tapper, which resembles a small file with a handle. This useful tool can quickly restore your tip to playability when it becomes compacted from constant contact with the cue ball.

Special Glasses - If you wear glasses like I do, you can appreciate the difficulty of sighting certain pool shots, especially when you need to get down low on the cue. One solution is to wear special glasses with high frames that allow you to easily shift your eyes back and forth between the cue ball and the object ball without having the frames obscure your vision. Perhaps your game can benefit from using the glasses I wear, which are manufactured by Decot Hy-Wyd Sport Glasses (4128 N. 36th St., Phoenix, AZ 85018).

Practicing Your Aim - The toughest thing to do is to aim properly, especially for newer players. I found that the Aim Trainer (Elephant Balls - 7723 Southwick Dr., Dublin OH 43017) can help you easily visualize the correct point of contact with the object ball. A specially designed card is placed underneath the object ball. It extends out to show you precisely where the cue ball needs to be at contact for a successful shot. The same manufacturer has also produced a set of training balls that are ideal for practicing your aim and stroke. The cue ball has special markings that make it easy to tell if you are hitting the cue ball where intended.

Practicing Your Aim and Stroke - The Laser Shark (Tac Star Industries, Inc., P.O. Box 70, Cottonwood, AZ 86326) is a device that fits on the top of your cue, much like a gun sight. It emits a bright red beam of light. You can use the laser to practice your aim. In addition, I found it particularly useful in checking the accuracy of my stroke. The laser will detect any sideways movement.

Cue Maintenance - The Blue Book of Pool Cues will put cue owners in touch with the repair services of the leading cuemakers.   It includes information on which repair services are offered and their cost.   The book also lists the approximate value of a number of custom cues (Blue Book Publications, One Appletree Square, Minneapolis, MN, 55425).

APPENDIX

Playing on Bar Tables

The strategies covered throughout this book are applicable for those who play on either size of table. However, there are some special considerations that should be recognized for those who play on bar tables exclusively and for the many players who switch back and forth between the big table and the bar table.

Shotmaking:

Get comfortable shooting over balls.

Allow for the more forgiving corner pockets.

Avoid sharp angled cuts into the side. Play to the more distant corner pockets.

Master the basic short rail banks and become proficient at long rail banks.

Learn the specialty shots (combos, billiards, caroms and rail first) as you will use them often due to the congested conditions.

The smaller available landing area means you must exercise great care when shooting jump shots.

Learn to play in congested quarters and with a short cue.

Take advantage of opportunities to luck a money ball into the pocket.

Position Play:

Play shape with great precision.

On open shots it's OK to play longer distance position.

Take extra care to avoid scratching.

Make sure to at least leave yourself a makeable shot (vs. precision shape and getting hooked).

The proper use of english (both inside and outside) can enable you to move the cue ball with great precision.

Don't force your shape to avoid a specialty shot such as a combo.

Safety Play:

The congestion factor creates many more hiding places.

Clusters can be especially effective hiding places.

Hook safeties can be especially effective when other balls interfere with the cue ball's path.

The Big Ball:

Aim for a thinner hit on cut shots to compensate for the larger ball.

Use plenty of draw from more than a couple of feet away when your objective is to play a stop shot.

On follow shots, be prepared to have the cue ball follow much further than you think it will.

Avoid long draw shots whenever possible.

Shoot with confidence as the big ball will hold its line better due to the extra weight.

Use very little english unless you shoot regularly with the big ball.

Recommended Books

There are a number of fine books on pool that cover the history of the game and that provide useful instruction. Each book has something to offer every player. Below is a list of my personal favorites.

The Billiard Encyclopedia
by: Victor Stein & Paul Rubino (550 pages)
A beautiful and lavish book that chronicles every part of the game. Nearly 800 illustrations (over 525 in color). Covers tables and artifacts from private collections and museums. Cue collectors will especially appreciate the large section on the master craftsman of the trade. Blue Book Publications, Inc.; 8009 34th Ave. Ste.1391, Minneapolis, MN 55425

Buddy Hall: Rags to Rifleman, Then What?
by: W.W. Woody (359 Pages)
This book tells the story of one of the greatest players in history with colorful descriptions of his encounters with legendary characters in the game. It's an honest portrayal of Mr. Hall's life as a road player who, along the way, gains a sense of spiritual awareness as he turns to tournament pool. The book offers lots of solid advice on the thinking that goes into a champion's play, which can obviously help any player. The book also contains a list of nicknames of the games' leading players, numberous photos of the players, as well as a glossary of colorful terms. I recommend it highly. Huckleberry Publishing Co.; P.O. Box 1104, Lebanon, TN 37087

Willie Mosconi on Pocket Billiards
by: Willie Mosconi   (143 Pages)
A sentimental favorite. Excellent photos and advice on the fundamentals of the game. Photos and descriptions of how to play straight pool by the greatest straight pool player in the history of the game. Crown Publishers, Inc.; 201 E. 50th St., New York, NY 10022

Billiards - The Official Rules and Records Book
by: The Billiard Congress of America (160 pages)
This is a very practical book that will settle any disputes regarding the rules of pool. Complete rules on more than 20 pool games. The book also contains a discussion on the fundamentals, biographies and members of the Hall of Fame and a listing of tournament results and records. Billiard Congress of America; 1700 S. First. Ave., Iowa City, IA 52240

Byrne's Standard Book of Pool and Billiards
by: Robert Byrne (332 Pages)
Excellent coverage of a wide variety of shots that come up over and over again in actual play. Good advice on how to practice and on straight pool. The second half of the book presents a comprehensive discussion of three cushion billiards. The graphics are top quality and the writing is both informative and entertaining. A must for all players. Harcourt Brace Jovanovich; 25 "B" Street, San Diego, Ca 92101

The Science of Pocket Billiards
by: Jack H. Koehler (262 pages)
There is much to be learned from this fine book as it presents a complete discussion on all aspects of the game. The author has conducted numerous studies on the game and presents his findings. The book is heavily illustrated throughout. Sportology Publications; 25832 Evergreen Rd., Laguna Hills, CA 92653

The 99 Critical Shots
by: Ray Martin and Rosser Reeves (220 Pages)
One of the great straight pool champions gives a recap of how to play some of the most important shots in the game. All are fully illustrated. There is also a discussion of the fundamentals with plenty of photos. Times Books/Random House; 201 E. 50th St., New York, NY 10022

Steve Mizerak's Complete Book of Pool
by: Steve Mizerak with Michael Panozzo (195 Pages)
The book has lots of sound advice on the fundamentals and several of the popular pool games. The author also gives tips on selecting equipment. The games' history is presented throughout the book with short stories and photos. Contemporary Books, Inc.; 2 Prudential Plaza, Chicago, IL 60601

Pool - History, Strategy, and Legends
by: Mike Shamos (128 Pages)
The author states accurately that if Pool "was offered as a University course, it might be called 'Pool Appreciation'". This informative and well written book offers a history of the game, with biographies of 27 of the all time greats. It also covers techniques, equipment and a colorful section on hustling. Pool is beautifully illustrated, with the majority of photos in color. A very enjoyable book. Friedmann/Fairfax Publishers; 15 W. 26th St., New York, NY 10010

The 8-Ball Book
by: The Monk (86 Pages)
The author is very supportive of your efforts to improve your game. The book offers advice on a variety of topics, including the mental game. A series of 75 affirmations will help to program your mind for success. Samsara Publishing; P.O. Box 365, Orange, MA 01364

Shots, Moves, & Strategies
by: Eddie Robin and a number of great players (308 pages)
One-pocket players will simply love this book. The authors provide hundreds of problems to teach the reader how to think the game like a pro. Solutions are then provided on the following page. The book contains a number of colorful stories of great champions and detailed glossary. Nicely illustrated. Billiard World Publishing; P.O. Box 12417, Las Vegas, NV 89112

Advanced Pool
by: George Fels (180 pages)
Anyone who wishes to run racks of straight pool (and who wouldn't?) can benefit from Mr. Fel's advice on pattern play, break shots, and how to get in dead stroke. Also offers tips on how to practice and strategies for 8-ball and 9-ball. Very well written. Contemporary Books; Two Prudential Plaza, Chicago, IL 60601

Cornbread Red
by: Bob Henning (228 pages)
This book recalls the life and times of a top money player. It is a fast paced tale that will make you feel like you are part of the action and it will teach you a few things about the mental side of the game as well. Very enjoyable. Bebob Publishing; P.O. Box 530411, Livonia, MI 48153

Where to Play

The organizations listed below can provide pool players of all levels and skills with the opportunity to gain valuable competitive experience. Players looking for a instructor in their area should contact the Billiard Congress of America for a list of their Certified Instructors.

For Amateur Players:

American Poolplayers Ass., Inc.
1000 Lake St. Louis Blvd., Suite 325
Lake St. Louis, MO 63367

Billiard Congress of America
1700 First Avenue, Suite 25A
Iowa City, IA 52240

Valley Ntl. Eight Ball League Ass., Inc.
333 Morton Street
Bay City, MI 48706

Professional and Semi-Pro:

Pro Billiards Tour
P.O. Box 5599
Spring Hill, FL 34606

Women's Professional Billiard Ass.
1411 Pierce Street
Sioux City, IA 51105

McDermott Ntl. Nine-Ball Tour
P.O. Box 87081 4
Dallas, TX 75287

Publications

The leading industry publications can provide you with tips to improve your game, results of professional tournaments, play profiles, exciting new products and other items of interest to the pool player. They are all relatively inexpensive and are well worth the price of a subscription.

Magazines:

Billiards Digest
200 So. Michigan Ave., Suite 1430
Chicago, IL 60604

Pool & Billiard Magazine
1701 Bloomingdale Road
Glendale Heights, IL 60139

The American Cueist
8020 Carr Street
Dallas, TX 75227

Periodicals:

National Billiard News
Box 807
Northville, MI 48167-0807

Regional Publications:

Breaking News
4701 N. Walnut Avenue
Long Beach, CA 90807

The Player
P.O. Box 907-210 W. Main
Chouteau, OK 74337

All About Pool
Academy Plaza
717 South Main Street
Bradford, MA 01835

Billiards Connection
10606-8 Camino Ruiz # 164
San Diego, CA 92126

Cue Ball Gazette
1001 Cooper Point Road SW
140-164
Olympia, WA 98502

Glossary

Action - When a money game is in progress.

Ahead Session - A money match in which the winner must be a predetermined number of games ahead.

Air Barrel - When the losing player plays a final game even through he/she has run out of money.

Backer - One who finances a money game in exchange for a percentage of the winnings.

Bad Hit - Failing to hit the designated object ball first. It's a foul.

Balance Point - The point where the cue is in balance.

Ball in Hand - A rule that allows a player to place the cue ball anywhere on the table after his/her opponent has committed a foul.

Bank Pool - A pool game scored on bank shots only.

Bank Shot - A shot in which the object ball contacts one or more cushions before going into the pocket.

Bar Box - Tavern size tables. 3½' x 7'. Coin Operated.

Barrel - A gambling unit, (ie., $20 equals four $5 barrels).

Bed - The playing surface of the table.

Behind the Line - Any ball that is between the head string and the head rail.

Big Ball - An oversized cue ball that's used on bar tables.

Billiard - A shot in which the cue ball glances off one ball before driving another object ball into the pocket.

Body English - Twisting and turning the arms and/or body in an attempt to influence the shot.

Break (The) - The first shot of any pool game.

Break Out - A shot that removes a ball(s) from a cluster.

Bridge - Using the front hand to hold the shaft of the cue.

Bridge Hand - For a righthanded player it's their lefthand. Vice versa for lefthanders.

Broken Down - A player who is mentally defeated before the contest is over.

Bust - A wide open break shot.

Busted - A gambler who has lost all of his/her money.

Butt - The back half of the cue stick.

Bye - In a tournament a player without an opponent advances to the next round.

Calcutta - Selling players at a tournament through an auction to create a separate prize fund.

Call - The act of designating a specific pocket for a shot.

Called Ball - The designated shot.

Call the Hit - A referee or neutral party judges whether a hit is good or a foul (bad hit).

Called Pocket - The designated pocket for the called ball.

Carom - A shot in which the object ball glances off another ball on its way to the pocket.

Chalk - A small cube with a tacky substance that is applied regularly to the cue tip to help prevent miscues.

Cheating the Pocket - Shooting the object ball into either side of the pocket.

Cheese (The) - A money ball in Nine Ball.

Choke - When a player folds under the pressure, misses ball(s) and plays well below their usual game.

Closed Bridge - A bridge with a loop for the cue, formed by connecting the tips of the thumb and index finger on the middle finger.

Close the Angle - When the cue ball rebounds off the cushion at a greater angle than the approach angle.

Cluster - A group of object balls that are touching or very close together.

Combination - A shot that involves two or more object balls. Two ball combinations are most common.

Contact Induced Throw - Friction between the cue ball and object ball on cut shots that alters the path of the object ball.

Contact Point - The spot on the object ball that the cue ball must strike to make the shot.

Corner Hooked - A cue ball that's deep in the pocket. When the edge of the pocket blocks the cue ball's path to the object ball.

Cross-Corner - A bank shot into the corner pocket.

Cross-Side - A bank shot into the side pocket.

Crutch - (See mechanical bridge).

Cue - The stick with which you shoot.

Cue Ball - The all white ball which you shoot with the cue.

Curve - What happens when you hit down on the cue ball with english.

Cushion - The raised surface that surrounds the playing surface.

Cut Shot - Any shot that has an angle to it.

Dead Combination - A combination shot that's lined up to the pocket which virtually can't be missed (Note - it can!).

Dead Shot - A shot that's lined up to the pocket. Tough to miss.

Dead Stroke - When a pool player is playing at peak levels and his/her stroke is on automatic pilot.

Deflection - Caused by using english. It throws the cue ball onto a different course.

Diamonds - Markings along the top of the rails.

Dirty Pool - Using underhanded tactics.

Dogged It - When a player misses because of choking.

Double Elimination - A tournament in which a player must lose twice to be eliminated.

Double Hit - Hitting the cue ball two or more times in succession. It's a foul.

Draw (The) - Used to determine the pairings at a tournament.

Draw Shot - Hitting the cue ball below center and applying backspin. On a straight shot the cue ball will come directly back toward you.

Duck - A very easy shot.

Ducking - Playing a safety instead of a tough shot.

Eight Ball - A game in which each player shoots either the solids or stripes and both win on the eight ball.

Elevated Bridge - Raising the palm of the bridge hand off the table so you can shoot over an obstructing object ball.

End Rail - Either the head rail or the foot rail. The rails between the corner pockets.

English - Side spin that results from stroking the cue ball on either side of its vertical axis.

Fan It In - To make a very thin cut shot.

Feather Shot - A very thin cut shot.

Ferrule - The hard white piece of plastic or ivory at the end of the shaft to which the tip is attached.

Fish - Somebody who loses money over and over again.

Flow Chart - Used to keep track of the progress of a tournament.

Flush - A player (gambler) who has a lot of money.

Follow - Top spin that causes the cue ball to roll forward after contacting the object ball. It's applied by striking the cue ball above the horizontal axis (above center).

Follow Through - The final phase of the stroke. Extending the cue tip past the cue ball's original location.

Foot of the Table - The end of the table on which the balls are racked.

Foot Rail - The rail at the end of the table where the balls are racked.

Foot Spot - The spot on the table that's on the middle of the foot string. It's where the head ball of a rack is located and where balls are spotted.

Foot String - An imaginary line that crosses the table two diamonds up from the foot rail. It goes directly over the foot spot.

Force Follow - Hitting the cue ball extra hard above center creating lots of top spin.

Force Shot - Making the cue ball travel a good distance sideways with only a small cut angle with which to work.

Foul - Scratching or not making the requirements of a legal shot or legal safety.

Frame - A player's turn at the table.

Free Shot - A shot that does not hurt a player if he/she misses. It usually results in a safety if missed.

Free Wheeling - Very close to dead stroke. When a player is loose and confident, partly due to his/her opponent's poor play.

Frozen Ball - A ball that is in contact with another ball on the cushion.

Full Ball - Sending the cue ball into 100% contact with the object ball (ie., not a cut shot).

Getting Down - When two players agree to a serious money match.

Getting in Line - A demanding shot that puts the cue ball into good position for the next shot.

Going Off - Losing a bunch of money, possibly all of a player's bankroll.

Good Hit - When the cue ball makes contact first with the intended object ball.

Grip - How you hold the cue with your backhand (your shooting hand).

Hanger - A ball that's sitting in the lip of the pocket.

Head of the Table - The end of the table from which you break.

Head Rail - The rail between the two corner pockets on the end of the table from which you break.

Head Spot - A spot that's located in the middle of the imaginary head string.

Head String - An imaginary line that runs across the table two diamonds up from the head rail. You must break from behind the head string.

Heart - The quality of mental toughness. The ability to come through in the clutch. All great players have it.

Heat (The) - Playing competitive pool under pressure.

High Roller - A gambler who likes to play for large stakes.

High Run - The most consecutive balls made by a player in a game of straight pool. Can also be a person's career best run.

Hit (The) - The sensation a player feels from using a particular cue (ie., it hits well).

Hold-up English - Spin that sharpens the cue ball's rebound off the cushion. It slows the cue ball down.

Hooked - When another object ball is blocking the cue ball's direct access to the designated object ball.

Hot Seat - The winner of the winner's bracket in a double elimination tournament. He/she is guaranteed no worse than second place.

House Cue - A one piece cue provided by the establishment.

House Pro - The resident pro who usually gives lessons and runs tournaments.

House Rules - A set of local rules by which you are expected to abide.

Hug the Rail - When a ball frozen to the cushion remains frozen as it is shot into the pocket.

Hustle - Conning an opponent into playing a money game he/she has little or no chance of winning.

Inning - A player's turn at the table.

Inside English - Applying side spin on the same side of the cue ball as the direction of the cut shot.

Insurance Ball - A ball that's left for your next shot on a break shot.

Jacked Up - When you must raise your bridge to shoot over an obstructing ball. Raising the back hand and shooting a draw shot when the cue ball is near a rail. Shooting pool one handed without lying the cue on the rail.

Jam Up - When a player is shooting very well.

Jaws - The area of the playing surface that is inside the edges of the pocket.

Joint - The metal or ivory midsection of the cue that screws together to connect the butt with the shaft of the cue.

Jump Shot - A downward stroke that causes the cue ball to leave the bed of the table and sail over obstructing balls.

Jumped Ball - An obstructing ball that has been cleared.

Key Ball - A ball that's shot before the 8-ball that makes it easy to get good shape on the 8.

Kick Shot - Shooting the cue ball into one or more cushions before contacting the object ball.

Kill Shot - A type of draw shot the checks the cue ball's roll after it rebounds off the cushion. Sometimes english is also used with the draw.

Kiss - When an object ball glances off another ball.

Kitchen - The area of the playing surface between the head string and the head rail. It's the area from which you break.

Knock - When a player decides not to play a money game because he/she is told they can't win by a third party.

Lady's Aide - (See mechanical bridge).

Lag - A very soft stroke.

Lag for the Break - The player who rolls the cue ball to the foot rail and back closest to the head rail wins the first break.

Lamb Killer - A player who specializes in beating less skillful players for money.

Last Pocket Eight Ball - A variation of Eight Ball in which you must pocket the 8-ball in the same pocket as the last shot of your group.

Leave - The position of the balls that one player receives as a result of the other's shot.

Lemonading - The act of stalling or playing less than your best game in hopes of raising the bet.

Line - Getting the word on how well a stranger plays.

Lock - A game that is so one-sided that the better player has little or no chance of losing.

Locksmith - A player who specializes in only making games where he/she is the heavy favorite.

Long - When a bank shot misses to the far side of the pocket. Also when a player runs the cue ball past the ideal position zone.

Long Rail Bank - A table length bank shot.

Long String - An imaginary line that runs down the middle of the table. Balls are spotted along the long string, starting at the foot spot.

Mark - Someone who is known to lose money and is the target of a hustler.

Masse - A circular shot that results from a nearly vertical stroke on the cue ball.

Matching Up - The negotiations that precede a money game.

Mechanical Bridge - A long handled implement with an attachment that has several ridges on the end in which the cue is placed. It is used for shots that can't otherwise be reached.

Miscue - What occurs when the tip fails to stick properly on the cue ball at impact.

Miss - A shot that fails to go into the pocket.

Money Ball - A ball that when legally pocketed, results in victory.

Mushroom - When a tip spreads out and becomes wider than its original shape.

Nap - The degree to which parts of the cloth rise up above the rest of the playing surface.

Natural Position - Shape that results from allowing the cue ball to roll without using english.

Nine Ball - A pool game that's played in rotation, one through nine. The player who sinks the 9-ball at anytime on a legal shot wins the game.

Nip Draw - A special draw shot that uses a short bridge and a short punch-like stroke.

Nit - A player who always wants a lock and bets low even though he/she is a very good player.

Nut Artist - Someone who only plays when they have a game at which they can hardly lose .

Nuts (The) - When you've made a game that you have little or no chance of losing.

Object Ball - The ball at which you are shooting.

On the Hill - When you need to win only one more game to win a race (or an ahead session).

On the Break - Making the money ball or the first shot (the break shot) of the game.

On the Snap - (See on the break).

One Pocket - A pool game where each player only scores by pocketing a ball in one of the two corner pockets on the foot rail.

Open Bridge - A bridge formed by laying the hand flat on the table and placing the cue in a vee formed by the thumb and index finger.

Open Table - In a game of Eight Ball when the option is still available to choose either solids or stripes.

Open the Angle - English that causes the cue ball to rebound at less of an angle than the angle of approach.

Open your Nose - In a money game one player stubbornly continues to play even though he/she is losing. A loss, however, is not certainty.

Out of Stroke - When a player is off their game, not playing very well.

Out Shot - A difficult shot that, if made, should result in victory, even though several balls may be left to pocket.

Outside English - Applying side spin on the opposite side of the cue ball than the object ball is traveling.

Over Cut - Missing a cut shot because the object ball was hit too thinly.

Pattern Play - Playing the balls in a specific order and/or a certain style of playing position.

Pinch - Using inside english to make a bank shot that could not otherwise be made.

Player - (As in he/she's a player) A person who plays very well, especially under competitive conditions.

Pocket Billiards - The formal expression of pool.

Pool - A game(s) that is played on a rectangular table with six pockets, a cue ball and several colored balls.

Pool Detective - A person who makes it a point to know various players' games and who passes that information on the others.

Pool Gods - Mythical characters who control the rolls and the luck factor in each contest. It is not wise to upset them.

Position - Where the cue ball is located in relation to the next shot. You can have good position, poor position and even no position.

Powder - A substance that is placed on the bridge hand so that the cue will slide with less friction.

Proposition - Offering a wager on an unusual and/or difficult shot that the person offering knows very well. Also can be an offer to play a variation of a regular pool game.

Pumped Up - When a gambler has a bunch of cash.

Push Out - A maneuver that follows immediately after the break in Nine Ball. When a player pushes out, his/her opponent has the option of accepting or declining the shot.

Push Shot - An illegal shot that results from hitting the cue ball more than once. It usually takes place when the balls are very close together or frozen.

Pyramid - A full rack of balls at the start of a game. The front ball is located on the foot spot.

Race - A match that's decided by the first player to win a specific number of games (ie., a race to seven).

Rack - A triangular shaped piece of equipment that's made out of wood or plastic. It is used to put the balls in position at the start of a game. Also refers to the position of the balls once they've been placed in position and the rack has been removed.

Rake - (See mechanical bridge).

Rail - The raised surface that surrounds the playing surface. It includes the cushions.

Rail Bridge - A bridge that's formed by placing the bridge hand on the rail.

Rail Shot - When the cue ball is frozen to the cushion or very close to it.

Regulation Size Table - A 4½' x 9' sized table.

Reverse English - Side spin that causes the cue ball to rebound off the cushion at a sharper angle than the approach angle.

Riding the Cash - A powerful stroke at the money ball. The goal is to slop the money ball wherever possible.

Ring Game - A money game of Nine Ball with three or more players .

Road Player - A hustler or player who travels around the country playing pool for money.

Rock - The cue ball.

Roll Off - When an irregularity in the table or a not perfectly level playing surface causes a slow moving object ball to veer off-line.

Rolls - The breaks of the game. There are good rolls and bad rolls.

Rotation - A pool game that uses all fifteen balls. They are played in order, 7 through 15.

Running English - Side spin on the cue ball that causes it to pick up speed after it contacts the cushion. It also reduces the rebound angle off the cushion.

Run Out - Making several balls in succession to win the game.

Run Out Player - A player who runs out with great regularity.

Run The Rack - Breaking and running out the entire rack.

Safety - A defensive maneuver that's designed to leave your opponent with a tough shot or safety, or perhaps no shot at all.

Score - How a match stands. When someone wins a lot of money.

Scratch - When the cue ball disappears into any of the six pockets.

Scratch Shot - A shot in which a scratch is very likely or unavoidable.

Session - An extended money game.

Set - One race within a series of races. Also could refer to playing under the ahead format.

Shaft - The half of the cue to which the tip is attached. The front part of the cue.

Shape - (See position).

Shark - A tactic that's designed to distract or throw your opponent off their game. A player who hustles pool.

Sharking - The act of using shark tactics .

Shooting the Lights Out - When you are shooting very straight and playing perfect pool. Similar to dead stroke.

Short - A bank shot that misses on the near side of the pocket. When the cue ball fails to reach the intended location for good position (comes up short).

Short Side Shape - Position for the more distant pocket.

Short Stop - A very capable and experienced player who is just a couple of notches below the very best.

Shotmaker - A very straight shooter who emphasizes making balls over playing position.

Short Rail Bank - A bank across the width of the table.

Side Rail - The rails that run along the length of the table.

Slate - The hard playing surface that rests under the cloth.

Slop - A lucky shot. Unintentionally pocketing a ball in whatever pocket at which it happens to arrive.

Slug - A loose rack. It's often given on purpose to neutralize an opponent's break.

Sneaky Pete - A two- piece cue that looks like a house cue, often used by hustlers.

Snookered - When the cue ball rests behind a ball which blocks a direct hit on the designated ball.

Solids - Balls numbered 1 through 7.

Speed - How well a player typically plays. His or her normal game.

Speed Control - The ability to control the cue ball's rolling distance. Good speed control is essential for playing good position.

Spin Your Rock - Applying english to the cue ball.

Spot - A location on the table. The foot spot and the head spot. A handicap to even out a match.

Spot Shot - The cue ball is placed behind the head string for a shot at an object ball that's placed on the foot spot.

Spot Up - Placing a ball on the foot spot. Usually occurs after a ball has been pocketed and a foul has been committed.

Stack - Same as the rack. The group of balls prior to the opening break.

Stakehorse - A person who finances money matches.

Stance - The position that you take for a shot.

Stall - Playing less than your best in the hopes of raising the bet.

Stick - (See cue).

Stick It - Stopping the cue ball dead in its tracks upon contact with the object ball.

Stone - Slang for the cue ball.

Stop Shot - (see stick it).

Straight In - Refers to a shot where the cue ball and object ball are lined up directly at the pocket.

Straight Pool - Also known as 14.1. A game which is played to a specific number of points, usually in multiples of 25 (ie., 75, 100, 125). One point is scored for each ball pocketed. The player can call any ball in any pocket.

Stripes - Balls numbered 9 through 15. The term is usually used when playing Eight Ball.

Stroke - The swing of the arm, wrist and hand that propels the cue through the cue ball.

Stun Shot - The absence of spin on the cue ball when it contacts the object ball. The shot is played with a firm stroke.

Sweat - Watching a pool game. For example, sweating the action.

Sweater - A person who is watching a pool game.

Table Roll - (See roll off).

Thin Cut - A shot that requires that very little of the cue ball comes in contact with the object ball.

Throw - Friction between the object ball and cue ball that changes the path of the object ball. English can throw a ball. Contact can also throw a ball.

Tip - The small round leather item that is attached to the ferrule. It comes in contact with the cue ball. Also refers to use of english (ie., ½ tip off center) and draw or follow (ie., 1 tip of draw).

Trap - When a player is locked up in a losing game.

Triangle - Another term for the wooden or plastic device which is used to rack the balls.

Through Traffic - Skillfully maneuvering the cue ball past a number of potentially obstructing balls.

Two- Piece Cue - A cue that has a joint in the middle. It can be broken down into two equal length pieces.

Under Cut - Missing a shot because the object ball was hit too fully.

Warm Up Strokes - A series of back and forth movements of the arm, hand and wrist that prepares the shooter for the actual stroke.

Weight - A handicap that one player gives another in a money game.

Wild Ball - A spot ball that does not have to be called.

Whitey - Slang for the cue ball.

Wire (On the) - A string above the table with beads or balls for keeping score.

Woofing - When one player verbally abuses another in the hopes of getting him/her to play for money.

Wrap - The part of the butt end of the cue that's normally covered with irish linen or leather.

About the Author

Mr. Capelle has been a player and a student of the game since 1969. He has won numerous local tournaments as well as a major southern California Amateur Eight Ball Championship. Mr. Capelle is a certified instructor with the Billiard Congress of America. He has overseen several tournaments, including the 1993 Orange County Bar Table Nine Ball Championship. He has spent a good part of his time balancing his pool playing activities with a career in the financial services industry. He has edited and published a stock market advisory service and served as a financial columnist for the Orange County Business Journal. Play Your Best Pool is his second book. He previously authored Investing in Growth (Probus, 1992).

Mr. Capelle resides in Huntington Beach, California where he enjoys golf, reading, music, movies and sports when he's not playing, watching and teaching pool.

For More Information

Readers who are interested in being kept informed of further publications by Philip Capelle and/or are interested in finding out more about his services (lessons, clinics, appearances, etc) please send your inquiries to the address below. I also welcome your comments on the book as well as your suggestions for improving future editions:

Play Your Best Pool
Philip B. Capelle
P.O. Box 400
Midway City, CA 92655